Identifying and Exploring Security Essentials

Mary Clifford, Ph.D.

Associate Professor of Criminal Justice
St. Cloud State University

PEARSON

Prentice
Hall

Upper Saddle River, New Jersey 07458

Library of Congress Cataloging-in-Publication Data

Clifford, Mary
  Identifying and exploring security essentials / Mary Clifford.
    p. cm.
  ISBN 0-13-112620-2
  1. Security systems. 2. Crime prevention. 3. Safety education. I.
Title.
  HV8290 .C58 2004
  658.4'7--dc22

                                                        2003015931

Publisher: Stephen Helba
Executive Editor: Frank Mortimer, Jr.
Assistant Editor: Korrine Dorsey
Production Editor: John Shannon, Pine Tree Composition, Inc.
Production Liaison: Barbara Marttine Cappuccio
Director of Manufacturing and Production: Bruce Johnson
Managing Editor: Mary Carnis
Creative Director: Cheryl Asherman
Cover Design Coordinator: Miguel Ortiz
Cover Designer: Cheryl Asherman
Cover Image: Frederic Pitchal, Corbis
Marketing Manager: Tim Peyton
Formatting and Interior Design: Pine Tree Composition, Inc.
Printing and Binding: R.R. Donnelley & Sons

Pearson Education LTD
Pearson Education Singapore, Pte. Ltd.
Pearson Education, Canda, Ltd
Pearson Education—Japan
Pearson Education Australia PTY, Limited
Pearson Educaçion de Mexico, S.A. de C.V.
Pearson Education Malaysia, Pte. Ltd.

10 9 8 7

ISBN 0-13-112620-2

This book is for every person who might benefit from a better understanding of security and security-related issues; most specifically I offer it for anyone who, like myself, aspires to live in a world where security can be found in a door or window left wide open.

Brief Contents

Contents

Preface

This text is offered to those interested in developing a better understanding of security and security-related concerns. On September 11, 2001 we saw clearly how security-related concerns affect everyone. The importance of the ideas presented here have been eerily illustrated in horrific fashion by the events on that day and in the days since. As a result, how we think about security concerns as a nation has changed in the United States and throughout the world. Security as a discipline and as a popular concern has been changed and awareness everywhere has been heightened.

The security-related themes presented here were originally organized for students in an upper-level security course. The information included here, however, will prove useful to anyone interested in security. Readers will see how to begin thinking strategically not only about security options but also about how to assess their own environment to determine which option will be most effective for them under what circumstances. More than a "how-to" book, this is a "how-to-think-about" book.

After reviewing and integrating years of security-related information from various security texts, articles, and trade journals, teaching security and crime prevention classes, and talking with security professionals, I came to realize that people (including security professionals) often use the same words and terms to describe different security-related issues and concepts. This can be confusing. Furthermore, the few social science research studies that have been done in this area suggest that even security practitioners do not agree about what *security* means. In an effort to provide better service to students, I began offering them a collection of ideas, rather than espousing one particular definition. I decided to focus on providing a definition supplemented by a presentation of, and discussion about, general security concepts. This text is the result of my effort to take various uses of security-related terms, concepts, and activities and synthesize these ideas into what I am calling "security essentials."

One factor motivating me to put together a textbook was my own frustration when reading and researching within the field. My initial goal was to find a means by which I could define terms easily for students who were just learning the field while at the same time not create confusion for them when they began reading security materials on their own. One of my concerns, however, is the importance of organizing and discussing the material in a way that makes sense to both researchers and academic types and security practitioners.

The reader should be aware that similar efforts to synthesize and prioritize security-related material are under way from within one of the largest, and perhaps most well-known, international security organizations, the American Society for Industrial Security (ASIS). Although I decided this text should reflect my academic leanings, I also try to acknowledge the importance of the practitioner perspective. Information from the ASIS organization's education committee should also prove useful. My hope is that by making comparisons between the efforts of academics and the efforts of practitioners, we can move a step closer to a fuller integration of what have traditionally been separate orientations to security-related information.

Some security concepts discussed throughout this text can and should be applied to any and all settings, but it is essential to highlight the fact that each secured environment is different. For students, this is a critical concept. No one book can speak to every security issue. People who look exclusively to textbooks for their security solutions are not utilizing the one thing that they may know the most about: the specific and specialized environmental conditions in the "target environment," or the setting they seek to protect. Security professionals responsible for a specific environment should know that environment better than anyone else. When the environmental conditions change, so then do the security needs. While a professional may understand a particular type of security (hospital security, for example), if he or she overlooks important environmental factors unique to a specific hospital or clinic, the system can be left vulnerable. I want students to think about both the information they are learning (e.g., hospital security) and how it is applied within the target environment (e.g., a specific clinic). The interaction between information and environmental conditions requires constant evaluation and reevaluation, and this reflects the ongoing *process* of review required when providing security.

I find students least prepared to deal with the fluid nature of the security process. So I began directing student attention toward the process of assessing security in various settings and then asking students to think about what a secure setting might mean under different circumstances. It became clear that once they could concentrate on what they knew about the conditions in the target environment, the better prepared they felt they were for making decisions about appropriate security options. The more environments they considered, the easier this became and the more confident they became in the evaluation and assessment processes. As they began to feel more comfortable assessing environmental conditions and thinking about security options, they realized how important it is to find a way to make a decision they can feel good about to meet both immediate needs and to address concerns for the long term.

Efforts to identify, explore, implement, and evaluate security objectives require constant oversight, exploration, evaluation, and reevaluation of the environmental conditions. I tell my students it is like doing a puzzle when the picture you are putting together is constantly changing. Keeping a step ahead is essential for ensuring adequate protection. This is a tough charge for security professionals and can initially be overwhelming for students.

Environmental changes may leave a system vulnerable. The minute a system is deemed "foolproof," someone somewhere will see it as a challenge to exploit that system's vulnerability. This is as true for crime fighting as it is for crime prevention. Those who follow crime and related issues know the use of DNA has been touted as a foolproof method for determining a person's guilt or innocence. *USA Today* ran a front-page story titled "Criminals Try To Outwit DNA." It explained that alleged criminals are "coaching each other on how to spread blood and semen samples from other people around crime scenes to try and fool DNA analysts."[p.1A] The minute you think you have the answers, the setting changes and requires a fresh review of the conditions you are addressing.

Traditional security textbooks have emphasized specific security options. This information is important; however, my approach to the material about security is a bit different. More traditional approaches to discussions about security focus on a specific, often competing, assessment of what security is, and then they tell the reader what is needed to achieve "it," maximum security. This text is an effort to provide opportunities and examples to illustrate the fluid nature of security as an ongoing process and to highlight the importance of knowing the target environment. From there readers must begin to engage their own understandings of what it is they want to secure. Whether coordinating the implementation of their own security protocol or seeking out assistance from other security professionals, readers will benefit from an introduction to this basic framework that can be understood easily and is followed by a step-by-step review of the fundamental aspects of the framework. Once readers learn these "basics," they then have the opportunity to think about how this framework is best applied to different target environments, and this acts as a useful transitional point for applying these ideas at home, at work, or anywhere.

OVERVIEW

Part I, "Reviewing the Basics," provides a thorough discussion of existing concepts, terms, and phrases. The introduction sets the stage by introducing several controversial issues in the field of security. A brief history of private security is presented in Chapter 1, followed by a discussion of fundamental security terms in Chapter 2. Chapter 3 provides an opportunity to think about applying the principles from Chapters 1 and 2 in different settings. Chapter 4 introduces five basic concepts central to security within a given environment. These themes become the focus of Part II, where they are considered in more explicit detail.

Part II, "Resources from Within," highlights the important elements of a security program introduced in Part I and takes those elements further. Physical security and asset protection, information and computer security, and personnel and security management are considered individually in Chapters 5, 6, and 7 respectively. Chapter 8 introduces the idea that these "essential" features of an overall security system do not operate in a vacuum. In fact, they interact. The idea of an integrated approach to security systems adds an additional layer of security protection for an environment. Chapter 9 provides sample target settings. Students are invited to apply the ideas introduced in Parts I and II.

Part III, "Making Essential External Connections," highlights the importance of activities that happen off site. Open and active communication with law enforcement is discussed in Chapter 10. Chapter 11 provides an elementary discussion of liability issues. Protection against liability is really the backbone of any security organization. Damage to the backbone will have a crippling effect on the business and perhaps on the industry as a whole. Chapter 12 discusses accidents and emergencies. While the chapter provides some basic information about resources for accident prevention and disaster management and planning, it also highlights the importance of paying attention to the aspects of an environment that may require specific attention and additional research. Chapter 13 outlines three security settings that demonstrate the integration of public and private policing efforts and a discussion of the future of security. Finally, Chapter 14 invites students to think about the settings provided in Chapter 9, with an eye toward addressing the external security needs.

In closing, I would like to invite you to enjoy playing with the ideas presented in this book. I hope anyone who is interested in developing a better understanding of security will have fun thinking through these security-related ideas. More important, I hope they find application of these ideas in their everyday lives. Helping students, small business owners, neighbors, and community members think about the realistic security threats present in their target environment is one of my goals. Having practitioners challenge the way they view their assumptions about security is another goal.

When it comes to understanding security, reading as much as you can is helpful. Conducting research to find solutions is helpful. Learning how to think critically about options is crucial. Readers can use each part of the text, building on previous sections, to develop a deeper understanding of the application of these ideas. I hope academics find this text helpful for thinking about scientifically useful and discipline-specific terms and concepts that are able to be measured and tested. I offer the terms and concepts presented here as a sort of practical and intellectual dartboard. Anybody want to play?

ENDNOTES

D. H. Gilmore and M. L. Garcia, "Coming to Terms with the Security Body of Knowledge" (paper presented at the ASIS International Seminar, Las Vegas, NV, September 1999), tape 91, 3–4.

R. Willing, "Criminals Try to Outwit DNA." *USA Today,* August 28, 2000, 1A.

ACKNOWLEDGMENTS

Like any academic work, this text represents a combination of ideas, combining a collection of existing ideas with my own effort to critically evaluate and revisit the concept of security. I see great efforts being made within the security community to outline a structure for existing security-related information with an eye toward creating an academically rigorous discipline of study. While continuing to highlight the importance of the experienced security practitioner, professionals within the security industry have elected to seek out ways to enhance their professional status by adding the essential academic piece. This is great news for the discipline, for practitioners and for people who are interested in developing a better understanding of security for themselves and their families where they live and work.

Security professionals are no longer satisfied with second-class status as "security guards" or "rent-a-cops." Security professionals are evolving into an innovative and creative group of professionals who seek to understand the security process within a global context. I am proud to be associated with such an esteemed, inspired group of professionals who have embraced these tough, challenging activities. Their individual and collective attempts to expand and enhance the present conception of security and security-related concepts have earned my deepest level of gratitude and positively affected their industry and the security of people everywhere.

On a more personal note, I must thank, first and foremost, my support personnel: my partner Mark VanGelder, and my daughter, Autumn. They have endured many nights and weekends without 'Mom' so that I could finish this project. I am deeply grateful to them for the sacrifices they have made in this process. I look forward to catching up on precious time. Second, I would like to thank Chuck Thibodeau, of Thibodeau and Associates, a security consulting firm based in Minneapolis, Minnesota. His "practitioner perspective" was invaluable as I was making choices about how to best serve the security community with this text. In spite of the fact that his work commitments did not allow a more active role in the production of this text, his comments and support for the project can be seen throughout. Third, I am especially thankful to an extremely competent, self-motivated undergraduate student at St. Cloud State University, Jesse Lane, who took it upon himself to help me polish up some of the important details as the project came to a close. His performance was exceptional, and the final stages of the project were immeasurably easier for me because of his willingness to work hard and his ability to learn the process quickly. Thanks, Jesse.

Some general thanks go to members of the St. Cloud State University community and to faculty and staff within the Department of Criminal Justice. The office staff always assumes additional burdens with a project like this, and I want to thank Deb Yorek for the hard work that she does everyday and for putting up with the shuffling that was required with this project. Thanks to Dean Richard Lewis, for much needed reassigned time, and to several of my faculty colleagues who either reviewed chapters or assisted, sometimes casually and sometimes more fully, with topical questions and resource support. Richard Lawrence, Kathy Sweet, Barry Schreiber, Dick Setter, John Campbell and Chuck Seefeldt were all helpful in that process and I am grateful to them for their assistance. Thanks also to my folks, whose love and support mean the world and who have helped me learn to feel secure in the world, regardless of the identified risk levels . . . wink. I love you both.

Thanks to the folks at Prentice Hall, Frank Mortimer, Korrine Dorsey, John Shannon, and the nameless others, for helping to finish up the details. Finally, I would like to thank Monica Hincken and Susan Beauchamp, whom I had the pleasure to work with early on in this project. I owe you both dinner, at least, and I can't wait to make good on the offer.

The author would also like to thank reviewers Shaun L. Gabbidon, Penn State Harrisburg Middletown, Pennsylvania; Christopher Hertig, York College of Pennsylvania, York, Pennsylvania; and Michael D. Moberly, Southern Illinois University, Carbondale, Illinois.

Mary Clifford
St. Cloud State University

Reviewing the Basics

*Problems cannot be solved at the same level of aware-
ness that created them.*

—Albert Einstein

Part I of *Identifying and Exploring Security Essentials* is focused on determining a common starting point. I offer readers an introduction outlining a
series of discussions unique to the security industry. The issues of whether security is a discipline of study, whether security practitioners need to professionalize their industry, and whether security systems make a target environment more safe or simply make the people in that environment *feel* more safe
will all be presented for consideration. The difficult and sometimes tenuous relationship between law enforcement and private security professionals is introduced briefly along with a discussion about the challenges that come with attempts to integrate the many levels of security. Are security professionals
expected to protect us from physical harm and keep us safe, or are they also
equally responsible to make sure that a greedy corporate financial officer
(CFO) doesn't walk away with billions of dollars in corporate assets? While reviewing the Introduction, readers may want to think about any assumptions
they bring with them to this discussion of security and security-related concepts.

Chapter 1 presents a very brief history of security. Because the history of
security-related efforts shadows in some places the development of public protection agencies, various aspects of these histories are also included. Chapter 2
is a review of terms. Some security resources use basic terms differently, and it
is important that readers understand how I am using the terms.

Once you have reviewed Chapters 1 and 2, Chapter 3 makes it possible to
look at different security settings and see how you would talk about these
terms in each of those scenarios. What is a threat? How does one determine a
risk level? Some readers may have had experiences that offered them an opportunity to think critically about security threats in a particular setting or target environment. An excellent exercise is to find some security-related issues
in your local paper. These can be excellent stories to review with the class or
with others interested in security.

Chapter 4 provides a security system overview, identifying security as both a system and a process. The system presented is basic but gives readers the opportunity to begin thinking about security as an integrated system with specific features or elements that work together.

Once readers begin critically reviewing various circumstances and start attaching security-related issues and concerns to different settings, they will likely find themselves analyzing even the most routine events throughout their day.

A quick story: The building I work in is locked after business hours. Because offices for both the student newspaper and the student radio are in the basement of the building, it is not uncommon to see students who want to get into the building hanging around until someone with a key comes along. This tactic must work fairly often, because students often linger by the doors. I always tell them I am not authorized to let them in, and encourage them to contact campus security for assistance. The students hate this because they say it's a hassle. One weekend afternoon I proceeded through the doorway and before the door closed, a student bolted for the door. No, he didn't ask if I would let him in; he was reading a paper outside. I assumed he was waiting for a ride. Still standing in the entryway, I turned ready to give my speech about unauthorized access, and I explained that I couldn't let him in, but we were both inside the building. Because the building had reported equipment losses, it was particularly important to control unauthorized access. He said, "You didn't let me in; I came in on my own." After we exchanged words, he tried to physically move me out of his way (I was about 10 months pregnant at the time, so this was no easy task). I called campus security and he was escorted from the building shortly thereafter. The security officer asked if I wanted to contact the local police and charge the student with assault. From a security standpoint, this story is interesting because instead of reducing the risk level associated with equipment losses, I found myself confronting a different threat with greater risk to my person. I have often seen students try and get in the building, so I didn't identify in my mind a scenario where a student would choose to force his or her way into the building. Again, opportunities to assess threats and related risk levels exist everywhere; it is just a question of whether or not you take notice of them.

By the end of Part I, I hope readers will have broadened their understanding of security as a concept. They will be prepared to think about some of the following questions: "Have I taken the opportunity to think about who or what I need to be 'protected' from?" "Why have I identified a need for protection?" "Do I only see security issues from the perspective of corporate America?" "Does my fear of victimization impact how I think about my security system?" "Why is it important to understand ideas from people across the globe who may have an entirely different orientation to security as a concept?" "Is it okay that the word *security* means different things to different security professionals?" If a person, perhaps another security professional, were to develop an understanding of security issues that differed from your own understanding, how is that connected to your decision to formulate a security response? Or is it connected at all?

Such questions or issues are likely to evoke a variety of different answers depending on the situation and the security professional. I am most interested in having students explore the unique, contextual characteristics of each situation.

I believe the contextual understandings of specific words (even if people are able to agree on the definitions of those words) will produce different meanings, or reactions, for different people. Yes, context is important, but it is also important to create generalized concepts not as easily subject to time, place, culture, and so forth. In this way we begin to define parameters for a discipline of study while also exploring the boundaries of those parameters as a function of that study. Regardless of people's thoughts on any given subject, I see value in the discussion and potential disagreements that will result. This is, after all, a big part of the academic/intellectual process, which like security is also ongoing. Such points of critical reflection are also a security essential. All encounters, be they readings, discussions, lectures, or field encounters, can be used to broaden your understanding of security. Although I admit to feeling frustrated when I confront something that is not consistent with existing literature or is out of place, these events always get me thinking. In a nutshell, this is the purpose of Part I: I hope to get the reader thinking about security in both general and specific ways.

Introducing Security Essentials: A Prelude

This book was designed to provide an overview of information essential to basic security system conceptualization. Having said that, it is important for the reader to understand that security professionals have not come to any concrete agreement about what constitutes the essential elements of a security system. In fact, security professionals have offered varied presentations of security-related concepts over the years. Even the parameters of "security" as a concept have yet to be clearly outlined.[1,2]

The more I teach, read about, and discuss security-related issues, the more I find an ongoing need to be clear about the preexisting assumptions made about basic security information. Security, as a concept, will mean different things to different people at different times. That fact alone is an essential aspect of security, and one we see clearly as a result of the September 11 attacks. Security in the United States means something markedly different today than it did before 9/11.

A good way to think about these existing differences is to open the discussion with a few questions about how people talk about security. For starters, there are researchers who study security and talk about it in abstract language, and then there are practitioners who work in specific target environments. These groups have talked differently about security, and even some of the most comprehensive research studies are summarily dismissed by practitioners who have had experiences in the field quite different from the outcomes presented in research findings. Also, a discussion about the importance of place will be highlighted. Certainly a good amount of technical expertise is required to implement specific features in a high-tech security system, for example, but it is also important to spend time thinking about the creative effort that goes into the construction of a security system. No matter how much information about security you have, there comes a time when you have to think creatively about your security system needs and the features unique to your target environment. This creative effort happens in the target setting, not in the pages of a textbook. For this reason, in this book you will see many opportunities to learn from example settings and scenarios.

This introduction discusses some of the issues in the field that warrant further consideration. I am sure, if you asked around, you would find others. As an introduction to the discussion about security in the following chapters, however, I would simply like to invite students and practitioners to use this presentation of security-related debates to consider *how* they think about security. People in their homes, citizens and community members, business owners, as well as security students and security professionals can identify and (re) consider their own suppositions about security and security-related information as a starting point for the discussions to come.

THE SECURITY BODY OF KNOWLEDGE: AN EMERGING ACADEMIC DISCIPLINE?

As I have spent more time studying security-related issues, several realities have become clear. First, quite a bit of information on security-related issues exists. Second, the security industry is constantly changing, and this creates even more information and a companion need to assess whether, or to what degree, existing information is outdated. Third, individual stories about security-related experiences abound. These three statements combine, feeding directly into the fourth and final consideration for the purposes here, the need for a clearly defined body of knowledge.

Making connections between certain periods in history and specific activities or breakthroughs in technology, philosophy, or ideology is one way to begin thinking about establishing parameters in any discipline of study. Historical periods of study have been established by scholars and researchers within a discipline for ease of reference and analysis. If I mention the Middle Ages, for example, the reader has a general understanding of the time period I wish to discuss. But people, even well-respected historians, disagree on the specific years when the Middle Ages began and ended. The finer points within these broad descriptions of historic periods are under constant discussion and sometimes hotly contested. Such is true with discussions about security, as a concept and as a discipline of study.

On one hand I seek to establish parameters around the security-related subjects under study, but on the other hand I want to debate and challenge the existing parameters that have been established. My interests might seem at odds. Nonetheless, you can rest assured; this is part of the academic process. Integrating ideas and exploring the applicability of a specific idea to different settings is certainly not unique to the study of security. Ongoing debates about basics and important reference points are found within any vital or expanding industry or discipline.

For almost 30 years the discipline of criminal justice has been outlining, defining, and redefining parameters within its area of study. Security is another example of an emerging area of study. Before that, many university programs did not have departments devoted to the study of criminal justice. Today that is different. Transformational solutions surface as additional research studies are completed and their results disseminated and incorporated into existing understandings. The example of criminal justice can serve as a strong motivational force, encouraging security practitioners to move toward a critical evaluation of the discipline's existing body of knowledge.

Charles Babbage, an early computer innovator, has been quoted as having said, "Errors using inadequate data are much less than those using no data at all." An organized, disciplined approach to the study of security is focused on decreasing errors of interpretation and application. The effort to define parameters for the field of security will require professionals, both practitioners and scholars, to work on various security-related topics for a number of years. The contributions to the security industry from such an ongoing discussion will be immeasurable. But before I can begin to study the concept of security, I'd like to talk a little bit about what the word has come to mean.

What Is Security?

Although the academic community has not established an extremely broad base of research in this area, it is helpful to review historical information about the security industry. Several stages of change or growth within the industry are apparent. Security has been discussed as a thing, an end, an objective somewhere "out there" to achieve or attain. In ways this is true; security professionals seek to establish a preconceived standard of security within a given environment. Either they achieve that level of security or they do not; the environment is secure or it is not. Right? Not so fast.

Critical commentary from security colleagues has called into question the notion of security as a duality, or something having only two aspects. In this case, it would be a duality to see an environment as being either secure or not secure. Rejecting this premise as oversimplified, security professionals then began to acknowledge security as a process rather than a thing that is either present or absent. Consequently, security professionals talk about where they are in the process of securing a target environment. Establishing a secure setting is an ongoing activity, one that can be constantly evaluated and revised but not something with a designated ending point.

Security professionals have also used the idea of security as a system. Focusing on the idea that security objectives are ongoing and constantly being reassessed, evaluated, and transformed as needs dictate, practitioners began to focus on the various elements or levels of security required to protect a specific environment. Emphasis is placed on security as a system or an orderly method for outlining arranging security issues and related practices. Because a security system consists of various aspects, commentary from the field began to emphasize the importance of making sure all those aspects are working together. The current trend is to talk about an integrated system, where the various components or arrangements within the systems overlap and work together within the setting to meet the overall security objective. More on this will be presented in Chapter 4 and throughout Part II.

In thinking about security, it makes sense to look at history. Some of the more traditional aspects of this history are discussed in Chapter 1. The history of private security has been told primarily around westward and industrial expansion in the United States, involving railroad police. The association of an emerging discipline of study, such as security, to a time-specific idea such as the railroad police is not uncommon as a discipline begins to find its form. But after the discussions in the discipline are expanded, a bigger picture of that idea (security) emerges. The history of security as a concept should reflect not only the eclectic nature of the disciplines used to outline the concept but also the changes in the way the concept has been viewed over time and in different areas of the country and the world.

A more comprehensive review of security in the United States, for example, would discuss a series of significant activities involving labor and labor relations. During nineteenth-century America, various labor disputes were controlled by calling in "security professionals." What do the numerous volumes of texts on labor relations say about security as it was applied in the labor disputes? Consider the following passage:

(*Source*: Patrick Corrigan, *The Toronto Star*)

The danger was terrible and real, and for a moment the American people stood appalled, not knowing how far the revolt might extend, or what character it might assume. Never since the days of the Civil War had the nation been so profoundly moved, or so painfully apprehensive. On all sides the determination was made plain that the outbreak must be put down; the laws must resume their sway; and the future of this great country must not be periled by mob violence. No man could tell how soon his home would be the mark of the rioter's torch, or his dear ones be at the mercy of an infuriated mob, and this thought brought hundreds of thousands to the support of the representatives of law and order. At the call of the civil authorities armed men came from all quarters, and it was soon apparent even to the most desperate rioters that the people were determined to preserve their institutions and property from violence at any cost. This formidable uprising of the people had the happiest effect, and the revolt succumbed before it. The disturbers of the peace slunk away, or were arrested, and the supremacy of the law reestablished. The very originators of the strikes, horrified at the capture and distortion of their movement by the mob of lawless ruffians, in many instances gave their assistance to the authorities in restoring order.[3]

Is the need for security determined from the perspective of the business professional? The worker? The government? The general public? How do these multiple perspectives impact the overall understanding of security? Traditional discussions of security emphasize protecting companies from striking workers. As Paul Harvey might say, it is always interesting to learn "the rest of the story."

Collective agreement might be found in the idea that security as a field of study pulls from other disciplines. The agreement is likely to cease there, however, particularly if someone attempts to provide a list of these disciplines. Contenders include criminology, sociology, psychology, human resource management, physiology, chemistry, physics, civil engineering, mechanical engineering, electrical engineering, computer engineering, landscape architecture, architecture, and architectural engineering.[4] I would love to read a more comprehensive review of the history of security as it has been discussed in all of these disciplines. Until then, the history of security will remain unnecessarily restricted.

In Chapter 2, I offer the Green and Farber definition of security for the reader to consider. According to that definition, security implies *a stable, relatively predictable environment in which an individual or group may pursue its ends without disruptions or harm and without fear of disturbance or injury.*[5] Many more definitions exist. For example, Mary Lynn Garcia (a Certified Protection Professional [CPP]) suggested that while security and safety have traditionally been talked about as if they were synonymous, this is inappropriate. She suggests that the words have different functions. *Security* concerns are limited to "malevolent human attacks."[6] Examples include the

September 11 attacks on the World Trade Center, the Oklahoma City bombing, and the shootings at Columbine High School in Littleton, Colorado. *Safety* issues, then, refer to "abnormal environments."[7] This might include electrical shorts, fires, hurricanes, chemical spills, and other kinds of accidents.[8]

DO YOU BELIEVE IN ANGELS?[1,2]

What started as the "Magnificent 13," a group of 13 individuals who were united by Curtis Sliwa and rode one of New York City's toughest subway lines (the number 4 train) during peak hours for crime, has grown into an organization with more than 5000 members in 67 cities in the United States, Canada, and Mexico. The group grew from the original 13 members to hundreds in a matter of months. This group is known today as the Alliance of Guardian Angels.

The mission of the Guardian Angel is simple: "Improve the quality of life in communities around the world." Their emphasis is on setting up community-based programs that target the ongoing issues of violence, crime, drugs, and gangs. The Guardian Angels are trained to make citizen's arrests when they see criminal activity taking place. They also provide positive role models for young people. Most of the people who are Guardian Angels work or go to school during the day and participate in the organization's activities in the evenings and on weekends.

The Guardian Angels are highly visible when they are on patrol. Clad in red berets and T-shirts bearing the organization's name, they hope to deter crime just by being noticed. The road to becoming an Angel is neither short nor easy. After being selected, a person must endure three months of training (10 hours per week) in various areas, such as self-defense, first aid and CPR, citizen's arrests, patrol techniques, and the penal code. A person does not have to be Superman to be a Guardian Angel. The organization is searching for the proper attitude, not big muscles.

The Guardian Angels patrol the streets of many large cities, sometimes in very dangerous areas. Unable to carry any type of weapon for protection, they must be fully competent to handle any situation. With the danger that the Guardian Angels face, one might expect that they would receive hazard pay or some kind of pension. But the organization is run on a completely volunteer basis. No one is paid a salary, so every dollar given to the Guardian Angels goes directly toward getting them out to protect more streets in more cities.

The Alliance of Guardian Angels has been such a success that it has branched out in efforts to protect more people from another type of danger. New to the scene are the Cyberangels. This subgroup was formed to find new ways to allow children to surf the Internet more safely. For this, the Cyberangels were awarded the 1998 President's Service Award for "outstanding achievement in protecting children and families on the Internet." People are realizing that crime and violence are getting out of hand. The Guardian Angels organization is an example of how one person felt he could help. He formed this Alliance, and others joined in with their support. They have become a large group of individuals who just "dare to care." Walking the streets at night, people feel a little bit safer knowing that they have Angels of their side.

References

1. "Guardian Angels," *http://www.guardianangels.org*
2. "Guardian Angels Safety Patrol," *http://www.ai.mit.edu/people/ericldab/ga.html*

Furthermore, at a recent international security conference, several security professionals agreed that attitudes about security as a concept are not necessarily shared among security practitioners. Along with Garcia, David Gilmore, also a CPP, focused on discussing the current body of security knowledge.[9] Gilmore addressed the questions "why isn't security accepted within the academic community?" and "why isn't it better accepted outside the industry?"[10] He presented findings from a study sponsored within the American Society of Industrial Security (ASIS); the findings suggested that even security practitioners have not reached any sort of consensus on what they believe to be included in the field of security. Furthermore, the security industry has "no common principles, no standards, no common language, [and] no common approach"[11] to developing an understanding of security as a concept and as a discipline. Lack of professional standards has become one of the biggest areas of criticism within the profession. In Garcia's words, there are no barriers to entry. "Anyone can hang a shingle and identify their objectives to be security-related."[12]

Professionalizing the Security Industry

Security professionals must establish a routine that will be followed, and they must be prepared to observe and make notations about any deviations or disruptions in routine. Security professionals are typically identified as either highly trained, well-paid professionals or extremely unskilled, underpaid individuals. The absence of industry standards has prolonged the debate about who even qualifies as a security professional.

Businesses choosing to emphasize the role of security in the overall health of the business seek out security professionals of the highest caliber. They see the value in utilizing these highly trained professionals to enhance the business's overall performance. But not all businesses are quick to embrace such a high standard. Some see security as an added expense they cannot afford. Too often the security professionals who come in contact with the public are in the latter category, known commonly as "rent-a-cops." Such an extreme dichotomy does not serve well the reputation of security professionals as a whole.

In an attempt to identify and determine essential professional standards for the security profession, in 1977, at the twenty-third ASIS Annual Seminar and Exhibits, ASIS awarded its first Certified Protection Professional (CPP) certification.[13] More than 8,000 security practitioners have worked through the professional certification program offered by ASIS and have earned the respected CPP designation.[14] While the issue of professional standards has been part of a long-standing debate, part of that discussion is linked with conversations about training and education. Training programs and certification processes have been used by security professionals to establish professional standards within the security industry. The security industry has been questioned as a discipline of study because it lacks a rigorous academic standard by which to evaluate security-related resources and academic and professional training. What type of training should be required of security professionals? Should it depend on their area of security expertise? Should it be offered in the context of a liberal arts education, similar to criminal justice or management programs, or should it be a topic-specific training format, such as computer training seminars available to the general public? These are all open questions. As of this writing, no definitive statements on these matters have been offered. But efforts are underway to address these kinds of discipline-specific issues. Members of ASIS are also leading the way in offering solutions for how to coordinate the individual efforts with more collective efforts to study and understand the security discipline.

Security Education

People taking actions to professionalize the security industry end up working with people trying to provide structure for an emerging security discipline. In fact, ASIS's Standing Committee on Academic Programs in Colleges and Universities has been wrestling with these and related issues for several years.[15] In fact, security practitioners in ASIS, arguably the most prestigious international security organization, are discussing what they believe are essential steps for establishing security as an academic discipline. In their presentation, David Gilmore, Carl Richards, and Martin Gill talked about the three-pronged approach that they have devised from within the ASIS organizational structure. First, they seek to develop a description of the field of security that can be used as a baseline for future security education development efforts. Second, they expect to review the status of baccalaureate and graduate security degree programs. Finally, they spend some time discussing the status of scholarly research in the area of security.[16]

Excellent Resources for Security Education

SCARMAN CENTRE[1]

The campus-based courses currently on offer, most of which can be taken one year full time or two years part time, are as follows:

- Msc/Postgraduate Diploma in Policing and Social Conflict
- Msc/Postgraduate Diploma in Crime Prevention and Community Safety
- Msc/Postgraduate Diploma in Criminology
- Msc/Postgraduate Diploma in Applied Criminology
- Msc/Postgraduate Diploma in Crime and Criminal Justice
- Msc/Postgraduate Diploma in Clinical Criminology
- Msc/Postgraduate Diploma in Security and Organizational Risk Management

The distance-learning courses currently on offer are as follows:

- Msc/Postgraduate Diploma in Community Safety
- Msc/Postgraduate Diploma in Criminal Justice
- Msc/Postgraduate Diploma in Health and Safety Management
- Msc/Postgraduate Diploma in Policing and Public Order Studies
- Msc/Postgraduate Diploma in Risk, Crisis, and Disaster Management
- Msc/Postgraduate Diploma in Security and Risk Management
- Msc/Postgraduate Diploma in Security Management
- Undergraduate Certificate and Diploma in Security Management

Aims of the program

- Provide you with a thorough grounding in theory and practice.
- Enable you to engage in informed debate about major issues in policing and social conflict.
- Inform you about recent developments in the field.
- Equip you to design, conduct and critically appraise research.
- Enhance your career by achieving a postgraduate degree from a prestigious university.

In addition, the MSc is designed to enable students to develop new and improved skills. These include the ability to

- Evaluate information critically.
- Communicate ideas clearly.
- Undertake advanced conceptual analysis.
- Understand and apply theories and models.
- Use information sources effectively.
- Report and interpret research critically.
- Develop new approaches to problem solving.

WEBSTER UNIVERSITY, ST. LOUIS, MO[2]

The curriculum of the program is based primarily on the social sciences. The program is designed to give maximum exposure to security management skills and to provide flexibility for the specific needs of the individual student. The content of the security management program complements and assists the student in preparation for the Certified Protection Professional Program.

(continued)

Program Curriculum

The 36 semester hours required for the master of arts or the 51 semester hours required for the master of business administration must include the following courses for a major/emphasis in security management:

- SECR 5000 Security Management (Requisite Course)
- SECR 5010 Legal and Ethical Issues in Security Management
- SECR 5020 Security Administration and Management
- SECR 5030 Business Assets Protection
- SECR 5060 Emergency Planning
- SECR 5080 Information Systems Security
- SECR 5090 Behavioral Issues
- SECR 6000 Integrated Studies in Security Management

In addition, the student chooses elective courses offered in the major and/or from the program curricula of other majors. If the requisite course is waived, the student must choose an elective course from this major or from the program curriculum of another major. Students pursuing dual majors who have the requisite course(s) waived will complete only the remaining required courses for the dual majors. The required courses and electives listed in this core may be taken as Directed Studies, subject to the conditions stated in the Directed Studies section listed under Academic Policies and Procedures.

Graduate Certificate Program

Security Management Issues (21 credit hours: 12 required and 9 elective)

The graduate certificate program in Security Management Issues is designed for the security professional who has or will acquire responsibilities for the management of security activities. It will also assist the individual who is relatively new to the security profession and needs to gain an understanding of the discipline. The program offers the student two distinct approaches to study and learning: theoretical and practical. The theoretical approach will provide the student with a broad overview, along with a basic understanding of the theory and critical concepts associated with the security field. The practical approach is designed to provide limited hands-on and observable experiences in specific areas of security as they relate to the public and/or private sectors. The student will complete the certificate program with an understanding and broad working knowledge of the security field that will allow him or her to carry out security responsibilities.

The student seeking the graduate certificate in Security Management Issues must hold a baccalaureate degree from a regionally accredited institution. Transfer credits and course substitutions are not applicable to graduate certificates. The 21 credit hours that make up the Graduate Certificate Program may be transferred and used by the student as a basis for pursuing a Master of Arts Degree in Security Management at an established Webster University site offering the Security Management major.

Requirements

Twelve hours Security Management core courses:

- SECR 5000 Security Management
- SECR 5010 Legal and Ethical Issues in Security Management
- SECR 5030 Business Assets Protection

In addition, all students will be required to take either

- SECR 5070 Information Security, or
- SECR 5076 Proprietary Information

Nine hours of elective courses from Security Management Issues (SECR 5070 series):

- Access Controls
- Risk Management
- Investigations
- Violence in the Workplace
- Terrorism
- Physical Security Planning
- Security in Hospitals, Schools, and Retail Establishments

The student seeking the graduate certificate should consult the Admission, Enrollment, Academic Policies, and Graduate Certificates sections of this catalog for information regarding application, admission, registration, and the academic policies of Webster University.

References

1. *http://www.le.ac.uk/scarman/teach/courses.html*
2. *http://www.webster.edu*

Preferred models of security have included physical security, personnel security, information systems security, investigations, loss prevention, risk management or analysis, legal aspects, and emergency planning. Three essential disciplines were mentioned in this discussion about the future of security education: criminology, risk, and management. Garcia reminds readers that the goal here is not to decide how to exclude anyone but to determine how the different disciplines contribute to the final security solution.[17] Yet some problems do exist when information is accumulated exclusively within a privatized professional organization. ASIS was organized with a unique purpose. Attention must be given to the conceptualization of security as a concept outside of large privatized corporations. This assessment is made without judgment. The worst outcome of this ongoing debate is the possibility that one group of security professionals might assume intellectual, technical, or professional superiority over another security group, when the fact is that different aspects of security can be quite specialized and require expertise on various levels. The current activities being undertaken by ASIS suggest that efforts to discuss basic assumptions about security as a concept are timely, and the industry will benefit tremendously by establishing both some common terms and a means by which to explore these terms theoretically.

Moving Beyond Anecdotal Research: A Focus on Method

Many authors of trade-journal security articles offer security professionals examples of a problem and then outline the related solution, a solution that worked *for them*. The story becomes a snapshot of an issue, often without a deeper understanding of the target environment, and often without a significant period of follow-up to see if the changes had both an immediate effect and an impact over time. While the information may be interesting, it is not always applicable to the readers' security setting. This highlights the importance of establishing objective measures for determining whether the experience is transferable to other security settings, and under what conditions. In this way, academic research studies are making important contributions to the security body of knowledge.

In this text, I emphasize the fact that all security professionals, whether new to an environment or revising an existing security system, must find a place to begin thinking about or rethinking the security objectives they want to highlight within any given target environment. It is not enough to say "Fischer and Green recommend this," even if we know Fischer and Green to be respected security professionals. Security professionals who have worked in a given environment know more about their environment than any security reference manual does. Learning to think through critical evaluations of existing resources and becoming more familiar with the environment you seek to secure will be as important as attending security training seminars. Once security professionals find a basic list of essential security information, it is their responsibility to adapt the information to their environment.

Another important, related point is the need to integrate information from other disciplines, like leadership studies, that might appear at first review to be unrelated to the study of security. I have attended a security training seminars on various topics. Typically the moderator is an experienced security professional. In one case, the topic was leadership and the presenter had an impressive, multifaceted 30-year history in the industry. At one point in his presentation, he was speaking about the importance of leadership and leadership types. He had compiled a list of leadership types based on his experience dealing with people throughout his career. While interesting and informative, the list was not linked in any way to the entire body of research on leadership theory, an extensive (and expanding) body of research. This disconnect between the existing body of research and the experiences of practitioners within the security field highlights, again, the benefits to be derived from broader academic involvement.

Security practitioners will benefit tremendously from academic efforts to seek out and integrate information from the vast amount of applicable research from a variety of disciplinary specializations. Finding a niche for interdisciplinary topics like security within a broader bureaucratic structure as massive and complex as that of institutions of higher education can be problematic.[18] Security does not fit neatly into any one designated academic discipline. For example, when dealing with computer security issues it is as important to understand computers and computer systems as it is to understand laws, investigation techniques, and enforcement protocols. Consider again the area of computer security. Does a course on computer security belong in a security program or in a criminal justice program like mine, with a private security minor? There is no question that students in both programs would benefit from the course, but the question of where to place it varies from institution to institution.

Such disciplinary restrictions within academic institutions create difficulties that must be overcome if an emerging discipline is to gain credibility. Practitioners need information that is site specific and task oriented. As a consequence, they might not necessarily embrace the seemingly over analytical, sometimes long-winded contributions coming into the security field from the ivory tower. Academic efforts to understand the security objective are likely to focus on attempts to quantify specific terms, concepts, applications, technologies, environmental settings, and the like in an effort to establish a theoretical base for understanding more fully the security enterprise. Such efforts can easily be met with skepticism from security professionals, who see themselves as having a job to do.

Both security practitioners and academics or researchers need the expertise offered by the other group. Efforts to enhance the collective understanding of people within the security industry are useful only when the information can be used well by persons seeking assistance in developing a broader base or a deeper level of understanding about these security-related matters. While security professionals may need assistance with the research process, academics will benefit tremendously from hearing about security professionals' experiences and gaining intimate knowledge of how their security objectives come to be outlined within their unique target environments. Cooperative efforts are likely to produce research that is more user friendly and helpful to people in both groups.

EMPHASIZING A SENSE OF PLACE

While security practitioners may spend a significant amount of time reading about new trends in security, I think it is critically important for students and people unfamiliar with the security industry to understand the importance of place. The degree to which people become involved in providing their own protection against a perceived threat will change depending on the setting. Preliminary studies I have done with college students suggest support for this.[19] At home, at work, at an airport, or even at the local Little League ball park, security threats and threats to safety exist. People's willingness to assume responsibility for their own protection depends on their perception of threats, their level of awareness about threats, and their familiarity with the setting.

Even a basic discussion about essential security information must consider the target environment. Take, as an example, a security professional who has been responsible for managing security at a local hospital for 10 years. The individual has the opportunity to relocate and finds himself coordinating security for a different hospital. Because every environment is unique, his understanding of hospital security issues will be useful only to the degree that he understands the new hospital environment. The physical layout, the "hotspots," the employee attitudes, the computer system and access protocol, the culture, the services provided, the security policies and procedures, and many other details about the environment will be site specific. Perhaps this hospital has more resources for security, and so the practitioner decides to take advantage of some of the latest innovations in the field and replace out-of-date equipment or update management practices. To effectively update the hospital's existing security system, the security professional must first develop a comprehensive awareness of the new target environment. To underestimate the importance of a comprehensive awareness of the environment to be secured is to underestimate the power of place. In the field of security, understanding the power of place is essential.

Site-Specific Attention and Attention to Security Themes

Security professionals are making publishing companies rich with their creative efforts outlining various ways to discuss security issues. Books on specialized security topics abound: hospital security, airport security, high-rise security, hotel security, big event security, executive protection, retail security, mall security, school security, security on college campuses, supermarket security, security during travel, home security, biometrics, access control systems, transport services, bank security, casino security, computer security, security for churches and other religious institutions, national park security, terrorism (domestic and international), check fraud prevention, and so on—the list is long. As the result of September 11, it becomes clear that homeland security issues add another dimension to that list.

Information about each of these areas of security is excellent for professional security practitioners working within a particular specialization. They will be the ones people call for help on those specific security issues. But for the novice security student or for people new to the security industry, directing the discussion toward the conditions of their unique target environment becomes an equally important yet a much more manageable task. Thorough review of the environment may seem simplistic, but it can have huge implications for determining what security-related information gets integrated into the overall security design.

Ideas from 10 books in any specialized security area taken from the preceding list will not be enough. You must know the environmental conditions in the target environment. Of course, for a textbook writer, the difficult issue is the fact that it is nearly impossible to talk in general terms about environmental features because there are so many different settings with so many different characteristics. This is where the reader must assume his or her own responsibility for the security process. I can offer general thoughts on security and provide a framework for discussing security-related issues, but then readers must feel empowered to make critical decisions about their own security-related needs. The general information must be modified to fit their particular environments.

As I begin talking about specific security issues, I want readers to think about how and why they would justify their decisions to include or not include certain information in their own environment. Not every security protocol is appropriate for every target environment. To make these decisions confidently, readers must find a balance between the security-related information they are reading about and the characteristics of their own environment.

Security as a Relative Concept

Another important consideration for security practitioners, particularly in the expanding global marketplace, is the way security as a concept is presented and understood. I maintain that security as it is understood in China is different (not better or worse, just understood differently) from security in the United States. Security practitioners make efforts to quantify abstract ideas such as what a threat is. (Chapter 2 discusses how to assess a threat.) A specific threat is likely to be rated, based in large part, on environmental conditions. Different security professionals are likely to assess threats based on individual priorities, industry research, professional consultation, professional preferences, and the like. This may result in two security practitioners evaluating the same environment and coming up with a different outcome. Does this mean one of them is wrong? Not necessarily. Many theories of crime have been offered, and various theories about how to best protect a given area will also be offered. The critical factor for determining which theory is better is to thoroughly review the research relevant to the situation and then consider how that research is useful given the unique environmental conditions.

Let us say that a new security professional is responsible for operations at a local retail mall. There is an incident in the parking lot after dark, and someone raises questions about whether appropriate standards for lighting in that parking lot are being maintained. How should you respond? Where can you find that information? Once you find a source of information, how can you determine if that source is appropriate for the specific parking setting (whether a large lot, a parking garage, or both)?

Go to the library or the Internet and do your own research. The National Parking Association recommends illumination of 6 foot candles (fc, a unit for measuring illumination: the amount of light a single candle provides over 1 square foot), at 30 inches above the parking floor in covered facilities. Open parking areas can get by with 2 fc, according to the Illinois Engineers Society North America.[20] Even the Code of Federal Regulations lists specific requirements of 0.2 fc for lighting protected areas within a perimeter.[21] These are standards presented by the federal government and U.S. organizations. But what might lighting standards be in Brazil? Japan? Academics and security practitioners about to open offices in other countries might ask these types of questions, but most working professionals within the United States will only need to concern themselves (usually) with U.S. standards governing particular matters such as the lighting in parking lots. For a security professional explaining a decision about parking lot lighting, it would be enough to reference the industry standard and the National Parking Association. A more thorough discussion of these security standards and professional guidelines would be necessary if the company's security issues required determining legal standards in other countries, or if the company determined the need to have a higher standard, for example.

Inviting commentary about different interpretations of what *security* means may be uncomfortable. The effect, however, is a more thorough review of the essential information. If environmental conditions are to be fully examined, then security professionals must make sure it is acceptable to discuss the conditions as a construct, a collective definition of what it means to be secure, created by the collective efforts of employees, managers, customers, security practitioners, and anyone else impacted by the security-related decisions.

Security as a concept must be openly debated in relative terms, right alongside the discussions about legal directives that guide the security industry. Not everyone welcomes debates about security as a concept. While it may not be comfortable to identify security as a concept that cannot be adequately assessed or even defined until a target environment is well known, the reality of this is clear. Discussing any concept in relative terms broadens the dialogue in ways that are difficult to manage. For this reason, people simply do not like to do it. It is easier to think of a concept within definite, identifiable parameters. As an academic, my training suggests that few concepts have neatly outlined parameters. Security is no exception. It is too easy to see security as a static enterprise, when—as stated before—security is a dynamic, interactive process.

If I, as a security practitioner, said, "I want to make you secure in your home," what would you think? Perhaps I even suggested that to feel safe and secure in your home, you would need to establish a stable, predictable environment. How would that sound? Good? Context is important here. What visual representation of the word *home* do you have? Does it matter whether the home is located in the middle of a public housing project or in a suburban neighborhood? Does it help to put locks on the doors and windows if physical abuse commonly takes place inside the home? How does one provide security when the problem exists within the target environment? Efforts to provide security under these circumstances would be quite different from efforts to provide security for a household without internal troubles. Imagine a security professional saying to you, "In order to maintain a predictable environment in the home, no one other than family members will be allowed into the house without a written request, received two weeks in advance of their visit. The two weeks is essential to assess the implications of that visit on the security of the home." Tell your kids or your kid's friends that they have to request permission to come over, and see what happens. Clearly, the security protocol put in place has to make sense to the people who will be using it most often.

Another example of the relativity of security-related issues can be found in something as specific as airport security standards. No one industry was as dramatically affected by the events of 9/11 than the airline industry. But even before the dramatic hijacking of these aircrafts, the standards for airline security have been maintained differently in different countries. El Al Israel Airlines is known internationally for its military-style security. With only one flight a day, El Al carries about 150,000 people annually to 23 destinations.[22] There are 20 aircraft in the airline's fleet. Contrast this with the 300 to 500 aircraft of major U.S. carriers, with hundreds of flights departing out of major airports each day.[23] Extra security precautions can be taken when there is only one flight per day. In the United States, before 9/11, it was believed that the expense of the extra security precautions would put most airlines out of business. Now, as the impact of 9/11 becomes more clear with time, it appears that the significant changes in airport security are going to be longstanding.

A security professional who imposes a packaged understanding of what is required to provide security in a given setting makes a series of assumptions about that setting. Martin Gill talked about this in a recent national meeting: "Can you imagine a situation where a company says to someone, 'Can you tell me whether my CCTV [closed-circuit television] works?' And then someone goes back and says yes or no?"[24] The answer to the question depends on multiple variables, not the least of which is a clear understanding of the role CCTV is intended to play within the overall security system outlined for that target environment. Does the United States have adequate aviation security since 9/11? Because the United States beefed up its aviation security after 9/11, does that mean that El Al Israel Airlines should do the same? How does assessment of aviation security change as a result of 9/11? Does an increased response in airline security leave vulnerable other areas? None of these questions can be answered well without understanding the context around which these two aviation systems, the U.S. and Israel's, were developed and then modified to meet additional security threats.

Again, we see that place and context are important features for studying security as a concept. For this reason, rather than just providing a definition of security, I talk with students more directly about how a plethora of variables, including time, place, regional socioeconomic status, culture, predominant religious affiliations, race, geographic location, just to name a few, might impact discussions of security. Establishing a common definition for the term *security* is not good enough; people must go beyond the definition of the term to include features of the setting they seek to make secure. Important, too, is the responsibility to assess threats and risk levels while also acknowledging an individual's need to achieve a specific level of security. In fact, the concept that represents the absence of security, fear or fearfulness, is likely to lead to emotional reactions rather than objective, carefully planned responses. The following paragraphs discuss the role of fear in security and crime prevention.

DISTINGUISHING BETWEEN CRIME AND THE FEAR OF CRIME

Crime and the fear of crime affect the everyday lives of people in the United States and across the globe. Of particular interest to me, as a researcher and an academic professional, is the gap between actual recorded crime and the fear of crime. Security professionals and others interested in security must attempt to better understand not only the facts about crime but also the fears that result from erroneous perceptions about crime. Security professionals are becoming the resource people go to when they are looking for information about appropriate, realistic responses to a crime or the fear of crime. Often the best efforts to collect information about crime do not alleviate a person's fear of that crime. According to the National Crime Victimization Survey, violent crime rates continue to decrease. Falling to the lowest levels since the government began measuring violent crime victimization in 1973, violent crime affected 33.7 of every 1,000 Americans age 12 or older in 1999.[25]

While people tend to pay steady attention to the issues of the day that affect them in their everyday lives, attention given to security-related issues is likely to fluctuate with individual and/or community perception about crime and victimization. Excellent research has been offered to remind people that their fears of being the victim of a violent crime are often misplaced.[26] For example, although women and older people fear crime because they believe themselves to be among the most heavily victimized of all groups, the rates of victimization are higher for men than women and for younger people than older people.[27] Also, women have been taught to fear attacks from strangers on the street, when in fact research has shown that perpetrators of assault and rape are most often people who know the victim.

It is important for security professionals to compare perceptions of crime against reality. The more a security response to an identified threat is based on realistic assessments of the threats, rather than cultural myths, the more appropriate those security protection efforts will be. Whether the fear of crime is based on personal experience, research analysis and findings, or simply a result of news stories or violence on television, fear can be a powerful motivator. People want to feel safe, and trends suggest that people in the United States are increasingly willing to pay to ensure or enhance their sense of security. The need to feel safe is a strong motivator. The question is, If a person comes across excellent research suggesting that his or her fears are unfounded, what would that person do? Would he or she change the fears or disbelieve the research?

Fear assessment and fear management may be an important activity for a security management team. How should a security professional assess a fear expressed by a coworker? Perhaps there is information about someone who is acting erratically. How should the security professional respond? What factors influence the security professional's decision about how to gather information and then how to respond? Security professionals must understand what fear means and how the perception of fear affects attitudes about threats and risk levels.

LINKS WITH LAW ENFORCEMENT: A TENUOUS RELATIONSHIP?

Crime rates and crime trends offer some insight into the likelihood that certain types of events will impact a target environment. Having accurate information about crime and the fear of crime is only one part of what is required to establish a secure setting. Like public policing agencies of yesteryear, security professionals are entering a time of professional transition. The proposed development of a body of literature and enhanced standards for security professionals is reminiscent of the transition of the criminal justice profession from a training program to a discipline of study—a transition that took place 25 to 30 years ago. The role of education in the professional life of both public and private police officers and other security professionals has been under constant debate.

Institutions of higher education offer a variety of degrees related to security; criminal justice, business, management, human relations, and computers are just a few. Few areas at the university are particularly well suited to absorb this "Excellent Resources for Security Education" interdisciplinary topic within the existing academic structure. At this point most academic programs do not offer security credentials, with few exceptions (see the "Excellent Resources for Security Education" box). In large part, the history of training within the security profession has been well defined by the professional certifications developed and conveyed within professional security organizations such as ASIS and the IFPO (International Foundation for Protection Officers). As a means of quality control, ensuring that only the best-prepared professionals are granted the certification, these organizations provide an ongoing training and security licensing service to the international professional community.

Security, as a profession, has not received the kind of policy and financial support offered to policing organizations that was offered to public law enforcement. The expansion of the study of criminal justice in universities has been largely attributed to the 1967 President's Commission on Law Enforcement and Administration of Justice and Congress' authorization of the Law Enforcement Assistance Administration in 1968.[28] Colleges raced to establish degree programs, although there were problems. In short, after 30 years, criminology and criminal justice studies programs are still seeking to define their place within a liberal arts educational setting.[29]

Security professionals are relegated, perhaps unfairly, to second-class status when compared with public police function. The expansion beyond public and private police histories to include various other factors associated with time, place, financing, and so forth may expose more fully the similarities and differences between public police and security professionals. Although some practitioners, in both police and security professions, see their roles as differing to various degrees, one serving private needs and one public needs, changes in the role of security professionals are resulting in connections linking private security professionals more directly with public safety services. Parallels between the history of law enforcement and the history of security have been, and continue to be, emphasized.*

The current understanding of security would be enhanced by including research highlighting the conception of security within certain places and times, such as the "Wild West" in the United States or a current-day Third World nation. The history of security is seldom discussed in terms of threats such as drive-by shootings, crack houses, criminal activity in low-income housing projects, hate crimes, and other matters directly related to the concept of security as it exists for many Americans each day. Actions that affect persons who cannot afford private security services are deemed the responsibility of public safety officials, such as the police. Community-oriented policing efforts are the most direct response to these kinds of community concerns.

The history of security is most often discussed in terms of the need for security in the business sector or within a corporate structure. To some degree,

---

*Various isolated studies have been done on this idea, some directly related to the idea that the public and private police histories overlap considerably and some less directly connected. As police services become more privatized, attention is being given to public police agencies that employ privately contracted security services to meet a public policing need. As I see it, this history is still intertwined, although, as suggested throughout this chapter, studies of security-related issues outside of law enforcement might also be quite instructive. See, for example, J. R. Greene et al., "Merging Public and Private Security for Collective Benefit," *American Journal of Police, 14,* no. 2 (1995): 3–20; A. Micucci, The Changing of the Guard: The Transformation of Private Security (paper presented at the National Academy of Criminal Justice Sciences, Boston, MA, May 1995); P. Palango, "On the Mean Streets: As Police Cut Back, Private Cops Are Moving In," *Maclean's, 111,* no. 2 (1995): 10–15. For more information on this subject, see Chapter 10.

9/11 changed that because each community understands that it might be vulnerable to a future terrorist attack, and measures need to be taken to protect the community. Names such as Pinkerton, Brinks, and Wells Fargo are identified as having the most significant role in the development of the U.S. security industry to date. Yet these are only a few of the many individuals who made it their job to secure themselves, their businesses, their homes, and their families without the additional financial resources necessary to acquire security through professional assistance. After 9/11, the average citizen understands that if he or she is standing in line at the airport or in a bus station and see a bag that is unattended, it is a security threat. The average citizen is called on to become a part of the community protection system. But what exactly can his or her role be? Is security as a concept discussed differently based on the definition and presentation of public and private space?

Definitions of Public and Private Space

Security professionals tend to emphasize a construction of security based largely on a business and corporate model. Security practices including technologies, management strategies, and integrated security designs have been discussed almost exclusively within private settings. It may also be important to think about how, or if, these efforts in private industry impact public law enforcement agency responsibilities.

If the decision about who pays for security is a factor in determining what security is, then only those who can pay can buy security. Following this logic, if I could not afford to buy a security system for my home, does that mean I could not enhance the security of my home? Private citizens, community members, and public safety officials (including law enforcement, emergency service crews, and other public service providers) are all working to enhance the safety and security of local community residents, yet in August 2000, hundreds of people attended the funeral of an 11-year-old boy who had been struck and killed by a stray bullet in South Minneapolis.[30] Speaking at the funeral, the pastor said, "It's time for us to police our own community."[31] Whose job was it to provide security for this little boy? Questions about the responsibility of a public official to protect the public on private property, or the responsibility of private police to protect the public on private property, are openly (sometimes heatedly) debated.

Discussions about the roles of public police and private police are ongoing. A fundamental theme of these conversations is whether public police are reactive or proactive. Police departments are expected to be reactive, whereas security practitioners focus more on proactive prevention. With the expansion of community policing initiatives, this model is clearly shifting. Police departments across the United States are, in fact, looking to the community for assistance with their policing objectives. A recent publication from a local community policing institute[32] suggests that a big part of the institute's job involves figuring out what factors make an area a crime hotspot. Once a factor is identified, efforts are concentrated toward trying to change them. This certainly reflects a proactive, or prevention, orientation in policing. The mission of this community policing institute is to build community partnerships to develop, implement, and strengthen community policing strategies.[33] A series of interesting research efforts could study whether the techniques and practices used in proactive police efforts are similar to proactive efforts initiated by security professionals in private settings. How are the models being used similar and how are they different?

Once again, a sense of place is important. Some interesting research has been produced to explore more fully the distinctions between public and private space, and public and private police.[34] Consider the Mall of America in Minnesota, or Disneyland. Both of these private industries are organized around the idea of attracting masses of customers. How does a public action in a private setting differ from the response one would see if that same action had taken place in a public setting? Security professionals and security management teams, in consultation with corporate boards or other corporate representatives, often determine whether—or to what extent—public law enforcement is involved when a law is broken on private property. How does one justify the fact that a private security professional who discovers a legal infraction may, with the support from the CEO or Board of Directors, choose not to report that infraction to the police. But would that same legal infraction committed by a person in public space lead to arrest and possibly jail time? What are the implications of such private actions on overall assessments of community safety and the role of the criminal justice system in society? Notions of private justice should be explored more fully.

If friends, relatives, and neighbors of the young man killed in south Minneapolis formed a group to combat violence in their neighborhood, maybe even established a means by which they could pay for a person's time to patrol the area, would this be a public or private organization? Do these community efforts impact people's understanding of public or private security services? If the group was organized with the assistance of the local law enforcement's community policing initiative, would that be different than if it was solely the initiative of a group of private citizens? What authority does this group have under law? If the group members' ultimate objective is to increase the security of their apartment building or neighborhood, does that make their working definition of *security* different from the definitions of *security* developed primarily within business and industry environments? Are the same models of security applicable to a community setting? While some of these issues are open questions, others are linked to legal definitions and contractual obligations that are ultimately resolved in the courts.

Responsibility for Self-Protection: A Personal Security Issue or a Police Issue?

One of the most intriguing security-related questions I have encountered to date is, "To what degree is a person responsible for his or her own security?" Of course, history suggests a much different answer than the one in the extremely litigious culture of the modern United States. Historically, people were responsible for their own protection and preservation. Today, if I slip on ice outside of an establishment in the middle of winter I can sue that establishment and win, even in Minnesota, where ice is common. Documentation within the security industry has focused on the profession itself or has been industry specific (e.g., labor relations) rather than embracing efforts to broaden the existing base of understanding within the industry and in academic research. The focus has been on corporations and efforts to protect capitalist interests.

Consider the case of Bernard Goetz (discussed in the highlight box). While much of the action he took was labeled "vigilante justice," and his motivations for the shooting were called into question in the courts, the case raises an interesting question about the conditions in which one may assume responsibility for responding to a perceived threat. This is particularly evident when the threat is presented in a public area, like the subway, rather than within one's home, which is considered a private residence. How much does the place matter when issues of security, particularly private security, are called into question? This case should indicate that security is a complex concept and should be explored more broadly than from within the corporate boardroom.

Self-Defense versus Criminal Activity[1-3]

There is a line between self-defense and criminal activity. The difficult part is trying to define that line accurately. In most cases, where the line is drawn is a matter of perspective, with a seemingly endless list of legitimate arguments for both sides. In the Bernhard Goetz case, the line between personal protection and aggravated assault was hotly contested.

On December 22, 1984, Bernhard Goetz boarded the downtown IRT train at the 14th Street station in Manhattan. It was 1 P.M., and he was carrying a loaded Smith and Wesson .38 caliber revolver. He sat down across from a group of four African-American young men. A few moments later, they tried to get some money out of him. Goetz pulled his gun and unloaded it on the men. He then jumped off the train, which had been stopped, and disappeared, only to turn himself in a few days later. Was this self-defense or attempted murder?

Most people in the United States were fascinated with Bernhard Goetz because he took it on himself to administer "justice" he believed was not being handled adequately by public officials. Each of the four young men he shot had committed serious crimes prior to the attempted robbery of Goetz. During an interview, one of the robbers admitted that he and the other men intended to rob Goetz because "he looked like easy bait." Goetz was not mistaken; the men were going to take his money. This, however, was not the first time Goetz had been approached by muggers. For example, he was once followed by a seemingly drug-crazed harasser who pulled a gun on him. He fired no shots; he only threatened the youth. Bernhard Goetz was said to have developed a fear of being attacked. A psychiatrist testified on his behalf about how desperate people become when they fear that their lives are in danger.

What about the other side of the story? What about the things Goetz said during the trial? Goetz admitted to going back to shoot one of the young men a second time, saying to him, "You look alright; here's another." He also made the comment that his actions could be viewed as a public service and he was trying to "get as many of them" as he could. These comments would have seemed to turn the case against Goetz, who was consequently labeled a racist. Was there any other way to stop this crime from occurring? The jury had to decide if he was a racist, guilty of cold-hearted attempted murder, or just someone who refused to be victimized by crime. Their decision was surprising. There were 18 charges. They jury found him innocent on 17; the only one they punished him for was a weapon charge, for which he would have to spend just 8.5 months in prison.

The case of Bernhard Goetz raises the issue of where to draw the line between personal protection and aggravated assault. What if Goetz had entered that subway car with a bodyguard who did the shooting? Would that have been viewed differently? Many celebrities have bodyguards around them at all times to protect them from crazy fans and other dangers. Is personal security only just when one person is paying another person for protection? Where are the limitations when it comes to protecting oneself? Bernhard Goetz was aware that he was going to be robbed and possibly physically beaten or something worse. The police were not there to protect him. A paid security professional was not there. Whose "job" was it to protect Bernhard Goetz?

References

1. "Cabey v. Goetz," http://www.courttv.com/casefiles/verdicts/goetz.html
2. "Subway Vigilante Admits Making Racist Remarks," April 12, 1996, http://www.cnn.com/US/9604/12/goetz/index.html
3. L. R. Cohen, "The Legitimacy of Vigilanteism," http://www.saf.org/LawReviews/Cohenl.html

THE CHALLENGES OF INTEGRATION: MANY LEVELS

Agencies and other community organizations with public safety functions, including 911 and other emergency response organizations, fire and rescue organizations, hazardous waste crews, public health agencies, and community watch groups, share a common interest in developing a better understanding of safety and security-related concepts. Security professionals and educators seek to integrate the academic understanding of security as a concept with the practitioner perspective of security as a concept. Law enforcement agencies share common interests with security professionals (and probably other public safety officials) because both are trying to provide stable and predictable environments within their communities. In the aftermath of 9/11, additional federal monies have been made available to assist local communities with their efforts to ensure that their community is protected. The forms these efforts to ensure protection will take are not at all clear.

Security professionals are trained to identify security-related issues within a target setting, and law enforcement professionals focus on a multitude of issues within their community. The number of problems a community is expected to confront is growing so much that law enforcement agencies are hiring contracted security personnel for specific duties. Furthermore, how does the integration of community-oriented programs (COPs) and other private citizen groups motivated to protect themselves because they do not feel secure in their homes or neighborhoods, like the Guardian Angels, impact the existing conceptualizations of security? These ideas about security, from both the public police and private security arenas, can work in tandem to assist researchers and practitioners in defining parameters for expanding the field of security-related study.

Security issues directly affect persons across the globe, not just students and professionals focusing on security for private industry, although that has been the primary focus of discussions of security to date. Efforts to integrate relevant security-related ideas have had some success, but it is still difficult to get security-related information into a form that researchers can easily track. Security practitioners are rising to meet the technological challenges in greater numbers as industry demands dictate. People working in security must know the industry and stay up to date on innovations. Security professionals specialize in developing unique security systems for any number of settings. Each environment is different and requires specialized responses. For this reason, business professionals are not the only people using security professionals as resources. People from the public sector, including law enforcement agencies, are electing to contract with security professionals for various public safety and security-related responsibilities.

Among other things, the job of the security professional is filled with relatively new technological challenges. CCTV cameras, access control, and em-

ployee monitoring devices are becoming essentials tools for security practitioners, but like other technological innovations, changes are happening so fast that
it is hard for businesses to keep up without the help of savvy security professionals.

Consider, for example, the case of computer security. The Energy Information Administration first collected household survey data on personal computers in 1990, when 16 percent of households owned one or more personal
computers. By 1997, that share had more than doubled, to 35 percent.[35] Most
workplaces cannot exist without computers. What people do to secure their
personal computers is largely up to them.

Depending on how they use their computers or how much they value the
information on their computers, some people may seek to provide more sophisticated protection from hackers. Businesses, for example, are likely to have
at least some antivirus programs, password access, or encryption programs. As
the information collected on the systems becomes more important, the level of
security deemed appropriate also increases. And, as the level of protection increases, so too does the likelihood that the company will utilize computer security experts to ensure that a more sophisticated protection system is put in
place and maintained. Yet to know about the security systems available is not
enough on its own. The decision to designate specific information as more or
less important is one made by the business, not the computer security professional. The ideal circumstance would find these professionals—a representative
from the business, a security professional, and a computer programmer—interacting and sharing their expertise as decisions about the security system protocol are identified and finalized.

Assessing Security in Everyday Life

All individuals have found themselves in circumstances where they feel the
need to assess their security. Whether staying late at work, parking a car in a
lot with inferior lighting, or asking questions about a fellow employee who
seems to be behaving in an unusual manner, people confront situations that
force them to think about the security of their person or property. Most individuals simply do not have the time, interest, or level of expertise necessary to
manage all their security-related concerns alone. To save money, or because
they see identifying security issues as a matter of common sense, a group of
business professionals may take it on themselves to determine their own security needs.

Because levels of fear are unique to individuals, industries, and environments, business professionals' ability to identify perceived threats will depend
on the information they characterize as being important. What they think they
know about security, more specifically, what they miss, can leave them vulnerable. Knowing everything about succeeding in a retail business is not necessar-

ily the same as knowing everything about protecting that business from threats. For this reason, the information provided throughout the text can provide a starting point for those interested in security issues. Those most familiar with the target environment will also provide an invaluable contribution as the efforts to plan the security response are drafted, refined, integrated into the setting, monitored, and reviewed. While the business professionals discussed previously may benefit from consulting a local security practitioner, they can also get a great head start by reviewing the material presented here.

Security as a Concept for the Powerful

A last note about how we think about and how we talk about security issues invites consideration of security as a concept alongside public safety, community policing initiatives, and even within the concept of community justice. Because much of the existing body of security literature focuses on corporations and organizations that can afford to enlist a full-time security response, it is clear to me that the discussion of security as a concept needs to be expanded to include issues identified and explored within communities and by individuals and groups who do not necessarily contract for services with a security professional. Is a drive-by shooting a security management issue? Does the fact that apartment complexes located in inner-city areas are not likely to employ a security professional in the building mean that all protection concerns must go to the public police? Are citizen groups performing a security function when they organize, seek out a security consultant to assist them, and patrol their community to rid it of drug houses, drug dealers, and gang activity?

The different responsibilities traditionally assigned to public police are becoming increasingly entangled in services provided by private security professionals because public law enforcement can't do everything. Not only do we continue to see traditional law enforcement roles assigned to a security professional, we are beginning to acknowledge the overlap within these public responsibilities, which suggests that these boundaries may be breaking down in interesting ways.

IDENTIFYING INFORMATION AS ESSENTIAL

Security as a profession is emerging from the shadows of public law enforcement. As communities across the United States maintain a state of readiness against future terroristic threats and as businesses expand into multinational corporations with significant capital to be gained and/or lost, it becomes obvious that the expertise security professionals offer us is essential. People want a better understanding of the role of security in their everyday lives and are seeking to go beyond the dark, murky, often mystical history of the security profession, where early security professionals were outlaws turned lawmen, hired guns, and renegade enforcers of justice. Both the academic and practitioner communities are calling for a structured review of existing security information and the creation of an agenda for this emerging discipline of study. Such efforts to better understand not only security efforts in practice but also security as a concept have the potential to change how the industry sees itself and how it is perceived by others.

Perhaps it goes without saying that a security expert is someone who has achieved advanced or specialized knowledge of security. Often, the "important" security-related work is thought to be the work done by security experts in the boardrooms of powerful corporations across the globe. Certainly some security professionals will find themselves in corporate boardrooms, but more will offer security services at retail stores, malls, nursing homes, hospitals, schools, theme parks, and airports; on college campuses; and in personal home security services, alarm companies, local police departments, and the like.

This introduction offers only a brief glimpse into the infinite number of security-related issues of critical importance to the researchers and security officers of tomorrow. Given the broad scope of these issues, a student in the field must identify someplace to begin. One of my favorite quotes, attributed to Nicholas Murray Butler, suggests that "an expert is one who knows more and more about less and less." This phrase should be instructive for anyone interested in security. People who become too focused on a specialized feature may miss the bigger picture. Security practitioners will have different objectives; some will require a broad understanding of existing security conditions, and others will be targeting very specialized security concerns. The same will be true with academic efforts.

In the chapters that follow, I offer some definitions and an overview of basic internal security resources common to just about any setting. The broader task is to highlight areas that can be used for research and analytical comparison. The more specific task is to offer useful information, or guidelines, for those working in the security profession. Research is fallible. When researching and working with a combination of factors, it is difficult to explain why a change in one variable in setting A has an effect, when changing that same variable in setting B may produce little change. These difficulties are, undoubtedly, what makes research in the social sciences so challenging and ultimately so important. If researchers can better understand how changes in security systems impact various settings, then the discipline of security will benefit tremendously.

CONCLUSION

My objective for this introduction is to get readers thinking: thinking about security as a concept, thinking about their own notions of what *security* means, thinking about where security happens, thinking about what constitutes a basic security system, thinking about how the environmental conditions change the application of a basic security system design. While I seek to provide a comprehensive review of essential security information, I also use this introduction to call attention to the need to explore more fully the existing ideas about security as a concept.

To develop a better understanding of security, students need to be exposed to some rather simple, easy-to-follow terms and explanations. But that is not enough. They must also have a willingness to understand that any of those basic concepts can take on a different form or function when environmental conditions change. The concept of home security will change, depending on the location and type of home (e.g., urban condominium in a 100-unit building, rural single-family detached dwelling on 10 acres of land).

People from diverse backgrounds with various security-related interests are looking to the security professional for information and resources. At a minimum, security professionals must justify their approach based on their knowledge of their environment, the security field, and the objectives established within their environment. While bridging the gap between practitioners and academics might require some focused attention, it is not an unattainable objective. Further commonalities can be found between the two loosely organized groups of professionals, law enforcement and security professionals. Professionals from both groups have an interest in security and are likely more directly linked to issues of public safety than either group, separately, has considered. Making a more robust delineation of security and its constructions is yet another justification for bringing academic practices to the existing practitioner-based perspectives.

A security professional can build features and checks and balances into a security system that complement the various aspects of the security program. An integrated approach that gives attention to the various aspects of an overall security plan makes sense. Using resources efficiently makes sense. Many of the strides being taken within the industry are good for the industry and make sense. While so many elements of existing security practices make sense, I also want readers to think about those things about security that are not well known or accepted as standard practice in the industry. There is no collective understanding of security as a concept. There is no common language for discussing security. There is little critical assessment of the impact of a security concept on different settings. And there has not been a full exploration of how security-related issues pertain to safety and security issues and the general objective of public safety. All these efforts need to be undertaken to expand, and hopefully advance, the emerging security discipline.

Throughout this book, I present for consideration the idea that traditional security discussions have focused on security management strategies and security technologies to the exclusion of important discussions about the settings in which these security strategies and technologies are implemented. Once you have found the ideal process, system, technology, or other security feature, you still have more work to do. Developing an understanding of the characteristics unique to the target environment you seek to protect is also a security essential.

REVIEW QUESTIONS

1. Outline the importance of understanding security as a process.
2. How are *security* concerns differentiated from *safety* concerns?
3. Outline the impact education, training and research on the need to professionalize the security industry.
4. One of the themes which will return throughout the text, is the importance of talking about "PLACE." How is a sense of place important to the overall security objective in a given target environment?
5. Are crime rates and people's perceptions of crime or fears about specific criminal activities a factor in assessing security needs? Why or why not? Be prepared to justify your response.
6. What relationships do you see between security practitioners and academics or formal educators? What differences exist?
7. What does the author mean by discussing the importance of integrating security concerns at various levels?
8. How is information described as "essential" for addressing security concerns?

DISCUSSION QUESTIONS

1. Early in their organization, the Guardian Angels were discussed by law enforcement agencies and others as a vigilante group. Please discuss how the Guardian Angels are or are not organized with a security function.
2. Security professionals are argued to be a supplement to regular policing forces, but there are those who believe a time is coming when security professionals will have more expertise and experience than local law enforcement agencies. Be prepared to discuss your ideas about the credibility you associate with security professionals now, and how you might assess their credibility in 10 years. How would your assessment be different in say 15 years? 20 years?
3. How are definitions of public and private space affected when discussing security?
4. Is it considered correct to assume an environment is either security or it is not secure?

5. Is it possible that two experienced security professionals will look at one environment and assess the security concerns in a different way? Discuss why this is so and what could be done to get closer to identifying the security concerns as they exist in that target environment.

6. What responsibility do people have to ensure their own protection? What conditions change a person's responsibility for their own protection?

7. What responsibility to police have for protecting a person who is extremely high profile within the national or international community? Are the responsibilities for protection held solely with the individual, who is required because of their celebrity to employ bodyguards rather than rely on local police agencies when they are at home and/or when they are visiting other parts of the country and the world?

REFERENCES

1. M. L. Garcia and D. L. Gilmore, "Coming to Terms with the Security Body of Knowledge" (papers presented at ASIS International Seminar, Las Vegas, NV, September 1999), tape #91.
2. D. Gilmore et al., "Academic/Practitioner Symposium: Moving Ahead on Three Fronts" (paper presented at ASIS International Seminar, Las Vegas, NV, September 1999), tape #102.
3. E. W. Martin, *The History of the Great Riots and of the Molly Maguires* (1877; reprint, New York: Augustus M. Kelley Publishers, 1971), 4–5.
4. D. Gilmore, "Coming to Terms," 3–4.
5. R. J. Fisher and G. Green, *Introduction to Security,* 6th ed. (Woburn, MA: Butterworth-Heinemann, 1998), 3.
6. Garcia, *Coming to Terms,* 12.
7. Garcia, *Coming to Terms,* 16.
8. Garcia, *Coming to Terms,* 16.
9. Garcia and Gilmore, "Coming to Terms."
10. Gilmore, "Coming to Terms," 3–4.
11. Garcia, "Coming to Terms," 16.
12. Garcia, "Coming to Terms," 16.
13. American Society for Industrial Security, ASIS home page, *http://www.asisonline.org/cpphistory.html*; accessed January 20, 2001.
14. American Society for Industrial Security, Certified Protection Professional promotion page, *http://www.asisonline.org/cpppromote.html*; accessed January 20, 2001.
15. Gilmore, 3–4.
16. Gilmore et al., "Academic/Practitioner Symposium," 9.
17. Garcia, "Coming to Terms," 16.
18. T. J. Flanagan, "Liberal Education and the Criminal Justice Major," *Journal of Criminal Justice Education 11,* no. 1 (2000): 1–14.

19. M. Clifford, "Security as a Sense of Place" (St. Cloud, MN: St. Cloud State University, 2000, photocopy).

20. R. Fischer and G. Green, *Introduction to Security*, 6th ed. (Woburn, MA: Butterworth-Heinemann, 1998), 201.

21. *Code of Federal Regulations Title 10* (Washington, DC: Government Printing Office, 1981).

22. K. Moore, *Airport, Aircraft, and Airline Security*, 2nd ed. (Stoneham, MA: Butterworth Heinemann, 1986), 51.

23. Moore, *Airport, Aircraft, and Airline Security*, 51.

24. Gilmore et al., "Academic/Practitioner Symposium," 39–40.

25. R. Willing, "Crime Rate Continues Descent: Better Policing Methods, Tougher Sentencing Guidelines and Strong Economy among Factors Credited," *USA Today*, August 28, 2000, 3A.

26. F. E. Hagan, *Research Methods in Criminal Justice and Criminology*, 5th ed. (Needham, MA: Allyn and Bacon, 2000), 14.

27. Hagan, *Research Methods*, ch. 1, pp. 3–17.

28. Flanagan, "Liberal Education," 4.

29. Flanagan, "Liberal Education," 1–14.

30. J. Powell, "At Boy's Funeral, Call Goes out to Witnesses," *Minneapolis Star Tribune*, August 12, 2000, A-1, B-1, B-5.

31. Powell, Joy, "At Boy's Funeral," *Minneapolis Star Tribune*, B-5.

32. Upper Midwest Community Policing Institute Newsletter, "New Commander Comes with Crime Busting Theory," September 2001.

33. Upper Midwest Community Policing Institute, p. 1.

34. M. Nalla and G. Newman, *A Primer in Private Security* (New York: Harrow and Heston, 1990).

35. *http://www.eia.doe.gov/oiaf/assum99/electricity.html*; last modified on February 2, 1999; accessed January 20, 2001.

CHAPTER

A History of Private Security
A Pervasive Enterprise

CHAPTER OUTLINE

Early Security and the Development of
Laws
  Prehistoric Security
  Development of Laws to Protect
  Citizens
  Early England
Early America: 1700s and 1800s
The Next 100 Years

World Wars I and II
Post–World War II
September 11, 2001
The Future of Security Is in Planning for
Tomorrow
Conclusion
  Review Questions
  Discussion Questions

CHAPTER HIGHLIGHTS

Prehistoric:
- responsibility of the individual
- use of whatever means available:
  1. tools
  2. natural boundaries as physical
     security
  3. small groups
- cultural and class emphasis of security objectives

*Development of laws to punish and
protect citizens.*
- legal time line:
  1. Sumerians represent first writ-
     ten history
  2. Code of Hammurabi

3. Draco's Law
4. Law of the Twelve Tables
5. Justinian Codes
6. Magna Carta
- Statute of Westminster:
  - watch and ward
  - hue and cry
  - assize of arms

People to know:
- Henry Fielding
- John Fielding
- King John
- Molly McGuires
- Robert Peel
- Allan Pinkerton

KEY WORDS

Assize of arms
Bow Street Runners
Code of Hammurabi
Draco's Law
Executive protection

Feudalism
Great Riots of 1877
Hue and Cry
Justinian Code
Law of the Twelve Tables

Lex Talionis (Law of Retaliation)   Statute of Westminster
Magna Carta   Sumerians
Moat   Urban Cohorts
Pinkerton Protective Patrol   Vigiles
Praetorian Guard   Watch and ward

The history of private security is integrated within the collective histories of civilizations throughout the world. Historical accounts of communities as different as self-supporting tribal cultures and capitalistic urban centers can provide the security aficionado with an abundance of security-related information. Activities undertaken to enhance protection efforts, for both individuals and groups, are documented in the rich historical traditions of vastly diverse cultures and communities across the globe.

A history of security concerns in India may not include any information about the railroad police or Allan Pinkerton, as they will be discussed later in this chapter about history of security in the United States. Each country has its own history of security-related activities as they have evolved into contemporary security-related issues. Information about the development of security practices in other countries (and/or geographic regions) would supplement nicely the history of the United States presented here. Citizens of Russia have different security interests from citizens of South Africa. In the United States, cities in the 1930s had different security concerns when compared with U.S. cities in the 1990s. Interest in, and attention given to, terrorist networks has shifted dramatically in the United States and across many parts of the globe since September 11, 2001 when compared with security-related interests prior to that day.

The historical review provided here is focused almost exclusively on the United States and as a result follows the traditional Eurocentric story describing the settlement of the United States. Yet it is essential to remember that important security efforts predate this written history or have been found in other areas of the globe as early as the fifth century. Important links have been made between the origins of both public and private security in the United States and Anglo-Saxon settlements in England dating back to A.D. 400.[1-4] It is easy to forget the simple fact that people were attentive to security issues well before elements of more formalized security and public police practices were documented in historic England, or in any other country throughout the world for that matter. Individuals and small groups of people were constantly mindful of the need to protect themselves against any number of existing threats. Imagine how the native peoples living in North America might have identified security threats as the European settlers moved into the area of land now known as the United States.

Certainly no one would argue the fact that early civilizations protected themselves against anticipated and unanticipated threats using various innovative defenses. Those efforts, most likely, incorporated any and all resources available at the time. Some security threats, like floods and other violent weather conditions, are not new. Other security threats emerge alongside social and technological transformations, such as an emerging global economic system, advanced weapons systems, and an economy increasing dependent on computer systems. This will be important to remember when considering the emerging security threats in the modern era. For the modern security professional, particularly since 9/11, innovation is still the name of the game. To be protected, we need to have a good understanding of what it is we need to be protected against.

The existence of a global marketplace makes it necessary for transnational corporations and businesses to focus on related (and sometimes seemingly unrelated) global security concerns. Corporations based in two or more different cultures will confront two or more unique perspectives on security matters. To better ensure the combined success of their collaborative business ventures, the security objectives they create must be acceptable and appropriate to everyone. Government-related security interests and business-related security interests in the United States or any specific nation are not always going to coincide nicely. National security issues are related to the global economy through multinational business dealings and trade issues in ways security professionals are only just beginning to understand.

One last note to help provide a context for the chapter's historical information. As suggested previously, efforts to create a secure environment involve both individual (or private) actions and collective (or public) actions. Individuals take limited actions in an attempt to ensure their personal safety, and public agents (e.g., law enforcement officers, policy makers) take actions in an attempt to maintain a safe community. Therefore, efforts to explore the history of private security are inextricably linked with efforts to explore the history of public safety and public policing efforts. By educating themselves about past security practices in both the public arena and the private arena, security professionals can be better prepared to identify, understand, and interpret security management strategies designed to meet modern security needs. Security has many levels, and the public/private distinction is an important one.

Beginning with a brief review of security issues in prehistoric and ancient civilizations, including the Roman Empire, the discussion moves to historic England, Colonial America, and concludes with attention being given to life in today's global community after September 11. As the European colonization of the United States expanded west, specific security-related activities have been identified as marking significant turning points in how we talk about the evolution of "private" security in the United States.

Today, as in the past, there are always threats to individuals and communities. The *types* of threats and the related levels of risk are quite different, however, particularly after the attacks on September 11. The identification of public and private security interests can be important when essential interactions between people attempting to maintain personal protection needs (e.g., protection of self and personal property) conflict with public efforts to ensure protection of the larger group of citizens within a community. This introduces, clearly, the issue of power and the role power plays in determining whether specific security needs are met.

Historical references to personal protection and other security efforts have traditionally been associated with powerful people. In the past, these people were often royalty, but today they could be political figures, chief executive officers, or celebrities. As readers go through this chapter on the history of security, it might prove interesting to think about how well security-related concerns of poor and/or powerless people are being met in each time period and within each culture being discussed. Security, as it is presented as the history for a nation, does not necessarily reflect the experiences of all people within that nation who seek to achieve security for themselves and within their communities.

EARLY SECURITY AND THE DEVELOPMENT OF LAWS

Modern society challenges security professionals with unique, often unprecedented security-related anxieties. After what people witnessed on 9/11, those anxieties got even worse. Security objectives are often outlined within identified parameters and are set up to address specific threats and risks using contemporary versions of age-old ideas. In 1975, Americans were estimated to spend between $10 billion and $15 billion annually for security.[5] In 1985, the National Institute of Justice released a *Research in Brief* comparing 1980 estimates for private security to expenditures for public law enforcement. Security employed an estimated 1.1 million persons, at a cost (including estimates of total expenditures for products and services) of $22 billion. Estimated expenditures for local law enforcement peaked at only $14 billion.[6] Since 1977, spending for private security services has exceeded public spending for law enforcement services.[7] Although it is clear that the response to the terrorist attacks on 9/11 will impact these figures, the full impact of this event on both public and private security expenditures is still being determined.

Even before 9/11, the security industry was identified as a growth industry. Initial figures in response to 9/11 have included a total of $10.6 billion dedicated to homeland security.[8] It is hard to know how this will impact future budget comparisons between public and private police organizations.

Relations between public law enforcement agencies and private security professionals in more recent history have been strained, although this is said to be changing. In fact, various public law enforcement agents have suggested that "the growth of private security businesses is one key to falling crime rates" in the 1990s.[9] Public police are increasingly making connections with private security professionals to assist them with designated aspects of the policing function.

History provides various examples of how the security objective can be met by making use of creative minds, ingenious plans, and readily available tools. Modern society has produced an unprecedented demand for security measures. In 1800, few people would have imagined the need for airport security. As late as the 1950s few people would have predicted the need to protect individuals and financial institutions against ATM fraud. Due in part, perhaps, to technological innovation and the expansion of the global marketplace, security professionals are increasingly being asked to respond to both real and perceived threats.

As society changes, industries change to meet these new social demands. As businesses or agencies changes, security-related needs and objectives change with them. The security industry is likely to produce the most direct influence on both national and international security-related issues. Security professionals can take advantage of the lessons history provides. In fact, innovation may still be the best defense against emerging security threats. In this way, the modern security practitioners have much to learn from historical accounts provided not only from the United States but also in countries throughout the world.

Prehistoric Security

Evidence of efforts to protect community groups against various threats can be found in artifacts from the earliest civilizations. Many introductory police and security textbooks note this, but little (if any) research has been devoted to the analysis of archeological findings of security-related materials with the expressed intent of better understanding how the security objective has changed over time. The earliest forms of potential threats are likely to have been severe weather, sickness, and warring tribes or wild animals.

As certain civilizations developed tools, began farming, and became less migratory, more formalized efforts to develop protection were being discovered. Historical artifacts and ancient ruins, for example, show us that some Native American tribal communities in the United States protected themselves by living in natural caves on high cliffs. By utilizing natural barriers or boundaries, individuals and groups could increase protection with minimal effort. Their protection came from making themselves inaccessible to outsiders or wild animals. Ladders that were erected to make the cave dwellings accessible to community members could be retracted to increase protection from enemy groups, for example.[10]

Certain climates provided specific security risks as well as protections. Consider, for example, how security threats and the related security objectives in the Brazilian rain forests would differ from those in the frozen tundra of Northern Siberia. Throughout history, efforts to address threats posed by natural elements have been essential elements of any security plan. Natural structures such as the caves in the preceding example have long been useful as a means for providing security. Lake dwellings accessible only by boat were the result of another innovative effort to develop protection by integrating a natural barrier. The restricted access limited the number of people who could get to the dwelling and provided much-needed time to identify (and if necessary, prepare to meet) those who were approaching.

Remember, too, that before formal laws were drafted, efforts to maintain order were present. John Christman suggests that

> [the] earliest law was probably a combination of tribal custom and the wishes of tribal chiefs. It was passed on by word of mouth (not written or codified as it is today) and its sanctions, the implementation of which were probably overseen by the tribal chief or the entire tribe, were primarily personal, which is to say designed to satisfy the aggrieved party.[11]

Even after formal laws had been established in "civilized" countries like the United States, vigilante justice was a preferred alternative. Undocumented efforts to establish "law and order" have often taken the form of undocumented oral stories preserved and relayed as "legend." Many of these stories came directly from the U.S. frontier. With no mechanisms in place to enforce existing laws, it often remained up to individuals and community groups to ensure their own protection. An alleged offender's punishment was often swift and severe, with retribution the primary objective. In some cases, standards of proof and evidence collection were nonexistent. Today movies are made about the "outlaw turned lawman" handing out "his own brand of justice." There are grand tales about how Wyatt Earp, Bat Masterson, Pat Garrett, and Wild Bill Hickok administered "justice" in the Wild West.[12]

In times that predate documented history and places where laws could not readily be enforced (such as the American frontier), it is commonly accepted that security objectives were defined by tribal leaders or family members who would act on behalf of others. For those who did not enjoy formal security protections, individual safety could be ensured when individuals allied with others they knew and trusted. Retaliation and *lex talionis* (the law of vengeance) ruled.

Security Issues across the Globe

The following security-related issues in different countries are included to illustrate the diversity of issues across the globe.

Bogotá, Colombia. Uniformed left-wing guerrillas and their far-right paramilitary enemies are increasingly turning to kidnapping and extortion to finance their campaigns. In 1999, Colombia saw an average of eight abductions a day. So many people are missing that a weekly radio address has been established for use by families of kidnap victims in an attempt to get the message out to missing family members that they have not been forgotten back home and that someone is fighting for their freedom. "We [are] reaching out to everybody, including the kidnappers . . . [in an effort] to build a culture where kidnapping is simply unacceptable."[1]

Afghanistan. The Taliban arrested a United Nations aid worker born in Arizona and living in Afghanistan and issued an edict banning women from working for relief agencies operating inside the country. She was released a day later and the edict rescinded, but in the meantime, a Taliban official explained the logic behind the policy. Women working in relief agencies raised a "national security issue." How so? They might be recruited as spies. The Taliban require all women to wear a burqa, a body covering with a tiny mesh screen for the eyes, which would provide the sort of cover that would appeal to the Central Intelligence Agency and MI 5.[2]

Durban, South Africa. Former President Nelson Mandela made a plea for more attention and resources to fight the AIDS epidemic in Africa. The current president, Thabo Mbeki, has been under attack since the spring, when he convened a panel of scientists to explore whether HIV does indeed cause AIDS—a fact long accepted by the scientific community. AIDS has already claimed more lives than the total of all wars, famines, floods, and such deadly diseases as malaria on the African continent. Each day, 1800 babies are born with HIV, more than 6000 teenagers become infected, and thousands of children are orphaned. Truly shocking, Mandela said, are new data showing that within South Africa, "1 in 2—that is, half—of our young people will die of AIDS. . . . The most frightening thing is that all of these infections could have been, can be, prevented."[3] The world, Mandela said, must not underestimate the commitment and resources needed to fight the epidemic, which is sweeping this continent with seemingly unstoppable speed.

Australia. Nursing staff at Port Moresby General Hospital claimed that a shortage in funding was affecting staff security and resulted in an attack on a woman physician at a clinic. Armed police were posted at the hospital, and nursing staff decided to close the children's clinic until the situation was resolved. The hospital's management had been ordered to reduce the number of nonmedical staff, including security officers.[4]

Moscow, Russia. "The Russian mafia has direct control over 40,960 commercial enterprises, among them 449 banks, 37 stock exchanges, 678 markets, and 566 joint ventures with Western participation. About 55% of Russian capital is in the hands of 'the mafia.' Approximately 80% of all shares eligible to vote are in the hands of organized crime. Some 693 gangs have in the meantime founded their own 'legal' institutes for laundering money. Some mafia groups operate internationally, especially in Germany, Austria, Israel and the United States. Two-thirds of Soviet state property has been bought by mafia groups or their straw men. When housing space is 'privatized,' the legal occupants are often assassinated."[5] With strong regional mafias, the real nightmare scenario in Russia involves ruthless organized crime syndicates and corrupt government officials working in league to create new international markets for nuclear materials. The Federal Bureau of Investigation has been working with the

(continued)

Russian police in an undercover operation targeting Russian organized crime groups trying to sell nuclear materials. The challenge is big, and the stakes could not be higher.

After a five-month investigation by *U.S. News & World Report* and CBS's *60 Minutes,* staff claimed to have "irrefutable" proof that Russian organized crime was behind a mysterious shipment of beryllium, a valuable substance used in missile guidance systems, high-performance aircraft, and precision optical components. This is said to be the first hard evidence that Russian crime syndicates have attempted to smuggle nuclear materials from the former Soviet Union. Sold legally, beryllium goes for more than $600 a kilo and is a critical material for building a more efficient nuclear warhead or a smaller nuclear reactor.[6]

Israel. Agents from Mossad, the Israeli Secret Service, have refused missions in protest of what they describe as a lack of backing from their superiors.[7] On July 7, 2000, a Mossad operative was found guilty of charges, including wiretapping, entering the country using genuine papers with false names, political espionage, and carrying out illegal acts for a foreign state.[8] He was captured trying to install a telephone bug in an apartment block in the Swiss capital, Berne. Israel paid $2 million in bail and promised to return the operative to Switzerland for trial. Sources told Israel Radio that the Mossad operatives were striking because they "expect[ed] to receive the full backing of the Mossad leadership,"[9] whether or not their assigned missions succeeded.

Washington, DC, United States. The U.S. government is increasingly relying on private military companies to do difficult international jobs. "Over the past 10 years, private military companies, or PMCs, have quietly taken a central role in the exporting of security, strategy, and training for foreign militaries."[10] In a recent example, the State Department approved a license for a U.S.-based company to enhance security in Equatorial Guinea, an African country with a population of 1 million people that is run by a military dictator and has no U.S. embassy. "In the U.S., the training services are sometimes paid out of the annual foreign aid bill, doled out to friendly or promising countries that may have unstable governments of militaries, such as Nigeria and Colombia. Other times, companies are hired directly by the host country and approved by the U.S."[11]

References

1. M. Hodgson, "A Radio Lifeline in Colombia," *Christian Science Monitor,* July 7, 2000, 1, 9.
2. C. Power, "A Country in Collapse," *http://www.msnbc.com/news/432620.asp?cp1 =1#BODY, Newsweek* Web exclusive, July 13, 2000.
3. C. Laino, "A Moving Call to Arms against AIDS," *Newsweek,* July 14, 2000.
4. Radio Australia, "PNG Nurses Issue Ultimatum over Security at Hospital," *http://abc.net.au/ra/newsarchive/1999/apr/rael-29apr1999-46.htm,* 29 April 1999.
5. Quote from H. G. Huyn, *The Red Phoenix,* in W. F. Jasper, "Russian Mafia: Organized Crime Is Big Business for the KGB," *New American 12,* no. 4 (1996).
6. T. Zimmermann and A. Cooperman, "Beryllium Deal, Russian Mafia," *U.S. News & World Report,* October 23, 1995.
7. BBC News, "Israeli Spies Threaten Strike," *http://me.orientation.com,* July 5, 2000.
8. BBC News, "Mossad Spy Found Guilty," *http://me.orientation.com,* July 7, 2000.
9. BBC News, "Israeli Spies Threaten Strike."
10. J. Brown, "The Rise of the Private-Sector Military," *Christian Science Monitor,* July 5, 2000, 3.
11. Brown, "The Rise of the Private-Sector Military."

The process of documenting historical accounts takes several steps. The evidence must be collected and interpreted before it is presented to the masses. A large portion of the information commonly referred to as "historical fact" would more accurately be referred to as "informed theory." These theories are ideas developed by scientists and research professionals based on available evidence. Many existing historical interpretations have been called into question, in some cases debunked outright, when new evidence is discovered. Keeping in mind the fact that historical evidence is sometimes limited, let us review some significant events that have been linked to today's security-related issues.

Development of Laws to Protect Citizens

Artifacts (e.g., items uncovered in archeological digs) suggest that laws were designed and enforced by communities in an effort to identify appropriate behavior within a community as early as 5000 years before the birth of Christ.[13] The collection of taxes has been identified as being probably "the oldest function of policing on behalf of the state."[14] To supplement military objectives, kings and rulers of ancient societies selected knights and other noblemen to pledge their allegiance to the kingdom for the expressed purpose of protecting the royalty and their holdings. This early version of **executive protection,** the hiring of elite, highly trained professionals for personal security, is only one example of a modern security practice with historical origins.

One of the earliest documented efforts to develop a set of standards has been attributed to the **Sumerians,** perhaps as early as 5000 B.C.[15] Located in what is today Iraq, the Sumerians of Mesopotamia established the earliest known society in which people utilized written forms of communication, archeological evidence has shown. Some documentation suggests that legal codes were outlined and enforced in other societies, but the specific documents have not been found.[16] The most widely accepted theory is that writing evolved to keep track of property.[17] Clay envelopes marked with the owner's rolled seal were used to hold tokens for goods, and the tokens represented specific transactions. Later on, symbols were scratched into clay to record transactions, such as the selling of two bunches of wheat or six cows.[18]

The Babylonian **Code of Hammurabi** (1750 B.C.) was established by King Hammurabi and discovered almost intact in 1901. While almost certainly not the first legal code, it was clearly developed from earlier Sumerian codes and is quite remarkable for what it tells us about ancient Mesopotamian society.[19] The expression "an eye for an eye" has come to symbolize the principle behind Hammurabi's code. It contains 282 clauses regulating a vast array of obligations, professions, and rights, including clauses concerning commerce, slavery, marriage, theft, and debts. The punishments are, by modern standards, barbaric.[20] The principles outlined are in the form of **lex talionis,** or the law of retaliation (mentioned previously).

Draco's Law (621 B.C.) is named for the Greek citizen who was chosen to write a code of law for Athens.[21] The penalty for many offenses was death—a penalty so severe that the word *draconian* is used today to describe an unreasonably harsh law. His laws were the first written laws in Greece. These laws are highlighted because they introduce the notion that the state, not private citizens, is responsible for punishing persons accused of crimes.[22]

The **Law of the Twelve Tables** (450 B.C.) originally included 10 laws. Two statutes were added later.[23] Ten Roman men were given wide powers to write the laws that were to govern Romans. These laws are considered to form the foundation of modern public and private law. They helped organize how crimes would be prosecuted publicly and instituted a system whereby injured parties could seek compensation from their aggressors. The laws were designed to protect the lower classes from the legal abuses of the ruling class, especially in the enforcement of debts.[24] From that point on, a basic principle of Roman law was that the law must be written and that justice could not be left in the hands of judges alone to interpret.[25] Among its proscriptions, the law prohibited interclass marriages, seriously punished thieves, and gave fathers rights of life or death over their sons.[26]

In 27 B.C., Roman emperor Augustus (31 B.C.–A.D. 14) reorganized the Roman armed forces to include an elite military unit called the **Praetorian Guard.** Expanding Julius Caesar's practice of assigning a guard of honor as bodyguards for Roman generals, Augustus expanded that guard from one cohort to nine, each with 500 men, and stationed them around Rome.[27] Augustus wanted permanent bodyguards (the Praetorians) stationed partly in Rome and partly in other Italian towns to maintain internal order and facilitate trade; the result was an efficient fleet to police the Mediterranean.[28] Their primary responsibility was to escort and protect Augustus, although he attempted to mask their military role by having them wear togas rather than military uniforms.[29]

After several unsuccessful efforts to address rising disruptions by establishing private fire brigades using slaves, Augustus divided Rome into 14 regions and 265 wards. Then, in A.D. 6, he established a corps of professional firemen referred to as **Vigiles;** there were seven squads each numbering 1000 freedmen. The Vigiles also had minor police duties, especially at night. Their main duty was to keep order in the city, and they could call on the Praetorian Guard for help if necessary.[30] Because historical accounts refer to the Praetorians as bodyguards utilized both in the private service of Roman military officials and in public service and military service, it is unclear whether they were primarily responsible for private or public security. The Vigiles were maintained separate from the military and organized by the state to serve the public good. This information has been used to suggest that the Vigiles were the first public police force, although around A.D. 13 Augustus instituted a force—known as the

Urban Cohorts—specifically to police Rome.[31] The Urban Cohorts were organized like the Praetorian Guard, and personnel were typically moved through
the Vigiles, to the Urban Cohorts, and then to the Praetorian Guard.[32] In short,
early security efforts such as identifying specific policing districts, having a military organizational structure, using public monies to protect the community,
and having elaborate watch systems have been credited to Augustus.

Justinian Code (A.D. 529) provides another example of early codified law.
Justinian, Emperor of Byzantium, is best remembered for his codification of Roman law in a series of books called *Corpus Juris Civilis*. Legal maxims still in
use today are derived from Justinian Code. His work inspired the modern concept of justice, a word that comes from the emperor's name. This Roman code
formed the foundation of civil law, one of the two main legal systems (the other
being English common law) that govern modern Western civilization.[33]

Early England

The Dark Ages is the period after the fall of the Roman and Greek empires.
During this time, as people joined together in response to common threats, including foreign invaders and food shortages, **feudalism** became the predominant means by which communities were organized.[34] The feudal system is said
to have provided a "very high degree of security for both the individual and the
group."[35] Feudal states were usually located around a castle or cathedral and
consisted of farmers, laborers, and craftspeople. These communities gave service to and sought protection from the local lord or noble.[36] Even then, security required registration, licensing, and a fee.[37]

Efforts to protect castles and their related holdings were enhanced by the
use of natural barriers. Castles, cities, and other fortresses were surrounded by
a deep ditch, usually filled with water and known as a **moat.** Moats reduced
the possibility of a surprise attack because access was available only by draw-
bridge. Large walls were erected to increase protection afforded the people and

---

The Great Wall[1]

One of the world's oldest and largest landmarks, the Great Wall of China, was erected
by the first emperor of the Qin dynasty as a defense against raids by nomadic peoples.
Work on the wall was begun about 221 B.C., and the original structure was completed
in approximately 204 B.C. Sections of the wall were repaired and extended during the
Ming dynasty (A.D. 1368–1644), after which the total length of the wall was about
2400 km (1500 miles) and extended between Mongolia and China.

References

1. Encarta Online, *http://encarta.msn.com/find/Concise.asp?ti=046F6000*

property contained within. Typically, these large walls would have only a central entrance, accessible through a heavy gate.

The high point of the Middle Ages—for security professionals, anyway—occurred under **King John** (1199–1216), with the creation of the **Magna Carta** (1215). In short, the Magna Carta established English "due process." The Magna Carta had 61 clauses, the most important of which may have been the 39th: "No freeman shall be captured or imprisoned . . . except by lawful judgement of his peers or by the law of the land."[38] This afforded significant personal protections for all people, and the idea of due process became one of the foundations for the modern U.S. justice system. Within 70 years, England produced the next significant contribution to the system of law enforcement in developing the **Statute of Westminster** (1285). King Edward *involved citizens* in crime prevention and apprehension. The Statute of Westminster established three practical measures focusing on the security of affected citizens: (1) the watch and ward, (2) the hue and cry, and (3) the assize of arms.[39] The **watch and ward,** an outcome of the Statute of Westminster, required night watchmen or bailiffs (selected from the citizenry) to maintain order and prevent crime.[40] Citizens were required to raise a **hue and cry** if a felony had been committed.[41] Ordered by law, by command of the constable, every person had to pursue the felon. Those who did not were punished or fined.[42] The **assize of arms,** established to enforce the hue and cry, required every male between the ages of 15 and 60 to keep a weapon in his home.[43]

Beginning in the 1500s, the system of feudalism was gradually replaced with the state church as a form of local government in rural areas. By the late 1600s in England, various groups of private police officers were utilized, including merchant police, parish police, dock police, and warehouse police.[44] Many of the other watchmen remained unpaid, untrained, and poorly respected citizens who were responsible for guarding the life and property of other English citizens until as late as 1829.[45] This period witnessed the breakdown of the watch system because people had little interest in being unpaid police officers in addition to handling their own personal obligations. If they could afford to, people hired someone else to take their turn at watch.[46] The quality of the replacements got lower and lower, until King Charles II (1660–1685) made arrangements for a force of 1000 paid watchmen or bellmen to protect his holdings during his reign. They were commonly referred to as the "Charlies," after the reigning king.[47] Although people were distrustful of paid police forces because they had become subject to corruption, watchmen became involved in aiding, abetting, or concealing crimes rather than detecting and suppressing them.[48]

In 1748, **Henry Fielding** was appointed as a magistrate at Bow Street in London. Fielding worked with his brother **John,** who succeeded him at Bow Street as magistrate. The idea of a unified, mobile police force is attributed to the Fieldings.[49] Known as honorable and honest men at a time when magistrates were often considered "scum of the earth, the Fieldings help to put in place a group of people to pursue crime who were paid by the government."[50] Two years after his appointment at Bow Street, Henry Fielding conducted what some consider to be the first inventory of security issues and published the findings in 1751 in a publication titled "An Enquiry into the Causes of the Late Increase of Robberies." With the financial support of the English government, Henry Fielding established (and John Fielding worked to maintain) a force of men, known as the **Bow Street Runners,** to investigate crime and pursue criminals.

EARLY AMERICA: 1700s AND 1800s

The systems being implemented for community protection in England were, in many cases, replicated in the United States. The constable remained responsible for law enforcement in the towns; sheriffs were responsible for law enforcement in the counties and were usually chosen from landowners who were loyal to the king. Efforts to meet security objectives in the New World were quite simple.

> The colonists learned quite a lot about taking care of themselves. The cornerstone of their protection was the simple law enforcement concept that the maintenance of law and order was the individual responsibility of each person, and that every citizen was accountable not only for his own actions but for those of his neighbor as well.[51]

Even after emancipation from England, huge areas of the United States were not affected by early efforts to develop formalized policing structures. Formal structures may have been in place to protect individual or community interests, but individuals acting on behalf of any governing body were not trusted. Cities and townships developed their own form of social order, and people trusted only those they knew within that structure.

Robert Peel and the development of the London Metropolitan Police cannot go without mention here. Policing organizations following this model began to emerge in the United States in the mid-1840s. Large cities began to organize police forces paid for by tax dollars. The need for protection, however, was not fully met by these early efforts. A few entrepreneurial types developed their own private police establishments in an effort to meet the increasing need, and they were highly successful. The mayor in the city of Chicago publicized his concerns in a local paper of the times:

Security Snapshot: Castle Design

Castles were designed to protect kings, queens, and other royalty. Castle designers employed various security tactics to ward off would-be trouble. Some castles were built on hilltops. The location provided defenders with a superior view of the land, allowing early detection of oncoming danger. The hills also slowed down the attackers, as they were required to run up the hills in order to reach the castles. Some castles were surrounded by large moats, which provided mighty obstacles for enemies to cross. Drawbridges were usually standard when castles had moats. Drawbridges allowed welcome visitors to enter the castle grounds and also let people leave with relative ease. Drawbridges also increased security. They were often massive and could be raised and lowered only from the inside. This would prohibit unwanted intruders from entering through the main access. Large, reinforced walls were built to surround the castles, which would make them nearly indestructible and difficult to scale in an attempt to gain entry. If an enemy were to get past the moat and the wall, many times there awaited additional moats and walls. If these were not troublesome to get past, then they at least slowed down the trespassers enough that a counterattack could be mounted. The outer walls had walkways around the tops that allowed the defenders of the castle to attack from an advantageous position. Along the walkways there were large openings between two tall areas of stone. These openings, called battlements, were a defensive feature that allowed for a wide range of vision and use of large defense equipment, such as catapults and cannons. Towers are another security feature of many castles. These towers were equipped with arrow slits, which provided an archer with a relatively good range for selecting targets while also providing the archer with a great deal of protection.

Military forts used some of the same security strategies as castles while adding new ones to suit their own needs. Reinforced walls with only one entrance surrounded many forts. This prevented a lot of side attacks and allowed for careful monitoring of who was coming into and leaving the grounds. Forts also employed the tactics of towers, which gave the people who were positioned there a good view of what was going on around the fort, both inside and out. Most forts were heavily armed, as they were especially used during times of war. Ditches and bunkers were placed within the fort, allowing for some cover in case the enemy did get in. Tunnels were often used to allow the defenders of the fort to move to different areas of defense. Newer forts have bombproof areas, which provide protection from heavy artillery. All forts have a place that is used as a last defense. Many have this area on a nearby hilltop, giving the defenders some help in slowing down the attackers and allowing them more opportunity to protect what little they may have left of the fort.

It is a lamentable fact that whilst our citizens are heavily taxed to support a large police force, a highly respectable private police is doing a lucrative business. Our citizens have ceased to look to the public police for protection, for the detection of culprits, or the recovery of stolen property.[52]

In spite of efforts to address the rising crime rates of that time, infighting between the private police and the public police was becoming more evident. The public police were largely seen as inadequate, and it became clear to **Allan**

Pinkerton and others that providing additional security services, services the public police could not supply, could be a lucrative enterprise.

On February 1, 1855, Pinkerton was asked by six midwestern railroad company representatives to establish a railroad police agency known as the North West Police Agency. Pinkerton was 35 and deputy to the Cook County, Chicago sheriff.[53] In addition to his work with the railroad police, Pinkerton was under contract with the federal government to investigate counterfeiting and protect the Post Office from robbery, and he was called on repeatedly for specific detective tasks. Much of Pinkerton's work as a detective involved covert activities to ensure that Post Office and railway industry employees remained honest. Pinkerton was given $10,000 to establish the railroad police.[54]

In 1858, Pinkerton formed the **Pinkerton Protective Patrol,** a small group of uniformed night watchmen, and contracted with various businesses to offer night protection. In its first year of operation, 751 documented instances of doors either open or not secured and 454 cases of improper employee conduct were discovered by Pinkerton spies (men on the inside).[55] Interestingly, the next mayor of Chicago used Pinkerton patrols to supplement existing public police efforts.[56]

Much of the work being done at that time by the private police was considered suspect. Violations of civil liberties, entrapment, and other forms of deception were tactics used to "get their man." In 1873, Pinkerton's agency was sued for $10,000 for allegedly intimidating the wife of an alleged mail robber without proper legal authority.[57] Organized labor was infuriated when a Pinkerton detective infiltrated the **Molly Maguires,** a group of miners Pinkerton believed was "murdering and intimidating mine owners."[58] A rendition of this story is portrayed in the 1970 movie starring Sean Connery and Richard Harris, *The Molly Maguires.* These issues highlighted the problems Pinkerton had trying to separate himself from disreputable detectives and establish respectability within his ranks. In 1867, he wrote a handbook titled *General Principles of Pinkerton's National Police Agency,* where he emphasized the honorable nature of the work his detectives performed and established specific rules of conduct and responsibility for his employees.[59]

As businesses in the United States expanded, so did the private security industry. Pinkerton's attempts to secure the railroad industry may have been the most notorious of these efforts. After Pinkerton's death, his sons carried on the business, and a noticeable shift from detection to prevention began to take place.[60] Labor problems produced volatile riots and left industry leaders relying on private protection agents to ensure protection of their industry and related property. Efforts to protect high-profile business leaders became financially advantageous. Within a decade of Allan's death, his sons opened six new offices, and preventive patrol efforts comprised a significant source of revenue for the company.[61] Throughout his career Allan Pinkerton emphasized the respectability of the private security profession, but the clear response to the profit motive has raised a question about the legitimacy of these "protection" efforts—a question still asked today.

As immigrants moved west with the railroad, individuals and companies increasingly sought additional protection for their expanding interests. In some cases, this protection came from a Native American.[62] Some Native Americans were hired to enforce white men's laws on reservations and protect coal companies, railroads, timber stands, and various other enterprises. The Indian Police Force was officially authorized in the late nineteenth century, but until that time "almost any mounted and armed Indian, working under the instructions and authority of the local Indian Agent, was utilized as a policeman."[63]

Outside the highly publicized efforts to establish a more effective law enforcement system, individuals offered their protection services for the right price. Those interested in paying for increased security could not always trust the people they sought to hire. Anyone seeking additional money could find it by becoming a watchman. Once a person obtained a watchman's permit, he or she had it forever.[64]

As the nineteenth century continued, the integration of public, private, and military police could be seen in various private uprisings, most often worker strikes. The tone of the time was aggressive. Industrial expansion was taking hold, yet "the new wealth of the nation did not filter down to its producers . . . and the labor movement gave battle."[65] Business owners attempted to take actions to import laborers from other countries in an effort to replace disgruntled U.S. workers. These efforts were blocked by legislation, but the stage was set for people to "go to war" over the distribution of wealth. Public police simply could not handle the massive riots that resulted. In the attempts to quell these worker rebellions, three factions were called into play: (1) the private detective agencies, (2) the courts, and (3) the military.[66]

The response to the **Great Riots of 1877** provides an example.

[The] Pinkertons [were] retained by the Balitmore & Ohio and the Philadelphia & Reading railroads, though they were no match for the ground swell of revolt that carried sections of the militia along with it. In May the Philadelphia & Reading ordered its employees to quit the Brotherhood of Locomotive Engineers (their union). The workers promised to obey but instead made plans for a surprise strike only to discover that the Pinkertons, fully informed, had prepared an army of strikebreakers. This strike was called off, but broke forth three months later in the full fury of accumulated and pent-up grievances. . . . Seventy five lives were lost before the military put down the strikers. Through the riots Pinkerton's business became a prescribed one, though now a formidable competitor appeared in the shape of the military.[67]

"'Pinkerton men' became a household word, a word of hate in the streets and a word of comfort in the mansions."[68] In July 1892, the Pinkertons responded to a strike in Homestead via boat.

> Strikers on the shore flourished weapons, signaling to the boat and the Pinkertons to turn about. In answer, the Pinkertons turned the Winchesters on the men. Firing began. The Pinkertons finally surrendered but not until twelve men, most of them strikers, had been killed. That night the detectives were beaten and shipped out of town by a mob of strikers [via train]. . . . Crowds of workers awaited them at Harrisburg and other cities to speed them on their way with curses. Bricks were hurled through the windows as their train passed. . . . Populists in the House and Senate raised their voices against the "murderous Pinkerton men."[69]

In response to the social outcry that resulted, the Pinkertons were investigated by both branches of Congress. The Senate committee argued that the Pinkertons were certainly "not of the highest order of morals or intellect"[70] and recommended that industry owners seek injunctions in the courts and protection from the sheriffs or the military if needed. The use of armed guards was strongly deprecated, but even in the wake of these congressional actions, Pinkerton was still responding to requests for strikebreakers. Huge numbers (as many as 3600 in the Pullman strike of 1894) were sworn in as deputies, by either the private Pinkerton agency or county sheriffs, in an attempt to quell the violence. It appears that many groups, including business leaders, workers, law enforcement officers, and government officials, were all trying to determine what might be the best approach to counter the violence that had become commonplace throughout the United States at this time.

THE NEXT 100 YEARS

Anyone employed in security-related professions at the beginning of the twentieth century simply could not have imagined the dramatic changes that would affect the profession over the next 100 years, including two world wars; an economic depression; the dust bowl; Prohibition; a global illicit drug trade; a dramatic terrorist attack; and the introduction of various new technologies, including electricity, the telephone, radio and television, airplanes, space travel, computers, satellites, and advanced weapons systems. Each of these technologies has impacted the way security professionals do their work.

It can easily be argued that the impact of recent rapid social transformations has not been fully realized, nor are the related (but often unanticipated) outcomes fully identified or understood. Nowhere is this more clearly illustrated than in the aftermath a single event, the World Trade Center attacks in

New York City. It is unclear whether terrorist attacks are going to require a community-specific response or a national response, or both.

In this section, attention is directed toward a few examples of dramatic actions taken by nations and expanding industries that had a clear impact on how we, as a nation, think about the security profession. A more comprehensive review of the twentieth century would be instructive, but it is an undertaking more appropriately assigned to a research historian. At a minimum, the aspiring security professional will want to review the world wars and their effect on post–World War II industry.

World Wars I and II

One of the most easily identifiable justifications for providing covert security measures can be found in the efforts to protect companies involved in the war effort. During wartime, security forces from all sectors worked together in an effort to provide an effective response to external threats. Businesses learned firsthand of the devastation that could be wrought by enemy agents from other countries. Munitions factories, transport ships, and other war-related enterprises were targeted in an effort to reduce their contribution to the overall war effort. Those involved in the targeted businesses used military and other resources to assist with the protection of their businesses, in the interest of national security.

While sabotage and espionage were identified as threats for businesses producing materials used in World War I, many of these businesses discontinued related security practices when the war ended in 1918.[71] For the 20 years between the two wars, strikes were not uncommon. Labor relations were typically spearheaded by employing strikebreakers. Employees were considered the biggest security concern for business, and business leaders did not worry much about other security issues.

In December 1941, after the bombing of Pearl Harbor, other security matters became an immediate concern once again. A change in law after World War I made it impossible for soldiers to guard private industry, so thousands of people were employed to provide protection for businesses involved in the war effort. By the end of the war, more than 200,000 men were responsible for protecting war goods, products, supplies, equipment, and personnel at over 10,000 industrial plants and factories.[72] Interestingly enough, local police departments were responsible for their training. Although they were technically in the army, their responsibilities were auxiliary military police.[73]

Military, public, and private policing objectives can easily become intertwined. When significant security threats are identified, enforcement and protection resources are accumulated from every sector. The cases of Caesar's

Praetorian Guard, the strikebreakers, and the war efforts remind us that the specific responsibilities of police, private security, and the military are not as distinct as is often believed.

Post–World War II

The devastating effects of sabotage and other wartime threats are said to be responsible for a primary shift in the climate of many large industries in the United States and across the globe. Industries were expanding at phenomenal rates. Individuals and business professionals identified constant threats and began to see the need for ongoing security protocols as an essential element within the successful corporate structure. Needs specific to their industry, expanding markets, and large capital investments continued to convince business professionals that they could not afford to rely on public police efforts. They sought instead expertise from people who had essential knowledge specific to their protection needs.

And so America, facing the end of the twentieth century bigger and more prosperous and possibly in greater danger than ever before, saw its best security officers seeking other employment because law enforcement did not pay a living wage.[74]

Industrial expansion provided opportunities for individuals who were interested in law enforcement but also interested in making a decent wage. At the end of the twentieth century, the outlook for the private security professional seemed better than ever. The lessons people take from history may be telling. Research in multiple areas of security has been used to remind people, at a minimum, that the history of security-related activities extends well beyond the recorded history of organized public policing efforts. While the relationship between public and private policing efforts is intertwined, members of each group have their own perspectives about how well that integration serves the public safety objective they likely share.

Until recently, much of the history of security was anecdotal. For this reason, the exploration of security-related concepts in academic settings is producing academically rigorous research, which will likely result in a more comprehensive evaluation and understanding of the role of police, particularly private security, in meeting public safety objectives. Some recent research suggests that various common perceptions about security are developed with a bad case of "historical amnesia."[75] As a result, much of what the general public (and, in some cases, security professionals and public law enforcement officers) believes about private security is "ill-informed and theoretically unsophisticated."[76]

September 11, 2001

The nation and the world are still recovering from the devastating effects of the terrorist attack on the World Trade Center in New York City on September 11, 2001. The threat of terrorism was very real before 9/11, however the risk levels associated with such attacks in the United States were not considered to be very high. As a direct result of the attacks, on October 8th by Executive Order, President George W. Bush established the Office of Homeland Security. Pennsylvania Governor Tom Ridge was sworn in to lead the effort to enhance domestic security. Since that time specific attention has been given to the role of law enforcement agencies and other first responders, border and port security, transportation security, health and food security, environmental and energy security, and citizen engagement.[77]

One of the most visible outcomes to assist local communities with preparation for and prevention against terrorist attacks is the Homeland Security Advisory System, introduced on March 12, 2002. The system was designed and implemented to ensure effective communications between all levels of government to disseminate information regarding emerging threats and/or risks of attacks. The five levels are color coded and intended to reflect specific states of alert necessary to protect against possible terrorist attacks. Red, or "Severe" is the highest level of alert. Orange is the second highest level of alert, labeled "High." Yellow or "Elevated," represents a significant risk of terrorism. Blue is a "Guarded" risk, and represents a general risk of terrorism, with Green representing a "Low" risk of terrorist attacks.[78]

In January of 2002, President Bush proposed an additional $38 billion dollars a year go toward the Homeland Security budget. In February, the President announced increases in funding for research on bioterrorism. In March, he promoted his administration's efforts to increase funding allocations to first responders. In June, he proposed a new Cabinet-level Department of Homeland Security. The effect of these new initiatives will be revealed over time. It is clear, however, that the use of the public law enforcement agencies to prevent and protect against future terrorism is going to be a priority. Border controls, disaster response, bioterrorism research, and domestic intelligence analysis will be central themes in future security-related efforts.

THE FUTURE OF SECURITY IS IN PLANNING FOR TOMORROW

In 1971, John Donald Peel wrote *The Story of Private Security*. In his concluding section, titled appropriately "The Future," he argues that public police simply cannot do the job the public wants them to do. He writes,

> The prospect is not pleasing, but the persistent atmosphere of violence in which we are living seems likely to get worse before it gets better. It seems a

fair statement that the police cannot much longer protect the public as the police would like to do, and continue at the same time to provide all the other services—the social work, the public health duties, the child guidance—the public insistently demands of them. At what point in such a situation may the thin blue line of protection provided by our police officers, already stretched to the danger point, possibly give way? If it does give way, where will the law abiding turn? As we have seen, it is useless to look to the community for protection.[79]

In saying "it is useless to look to the community for protection," Peel refers to the fact that neighbors typically don't resolve disputes, they take the issue to the police with the expectation that a local law enforcement officer will solve the problem.

In addition to the expectation that police be social workers, public health professionals, and role models for our children, today's police officers face pressing public safety and protection issues including threats of terrorism, gun violence, drugs, gangs, organized crime, white-collar crime, environmental crime, and computer crime, as examples. We can begin to see how much security concerns may change in a matter of only 20 or 30 years, or even after one specific day.

While these types of crime were likely to have existed years ago, the age of information, technology, and transportation makes it more likely that public and private security will be involved in a systemic response toward prevention of harm from these criminal activities and criminal networks. Unfortunately, local communities have not had the resources to protect against catastrophic events. Until 9/11, resources to do much within local communities was extremely limited. President Bush has publicly highlighted many times since 9/11, the importance of a well prepared first responder team. This is hard to do with limited resources, and so the President seeks to make monies available to local communities for first responder training and prevention planning.[80]

The full effect of this financial infusion into local communities for first responders will not be clear for some time. Even before 9/11, many argue that public police simply cannot be expected to provide the levels of safety and security that citizens in communities across the country have come to expect. As noted above, history also tells us that people who do not feel protected within their community will seek their own version of security, which can unleash a whole new type of security threat.

CONCLUSION

The history of private security is a history of eclectic efforts to provide protection in various environments as threats are identified. Efforts to police public space and private property overlap and are even intertwined in ways that suggesting more attention should be given to the integration of services provided by public and private policing agencies, perhaps using a collective phrase like "public safety." It is true that many retired law enforcement officers take jobs in the security industry, and some working police officers assume positions within the security industry when they finish their shift with the department. Furthermore, police departments contract with private agencies for specialized services; and in some cities, public and private police work together on the same cases and/or issues. Because this is such an important concept, there is more discussion about the integrated role of public and private police in Chapter 9.

New security-related issues of the modern, computerized, global economy have resulted in the increasing need for an ever-vigilant, highly trained, and well-educated community of security professionals. While many of the security technologies, techniques, and protocols are advertised as "new," a closer inspection reminds us that although the technology is innovative, the ideas behind these products have been around for a while. Computers, for example, use multiple layers of defenses to protect the important information in the computer system; this idea is similar to how forts or castles created multiple layers of defense, such as moats and other perimeter protections, as a way to deter or prevent entry.

This chapter has highlighted several notable events impacting the modern-day concept of public and private policing in the United States. But it is not enough for students to limit their understanding of security to the modern day, or to England and the United States. It is important to remember that time and place are important in understanding how security objectives are identified and how measures are taken to ensure that protection efforts are implemented. This text focuses on the European and American communities, so the history lesson has been focused on Europe and the United States. It is essential to understand that a comprehensive assessment of security requires attention to the dominant culture from within which the security objectives are being developed.

As is the case with many historical accounts, the view presented here may overlook the experiences of less dominant groups, and it does not incorporate cultural experiences outside the history of the United States. Highlight boxes throughout the chapter emphasized some security-related issues throughout the globe. Consideration should also be given to the impact of such security concerns on these groups outside the mainstream. Reviewing the respective histories of other countries and geographic regions should provide the practitioner with a more comprehensive understanding of global security-related issues.

History suggests, arguably, that initial laws introduced to provide protection were structured to enhance the protection of kings and noblemen. Even today, protection services are more available to those who have money and power. Efforts to protect "average" citizens came later. When circumstances suggest that personal protection is the only protection an individual has, skepticism about public police efforts increases and entrepreneurial enterprises in private protection are likely to flourish. Yet, as stated previously, private protection comes at a cost. People who educate themselves and develop a better understanding of the existing threats and security-related issues become resource providers rather than consumers. The more they know, the better able they are to protect themselves and others rather than need protection.

Security professionals who understand that they do not have to "reinvent the wheel" (chances are pretty good the wheel is out there already) also understand that they need not spend time spinning their wheels. This chapter encourages readers to study history, learn about various cultures and security climates, and learn about security trends and perceptions of threats—activities essential for someone interested in the security field. The emphasis on history, diversity, and social context will prove useful whether readers are preparing for a career in the security industry or seeking to protect a certain environment.

REVIEW QUESTIONS

1. What types of security-related activities took place in prehistoric communities?
2. As early as 5000 B.C., Sumerians were one of the oldest recorded societies to have what?
3. What was the purpose of the Praetorian Guard?
4. Established under the rule of King John, the Magna Carta is said to be one of the most important legal documents concerning personal protection. What specific contributions did the Magna Carta make to the evolution of personal protection?
5. What was the role of the citizen in law enforcement after the implementation of the Statute of Westminster?
6. What was the relationship between Henry Fielding and the Bow Street Runners?
7. How did Allan Pinkerton advance the security industry in the United States?
8. Who had the primary responsibility for protecting individuals in the U.S. frontier?

DISCUSSION QUESTIONS

1. Consider the information presented throughout this chapter. Throughout history, have more affluent members of society had better access to security than less affluent members of society? Provide evidence to support your position.

2. Security professionals have been described as a "support service" to local police. Do you agree or disagree with such a statement? What information included in the chapter supports your opinion?

3. Consider the following statement made by Peel: "The community cannot control the behavior of its members when the population grows beyond a few hundred."
   - How would you assess his evaluation of society's ability to police itself?
   - What does such a statement mean today, in an era of computer networks that allow both legitimate and illegitimate businesses to span the globe?
   - What do we learn from history about the "rogue players"— people some might call "entrepreneurs"— who participated in early efforts to capitalize on the "selling" of security services?
   - What does this statement mean to you today, when you can transfer money electronically, via satellite, from just about anywhere on the globe?

4. Consider a 10-year-old boy living in a downtown area of a large urban center. Consider another 10-year-old boy living in a rather exclusive gated community within that same urban center. How would the security concerns for each of these children differ? What if they were girls rather than boys? What if they were 15 years old? What if they were 18 years old?

REFERENCES

1. N. South, "Law, Profit, and 'Private Persons': Private and Public Policing in English History," in *Private Policing,* ed. C. D. Shearing and P. C. Stenning (Newbury Park, CA: Sage, 1987), 72–109.

2. R. Fischer and G. Green, *Introduction to Security,* 6th ed. (Boston: Butterworth-Heinemann, 1998), 3–6.

3. M. Nalla and G. Newman, *A Primer in Private Security* (New York: Harrow and Heston, 1990).

4. J. P. Peel, *The Story of Private Security* (Springfield, IL: Charles C. Thomas, 1971).

5. R. Stuart, *New York Times,* March 30, 1975, Section 3, p. 1.

6. W. C. Cunningham and T. H. Taylor, *The Growing Role of Private Security: Research in Brief* (Washington, DC: U.S. Department of Justice, National Institute of Justice, 1984) p. 239.

7. Cunningham and Taylor, *Growing Role,* 239.

8. Office of the Press Secretary, "Strengthening Homeland Security Since 9/11," *http://www.whitehouse.gov/homeland/six_month_update.html* site created April 11, 2002, last visited 08/15/02.

9. J. Rakowsky, "Bratton Lauds Community Policing Effort," *Boston Globe,* October 19, 1996, G10.

10. R. Healy, *Design for Security* (New York: John Wiley and Sons, 1968), 1–7.

11. J. H. Christman, "History of Private Security," in *Protection Officer Training Manual,* ed. International Foundation for Protection Officers (Boston: Butterworth-Heinemann, 1998), 89.

12. C. E. Simonsen, *Private Security in America: An Introduction* (Upper Saddle River, NJ: Prentice Hall, 1998), 14–22.

13. "Ancient Civilizations and Lost Cities," *http://www.eliki.com/ancient/civilizations/sumerian/.*, dated 1997, designed and maintained by Interactive Technologies, LLC; accessed on January 20, 2001.

14. Nalla and Newman, *Primer in Private Security,* p. 16.

15. Interactive Technologies, "The Sumerians of Mesopotamia."

16. At http://www.wwlia.org, the following information is available: "2350 BC: Urukagina's Code: This code has never been discovered but it is mentioned in other documents as a consolidation of existing 'ordinances' or laws laid down by Mesopotamian kings." "2050 BC: Ur-Nammu's Code: The earliest known written legal code of which a copy has been found, albeit a copy in such poor shape that only five articles can be deciphered. The Code allowed for the dismissal of corrupt men, protection for the poor and a punishment system where the punishment is proportionate to the crime."

17. L. Duhaime, "The Timetable of World Legal History," *http://www.wwlia.org/hist.htm#1700bc*, created 1994, accessed October 23, 1999.

18. Interactive Technologies, "The Sumerians of Mesopotamia."

19. R. T. McConnell, Jr., "The Formation of Near Eastern Civilizations," *http://www.colacoll.edu/academic/cccc/history/hist101/geo.htm* (May 20, 1997), accessed October 17, 1999.

20. Duhaime, "The Timetable of World Legal History."

21. Duhaime, "The Timetable of World Legal History."

22. Duhaime, "The Timetable of World Legal History."

23. L. Duhaime, "The Timetable of World Legal History," *http://www.wwlia.org/hist.htm#1700bc*, created 1994, accessed October 23, 1999. The tables are listed as follows: Table I: preliminaries to a trial, rules for a trial; Table II: the trial; Table III: debt; Table IV: rights of fathers; Table V: guardianship; Table VI: acquisition, possession; Table VII: rights concerning land; Table VIII: torts or delicts; Table IX: public law; Table X: sacred law; Table XI: supplementary laws; Table XII: supplementary laws.

24. Duhaime, "The Timetable of World Legal History."

25. Duhaime, "The Timetable of World Legal History."

26. Duhaime, "The Timetable of World Legal History."

27. Encyclopædia Brittanica, "Praetorian Guard," *http://www.eb.com:180/bol/ topic?idxref=390647*, created 1994, accessed June 23, 1999.

28. Encyclopædia Britannica, "Augustus, Caesar," *http://www.eb.com:180/bol/ topic?artcl=109389&seq_nbr=1&page=n&isctn=2>*, created 1994, accessed June 23, 1999.

29. R. W. Davies, "Augustus Caesar: A Police System in the Ancient World," in *Pioneers in Policing,* ed. J. P. Stead (Montclair, NJ: Patterson Smith Publishing Company, 1977), 14–20, 25.

30. Encyclopædia Britannica, "Rome," *http://www.eb.com:180/bol/topic?eu= 117431&sctn=5*, created 1994, accessed June 23, 1999.

31. Davies, "Augustus Caesar," 16–17.

32. Davies, "Augustus Caesar," 17.

33. Duhaime, "The Timetable of World Legal History."

34. "Feudalism", *www.eb.com: 180/bol/topic?eu=3476&sctn=1*, created 1994, accessed January 20, 2001.

35. Fischer and Green, *Introduction to Security,* 5.

36. "Feudalism."

37. P. Purpura, *Security and Loss Prevention: An Introduction,* 3rd ed. (Woburn, MA: Butterworth-Heinemann, 1998), 7–8.

38. Duhaime, "The Timetable of World Legal History."

39. K. Hess and H. M. Wrobleski, *Introduction to Private Security,* 4th ed. (Minneapolis, MN: West Publishing Company, 1998), 6.

40. J. H. Christman, "History of Private Security," in *Protection Officer Training Manual,* ed. International Foundation for Protection Officers (Boston: Butterworth-Heinemann, 1998), 30–36.

41. Peel, *Story of Private Security,* 10.

42. Peel, *Story of Private Security,* 10.

43. Hess and Wrobleski, *Introduction to Private Security,* 8.

44. J. H. Christman, "History of Private Security," in *Protection Officer Training Manual,* ed. International Foundation for Protection Officers (Boston: Butterworth-Heinemann, 1998), 30–36.

45. Peel, *Story of Private Security,* 11.

46. Peel, *Story of Private Security,* 13.

47. Peel, *Story of Private Security,* 13.

48. Peel, *Story of Private Security,* 11.

49. J. B. Rubenstein, "Henry and John Fielding: Police Philosophy and Police Technique," in *Pioneers in Policing,* ed. J. P. Stead (Montclair, NJ: Patterson Smith Publishing Company, 1977).

50. Rubenstein, "Henry and John Fielding," 35.

51. Peel, *Story of Private Security,* 14.

52. Quote from *The Chicago Daily Democratic Press,* March 11, 1857, in J. P. Stead, *Pioneers in Policing* (Montclair, NJ: Patterson Smith Publishing Company, 1977), 106.

53. F. T. Morn, "Allan Pinkerton. Private Police Influence on Police Development," in *Pioneers in Policing,* ed. J. P. Stead (Montclair, NJ: Patterson Smith Publishing Company, 1977), 96–120.

54. Morn, "Allan Pinkerton," 96.

55. Morn, "Allan Pinkerton," 106–107.

56. Morn, "Allan Pinkerton," 107.

57. Morn, "Allan Pinkerton," 108.

58. Morn, "Allan Pinkerton," 108.

59. Morn, "Allan Pinkerton," 109.

60. Morn, "Allan Pinkerton," 112.

61. Morn, "Allan Pinkerton," 112.

62. Peel, *Story of Private Security,* 21.

63. Peel, *Story of Private Security,* 21.

64. Peel, *Story of Private Security,* 21.

65. E. Levinson, *I Break Strikes! The Technique of Pearl L. Bergoff* (New York: Robert M. McBride, 1969), 18.

66. Levinson, *I Break Strikes!* 18.

67. Levinson, *I Break Strikes!* 19.

68. Levinson, *I Break Strikes!* 20.

69. Levinson, *I Break Strikes!* 20.

70. Levinson, *I Break Strikes!* 23.

71. Peel, *Story of Private Security,* 22.

72. Peel, *Story of Private Security,* 22.

73. Peel, *Story of Private Security,* 23.

74. Peel, *Story of Private Security,* 25.

75. Prenszler et al., "The Case for Non-Police Private Security," *Journal of Security Administration* (1996): 16–33.

76. Prenszler et al., "The Case for Non-Police Private Security," 16.

77. The White House, Office of the Press Secretary. Created 04-11-02. Last accessed 08-15-02. *http://www.whitehouse.gov/homeland/six_month_update.html*

78. The White House, Office of the Press Secretary. Cite created 03.12.2002. Last accessed 08.15.02 *http://www.whitehouse.gov/nows/releases/2002/03/20020312-1.html*

79. Prenszler et al., "The Case for Non-Police Private Security," 147.

80. "President promotes funding for emergency first responders." The White House. Office of the Press Secretary. Cite created 04-27-02. Last accessed, 08.15.02. *www.whitehouse.gov/news/releases/2002/03/20020327-6.html*

Identifying the Essentials

CHAPTER OUTLINE

Beginning with the Basics: Ever Changing and Never Ending
Studies in Human Behavior: An Essential Need for Security
Outlining and Defining *Security*
  Creating and Maintaining a Stable and Predictable Environment
  Threats, Risk, and Vulnerabilities
Introducing Essential Security Tools: Identifying Threats, Risks, and Vulnerabilities
  Threats and Related Risk Levels

Identifying Vulnerabilities and Determining Countermeasures
A Final, All-Important Term
A Few Essential Elements
  Proactive versus Reactive Response
  Contract Officers versus Proprietary Officers
  Contract Outsourcing Decisions
Conclusion
  Review Questions
  Discussion Questions

CHAPTER HIGHLIGHTS

Security basics:
- The security objective is a never-ending process.
- Security needs change over time.

Contributions from psychology:
- Adler: Humans are, above all else, social.
- Maslow and the hierarchy of needs: Security is a fundamental human need.

Defining security:
- stability
- predictability

Useful terms:
- threat
- risk:
  1. probability
  2. criticality
- vulnerability

Essential tools:
- threat assessment
- vulnerability assessment
- security survey (security audit)
- risk assessment
- risk analysis

KEY WORDS

American Society for Industrial Security (ASIS)
Certified Protection Professional (CPP)
Contingency plan
Contract

Countermeasures
Criticality
Loss event
Predictable environment
Proactive

Probability	Security survey
Proprietary	Stable environment
Reactive	Threat
Risk	Threat assessment
Risk analysis	Vulnerability
Risk assessment	Vulnerability assessment
Security audit	Vulnerability gap

Everyone is interested in security issues at one point or another. In any local newspaper on any given day, a person will read stories that may affect how they interpret their own sense of security. My local newspaper today included a story about a sex offender who escaped from a privately owned inmate transportation service while being relocated from one prison facility to another. In another article, a suburban home was destroyed by a fire whose cause had yet to be determined. Another story told of a local manufacturing company evacuating workers, canceling some shifts, and delaying other shifts because of a bomb threat. The building was cleared, no bomb was found, and workers returned to their duties without further incident.

One of the most unusual stories told of a series of car thefts: In various neighborhoods all over town, thieves were finding open entrances, entering homes, and attempting to find people's car keys. Once the keys were found, the thieves would then drive away with the victim's car. Because of the number of similar incidents all over town, police issued a warning asking people to make sure they lock up their homes and cars in an attempt to prevent future opportunities for similar crimes.

Any number of stories from communities across the country can be used to illustrate the various kinds of security-related information individuals are confronted with every day. Different people respond differently to the news of a potential threat. Some people may respond by taking certain actions to protect themselves and their families. Others may simply note the incident, assume their chances of being impacted by the reported threat are small, and do nothing at all. Perhaps Jody just bought her dream car after several years of hard work. She might have been extremely interested in the news story about random car thefts. On the other hand, maybe Jody's car spends more time in the repair shop than it does in the garage. In this case, she would probably not be overly concerned after learning about the thefts.

Business professionals and other community members will inevitably focus their attention on any number of safety and security concerns over time. The

A special thanks to Chuck Thibodeau of Thibodeau and Associates in Minneapolis, Minnesota for his contribution and comments throughout this chapter.

response to a perceived security threat, as suggested previously, varies with the individual and the circumstances. Think about your own reaction to some of the news stories introduced earlier. After reading about the house fire, did you think about how well your own home is protected against fire? Or were you relatively unaffected by the story because you know your home is protected? Or did you think, "Gee, I am glad that will never happen to me"? If so, have you taken steps to ensure the risk levels linked to the threat of fire are low?

The average person may increase his or her level of awareness about a specific security-related issue after identifying it as a possible threat. But again, a person's interest in security fluctuates with his or her perception of the world. People are increasingly spending time, energy, and money to keep their person and property safe. It is difficult, however, to conclude logically from this increased interest in personal security that these individuals are *in fact* more secure. Interestingly, the threats people fear the most are not always the threats most likely to materialize.

How people use security technologies and security devices is also interesting. Everyone has heard stories of people who buy smoke detectors and then do not change the batteries. Other people have home security systems but do not activate them because they find the systems inconvenient. Some female college students buy personal protection devices, such as pepper spray or mace, to carry as they walk to and from night classes, but they keep the devices in their backpacks, where they are harder to get on a moment's notice than if held in the hand. Just because people invest in security devices does not mean their safety is enhanced. Security devices are effective only if used properly, and security professionals will attest that security protocols must be integrated into a routine that is useful, or people will not benefit from them.

Consider another example of the role of security issues in everyday life. Most people spend 40 or more hours a week in a building someone else owns. They do a specific job but typically give hardly a second thought to whether their workplace is secure. Most people are not interested in focusing on security issues at work. Some may have had thoughts about security issues in their workplace, but chances are good that the thoughts were fleeting and ended with assumptions about how adequate safeguards were probably put in place by someone else. How safe would you feel going back into a building after a bomb was reported? Would you react differently if you lived in Oklahoma City after the bombing of the Murrah Building, or in Littleton, Colorado, after the bomb devices were found in Columbine High?

In spite of the fact that not all threats can be anticipated, a security professional must make a proactive security plan while also reacting to changing local events and circumstances. The objective is to increase people's sense of safety and security while at the same time allowing for appropriate freedom of movement and interaction within the target environment. Although people may feel safer if specific steps are taken after a catastrophic event, sometimes such action is neither practical nor necessary because the threat is unlikely to be repeated and the risk level is so low. A responsible security professional must find the balance between real threat and perceived threat. This can be tricky. As circumstances in the immediate environment change, so should the security professional's response. These local changes, however, also reflect changes at a state and/or national level such as the effect of 9/11.

Consider the equally important fact that certain neighborhoods are perceived to be more likely to experience crime, while people living in other neighborhoods tend to feel safer. Neighborhoods in big cities are perceived to be dangerous while rural areas are assumed to be safe. Depending on geographic location and time of year, this may or may not be true. Communities across the country have different levels of security concern, and these levels of concern often fluctuate over time. Concern may be related to drug activities, drive-by shootings, gang activity, an increase in robberies, or simply an attempt to provide a collective sense of greater security within the neighborhood. Neighborhood watch groups are one example of a collective community effort to enhance security in a particular area. Individuals in neighborhoods band together

(*Source:* Cartoonists and Writers Syndicate.)

to protect themselves against a specific community concern. Often coordinating their efforts with local police departments, individual community members work to target and eliminate various activities they believe pose threats to their homes and families.

It is clear that one person's reaction to security issues may differ dramatically from another person's. Fear of crime is considered one of the factors driving up interest in security-related professions.[1] While violent crime in general may be on the decline, the stories increasingly making headline news involve workplaces, schools, and homes across the country that have been directly affected by unanticipated security threats. The security professional's job is to reduce the likelihood that such threats will manifest themselves.

This chapter discusses basic terms and tools that anyone who is interested in security should know about and understand. Attention is given to some basic information about the security process, the impact of security on human behavior, and the importance of creating and maintaining a stable and predictable environment. A brief review of terms and definitions commonly used by security professionals is presented. The differences between proactive and reactive response and between "contract" and "proprietary" guard services are outlined.

BEGINNING WITH THE BASICS: EVER CHANGING AND NEVER ENDING

To get a better understanding of security objectives at the most basic level, any interested person should be clear about two things: (1) The effort to achieve a secure environment is a never-ending process, and (2) security objectives change over time. While efforts to create a safe environment can begin at a predetermined point, the *process* of maintaining effective security protection must remain lively and interactive ad infinitum. Once the security objectives are outlined, specific needs and available resources can be itemized and analyzed. But implementing the plan is just the beginning. Establishing a security program is anything but a short-term proposition.

The second fact, that security objectives change over time, is integrally connected to the first point. The process of achieving a secure environment must be ongoing, because the relevant people, tools, practices, justifications, and intended outcomes are all subject to various external factors. Society is constantly changing. People are constantly reacting to these changes. Social issues; individual, community, and corporate attitudes; and perceived threats will all change over time. New security threats and risks emerge regularly. Most, if not all, security protocols outlined for maintaining the integrity of a security management program will require anything from regular, relatively minor updates to major technological modifications.

As readers begin identifying and exploring security essentials, it is of critical importance that they see the security objective as a dynamic, interactive, multidimensional process. The development of a secure environment is contingent on multiple factors. Some people or businesses simply consider security concerns a higher priority than other people or businesses do. Professionals in some environments, for example, may invest heavily in protecting the company's employees, products, facility, and equipment. Individuals in other environments may address a particular concern only after they are forced to confront that security threat. People seek security for a variety of reasons, some more clear than others. Security professionals must understand the motivations of the people with whom they work, in addition to the people they will encounter on any given day.

STUDIES IN HUMAN BEHAVIOR: AN ESSENTIAL NEED FOR SECURITY

Professionals in the security industry benefit from reviewing existing research on human behavior as it is presented within the social and behavioral sciences. Understanding the relationship between research in the field of human behavior and the need for humans to create a secure space proves to be an important starting point for considering the overall security objective. In fact, it is so important that **ASIS** (the American Society for Industrial Security, pronounced "as is"), the largest training organization for security professionals in the world, makes references to the importance of the study of human behavior in its manual for the **CPP** (Certified Protection Professional) training course.[2]

A study of human behavior as it relates to the security objective can be found in the work of Alfred Adler. Known as the "father of individual psychology," Adler devoted a lot of time and energy at the turn of the twentieth century to developing the field of psychotherapy that he called "individual psychology."[3,4] In short, Adler concluded that humans, above all else, are social. He argued that humans are bound together in mutually beneficial societies by a fundamental need to belong. In other words, his work demonstrated that humans feel more secure psychologically when they are a part of society rather than acting separately as isolated individuals. People behave in certain ways and pursue particular courses of action in order to satisfy social needs. Adler argued all human behavior has purpose, and the purpose of that behavior involves need satisfaction.

Expanding on Adler's work, Abraham Maslow became another prolific scholar on psychological development and human behavior.[5] Maslow studied and wrote about specific human needs, identifying certain needs as being central to healthy human functioning. He described these needs in the form of a pyramid with five different levels, arranged in an ascending order of priorities (Figure 2–1).[6]

Maslow's work suggests that needs located higher in the hierarchy cannot be achieved until the needs on the lower levels have been satisfied. The

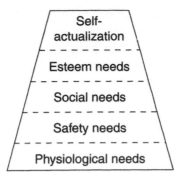

FIGURE 2–1 Maslow's Hierarchy of Needs

lowest-level needs are physiological. This includes the need for food, clothing, and shelter. Once these needs are maintained, a person will naturally begin to think about the next level. The next level is the need for safety and security. Continuing up the pyramid to level three, there are social needs, or the need to belong—an idea central to Adlerian psychology. The fourth and fifth levels on Maslow's hierarchy are the need for recognition of accomplishments (esteem needs), then the need for self-actualization.

This brief review of some of the landmark research in human behavior is a reminder that security issues are recognized as primary, goal-directed needs that are essential elements of human psychological wellness. Safety needs involve establishing stability and consistency in a chaotic world.[7] These needs are primarily psychological. The research in human development, introduced only briefly here, suggests that people generally seek to protect and preserve life and property by creating safe, stable, even predictable environments.

Maslow's research suggests that people who face violence or live in circumstances where their personal welfare cannot be ensured will not be able to devote as much time to psychological and moral development.[8] Adler's work helps clarify why humans have typically identified and addressed safety and security objectives within community structures, rather than leaving them to individual efforts. People increasingly demand law and order when they do not feel safe in their neighborhoods or communities. In short, the need for stability in the area of safety and security is so important to humans, both as individuals and within social groupings, that they are not expected to proceed to higher levels of psychological development until fundamental aspects of these needs for safety and security are fulfilled.

The work of Adler and Maslow is briefly touched on to help introduce the idea of security as a primary human need. For security professionals and students learning about security issues, it becomes even more important to think about what the term *security* means. Does the word *security* mean the same thing to security professionals as it does to people on the street? Remember the newspaper story (mentioned previously) about a building being evacuated because of a bomb threat? After such an event, after the company's security professionals and local police complete the sweep of the facility, the business owners are informed that the building is safe for normal operations. As an employee of the company, would you be comfortable returning to the facility? What information about the incident would help you feel secure in that work environment after such an event?

Anyone with even a limited understanding of the security industry can provide impressions about what it means to feel secure. For the security professional, the critical point is that *feeling* secure can be quite different from actually *being* secure. In this case, the responsibility of the security professionals does not end after the building is declared "all clear." Security professionals can also provide a tremendous service to the facility management by helping the returning workers feel secure as they report back to work. Security professionals are focused on making sure certain target environments *are* secure and that the people—usually customers or employees, or both—in this environment *feel* secure.

OUTLINING AND DEFINING "SECURITY"

No one would deny the fact that the term *security* refers to a complex set of ideas. *Security* has multiple, sometimes extremely different, meanings. Consider something as specific as a security alarm or a phrase as broad as *national security.* Definitions of *private security, private police,* and even *public space* and *private space* continue to be redefined and publicly debated.[9] In spite of the multiplicity of definitions, some degree of collective agreement has been reached among scholars and security professionals. The late 1970s produced one of the most widely referenced definitions of security. Today the definition is still widely referenced, and many people who use the term *security* incorporate the central concepts outlined in that early definition. In short, the definition is as follows: "Security, in its semantic and philosophical sense, implies a stable, relatively predictable environment in which an individual or group may pursue its ends without disruptions or harm, and without fear of such disturbance or injury."[10]

Upon closer examination, it is easy to see that this definition of *security* reflects some of the same ideas from the field of human development highlighted earlier. If individuals or groups do not fear disturbance or injury, if they feel safe, they can pursue their ends without disruption. At its essence, the Green and Farber definition identifies the need for security more specifically as achieving two things. A secure environment should be (1) stable and (2) predictable.[11]

Creating and Maintaining a Stable and Predictable Environment

Security managers who design and implement security management strategies are, at a basic level, interested in establishing and maintaining a stable environment. A **stable environment** is one resistant to sudden changes. An unstable environment is susceptible to unanticipated change. Stability within a secured environment has long-term implications. Establishing and maintaining a crime-free, tranquil environment as a safe and secure workplace, for example, means little to employees if the environment is not likely to remain crime-free and tranquil over time. To provide a stable environment means to make sure unanticipated events do not disrupt the safety and security of a target environment—in this case a workplace. Stability, therefore, is key to establishing or maintaining the integrity of the security system put in place.

A **predictable environment** is one in which the security professionals can know, with a significant degree of certainty, what will happen within that environment on a given day. The process of establishing predictability, like stability, is ongoing. Predictability is brought about through a process of constant observation and reporting. By identifying an expected pattern of behavior, security professionals can be more attuned to anything that might appear to threaten the stability of the target environment. After daily routines have been established and personnel have been responsible for observing and cataloguing typical conditions within a workplace setting, for example, members of the security management team can get a pretty good picture of potential threats and risks because they have established a baseline of typical daily activities.

As suggested in the Green and Farber definition, stability and predictability go hand in hand. It is difficult, for example, to predict what might happen in an unstable environment. When an environment is stable, specific irregularities are more easily notable and, therefore, more easily addressed by security professionals. Disruptions occur in the form of anticipated and unanticipated threats. Thus relative predictability can be established and maintained by security personnel working together with company employees to observe, report, and take action on problems that threaten the stability of their work environment. It is very important to remember that no matter how efficient the security efforts, every peaceful environment is threatened by an unwelcome disturbance occasionally. No environment can ever be completely free from threats. This is key. We saw this on September 11. Depending on the interaction or activity, the risk of threat may range from low to high, but all interactions and activities involve potential threats. The question is how well we can be prepared to prevent anticipated threats or to respond in the face of unanticipated threats.

Threats, Risk, and Vulnerabilities

To help simplify the discussion about threats and risk levels, and in an effort to better classify and assess the impact of threats and the related risk level on a target environment, we introduce two relatively simple definitions. First, a **threat** is an impending or potential danger or harm. Second, **risk** actually refers to two things: (1) the likelihood of a threat materializing, and (2) the degree of damage that can be expected if the threat does occur. For security professionals, these two aspects of risk are referred to as a threat's probability and criticality. **Probability** refers to the likelihood a threat will actually happen. **Criticality** is used to indicate the extent of damage likely if that threat occurs.

After determining the probability and criticality associated with a threat, the risk is identified by assigning a level (low, medium, or high) or a number (1 through 10) to each of these two aspects of risk. We will discuss more specifics associated with this assessment process throughout subsequent chapters; the purpose here is only to introduce the idea.

Once threats are identified and risk levels are assessed, security professionals must also account for **vulnerabilities.** Clifford Simonsen defines a vulnerability as "any weakness or flaw in the physical layout, organization, procedures, management, administration, hardware, or software that may be exploited to cause harm to the institution, business or activity."[12] A **vulnerability gap** is the difference between the level of security in place and the level of security needed for appropriate protection in a target environment. The larger the vulnerability gap, the higher the risk factors (in terms of probability and/or criticality) associated with that threat.

Consultation with various security professionals suggests that the definitions of the terms *threat* and *risk* have suffered a fate similar to the terms *safety* and *security*. People use these terms interchangeably. The tendency to overuse these words detracts from security-related efforts within the discipline to ensure that practitioners and researchers are using the terms in the same way. This precision is particularly important in the case of *threat* and *risk,* which refer to two very different things. While this distinction may seem unimportant to some, such definitional specificity is essential within an academic environment for research purposes. Furthermore, such clarification is important for professionals in the field, who continue to learn from each other.

A threat is simply an item that is identified and placed on a list of specific events that may emerge in a target environment and that is likely to cause some form of loss to the target environment. A threat is inherently a negative-impact event, a possibility at some future time. It can be said that every threat has a risk component, but it is not equally accurate to refer to risk as if it has varying threat levels. This is simply inaccurate. There are only threats, and these threats will be discussed as having varying levels of occurrence risk.

The risk factor associated with a particular threat is almost always determined by environmental conditions. The common threat of fire does not always have the same risk level. The risk of fire changes depending upon conditions in the target environment. In other words, characteristics associated with a given environment will be a factor in determining the level of risk attached to a given threat—in this case the threat of fire. Risk will most often be referred to as a "level" or "factor."

Security professionals spend a considerable amount of time trying to assess the risk levels associated with each threat identified as a possible danger to the target environment they are responsible for protecting. The moment a threat manifests itself, it is likely to produce another security term: a **loss event.** The term *loss event* refers to damage, or loss, to the target environment. Once a threat materializes, the risk concern shifts from probability (likelihood) to criticality (degree of damage). Typically, damage translates into some type of monetary loss to the company. It is the job of every security professional to make certain a plan is in place not only to prevent the threat from happening, but to minimize the damage the threat can do if it does happen. Remember, no environment is ever 100 percent threat free. Security professionals must, therefore, identify possible threats and assess risk levels in an effort to successfully establish a security plan that will minimize loss events.

INTRODUCING ESSENTIAL SECURITY TOOLS: IDENTIFYING THREATS, RISKS, AND VULNERABILITIES

It should be clear that threats and their related risk levels directly affect the stability and predictability of a target environment. Be clear about this, because it is important. The process of identifying threats and reducing the risk levels associated with those threats is a large part of the security objective, for both individuals and businesses.

Threats and Related Risk Levels

It may sound overly dramatic to state without reservation the reality that humans are continuously facing some level of threat. The trick for security professionals is to identify potential threats and assess their likelihood of materializing. Security practitioners must develop a working list of threats they believe might impact their target environment. Exhibit 2–1 contains a fairly comprehensive list of threats that are common in at least one form or another to just about every possible environment. This list should be used as a starting point

Exhibit 2–1   List of Potential Threats

Americans with Disabilities Act	Internal strife
Arson	Loss of power
Assault/battery	Medical emergency
Burglary	Occupational Safety and Health
Chemical spill	Administration violation
Civil lawsuit	Organized gambling
Drug-related incident	Parking lot crime
Embezzlement	Personal injury accident
Environmental Protection Agency	Sabotage
violation	Severe weather (flood, tornado,
Equal Employment Opportunity	earthquake, hurricane)
Commission violation	Sexual assault
Explosion	Sexual harassment
Extortion	Shoplifting
Firearm threat (internal or external)	Terrorism
Firearm violation	Theft (petty and major)
Fire emergency	Union strife
HVAC failure	Vendor theft

for identifying specific threats within a target environment. For example, in a multinational corporation that has responsibilities for protecting a particular trade secret, security measures must be put in place to protect that secret, and, more important, the security professional must assess *all* possible scenarios for how someone might breach that system and make off with the information. The company's success depends on it.

One of the responsibilities of a security professional is to conduct an inventory of security threats. This is sometimes referred to as a **threat assessment** or threat analysis. These two terms refer to the same activity: assessing the likelihood that a threat will occur in a target environment. Companies, national parks, schools, hospitals, and other public and private agencies all over the world deal very effectively with the threats itemized in Exhibit 2–1 every day. A very basic threat assessment would involve reviewing the list of threats in the exhibit and determining which threats might impact a particular business. After identifying a basic list of threats, the threat identification process continues by examining the history of events in and around the target environment. An examination of 911 reports from the local police department and a review of internal incident reports will reveal past threats. Interviews with employees and others who frequent the environment can be another way of identifying additional threats that may pose problems down the road.

Take a few minutes to review Exhibit 2–1, keeping in mind the fact that no list can include every potential threat and each threat list should be tailored to the target environment. Think of an environment you might wish to secure. Are all the threats to your environment listed here? What would you need to add to the list?

Does the list in Exhibit 2–1 provide an easy, efficient, accessible means for you to review and prepare for the threats to your target environment? If not, how might you change the format to make this threat analysis more useful to your agency, or the people working with you, and ensure the security of the environment? Consider the organization of threats in Exhibit 2–2.

Once a security professional sees a clear list of examples of threats, he or she will begin to see the relationship between these threats and the risk levels associated with them. Remember, risks refer to the probability (likelihood of the threat materializing) and criticality (degree of damage possible) associated with each threat. A security professional must be aware of potential threats in order to reduce the risk levels associated with those threats. When threats have been identified, a **risk assessment** can be used to determine the level of risk

Exhibit 2–2   List of Potential Threats Arranged Topically

Emergencies
  Arson/fire
  Bomb threat
  Chemical spill
  Explosion
  Loss of power
  Medical emergency
    Customer
    Work-related injury
  Severe weather
    Earthquake
    Flood
    Hurricane
    Tornado
  Workplace violence
Information/computers
  Crackers
  Hackers
  Internal sabotage
  System failure
  Electricity outage
  Unknown virus attack
Liability
  Americans with Disabilities Act
    violation
  Civil lawsuit
  Environmental Protection Agency
    violation
  Equal Employment Opportunity
    Commission violation

  Occupational Safety and Health
    Administration violation
  Sexual harassment
Miscellaneous threats
  Assault/battery
  Firearm violation
  Sexual assault
  Stalking
  Burglary
  Drug-related incident
  Embezzlement
  Employee theft
  Extortion
  Sabotage
  Shoplifting
  Terrorism
  Theft (petty and major)
  Vendor theft
Personnel and security management
  Domestic violence
  Internal strife
  Organized gambling
  Union strife
Physical security
  Access control
    Guards
    Alarms
    Gates
  Parking lot crime
  Parking lot lighting

associated with each threat. Proactive prevention involves spending a considerable amount of time evaluating risks. The risk assessment requires consideration of the probability and criticality. After a threat assessment has been completed, a risk assessment can be done on each risk to determine the probability and criticality associated with that threat within a target environment. See Figure 2–2 for an example of this.

Threats are listed in the left column, with room to add a number to represent the probability and criticality associated with each threat. The total or combined risk measure can be compiled, if this is desirable. Consider the following structure for interpreting risk. Assume the reader elects to outline a risk scale using numbers from 0 to 100 (1 through 10 can be used instead, if you prefer). If the risk of a particular threat is identified to be 90 (or 9) on that scale, the threat is extremely likely to result in a loss event—an event that costs the company money. A 10 (or 1) on that same scale indicates the threat poses minimal risk. A "no risk" classification is rare. If a threat is identified, inevitably there will be an accompanying risk level (probability and criticality) related to that threat.

The risk of certain threats can increase or decrease under different circumstances. When a person drives a car, there are various potential threats, including running out of gas, being carjacked, colliding with another car, or experiencing engine failure. The probability, or likelihood, of one of these things happening will range from high to low depending on the circumstances. If a person is driving along a rural country road, the chances that the car will be taken at gunpoint are probably lower than if the person is in a large urban area where carjackings have been reported. Therefore, when assessing the probability and

THREAT	Risk / Probability / Criticality / Total		
Threat 1			
Threat 2			
Threat 3			
Threat 4			
Threat 5			
Threat 6			
Threat 7			
Threat 8			
Threat 9			
Threat 10			

FIGURE 2–2 Threat List with Attached Risk Assessment
(*Source:* Charles T. Thibodeau, M. Ed., CPP, CSS, CPO.)

criticality associated with anticipated threats, it is important to focus exclusively on the assessment of risk as it exists within a particular environment.

Consider a threat inventory and risk assessment for a high school. What threats listed in either Exhibit 2–1 or Exhibit 2–2 are most applicable to this environment? Are there additional threats? Lists for schools in different communities will contain different threats. Also, recent events in the news may affect the list. Would the list of threats identified for high schools be any different before and after the shootings in Littleton, Colorado?

One common threat is fire. Business owners, school administrators, home owners, and almost everyone else must address the threat posed by fire. Depending on the building and its use, the time of year, and other environmental conditions, the risk of fire or the likelihood a fire will occur and the amount of damage it may cause will vary.

In a nutshell, perhaps the first order of business for security professionals is to develop a means by which they can forecast, with reasonable accuracy, the risk levels (probability and criticality) of each of the threats likely to negatively impact their stable, predictable target environment. The risk levels can then be mitigated, or reduced, by employing security countermeasures. Because no environment can ever be entirely risk free, a well-prepared security professional will also assess criticality, or cost associated with anticipated losses if the threat is not successfully countered.

Various techniques have been used by security professionals in an attempt to organize threat- and risk-related information. Figure 2–2 offered one example, and Figures 2–3, 2–4, and 2–5 offer alternative formats. Figure 2–2 could be used for the general categories of threats. A security professional would fill in the threats according to the needs of any given target environment. Figure 2–3 offers another format focused on a general listing of threats and the diagonal documenting of related risk levels. This format is perhaps a little easier to read at a glance because all of the threats and their attached risk levels can be

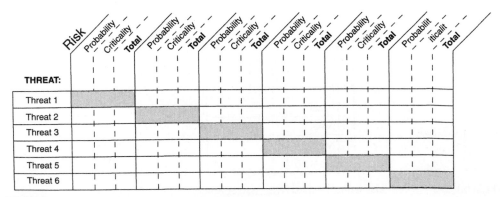

FIGURE 2–3 Threat List with Attached Risk Assessment
(*Source:* Charles T. Thibodeau, M. Ed., CPP, CSS, CPO.)

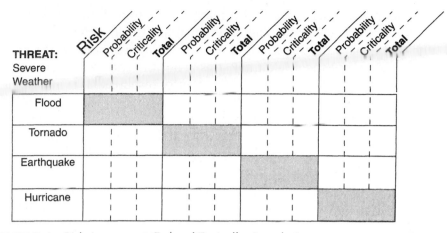

FIGURE 2–4 Risk Assessment Ordered Topically: Sample 1
(*Source:* Charles T. Thibodeau, M. Ed., CPP, CSS, CPO.)

compared. Figures 2–4 and 2–5 offer yet another way to organize important information. If, as in Exhibit 2–2, it seems most useful to put threats into categories, then perhaps breaking down the threat inventory and risk analysis by category also makes sense. Figure 2–4 shows the breakdown offered for severe weather, and Figure 2–5 the breakdown for information/computer systems. This grid can be read either as a straight column or on a diagonal (I prefer the diagonal option). So a threat inventory could have 5 to 10 pages of categories of threats that are broken down more thoroughly into subcategories.

As is clear from the variety of examples, there is no one right way to assess risk. The information included is almost always site specific. Depending on how

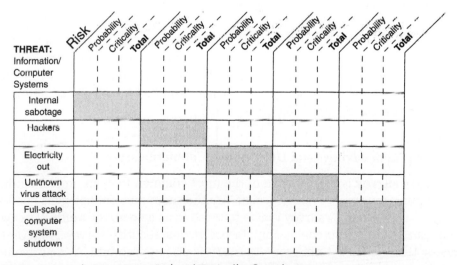

FIGURE 2–5 Risk Assessment Ordered Topically: Sample 2
(*Source:* Charles T. Thibodeau, M. Ed., CPP, CSS, CPO.)

the information will be used, the format may be more important. It is important to have an excellent understanding of an environment in order to conduct a thorough and exhaustive threat inventory and risk assessment. When assessments are made about the level of risk, this is not the end of the process. Decisions must be made about how to spend security resources. It is important to be thorough while conducting the threat inventory and related risk assessments, but it is also important to know that these inventories are only a beginning. Threats and their related risk levels change. Because of change, it will be necessary to review the list of threats you have identified and revisit the probability and criticality of each threat regularly.

Initially, becoming familiar with the process of identifying resources and consolidating the information collected from the various security assessment tools, some of which are presented in brief here, is essential. A number of these tools, and some additional examples, are included in Appendix A. But remember, while it is important to have a basic understanding of issues, security concerns that are specific to a security professional's target environment will emerge and the security professional will be responsible for addressing these concerns. Although it might initially seem complicated to divide risk into two concepts, probability and criticality, the two concepts make it easier to talk about the impact of identified threats.

The flexibility within the basic formula to identify threats and risks may seem awkward at first. I can provide the reader with ideas about how to proceed when identifying threats and assessing risks, but ultimately that is something dependent in large part on the characteristics of the target environment. To assume a rigid checklist for the environment is to miss some important details not on the checklist but present in the environment. A security professional must know the security objectives, know the target environment, find various examples of security tools intended to assist with threat analysis and risk assessment, and be flexible enough to modify those things irrelevant to the target environment. To understand better the impact of a specific threat on a target environment, a security professional must understand the environment well. The more a security professional learns, the better able he or she is to prepare for threats in the target environment.

Identifying Vulnerabilities and Determining Countermeasures

A **security survey** is perhaps one of the most common tools for implementing or evaluating an overall security design. Another note on terminology is needed here, because a security survey is also referred to as a **security audit.** The two terms can be used interchangeably. In essence, a security survey is an audit process; therefore, the term *security audit* is also appropriate. A security survey is a critical, on-site examination and analysis of a target environment to ascertain the present security status, to identify deficiencies or excesses, to determine the protection needed, and to make recommendations to improve overall security.[13] This tool is used to make note of both positive and negative issues as they relate to the overall security of that target environment. Its purpose is to draw out vulnerabilities and threats that might have been overlooked, so that the security practitioner can then do a more focused analysis on the perceived vulnerability gap, to ensure that the use of countermeasures is appropriate. A sample security survey can be found in Appendix A.

When addressing specific threats and their related risk levels, security professionals will institute **countermeasures.** A countermeasure, simply stated, is a practice put in place to reduce the risk associated with a given threat. The installation of sprinklers, for example, would be a countermeasure implemented to reduce the criticality (or potential damage) associated with the threat of fire. The documentation of countermeasure options and their impact on risk levels is also important. Consider the format for evaluating proposed countermeasures provided in Figure 2–6.

Once a countermeasure is in place, it is important to monitor the effectiveness of the threat response. As stated earlier, it is important to select a time period to review all elements of the threat list, the related risks, and the effectiveness of the countermeasures. A **vulnerability assessment** is used to examine the effectiveness of specific countermeasures put in place to protect against specific threats. Vulnerability assessments are used to address a very specific concern, such as the countermeasures used for one threat. For example, if tornadoes are a threat to a security professional's target environment, he or she would need to assess the level of risk, in terms of probability and criticality. Suppose that a given location has not had a tornado in over five years. Given this, the security professional decides to give this threat a probability of 4. The criticality factor would be much higher, maybe an 8 or more; if a tornado hits a target environment, it could do a devastating amount of damage. Then

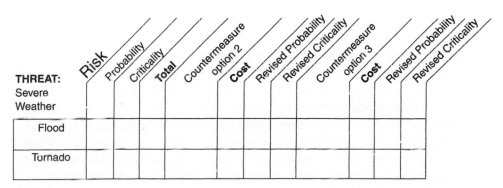

FIGURE 2–6   Countermeasure Options
(*Source:* Charles T. Thibodeau, M. Ed., CPP, CSS, CPO.)

the security professional would consider countermeasures. No countermeasure can affect the probability of a tornado. If a storm is coming, there is nothing anyone can do to change its course or speed. But certain countermeasures will help reduce loss if a storm does hit. For example, a storm shelter for employees would reduce the risk of personal injury resulting from the storm. Some companies in areas with hurricanes have underground storage areas large enough to hold their entire computer mainframes—at a minimum. If a storm is coming, they put everything below ground to reduce the potential loss. Depending on the size of the company and the size of the storm, this countermeasure may prove to be extremely effective at not only protecting the equipment from damage caused by the storm but allowing the company to continue operating during and immediately after the storm. These features alone suggest this countermeasure, under the right circumstances, could make the difference between a company surviving or being wiped out—literally.

Should it become necessary to make use of these underground facilities, the security team will have an excellent opportunity to do a vulnerability assessment. The vulnerability assessment is designed to produce an in-depth evaluation of the effectiveness of a countermeasure. Again, using the example of underground storage facilities, all problems will be documented for ongoing evaluation. Perhaps the transport of the equipment went really well, but the company lost power in the storm and did not have a backup source. Perhaps the storage area had limited space and the company had not decided before the onset of the storm which computer systems were the most important and in what order of priority they should be evacuated. A vulnerability assessment should involve this level of detail.

A FINAL, ALL-IMPORTANT TERM

Remember, security professionals have several responsibilities, most of which involve preventing or being prepared for possible threats. The identification of threats and the management of risk are the primary duties of security professionals. In short, security professionals analyze risks.

The term **risk analysis** is commonly used in security circles. A risk analysis is different from a risk assessment, which was discussed earlier. While the terms may seem similar, as is the case with various security terms, their difference is important to highlight. As noted previously, a risk assessment is used to determine the level of risk associated with each individual threat. A risk analysis, on the other hand, refers to the *entire process* of examining risk. Therefore, a complete risk analysis involves all of the evaluative tools discussed up to this point, including threat assessments, vulnerability studies, probability and criticality assessments, and security surveys. The risk analysis is a composite of all of these security tools and can be considered the final report on the state of a target environment with respect to its overall security needs. As stated earlier, it is important that security professionals working together are using terms the same way; unfortunately *risk analysis* and *risk assessment* are often confused or used interchangeably.

A FEW MISCELLANEOUS ESSENTIALS

While the bulk of this chapter is focused on introducing basic security terms and tools, it is also essential to provide a context for those terms and tools. Two more issues need to be introduced here. The first one is difference between proactivity and reactivity in the security planning process. Second is the difference between contract and proprietary guards. The last part of this section discusses contract outsourcing.

Proactive versus Reactive Response

Security departments confront most security threats on a **proactive,** or preventive, basis. This means the threat is anticipated, and measures to prevent the threat from becoming an emergency, critical incident, or crisis are undertaken. Ideally, a target environment will not be impacted, or will be minimally impacted, by a threat for which the security management team has developed and implemented a plan.

But security professionals are not always focused on proactive efforts. A **reactive plan** is often developed for use in the event prevention efforts fail. A reactive plan (also referred to as a **contingency plan**) is implemented after the fact. Rather than prevent the event, as in a proactive effort, a reactive plan outlines a course of action to be followed if a threat occurs.

Consider a common example. Security professionals and business owners understand that employees usually prove to be a more significant threat to the company's profit margins than customers do. A security management team will develop proactive plans to prevent various forms of employee theft. If a theft by an employee is detected, however, the company (often through the security department) must have a plan to respond to deal with the theft. This will often simply include a protocol for determining whether that individual will be dismissed or handed over to local police. When a security breach happens, the security management team must look at how the offense occurred and factor this new information into future strategies to ensure that the same kind of violation does not happen again.

Security management strategies include both proactive and reactive elements; this is to be expected. But both proactive and reactive security plans can fail. In the employee theft example (and others), the threat is so pervasive that the security management team expects some incidences of employee theft. The security objective is to minimize the risk levels associated with that threat.

Contract Officers versus Proprietary Officers

Business leaders, usually security managers, need to make decisions about whether they will hire their own protection officers (formerly referred to as security guards) or contract with outside companies to provide these services. **Proprietary** security services use in-house officers. **Contract** services are provided by firms or individuals from outside the business or target environment. Often the decision to use contract or proprietary security services involves the use of protection officers, security patrols, investigators, armed couriers, alarm respondents, specialists in risk analysis, and other types of security consultants.

Contract Outsourcing Decisions*

The search for a reliable contract-staffing agency is a nagging problem facing many American businesses. No matter what the need, to augment an existing workforce or to replace a proprietary workforce—whether for janitorial services, administrative assistants, or security officers—selecting the right agency is a challenge.

The challenge is fueled by the reality of running a contract-staffing business. Outsourcing companies have very small operating budgets because they operate on a very low profit margin, many times well below 3 percent of revenue. They require lots of people to meet the market demands, and their experiences often prove the old adage "good help is hard to find." They also face the pressures of having to provide services on very short notice and of having high employee turnover (in the contract security industry, well over 80 percent per year on average). This is both costly for the contract firm and a risk for the client.

In many cases the demand for eligible workers increases the pressure on the contract-staffing company to fill open slots at any cost. All too often, a company may lower its hiring standards in an attempt to fill that need for more peo-

---

*This section is a compilation of materials from the following sources: R. Colling, *Hospital Security,* 3rd ed. (Woburn, MA: Butterworth-Heinemann, 1992), 135–153; G. Craighead, *High-Rise Security and Fire Life Safety* (1996), 422; D. Dalton, *The Art of Successful Security Management* (Woburn, MA: Butterworth-Heinemann, 1998), 217–220; R. Fischer and G. Green, *Introduction to Security,* 6th ed. (Woburn, MA: Butterworth-Heinemann, 1998), 90–96; C. Nemeth, *Private Security and the Law,* 2nd ed. (Woburn, MA: Butterworth-Heinemann, 1995), 154–156 and other pages; P. Purpura, *Security and Loss Prevention: An Introduction,* 3rd ed. (Woburn, MA: Butterworth-Heinemann, 1998), 166–168.

ple. This results in the "warm-body guard" phenomenon. Hiring standards are sometimes reduced to the point where the next "warm body" that comes through that office door is going to be hired no matter what. This can prove to be a legal liability nightmare for the client.

When contracting for security personnel, managers must be aware of these problems. Rather than being discouraged during the agency selection process, the manager can avoid meeting the problems later by addressing these concerns in the contract. The contract language will determine whether the outsourcing experience is successful.

Request for Proposal

The contract-staffing agency selection process, which ultimately leads to a contract being drawn up, usually starts with a request for proposal (RFP). Before examining the outsourcing contract, security professionals must understand the RFP. The company seeking contract services uses an RFP and outlines with great detail and specificity what it is expecting to receive from a contract company in exchange for the company's money. Another way of looking at an RFP is that it is an invitation sent to any number of contractors asking them to bid on the specifications outlined in the RFP.

The RFP document contains a list of terms and conditions, a detailed scope of work, a request for a training syllabus, proof of legal requirements like copies of licenses and insurance, and specific conditions and expectations the contractor must meet to satisfy the contract. Some RFPs spell out the hours of operation, the job description of each type of worker sought, and the qualifications required of each contract employee. In addition, the RFP will contain an escape clause to allow for the termination of the contract by either side under certain conditions. For instance, if the company fails to pay the invoices of the contractor for a certain number of days, weeks, or months, the contract company may have the right to pull out of the contract without penalty. If, on the other hand, the contract company fails to live up to the performance expectations spelled out in the contract, the hiring company may elect to cancel the contract.

In the RFP the wise manager will include specifications on turnover limits and sustainable living wage levels, with a pay raise schedule and in some cases a signing bonus. The wise manager will include specifications on reasonable benefits, training requirements, and plans for promotional opportunities. The manager will tailor the RFP to produce the type of security officer that will be more than a warm-body guard. The wise manager will work with the contract company to ensure that marginal employees are not sent over. The wise manager will obtain the most cost-effective contract that he or she can without shorting the contractor to the point that the dreaded warm-body guard is the only option. Thus, the outsourcing program should have a healthy budget.

Examining the Contract

A contract must have seven features in order to satisfy the law.

1. It must contain an offer.
2. It must contain an acceptance.
3. It must contain a consideration.
4. It must contain mutual assent to the same proposition.
5. Its subject matter must be legal.
6. The contracting parties must be of legal age.
7. The contracting parties must be legally competent to enter into a contract.

For purposes of this chapter, I will assume that the subject matter of the outsourcing contract is legal and that the contracting parties are of legal age as well as legally sane and competent. Thus, I need only examine the first four components. This examination is important because the contract is the foundation of a successful outsourcing relationship. It is also important to keep in mind that each of these components is twofold. That is, there are two offers, two acceptances, and two parts to the consideration. In addition, all parties must arrive at the "assent to the same proposition" simultaneously, never unilaterally. Everyone must have the same understanding of the performance expectations specified in the contract.

Offer. The contract offer consists of the purchasing company first offering the opportunity to bid. The contract company responds, making what is called a "proposal for services" and offering to provide those services for a price. The services and the price for those services are the offers being made by the contracting company.

Acceptance. The acceptance is when the company responds to the proposal for services and accepts what the contract company proposes as its offer to satisfy the performance expectations set out in the RFP. Thus, the contract company is saying it will meet the expectations set out in the RFP for a price. The company that wants to purchase the services is saying that it agrees to pay the price requested in the proposal for services.

Consideration. The consideration paid by the contracting company is the services it provides. The consideration paid by the purchasing company is the money it pays for those services. Thus, there is two-way consideration in every contract.

Mutual Assent to the Same Proposition. The term *mutual assent* means that the parties who are making the contract are at the same level of understanding of the conditions and expectations regarding the terms of the contract. This becomes a critical issue when one party accuses the other party of failing its duty to perform on the contract. That is why the terms of the contract must be crystal clear to everyone involved. The less fine print, the better.

Linking Outsourcing to the Risk Analysis

There are many reasons for outsourcing, including saving money, transferring risk, ensuring quality service, and increasing management flexibility.[14] If the only reason for outsourcing is to save money and the company is sued, the courts may not be very kind to the company who put money ahead of safety and security. This would be especially true if it can be proven that the outsourcing efforts resulted in a number of marginal employees working in that security department at the time of a loss event.

Transferring risk is another reason for outsourcing. In theory, at least the contractor provides a barrier or "corporate veil" protecting the company from lawsuits. The idea is, if anything goes wrong, the contract company will get the lawsuit. But this logic is flawed; a lawyer in charge of a "deep-pocket" lawsuit usually can find a way to drive a Mack truck through any corporate veil of protection. Transferring risk may be one of the weakest reasons to outsource.

The use of contract outsourcing is known to raise questions about the ability of a particular environment to ensure quality service. This thinking suggests that a contract agent is not vested in the company and is therefore not likely to provide the kind of quality service that a proprietary service would. Again, much of this will depend on the priorities of the target environment. A final example for consideration when determining whether to use contract or proprietary security service can be found in the company's management flexibility. Some argue that a security professional can streamline an organization by making others responsible for particular security decisions, thus providing a depth, versatility, and level of coverage that might certainly raise the standard. Ultimately, the decisions about which services to provide from within an organization and which should be outsourced are not easy. But it should be clear that more and more security professionals are making a comfortable living by providing expert security services to any size agency or organization. This makes it important for the security professional to know what security needs exist in the target environment.

However, none of these reasons for outsourcing meets the legal obligation or duty to provide a safe, stable, and predictable environment in the way that the risk analysis reason for outsourcing does. When asked in court the reason for using contract security officers, the wise manager turns to the risk analysis for his or her primary explanation. The legal reason is in that procedure. The risk analysis, with its threat identification and analysis, will point to the need for security personnel to augment the threat-countermeasure design. It was the threat analysis that determined that security officers were needed and at what skill level they should be. Certainly if the threat analysis identified the need for armed security officers, the company would be better off hiring licensed police officers. If vehicular traffic control is indicated as a countermeasure based on the threat analysis, the wise manager will hire highly skilled and experienced individuals to stand in the road and direct traffic. If receptionist-type duty is all that is required to control access at the main entrance of a building, then the hired person will need only receptionist-type skills. Many times, a single contract firm can provide workers at all of these levels at the same time. In court, the wise manager will note that employees of several different skill levels were needed and that after careful shopping for the right contract security firm, he or she found the one that could supply all of these types of workers. The reason the wise manager chose contract over proprietary, he or she can explain, is that the risk analysis directed that choice.

Choices of Agencies

In most municipalities, there are a number of contract agencies to choose from. Of course, the closer one lives to a big city, the more choices there are. A choice that many businesses do not consider or do not even know exists is the local police station. Many police departments have contract security businesses right in the precinct house. There are a few drawbacks to using licensed police officers as security officers. First, they have no private security training, so they will apply their police training in any work environment. They cannot just stand by and watch felonies occur without taking some action. Of course, most American businesses simply suspend or fire employees that misbehave. Police can have a hard time doing only that.

In addition, there is the problem of split loyalty. With a proprietary security force or a contract security force, most often loyalty to the client becomes a part of each officer's regime. What happens when a police officer is guarding a client's property and that officer sees two men breaking into the building across the street? The police officer switch gets thrown and away the officer goes, possibly leaving the client's property unprotected for hours. Generally speaking, hiring public law enforcement officers to "moonlight" in a company's facility may be a very bad idea for both the company and the contractor.

CONCLUSION

This chapter has provided a fairly straightforward discussion of common terms and phrases in the security profession. This is a natural starting point for developing a clear and productive understanding of the mission and practices of security professionals. The security professional seeks to establish and maintain a stable, relatively predictable environment. The objective is to identify threats, assess risks, identify countermeasures, implement preferred countermeasures, and then review the existing structure. Achieving safety and security is a never-ending process that is always changing.

Green and Farber's definition of *security* helps to pinpoint the essence of the security objective. Creating a stable environment and predicting the potential for loss events accurately are parts of that ongoing process. The process of identifying and exploring security objectives will require security professionals to establish a balance between the efficient use of limited resources and an effective security plan. The practice of establishing a secure environment requires a concentrated effort with a focused, clear objective. People and resources must be assessed, and decisions must be made about how the target environment can best be organized and managed to achieve the desired security objectives. To maintain the integrity of a secure system requires a vigilant group of trained professionals with an aptitude for technological innovation and development, devotion to monitoring and assessing crime trends, an investment of financial resources, and a little bit of luck. To settle for anything less is to reduce the effectiveness of the overall security program.

REVIEW QUESTIONS
1. Discuss the difference between threat and risk.
2. Explain the difference between probability and criticality.
3. Discuss the relationship between threat and the related risk level.
4. Why is it important for a security professional to establish a stable and predictable environment?
5. How is the work of Adler and Maslow significant for the security industry?

DISCUSSION QUESTIONS
1. If you had just bought a new car, how would you go about identifying and managing the risks associated with car ownership?
2. What might be some threats that would impact a stable and predictable elementary school environment? How would those threats change if you

were attempting to provide a stable and predictable environment for a junior high school? A high school?

3. Is security the responsibility of each individual, the community, the police, or private security companies? Please explain your response.

4. As a security professional, you just implemented a series of security directives for a new business. Now what do you do?

REFERENCES

1. Cunningham, W. C., J. J. Strauchs, and C. Van Meter, Private Security Trends: 1970–2000. The Hallcrest Report II, 236.
2. For more information about the CPP program and materials, go online at *http://www.asisonline.org/cpp.html*.
3. E. Dreikers Ferguson, *Adlarian Theory: An Introduction* (Vancouver, BC: Adlerian Psychology Association of British Columbia, 1984).
4. R. R. Dreikurs, *Fundamentals of Adlerian Psychology* (Chicago, IL: Alfred Adler Institute, 1953).
5. R. Corsini, *Current Psychotherapies* (Chicago, IL: F. E. Peacock Publishers, 1973), 45.
6. R. L. Hilgert and T. Haimann, *Supervision: Concepts and Practices of Management,* 5th ed. (Cincinnati, OH: South-Western Publishing Co.).
7. "Maslow's Hierarchy of Needs," *http://chiron.valdosta.edu/whuitt/col/regsys/maslow.html*.
8. "Maslow's Hierarchy of Needs," *http://chiron.valdosta.edu/whuitt/col/regsys/maslow.html*.
9. Nalla & Newman.
10. Fisher & Green.
11. Fisher & Green.
12. C. E. Simonsen, *Private Security in America: An Introduction* (Upper Saddle River, NJ: Prentice Hall, 1998), 202.
13. R. M. Momboise, *Industrial Security for Strikes, Riots, and Disasters* (Springfield, IL: Charles C. Thomas, 1968), 13.
14. D. Dalton, *The Art of Successful Security Management* (Woburn, MA: Butterworth-Heinemann, 1998), 217–220.

CHAPTER

Studying Security Threats and the Related Risk Levels

CHAPTER OUTLINE

Prison Inmate Escapes from Private Security Transportation Firm

Tragic Portent: Slain Doctor Predicted Violent Abortion Protest

Turkey Farm Cries Foul over Parrots: Disease Threatens Pt. Arena Ranch

"Biotech Terrorist" Threats Taken Seriously: Iowa State, Pioneer Hi-Bred May be Targets

Teamsters Strike Overnight Trucking

Security professionals must be able to analyze risk from various levels. The following security scenarios have been included to help readers think about the concepts presented in Chapter 2. In each scenario, some of the facts are still under investigation and may be unclear. Work with what you know.

After reading the following cases, think about each situation and then review the "facts for consideration" section. These are hypotheticals, in most cases, but will provide additional facts for you to think about as you review the scenarios. Use this opportunity to begin identifying and exploring essential

---

Prison Inmate Escapes from Private Transportation Firm*

While state police and helicopters searched the New Mexico terrain Thursday for escaped convict Kyle Bell, North Dakota officials wondered why it took a private security firm transporting the killer 10 hours before it discovered he was no longer on the bus. "We have a lot of questions," Elaine Little, director of North Dakota's Department of Corrections said in an interview.

One prisoner told police that Bell unlocked leg irons and handcuffs with a key he had in his shoe, then another inmate helped him climb through a roof vent in the TransCor America bus. He escaped during a fuel stop in Santo Rosa, NM 110 miles east of Albuquerque. Bell apparently jumped off the bus after it left the gas station.

The bus, carrying 12 inmates, was operated by Nashville-based TransCor, the nation's largest prisoner transport company. Bell, who was convicted in the death of 11-year-old Jeanna North of Fargo, was being taken to an Oregon prison. Little said TransCor guards did not count the prisoners before the bus left the gas station, nor did they make counts after two additional stops during which some prisoners were transferred.

Bell was discovered missing during a stop in Arizona, between 1:00 and 1:30 P.M., or 10 hours after the fuel stop in Santa Rosa. TransCor staff members apparently spent up to three hours trying to determine if Bell had been accidentally let off during transfers before they notified North Dakota authorities of the escape at 4:30 P.M.

"We want to know from the beginning to the end what they did with Mr. Bell and how they could go so long without realizing he was not in the bus," Little said. She said she also wanted to know why a vent was unsecured. "We want to know whether there were procedures that weren't followed or if they don't exist."

TransCor issued a news release, saying "it appears that several procedural violations have occurred involving security policies." Those included "searching, counters and agent positioning," but the company did not elaborate. It said, "we are embarrassed by this incident" and that the bus crew had been relieved of duty. Bell received a life sentence for North's death in 1993. He was already serving a 30-year sentence for molesting two children in 1993 and 1994, said Birch Burdick, Cass County states attorney. TransCor was informed by North Dakota officials that Bell was a high risk, Little said, because he had tried to escape from the Cass County jail, and officials on another occasion had found a letter with an escape plan on it.

---

*Furst, Randy. October 15, 1999. "North Dakota Officials Have Lots of Questions About Bell's Escape." Minneapolis *Star Tribune*.

security information, threats, risk levels, and vulnerabilities for starters. You have the enviable task of planning with the benefit of hindsight. After reading each scenario, ask yourself if a security management team you worked with would have been better prepared for the threat outlined in each setting.

FACTS FOR CONSIDERATION

1. The company you work for is Van's Transport Service and you are hired to oversee the security of inmates being transported from one facility to another.
2. It is often the case that you transport an inmate a significant distance, requiring between two and eight stops on any given trip. On no occasion does your company allow for stops to include overnight lodging, but some trips may take as many as 48 hours to complete.
3. The company has been providing this service to public prison facilities for over seven years. In the history of the company, two inmates (on two separate occasions) have attempted to escape while the van was refueling, and one incident involved some friends of an inmate attempting to overtake the van on a highway. In the escape attempts, other inmates were involved in attempting to assist the escapee.

    In the case of the alleged attempt to overtake the van, the facts were never clear. The attempt failed because highway patrol officers responded to an alert, cautionary radio call from the driver, who believed she identified a potential problem after she noticed the same car make a second, then a third refueling stop with the transport van. Because of police intervention, the alleged suspects were picked up, questioned, and later released. While nothing could be proven, the circumstances resulted in the company's decision to arm all officers during transport.

Please respond to the following items:

1. Make a reasonable list of threats based on the facts presented.
2. Identify whether the probability of each risk is high, medium, or low.
3. Identify whether the criticality of each risk is high, medium, or low.
4. Would a reactive or contingency plan be required here? If yes, please describe one you believe appropriate to the circumstance. Be prepared to justify your response.

Tragic Portent: Slain Doctor Predicted Violent Abortion Protest

THE ASSOCIATED PRESS

**Buffalo, N.Y.—Dr. Barnett Slepian's own words signal
a chilling premonition of his own violent end.**

In an August 1994 letter to the editor reacting to his frequent run-ins with "nonviolent" anti-abortion forces, he wrote: "Please don't feign surprise, dismay and certainly not innocence when a more volatile and less restrained member of the group decides to react . . . by shooting an abortion provider."

And in a television interview, the father of four worried about how his family would cope if his work ultimately led to his death. Slepian, a 52-year-old obstetrician-gynecologist, was killed by a sniper who fired a rifle bullet through a window in his home Friday night. His was the first fatality among five sniper attacks on upstate New York or Canadian abortion providers in the last four years.

The killer remained at large yesterday as an international investigation continued. Police listed no suspects. All of the previous attacks have occurred within a few weeks of Nov. 11, Veterans Day, which is known as Remembrance Day in Canada. In the 1994 letter to *The Buffalo News*, Slepian said he did not begrudge anti-abortion demonstrators who "scream that I am a murderer and a killer when I enter the clinics at which they 'peacefully' exercise their First Amendment right of freedom of speech.

"They may also do the same when by chance they see me during the routine of my day," he wrote. "This may be at a restaurant, at a mall, in a store or, as they have done recently, while I was watching my young children play at [a children's restaurant]." But "they all share the blame," Slepian wrote, when "a more volatile and less restrained member of the group decides to react to their inflammatory rhetoric by shooting an abortion provider." Yesterday mourners left flowers by the door of Slepian's office and a banner that hung on a bush read: "We won't go back—defend the right to abortion!" Taped to his office door was a photo of Slepian and a baby he had delivered.

In a statement, the founder of Pro-Life Virginia called Slepian's killer "a hero," one who ended Slepian's "blood-thirsty practice." "We as Christians have a responsibility to protect the innocent from being murdered, the same way we would want someone to protect us. Who ever shot the shot protected the children," the Rev. Donald Spitz said.

Slepian often expressed his fears that abortion foes were encouraging violence. In a 1994 interview with Buffalo television station WIVB, Slepian said: "Maybe they are not going to perform it, but they're setting up their soldiers to perform the violence."

All of his children were home when Slepian's wife, Lynn, called 911 after the sniper's bullet entered the doctor's back, pierced his lungs, exited his body and ricocheted into another room. Fifteen-year-old Andy had been watching a Buffalo Sabres hockey game on TV and ran into the kitchen. "He saw blood in back of his dad," Andy Berger, 14, a friend of Andy Slepian, told *The Buffalo News*.

Generally, people on both sides of the abortion debate condemned the killing. The Revs. Rob and Paul Schenck of the National Clergy Council, who helped organize the massive "Spring of Life" abortion protest in Buffalo in 1992, urged "all people of conscience to defend life peacefully." "The murder of Barnett Slepian," they said, "is wrong, sinful and cowardly." Dr. George Tiller of Kansas, who was wounded in an August 1993 shooting in the parking lot of his clinic, called it "a well-orchestrated political Armageddon against women and their freedom."

FACTS FOR CONSIDERATION

1. You are the director of security for a women's health center that performs abortions. An antiabortion group has planned a four-day conference in your city in the next week. Several of the groups expected to participate in the conference have been indirectly associated with an activist group connected with several bombings of abortion clinics.
2. You have a staff of 9 officers. You have 5 doctors and 13 nurses and staff members. On any given day, your clinic may see as many as 135 women for various medical needs, including scheduled abortions.
3. Members of the staff have expressed concerns to you about rumors that their clinic might be a target during the conference.
4. You arrive at work to find fliers saying "The End Is Near" posted on the front door of your facility.

Please respond to the following items:

1. Make a reasonable list of threats based on the facts presented.
2. Identify whether the probability of each risk is high, medium, or low.
3. Identify whether the criticality of each risk is high, medium, or low.
4. Would a reactive or contingency plan be required here? If yes, please describe one you believe appropriate to the circumstance. Be prepared to justify your response.

Turkey Farm Cries Foul over Parrots; Disease Threatens Pt. Arena Ranch

BY TIM TESCONI

Press Democrat Staff Writer

Feathers are flying on the Mendocino Coast where a newly-established parrot preserve is threatening the survival of a turkey breeding farm that has operated for years in the remote hills of Point Arena. Nicholas Turkey Breeding Farms, an international, Sonoma County-based company that operates the turkey farm, has given notice that it will vacate the ranch if the neighboring parrot farm is not closed by the county. Simply stated, parrots and turkeys don't mix because of the transmission of fatal and highly contagious bird diseases.

The turkey breeding farm was established in Point Arena because the area is so isolated from pet birds and backyard chickens. "It does seem ironic that there's only one turkey ranch and only one parrot breeding farm in Mendocino County and they're next to each other in Point Arena," said Keith Faulder, a Ukiah attorney who has been hired by the Stornetta family. The Stornettas, longtime coastal dairy ranchers, own the property that Nicholas Turkey Breeding Farms leases in Point Arena. Barbara Gould said Thursday she and her parrots are not budging from her 17-acre farm in Point

(continued)

Arena, where she has established the Parrot Preservation Society, a nonprofit group dedicated to saving parrots around the world. She and her husband, Geoffrey, acquired the Mendocino Coast property this summer and began moving hundreds of parrots, many of them rescued birds, from her previous home in Arizona. "I'm gearing up for the fight of my life. They are after my life and livelihood," said Gould, 53.

The battle of the birds is raising issues of private property rights, zoning laws and the clash between agriculture and urban transplants that move into farming areas. Sources said millions of dollars are at stake for Nicholas Farms. The threat of disease from the parrots jeopardizes Nicholas's ability to ship fertile turkey eggs to its markets around the world. Nicholas is one of the world's primary turkey breeders, producing the parent-stock of turkeys raised for meat. "How someone can move in and ruin a business that has been here so long is just not right," said Walter R. Stornetta, a fourth-generation dairy rancher who owns the Point Arena ranch. "The parrot people are a classic example of what happens when people from urban areas move into agriculture areas and don't understand the ramifications of what they do to farming." Ed Merritt, an executive at Nicholas Farms, declined to comment on the parrot controversy.

The Mendocino County Planning and Building Department is investigating the parrot breeding operation, which, according to a preliminary ruling, is in violation of county zoning regulations. Nicholas Farms already has moved some of its 1,000 pedigreed turkeys off the Point Arena ranch to other North Coast sites because of the threat of disease from the hundreds of parrots on the neighboring property. Nicholas employs 10 people at the ranch. Scientists said the proximity of the turkeys and parrots is a serious health issue because diseases, such as exotic newcastle, Avian influenza and psittacosis, can be easily spread by the wild birds and rodents traveling between the two properties. The properties are only 1,500 feet from fence line to fence line but should be miles apart to prevent the spread of disease, according to avian specialists. "Both parties should be very concerned," said Dr. Francine Bradley, an avian specialist with the University of California Cooperative Extension at Davis. "There are a whole gamut of diseases that can be transferred between the turkeys and parrots when there is so little geographic separation," Bradley said that in poultry-producing counties, such as Fresno, Madera and Kings. There are strict county laws that regulate distances between poultry operations for disease control.

Bradley said Nicholas has an extensive "bio-security" system at its ranches to prevent the spread of disease. Turkeys are kept in environmentally-controlled houses and human visitors are strictly regulated. On the rare occasions that humans are allowed on Nicholas farms they are required to enter a sanitation chamber where they must shower and put on sterile coveralls. Gould questions Nicholas' bio-security system, saying Nicholas workers have moved freely between the two properties when they've told her she and her parrots had to move. Gould said she did extensive checking on zoning and land-use regulations before buying the property. She said she was assured by county planners that she could raise and breed parrots on the Point Arena property. Gould said now because of political pressure from the Stornetta family the county is saying she may be in violation of zoning laws. "They said parrots are not considered a bonafide agricultural endeavor," Gould said. A county zoning enforcement code inspector is scheduled to come to Gould's property today.

Gould expects to receive an order to remove the parrots from her property and is mustering community support. Alan Falleri, chief planner for the Mendocino County Planning and Building Department, said the county's preliminary decision is that Gould is in violation of zoning laws because parrots are not an agricultural activity and she is operating in an agricultural zone. "Unless she is raising parrots for meat, it is a violation of zoning regulations," he said. "There is a fine line between what is an agricultural and non-agricultural use. Generally, we consider an agricultural use to be the production of food and fiber." Falleri said today's inspection will determine what

(continued)

Gould is doing with the parrots and if there is a violation. Falleri said a cease and desist order will be issued if Gould is in violation. He said because of the disease potential of the parrots on the neighboring turkeys, she could receive an emergency order to immediately remove the parrots. Falleri also disputes Gould's claim she was told by members of the county's planning staff that she could establish the parrot breeding operation on agricultural land in Point Arena. "The testimony of our planners is that no one told her any such thing," Falleri said. Gould has her own lawyers working to protect her interests. "My attorneys in Arizona can't find the basis for the complaint" by the county, she said. The Mendocino County Farm Bureau is supporting Nicholas Farms in the battle and has sent a letter to the Planning Department urging that the county take swift action to get the parrots out of Point Arena.

FACTS FOR CONSIDERATION

1. It is your job, as the director of security at Acme Turkey Farm, to make sure the health of the birds is maintained.
2. Your boss, the head of the company, has indicated that losses of at least two birds have occurred over the last three weeks. Your boss asks if you can look into it.
3. The boss suspects an employee, but if the loss was caused by a person from the outside, the risk of contamination of the birds would be dramatically increased.
4. The company is a small operation and includes only about 200 turkeys per season. You are the only security officer working for the company.

Please respond to the following items:

1. Make a reasonable list of threats based on the facts presented.
2. Identify whether the probability of each risk is high, medium, or low.
3. Identify whether the criticality of each risk is high, medium, or low.
4. Would a reactive or contingency plan be required here? If yes, please describe one you believe appropriate to the circumstance. Be prepared to justify your response.

"Biotech Terrorist" Threats Taken Seriously:
Iowa State, Pioneer Hi-Bred May Be Targets

DES MOINES, IOWA

Iowa State University and Pioneer Hi-Bred International Inc. are on alert following an Internet threat of terrorism against biotech seed research and production facilities, the Des Moines Sunday Register reported.

"We're alerting everyone to the possibility" of some kind of attack, said Walt Fehr, an agronomist who heads Iowa State University's biotech-based agricultural research.

Faculty and staff members at ISU, the nation's oldest land-grant university, have been alerted and urged to notify campus security if they see strangers in buildings on campus or protesters gathered on campus, Fehr said.

At Des Moines-based Pioneer, the world's largest seed corn supplier, employees were notified of the threats Friday by e-mail.

"You don't know whether or not people are going to follow through on these kind of threats, but you want to take them seriously, and you want to make sure you're prepared," Pioneer spokesman Tim Martin said.

The anonymous message recently posted on the Internet said: "All of a sudden 'venture capitalist' scum realize that biotechnology is not such a great investment and they flee with their bags of cash with them. . . . Our view is that if corporations, governments and universities have any relationship to biotechnology, they are targets."

The message went on to say that U.S. Department of Agriculture test plots are the No. 1 target and that researchers receiving "corporate biotech money" are next.

Three years ago, Greenpeace members sprayed pink, milk-based paint on a soybean research plot near Atlantic, Iowa, destroying a year's worth of research by scientists working for Monsanto Co.–owned Asgrow Seed Co.

Anti-biotech activists contend that crop research sites have been sabotaged throughout the United States this year. Groups with such names as Reclaim the Seeds, Future Farmers and the Minnesota Bolt Weevils claimed attacks last month on:

- Genetically engineered sunflowers and corn growing at a Pioneer site in northern California.
- Biotech-based crops at a Pioneer facility near Mankato, Minn., and at a Novartis site in Goodhue County, Minn.
- Genetically engineered plants at a University of California–Berkeley research location.

Some of the harshest critics of the growing use of biotechnology by the seed industry are appalled by the call for violent protests.

"Clearly, harm to people is a sort of action which we totally deplore," said Rebecca Goldburg, senior scientist at the Environmental Defense Fund in New York City, adding that her group also opposes vandalizing property.

Biotechnology, which weds the study of living organisms with high-tech genetic engineering, is pushing the parameters of traditional plant breeding. Scientists can further enhance or suppress certain characteristics of crops. For example, they can make plants resist particular pests, tolerate application of certain herbicides that otherwise would kill the plants, and yield more nutritious food ingredients.

Opponents contend that the genetic changes may have unintended results that could be harmful. For example, earlier this year a laboratory study by Cornell University concluded that corn plants genetically designed to resist European corn borers were also capable of killing monarch butterfly larvae. Although the results of the study have been challenged, biotech opponents cite them to support their view.

FACTS FOR CONSIDERATION

1. Acts of domestic terrorism on biotech labs have increased 500 percent over the last five years. You are director of security for the largest biotech lab in the upper midwestern part of the United States.
2. Threats to your facility have been received at a rate of approximately three per week for the last month.
3. Three years ago an animal rights group broke into the facility and released 45 rats, mice, and monkeys and contaminated various samples in five areas of the facility.

Please respond to the following items:

1. Make a reasonable list of threats based on the facts presented.
2. Identify whether the probability of each risk is high, medium, or low.
3. Identify whether the criticality of each risk is high, medium, or low.
4. Would a reactive or contingency plan be required here? If yes, please describe one you believe appropriate to the circumstance. Be prepared to justify your response.

Teamsters Strike Overnight Trucking

OVERNITE-TEAMSTER NEWS RELEASE

Overnite Strike Goes Nationwide

(Washington DC)

Yesterday, Overnite workers at Teamsters Local 667 in Memphis Tennessee initiated an unfair labor practice strike against Overnite Transportation Company, the sixth largest LTL trucking company in the country.

By late Sunday afternoon, Overnite workers at South Holland, Palatine and Bedford Park, IL, Farmingdale, NY, Dallas, Fort Worth, Tyler and Garland, TX, Harrisburg and Bensalem, PA, Miami, FL, Sacramento, CA, Milwaukee, WI, Lexington, KY, Omaha, NE, Portland, OR, Little Rock, AR, Decatur, AL, Nashville TN, New Orleans, LA, St. Louis, Bridgeton and Springfield, MO, Toledo, Dayton, Richfield and Cincinnati, OH, Indianapolis, IN, Atlanta, N. Atlanta, Macon and Marietta, GA had joined the unfair labor practice strike in support of the Memphis Overnite workers. "The Teamsters had sought to avoid this strike," said James P. Hoffa, President of the Teamsters, "but Overnite has brought it upon itself. This strike is the bitter fruit of Overnite's unrepentant and unrelenting violation of its workers' federally protected rights."

Background

Since 1994, the Overnite workers have been struggling for justice against one of the worst labor law violators of our generation. The National Labor Relations Board has filed more than 1,000 complaints against Overnite Transportation Company. The charges include: unlawful withholding of wage increases, unlawful harassment, unlawful intimidation, unlawful surveillance, unlawful discharge and unlawful bad faith bargaining. Despite having to pay out tens of millions of dollars for its violations and legal fees, Overnite continues to contemptuously disregard the federal laws that protect American workers. Despite 4 years of negotiations, despite the Labor Board ordering the Company to bargain in good faith, Overnite refuses to do so. Over 150 negotiating sessions have yet to lead to a contract. The Overnite workers played by the rules but the Company will not. Currently, the Teamsters represent approximately 40–45 percent of Overnite's dock workers and drivers at 37 Overnite terminals (26 certified, 11 bargaining orders), including five of Overnite's largest seven terminals (Kansas City; Lexington; Memphis; Atlanta and Indianapolis). Overnite is a wholly-owned subsidiary of Union Pacific Corporation.

FACTS FOR CONSIDERATION

1. You are the security director for ACME Transport, which has 5 security personnel, 15 staff people, 30 packers, and 45 drivers. After an unsuccessful meeting with union officials, workers are threatening to strike.
2. Company officials are firm in their efforts to replace any striking workers and to keep the business open and operational until the contract discussions are resolved.
3. Your security personnel suggest that the packers are the most volatile group within the organization, with the staff and drivers well behind them. The drivers do not see their situation as similar to the packers', but they are planning to support them by not crossing the picket lines.
4. An anonymous phone message suggested that a takeover of the chief executive officer's office might be planned, and efforts to protect the upper management by removing them from the building "would not be tolerated."

Please respond to the following items:

1. Make a reasonable list of threats based on the facts presented.
2. Identify whether the probability of each risk is high, medium, or low.
3. Identify whether the criticality of each risk is high, medium, or low.
4. Would a reactive or contingency plan be required here? If yes, please describe one you believe appropriate to the circumstance. Be prepared to justify your response.

A Prevention System Overview:

Defining the Overall Security Objective

CHAPTER HIGHLIGHTS

Prevention system:
Overview:
1. Physical security
2. Personnel security
3. Information security
4. Liability
5. Interdepartmental dependencies

Risk management:
Options outlined:
1. Eliminate the risk.
2. Mitigate the risk.
3. Transfer the risk.
4. Spread the risk.
5. Accept the risk.

KEY WORDS

Assuming risk
Eliminating risk
Mitigating risk
Overall security objective
Personnel security
Physical security

Risk management
Seamless, integrated security design
Security objective
Spreading risk
Transferring risk

To begin the process of making an environment secure, one must establish a theoretical ideal of what it means to have security within a given target environment. Without a doubt, this security ideal will vary, depending on who is creating it and what their objectives are for the system. Once the theoretical realities have been considered, it is important to shift the focus to the various practical realities that exist within the target environment. The process of making a system secure, then, can be discussed as a process involving ongoing exchanges between the identified theoretical ideals and the practical realities within a target environment.

Both the theoretical ideal and the practical implementation realities within the target environment must be fully considered to determine whether or not the security plan is as effective as it can be. Consideration of these essential elements is ongoing and constantly interactive.

It might help to think of the field of security in two parts, almost as two separate things. Consider Figure 4–1. On the one hand you learn about various security-related issues that, in theory, might be appropriate for addressing your security-related concerns. On the other hand, you must identify the practical realities within your target environment that will impact the ability to implement the established security priorities. Say, for example, as a retail store owner you read in a security magazine about a loss prevention system that is identified as the most effective means for reducing shoplifting losses. You know that your unexplained losses are increasing, and you decide to make this a priority for your target environment (your retail shop). After you establish

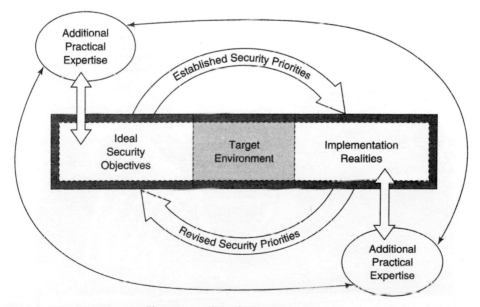

FIGURE 4–1 The Security Planning and Implementation Process

this as a priority, you move toward looking at the loss prevention system from a different perspective. Now you must consider the practical realities within your target environment and determine if the loss prevention system still looks like a good idea. Is the system too expensive for you to afford? Will the losses you prevent pay for the system? Is the product you sell easily tagged? Is it possible for your clerks to bypass the system and remove product undetected before tagging the merchandise and placing it on the shelf? Are the tags easily damaged and made ineffective? How much does it cost to replace damaged tags?

When security enhancements are discussed as a theoretical ideal, the practical realities are sometimes overlooked. If, as you assume, the threat is from shoplifters, perhaps this system is great. If, however, the threat is from your employees and the system makes the employees responsible for tagging items and they have unrestricted access to the product before it gets tagged, the practical realities in your target environment will eventually bear that out. The system is likely to have little effect on the problem.

On the other hand, if the practical concerns from the target environment take priority, then some theoretically viable possibilities are lost. In the example just presented, a retail professional learns quickly that the most likely threat to the bottom line is employees. In theory, the most common explanation for retail losses is the employees. Again, considering what the security body of knowledge has to teach us, we find some theoretical possibili-

(*Source:* Reprinted with special permission of North America Syndicate.)

ties that might warrant consideration in our target setting. Looking at this theory and seeing how it applies to the retail setting mentioned previously might help explain that the losses are due to an employee who is stealing from the store, rather than shoplifters. This practical reality might dictate the need to explore an entirely new set of theoretical options for catching the employee in the act of stealing. The security planning and implementation process continues.

This interactive process is the point at which you can begin to identify and modify your security objectives. A **security objective** is defined as a focused effort to seek out or establish stability and predictability within a target setting. In short, a basic security system can be outlined as issues related to (1) physical security, (2) personnel security, (3) information security, (4) liability issues, and (5) interdepartmental dependencies. But again, be clear. The seemingly independent aspects of a security system are not so independent. These simplified elements of a target environment must work together to ensure a seamless, integrated security design. For this reason, I suggest that the **overall security objective** will be a seamless, integrated security design including and accounting for all elements of the prevention system.

In this chapter, we will revisit the concept of risk. To provide readers with an opportunity to become comfortable with the critical risk-related terms, we will look not only at risk but at risk management. Five strategies for managing risk are introduced. Finally, more specific information is presented about security objectives.

REVISITING RISK

Although Chapter 2 introduced basic security concepts, it should be clear that a more concise understanding of security-related issues can be developed by listening to how individuals working in different security-related areas use the terms. The quest for an exact, concise definition of security-related terms may be valuable mostly as an academic pursuit. In other words, it might be most valuable in a theoretical context. Having all terms precisely defined and used in the same way by all people who discuss security is an idealized objective. For someone who is interested in developing a security plan, such intellectual pursuits may be of little use.

With this in mind, I offer a simplistic breakdown of risk and risk-related terms. As noted in Chapter 2, the use of the word *risk* can vary dramatically among security professionals. As used in this book, *risk* refers to (1) probability and (2) criticality. A risk assessment is done every time a threat has been identified and the security professional wants to assign it an appropriate level of risk. A risk assessment has two components: (1) a probability assessment and (2) a criticality assessment.

RISK MANAGEMENT OPTIONS

Any preliminary discussions about security, security planning, and security environments initiated in Chapter 3 will most likely be structured primarily around a relatively simple objective: identifying threats and assigning appropriate risk levels to those threats. Many security professionals would agree that an important part of the job, perhaps one of the most labor-intensive and time-consuming parts, is the process of identifying risk levels and from there implementing countermeasures to reduce or eliminate their impact on the target environment. This fact alone makes it necessary to take a few minutes to examine risk more closely. The higher the risk, the more likely a threat will turn into a loss event.

The presence of a threat is not always bad. In some cases, the risk associated with that threat is extremely low. In other cases, accepting or assuming risk is actually a valid practice. In the case where an item is not worth the money or time it will take to protect it from a threat, it is better to accept the consequences of not protecting it. An example might be an old used car worth only $500. The cost of a car alarm or full collision insurance coverage on the vehicle might easily exceed the value of the vehicle. Little incentive exists to expend money for increasing the security of this car. If the car is damaged, the loss is not great. But a person with a brand-new car worth $20,000 may be more willing to insure the car against damage or theft. Paying for full insurance coverage makes sense, because if there is an accident, the car can be fixed and the loss (damage to the car) is transferred to the insurance company.

This process of identifying and responding to risk is called **risk management.** Risk management plans provide a means by which security professionals can address threats and risks to meet the satisfaction of the company, agency, or organization. Security professionals have, in general, five ways to respond to risk: (1) eliminate the risk, (2) mitigate the risk, (3) transfer the risk, (4) spread the risk, and (5) accept the risk (Figure 4–2).

As suggested previously, when a threat is identified, evasive actions may be taken in the interest of **eliminating risk** associated with the threat being evaluated. This idea is most effective in the early stages of planning. Consider how much money a company would stand to lose if the planners decided to build a new factory, only to have the area impacted by a flood two years later. Part of the job of the security division could be to identify and eliminate potential risks to the sites being considered for the placement of this new factory. Their findings could reveal information documenting a huge flood in the area 10 years ago. Could a disastrous flood happen again? No one knows. The company now has more information, however, for determining whether it is still interested in building the new facility in this area. The risk associated with a flood could be reduced significantly if the company decided to locate the new factory on

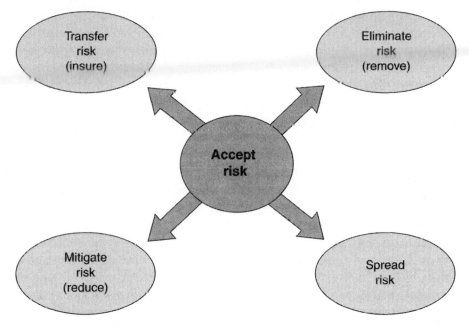

FIGURE 4–2   Five Risk Management Responses
(*Source:* Charles T. Thibodeau, M. Ed., CPP, CSS, CPO.)

higher ground. Careful site selection, in this example, would reduce the risk of a flood.

Security managers interested in **mitigating risk** are fully aware that the threat they seek to address cannot be completely eliminated. When mitigating a risk, the efforts shift to reducing the impact of the threat. The one risk every company wishes it could eliminate completely is the hiring of troubled or dangerous employees. Employee alcohol or drug use can prove to be problematic for a company in the long term. When drug and alcohol problems find their way into the work environment, other risks to companies increase. Low worker productivity, sick leave requests, and accidents on the job have all been related to employee drug use For some jobs, drug screening has become a routine part of the hiring process. Screening will identify a significant number of potential drug-related problems but certainly not all of them. Research suggests that 80 to 90 percent of the people who use drugs or alcohol inappropriately can be screened out.[1] Drug screening does not eliminate the problems associated with employee drug use, but it can be used to reduce the problem to an acceptable level.

Remember, corporate officials typically determine policies for the company. This can mean the company will have a policy about what an "acceptable level" of drug use will be. Something one company may determine to be acceptable may not be suitable for another company. In the case of drugs in the workplace, even if a zero tolerance policy were implemented, it is likely that a company might eventually be confronted with an employee believed to be using drugs. Zero tolerance policies do not necessarily produce zero risk, and how a company handles an employee suspected of using drugs has critically important liability implications for the company. The effort to reduce risks associated with people who have a substance abuse problem is an example of mitigating a risk.

Transferring risk simply amounts to outlining a backup strategy. Responsible security plans assume the eventual failure of the primary security objective. An easy way to understand transferring risk is to think about an insurance policy. Business continuity is essential for a company's survival. What would happen to a company if, in spite of its fire prevention plans, it experienced a catastrophic fire? The fire insurance would pick up the pieces and cover the cost of the building, its machinery, and lost assets as well as lost business income. The company covers the risk by transferring the responsibility for the risk to an insurance company. Everyone who drives a car carries insurance for the same reason. It costs us a relatively small amount of money in the short term, but if an accident happens we are protected. The transferral of risk does not reduce or eliminate risks; it simply provides a means for protecting against devastating losses. Common examples include health insurance, life insurance, and homeowner insurance. All of these insurance policies have one thing in common: They transfer the liability of a loss by transferring a large portion of the cost from the insured to the insurance company.

Spreading risk means spreading the company assets over multiple buildings, multiple locations, or, in some cases, multiple businesses. Companies diversify into many other businesses to protect against the possibility that a financial loss in one business will undermine the success of the larger corporate structure. While one business within the corporate structure may show losses, the overall outlook of the corporation remains good. Suppose a company's manufacturing processes were located in a single 10-story building that was seriously damaged as the result of a tornado. That company would be shut down for a significant time. Suppose losses from the storm are minimal, because the company had insurance. Even though the structural losses are covered, the loss of productivity (because of the amount of time it will take to rebuild) could be devastating.

A security management team that incorporated the risk of tornadoes into the original structural plans might have decided to construct the same square footage of floor space in five two-story buildings. It is easy to see why the impact of a tornado would probably be significantly reduced. Even if one building were completely destroyed, it is unlikely that all the buildings would be destroyed. Although business operations would be reduced in the aftermath of the storm and it might take time to repair the damage, relatively normal business operations would be maintained in the other buildings. The losses to the company could be absorbed more easily because the risk was spread out rather than concentrated.

In the preceding example of the old car, I talked about **assuming risk.** While assuming, or simply accepting, risk is a legitimate response to risk, it is *Midterm* not free from problems. It can be acceptable to assume some risk, but as a general rule no one should risk more than he or she can afford to lose. A person might leave a wallet in an unlocked car if the wallet holds only $10 and no credit cards, feeling willing to assume the risk. But if the wallet contains $200 and credit cards, chances are the person would not leave the wallet in the car.

As mentioned previously, five general methods are outlined here for addressing and managing risk: Eliminate the risk, mitigate the risk, transfer the risk, spread the risk, and assume the risk. Threats are real issues that impact the company, sometimes with devastating consequences. Successfully managing these threats and their related risk levels is a big part of the overall security objective.

The Sanctuary Has Been Broken—and Burned

In a world where the number of violent acts is constantly increasing, one has to wonder where a person can go in order to feel safe. One of the first places that comes to mind is church. One would think that a place that is a symbol of high moral standards would be safe form most vicious acts. Sadly, recent years have been witness to incidents at churches, many with horrible outcomes.

Gun violence has become a major concern in the nation, and churches are not immune. In March 1999, a man burst through the doors of a Louisiana church and fired two shots into the ceiling. After ordering everyone to the floor, he walked down the aisle, shooting between the benches. There were approximately 50 to 75 worshippers in the church at the time the firing started. The man's wife and two-year-old son were among the attendees. Three people were killed (including the gunman's wife and child), and four others were wounded, two of whom were in critical condition. The gunman fired off two clips from his semiautomatic pistol. As he left, the man was heard mumbling to himself, "That'll show you." This comment was seemingly directed toward his wife, with whom he had a rocky relationship. The tragedy was summed up best by the police chief: "The safest place in the world I always thought was a church, and now that sanctuary has been broken."[1]

In March 2000, during a small service of about 20 Hispanic individuals in Pasadena, Texas, a man walked into a church and shot four people, then turned the gun on himself—all because a woman in the church did not have amorous feelings for him, as he did for her. Only one of the four people was seriously wounded, and the lone fatality was the gunman.[2]

In September 1999, at a teen youth rally at a Baptist church in Fort Worth, Texas, a gunman walked in, pulled a gun, and started shooting. There were 150 teenagers in attendance. The man interrupted the gathering and challenged the group's religious beliefs. After the man started shooting, the group was overcome with panic. A pipe bomb also exploded in the church. When the man had finished firing, he sat in a back pew, put the gun to his head, and shot himself. In the end, eight people were confirmed dead and seven others were injured, at least two of them critically.[3]

(continued)

Shootings are not the only form of violence found in churches. Arson has also become a problem. In July 2000, a self-proclaimed "missionary of Lucifer" pleaded guilty to torching 26 churches over a five-year period. Fires were set in Alabama, California, Indiana, Kentucky, Missouri, Ohio, South Carolina, and Tennessee. Fortunately, most of these fires were started late at night or early in the morning, and no one was physically harmed. The emotional harm, however, was unavoidable. The arsonist had frequently expressed his hostility toward Christianity and tried to get people he met to sign a contract with the devil. He saw this as his mission.[4]

In Mobile, Alabama, in October 1997, three white individuals were convicted of burning a church. This was seen as racially motivated because the membership of the congregation was primarily African American and one of the three individuals had been seen at a Ku Klux Klan rally two days earlier.[5]

In May 1998, a church was bombed in Danville, Illinois. A pipe bomb was placed outside the church between a wall and an air-conditioning unit. It exploded just as the pastor was concluding his offering prayer. The blast blew open the church wall, injuring 33 worshippers. No threats were received prior to the incident.[6]

The need for security sometimes extends into unexpected settings. Different motivating factors, such as love, anger, distaste for a set of beliefs or an organization, and racial discrimination, can be associated with the examples of violence directed toward religious gatherings, affiliations, or institutions. Security practitioners must not allow assumptions or preconceived ideas about safety and security in sacred places to impact their role in providing security.

References

1. G. Coates, "Gunman Opens Fire in Church," *http://abcnews.go.com/sections/us/DailyNews/churchshooting9990311.htm.* March 11, 1999.
2. M. K. Stack, "4 Hurt in Church Shooting," *http://more.abcnews.go.com/sections/us/dailynews/churchshooting000323.htm.* March 23, 2000.
3. "Shooting at Teen Service," *http://more.abcnews.go.com/sections/us/dailynews/churchshooting_texas990915.html.* September 15, 1999.
4. "Church Arsonist Pleads Guilty," *http://more.abcnews.go.com/sections/us/dailynews/luciferarsonist000711.html.* July 11, 2000.
5. "Convicted of Conspiracy," *http://more.abcnews.go.com/sections/us/church1103/index.html.* October 3, 1997.
6. "Feds Probe Church Blast," *http://more.abcnews.go.com/sections/us/dailynews/bomb980526.html.* May 26, 1998.

THE SECURITY OBJECTIVE

People who are interested in identifying and exploring security-related concerns in a target environment must have the flexibility to outline their own objectives for the security plan. As discussed earlier, individuals and corporate executives react differently to potential security threats. Some people find themselves working as "security coordinators" for retail companies with no clear security guidelines. The information and resources the security professionals bring to the job will be useful, but the attitude of the company managers is often more important for determining how existing security guidelines will be administered and how proposed guidelines will be implemented.

Various environmental factors will affect a security professional's ability to develop a useful security plan, even if the security professional knows the characteristics and parameters of the target environment. When thinking about the security issues in the target environment, security professionals should think in terms of security objectives. Thinking in terms of objectives, the security professional will be better prepared to focus on what he or she wants the security plan to do. For purposes of discussion, a security objective can be any concern or problem within a target environment, for which efforts are undertaken to establish and maintain a stable and predictable environment.

Any limitations present in a target environment must be taken into account when developing a security plan. Restrictions or limitations might include a lack of allocated funding for security equipment or limited resources for ongoing security-related training. Various elements of the environment must be clearly understood for a security professional to best utilize the security tools and resources. By identifying a security objective, the security professional is forced to outline all of the things that can be used in developing and maintaining a stable, predictable set of conditions in a target environment.

Any good intention to develop or enhance an overall security plan is dependent on many factors, including finances, resources, personnel, business objectives, and other site-specific conditions. The likelihood that the predetermined security objective will be obtained will depend on those site-specific conditions. Be clear. A comprehensive understanding of security essentials requires an emphasis on the *process* of determining how to best achieve stability and predictability in a designated environment. If a company is looking to enhance safety and security in the parking ramps, for example, the question to answer is, How can we attain this security objective? In other words, How can we develop a stable, predictable environment in the parking ramps? Security professionals are responsible for developing the most comprehensive understanding of the conditions in which they intend to build (or enhance) the security plan. They can define and then outline ways to make sure the security objective can be maintained.

Instead of identifying a definition of *security* and attempting to create a secure environment by this definition, a security professional should actively involve him- or herself in deciding what security objectives make sense in the environment. It is not enough for security professionals to look at existing trends within the security industry and say "OK, if my business implements this security device, my business will be secure." The rather generic term *security objective* simply provides an identifiable goal for the specified aspects of that security plan.

The intricacies involved in addressing security-related concerns in a complex global economy are staggering. Very specialized operations require security plans that are tailored to meet those specialized needs. The ideas in this book are not intended to provide a security system to protect classified government information about biological warfare, for example. I believe, however, that even a highly sensitive security plan will adhere, in large part, to many of the essential security concepts discussed throughout this text. By developing a comprehensive understanding of these essential security tools, a security professional can enhance any target environment in a cost-effective manner. The end result is a stable, predictable, secure, environment.

One of the themes mentioned throughout this book is the need for regular communication between security professionals and business (or human resource) managers. The security-related themes mentioned here are certainly appropriate for use by a business professional who has decided to hire security professionals. Whether the business is retail sales or cement manufacturing, security concerns are part of the business manager's responsibilities, but the job is bigger than maintaining a secure work environment. To understand how security professionals fit into the overall security plan, the business manager can learn how security professionals assess and manage security concerns. As responsible consumers, business managers hiring security professionals are wise to get to know some of the fundamental security ideas being advanced by professionals in the security industry.

It is important to see the security objective as a balance between a stable, relatively predictable environment and a free flow of activity, information, and services. Initially, terms such as *threat, risk, probability,* and *criticality* may be confusing. Their role in the security objective, however, cannot be underestimated. If we can reduce the likelihood of a threat by assessing the likelihood of that threat (probability) and the critical impact or damage likely to result from that threat (criticality) and taking appropriate preventative actions, we will be reasonably assured that a stable and predictable environment can be maintained. This balancing act requires security management teams to set their sights on developing the perfect security protocol, while knowing all the while this "perfect" level of security can never be achieved. The assessment tools available to security professionals can be complicated, but the results can be extremely useful for developing or enhancing existing security protocols.

In spite of deliberate preparation and planning, a person may still become involved in a car accident. Perhaps the car was hit by a drunk driver's car, or unexpected mechanical problems caused the car to stall, then be hit by another car. How do people prepare for such unforeseen events? In short, sometimes they do not. Sometimes they cannot. A company can have a state-of-the-art security system, with all kinds of redundant backup systems and contingency plans, but the security management team may discover that a breach of the security system has occurred. This is not impossible to imagine. What if an earthquake occurred in a place where an earthquake had never been known to occur before? Even the best security management team is not likely to be fully prepared for such an unprecedented event. Identifying threats and assessing risk are at the heart of the overall security objective.

THE OVERALL SECURITY OBJECTIVE: A SEAMLESS, INTEGRATED SECURITY DESIGN

Maintaining the integrity of a secure system requires a vigilant group of trained professionals with an aptitude for technological innovation and development, an interest in monitoring and assessing crime trends, an investment of financial resources to fund efforts to meet the security objective, and a little bit of luck.

This prevailing scheme for security strategies emphasizes the need to create what is called a **seamless, integrated security design.** The objective in establishing a seamless, integrated security system is to be able to address the security objective from multiple angles (Figure 4–3, a pyramid as seen from above). All sides of the pyramid fit together and support each other. Legal liability issues are so critical to the overall security objective that they form the pyramid's base. Notice also that the four sides are built on a foundation. The seamless, integrated security design is the most effective and the most widely accepted security design in use today.

A seamless, integrated security system allows security professionals to make use of a wide variety of security concepts and accessories present in an environment. **Physical security** components include security hardware: alarms, closed-captioned television (CCTV), locks, and lighting. Security officers, and policy and procedure manuals for the entire security program, are also considered part of the physical security component within a comprehensive security plan. Locks and alarms are used to protect the majority of corporate assets—including people and property. CCTV is used to provide "eyes" to

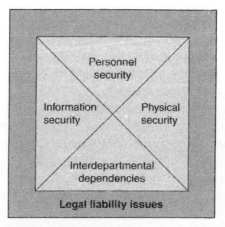

FIGURE 4–3 Seamless, Integrated Security Design
(*Source:* Charles T. Thibodeau, M. Ed., CPP, CSS, CPO.)

the system, and two-way intercoms prove useful as the "ears" of the system. Policy and procedure manuals outline the authority granted to the security professionals so they have the proper direction to perform the necessary security functions adequately.

While physical security proves to be a critical resource to the security management team, personnel security and information security are two equally important areas of an integrated security system. **Personnel security** involves the hiring (and firing) of employees and the control of employee movements and activities. A superior physical security system proves not very useful if the people working within the system pose the greatest security threat. Hiring highly skilled, reliable people (personnel security) helps protect the environment from inside threats, and physical security measures help protect the company from the outside threats.

Information security involves the essential policies and procedures for protecting important documents integral to maintaining the safety and security of the environment. Combinations to safes, alarm system codes, patented information, computer security, corporate secrets and data, and anything related to the integrity of the environment can be maintained under the heading of "information security."

A final interdependent element used to establish and maintain stability and predictability in a given environment comes in the form of **interdepartmental dependency.** Directors of security are integrally connected to the managers of specific corporate departments, for example. Different divisions within a protected environment must work together to ensure the security objective is met and maintained effectively. Information important to the overall functioning of the company, for example, will be found in a variety of departments. The result, therefore, is the use of a variety of physical security features by each of these departments, involving a number of personnel who identify and process information that needs to be protected. Secure systems that have worked well within specific areas of a company, for example, can be replicated and maintained at a relatively minor increase in cost. Involving carefully selected employees to assist with the task of attaining the security objective makes sense. Realize too, however, that it also brings risk.

It is easy to see that areas within the field of security that may have appeared only peripherally related can, in fact, be used together to create an extremely formidable security presence. The potential impact of a security design that does not work well must be made exceptionally clear. When accidents or injuries occur within a specific environment, the company (and, by implication, the security professionals) is sometimes held responsible for those incidents. Various measures within the corporate security strategy can be used to reduce the liability to the company. For now, it is important to understand the responsibilities associated with outlining and achieving a security objective that works well for the environment. It is not unusual for a company to be sued six months or even two years after an alleged incident, so the process should be thorough and retrievable.

Utilizing the ideas presented here can assist in developing a workable security objective for an individual, a company, or a security management team. People feel safer in a group of people with common objectives. People need to feel secure within their chosen environment. Identifying and controlling for security threats helps to produce a stable and predictable environment. Establishing an understanding of essential elements of the security objective within affected groups creates an interdependency between groups for maintaining that security. Remember, these aspects of the overall security objective all work together to ensure that persons who visit or work within a specific environment may pursue their ends without "disruptions or harm, and without fear of such disturbance or injury."[2] Trained professionals working with adequate resources can combine their efforts with personnel involved to ensure that a given environment remains secure. The quest for identifying and maintaining the best possible security objective for a target environment will provide an ongoing challenge.

The security objective must include attention to physical security, personnel security, information security, and, where possible, interdepartmental dependencies. These four elements are linked by the important legal and ethical problems that result when the elements are not accurately identified or integrated. In short, the security objective is simple: to develop a seamless, integrated security program that includes all persons involved and results in a stable and predictable environment. Security directors, security consultants, private investigators, security officers, security administrators, company officials, and individual employees all play a part in outlining the overall security objectives and making sure those objectives are maintained.

CONCLUSION

This chapter has been focused on introducing some final security essentials. The word *risk* and terms related to risk are explored more thoroughly. The terms *security objective* and *overall security objective* are introduced in an effort to assist the reader in understanding that security issues have multiple levels. One may envision the need to begin with the overall security objective to create a seamless, integrated security design, but typically specific (usually more concrete) security objectives become the focal point for specifically targeted security practices, such as a vulnerability assessment. In the end, a basic security design should include five areas: (1) physical security, (2) personnel security, (3) information security, (4) interdepartmental dependencies, and (5) liability issues. Once these aspects are addressed and integrated, security practitioners can more easily respond to critical issues as they arise within the target setting.

REVIEW QUESTIONS

1. Outline briefly the five risk management options discussed in the chapter.
2. Identify the five basic elements of a security system.
3. How does legal liability differ from the other four parts of an integrated security system design?
4. Outline the differences between one security objective and the overall security objective.

DISCUSSION QUESTIONS

1. What role does the target setting play in the five aspects of a security system?
2. What is the role of managers in ensuring that various elements of a security system are incorporated into a seamless, integrated security design?
3. Consider the following scenarios:
   - threat of computer virus
   - threat of bad weather
   - threat of drug-related violence
   - threat of drive-by shooting
   - threat of crime in a church

   Which of the five risk management options makes the most sense for each of these threats and settings? Please justify your response.
4. Do you see any difficulty using the model of integrated security system design outside of traditional corporate or business settings?

SUGGESTED READINGS

Brislin, R. F., and E. C. Lewis. 1994. *The Effective Security Supervision Manual.* Woburn, MA: Butterworth-Heinemann.

Burstein, H. 1995. *Security: A Management Perspective.* Englewood Cliffs, NJ: Prentice Hall.

Dalton, D. R. 1997. *The Art of Successful Security Management.* Woburn, MA: Butterworth-Heinemann.

Fay, J. 1993. *Encyclopedia of Security Management: Techniques and Technology.* Woburn, MA: Butterworth-Heinemann.

Robinson, R. 1999. *Issues in Security Management.* Woburn, MA: Butterworth-Heinemann.

Schreider, T. 1998. *Encyclopedia of Disaster Recovery, Security, and Risk Management.* Duluth, GA: Crucible Publishing Works.

Sennewald, C. A. 1998. *Effective Security Management.* Woburn, MA: Butterworth Heinemann.

REFERENCES

1. Green, G., and R. C. Farber, *Introduction to Security: Principles & Practices* (Security World Publishing Company, 1978), 3.
2. R. Fisher and G. Green, *Introduction to Private Security,* 6th ed. (Boston: Butterworth-Heinemann, 1998)

PART

II

Internal Resources and Integration: Identifying Resources from Within

Common sense is the collection of prejudices acquired by age eighteen.

—Albert Einstein

For individuals in specific settings—police officers, corrections officers, security officers, even a family on vacation—assessing their own security becomes a constant process, something they do automatically. A woman walking in an urban setting may have a high level of fear.[1] It makes sense for her to evaluate her surroundings, including the people, the place, the time of day, the types of trouble she is likely to confront, as often as she thinks is necessary. If she turns a corner, her setting changes, people change, and she will think about how these changes increase or lessen her fear.

We all do this to some degree. A person might decide to change a route or identify alternatives to a typical routine because of a fear or perceived threat. Within this process, the person is likely to evaluate his or her own abilities to address a given threat: Am I tired? Am I physically fit? Am I in an unfamiliar location? Do I have access to assistance? When something in the environment changes, a person reassesses his or her security. Some people argue that this process is easy, commonsensical, something we do without thinking. Security planning has often been discussed in a similar way, as if all a person needs to design a comprehensive security system is a healthy dose of common sense. In Part II we consider these ideas more fully.

It is true, perhaps, that some people have an innate, intuitive sense of threats and risk levels. It is also true, however, that a person who is reacting without preparation in a given setting might miss something important to consider in the future. The comfort, or "security," one finds in a planned response is found in the preparation. If a person has taken the time to think about possible threats, risk levels, and likely responses, then it is likely efforts will have been taken to avoid the most serious threats. In planning for a security threat, security professionals move the act of providing security away from a simple assessment based in "commonsense" toward a well-rehearsed proactive prevention strategy.

Part II is focused on helping readers design and evaluate security objectives, identify an overall security objective, and then begin to design a preliminary security plan. Although this is just a basic starting point, thinking in terms of an outline of basic elements can be helpful. The goal is not to react but to prevent.

One of the most important themes within any conversation focused on identifying and exploring security essentials is the relatively simple idea that security happens at multiple levels. Consider how a person would plan security for a family of five. What would that person want to know in order to advise the family about increasing its members' safety and security? What if security planning were more difficult? Consider the security concerns of a family of five (two parents, three children) moving west in the mid-1800s. The person in charge of this family's security would need to know that the family members (most likely) would travel in a covered wagon, acquire food and other supplies along the way as needed, carry weapons for personal protection, carry tools, pack personal goods (clothing, coats, shoes), and be on their own if there were medical problems. What else would a person want to know in order to advise the family members about how to protect themselves and each other? What about the weather? What time of year would the family be traveling? The weather (especially cold weather) could significantly impact the family members' ability to meet their basic needs for food, clothing, and shelter. What about the physical welfare of each person in the family? Are they healthy? Are there older people or small children? How might having older people or small children on the trip impact a security plan? What about the financial welfare of the family? How does this impact the options available to the family members as they travel west? What additional security threats might the family confront?

A person's ability to advise this family well will likely hinge on his or her ability to ask the right questions and anticipate the kinds of events this family is likely to encounter. When making suggestions, the security professional giving advice would need to keep in mind all the relevant details about the trip. In meeting their security concerns, the family members are left to their own resources. They have no global positioning system to guide them, and they have no cell phone to call for help.

Even if the family members had the benefit of reviewing a well-considered security plan before their trip west, the plan and the reality of the trip might not agree. They would be left to rely on their own wits and resources as they reacted to any unplanned situations. One might even say they would have to use common sense. In today's high-tech society, this example may seem a bit out of date, but it references basic security concerns reflected in just about every life circumstance. Most people do not hire security professionals; they protect themselves in day-to-day life. Government officials, celebrities, and other high-profile people may decide to contract with a security professional who can help them meet their personal protection needs. In a real sense, someone developing a security strategy may do everything right, but, as in the case of the family journeying west, unanticipated intervening variables may determine whether the security plan was sufficient. This is a constant reality in the security profession. It is a constant reality in life.

The security professional assumes the responsibility for making certain all practical methods for enhancing the existing level of security have been explored. But even the best security system is limited; almost all security plans or systems can be breached. The plan is to begin with basic coverage of essential security information, then integrate those security concerns with additional information about a particular target environment.

The essential elements of an overall security system design or security management strategy have been discussed in multiple ways in introductory textbooks. Part II provides an overview of a basic security design. The information is divided into three basic, yet essential, areas: (1) physical security and asset protection, (2) information and computer security, and (3) personnel and security management. Each area is explored in greater detail in Chapters 5, 6, and 7, respectively.

Chapter 8 is focused on the importance of integration. Because the three areas just outlined are working at different levels to address the overall security objective, it is important that they be put in place with an eye toward the overall operation. With specific attention being given to the conditions in the target environment, these three elements can be integrated in ways that will enhance the security contribution of each of the three central layers of security outlined. Good communication plays a critical role in efforts to unify the operational objectives.

Finally, Chapter 9 outlines several different settings to provide readers with an opportunity to begin thinking about how best to apply the materials presented throughout the text up to this point. A brief summary of information is provided about each area: a convenience store, a school, a hospital, an airport, and a bank. Recent information about each setting was collected from trade journals, academic studies, and generic information common to each setting. After reviewing the information presented, it is up to the readers to determine what information they need and how it is most appropriately applied to the environment they are reviewing.

The objective for students and anyone new to the field is to experiment with a few target environments before you go work in your own target environment. These chapters would be well utilized if readers assessed the settings in terms of the issues discussed in Chapters 5, 6, and 7. This would be an excellent way to see the various levels or layers of security for each of these settings. Then readers might think about the ease, or difficulty, with which these three types of security might be integrated.

Another excellent exercise would be for readers to consider their own target environments and review the information presented in Part I. Readers should think about the history of the setting, likely threats, and risk levels, and then overlay the information presented throughout Part II.

The emphasis throughout Part II is on the internal setting of a target environment. Basic information is followed by a presentation of various settings, to allow readers to explore their ability to assess a situation in a comprehensive way, on multiple levels in different settings.

As readers think about the individual layers and how the various pieces might fit together, they will naturally ask questions about the environments in which they are working. Readers are likely to develop a skill for seeing security as an ongoing process, with multiple layers and multiple objectives, all of which can impact, either directly or indirectly, the plan to meet security-related needs.

As readers begin developing their own skills in information gathering, application, and integration, I hope they will also be learning the importance of constant critical reassessment of existing security system designs. Well-informed communication between different divisions is another essential, particularly if your goal is an integrated security system. Although the basic security plan can be enhanced as resources and objectives dictate, it is important to think about how the multiple levels of the security program overlap. Cutting corners by using quick fixes can ultimately be more costly if security breaches continue.

It is not enough to incorporate the essential areas outlined in Part II, put some security technologies in place, and call it a security system. Many aspects of the overall security system design depend on the practical realities of the target environment. Space, financial restrictions, and risk levels are examples. Each security professional must decide what is appropriate for his or her setting. Security professionals must be dedicated to revisiting and revising information. If you don't think about relevant theoretical possibilities, you leave your setting vulnerable. If you don't pay attention to the practical realities, you also leave your setting vulnerable. Furthermore, if you prejudge a person, circumstance, or activity as nonthreatening before you have good information, your setting remains vulnerable. If you know your target environment is vulnerable, but the text didn't mention the areas you need to address, then you leave your setting vulnerable. The goal, of course, is *not* to leave your target environment vulnerable.

REFERENCE

1. C. Keane, "Evaluating the Influence of Fear of Crime as an Environmental Mobility Restrictor on Women's Routine Activities," *Environment and Behavior 30*, no. 1 (1998): 61.

CHAPTER

5

Physical Security and Asset Protection

CHAPTER OUTLINE

Early Academic Efforts: Crime Prevention through Environmental Design
Three Models for Discussing Physical Security
  The Three, Four, and Five Ds: The D Is for Defense
  Lines of Defense
  External and Internal Threats
The Role of Physical Security in the Overall Security Objective

Tools for a Basic Plan: Locks, Lights, Alarms, and Access Control
Other Aspects of a Physical Security Plan
  Asset Protection
  The Use of Technology as/in Physical Security
  Security Procedures Manuals
Conclusion
  Review Questions
  Discussion Questions

CHAPTER HIGHLIGHTS

Review of crime prevention through environmental design
Three prevailing models for thinking about physical security:
  1. the dynamic Ds
  2. lines of defense

  3. external/internal distinctions
Locks, lights, alarms, and access control
Policy and procedure manuals

KEY WORDS

Access control
Asset protection
"Broken windows" theory
Crime prevention through environmental design (CPTED)
Dynamic Ds
Environmental criminology
External loss prevention

Fence
Internal loss prevention
Intrusion detection system (IDS)
Limited action
Lines of defense
"Onion philosophy"
Physical security

Different security professionals have provided different models and methods for explaining what is meant by *physical security*. Various presentation styles or organizational models focused on examining physical security have been developed in an attempt to clarify the information. The combination of these efforts, I would argue, has had perhaps the opposite result. Anyone who is relatively new to the field of security may find that these various ideas about physical security make the process of moving forward seem difficult or confusing. Having said that, let's push forward with a discussion of physical security.

This chapter is focused on evaluating the aspects of physical security as this term has been defined by, and talked about in, the security profession. *Physical security* refers to the physical (tangible) measures put in place to safeguard personnel, equipment, facilities (or a portion thereof), and information—in any form—against espionage, sabotage, damage, and/or theft. That says it all. Anything that a security professional puts in place to address a security concern can be considered part of the physical security plan.

Physical security features refer to the measures put in place to contain (or better control) problems related to at least three things: property, information, and people. **Physical security** is anything "specifically concerned with the various physical measures designed (1) to safeguard personnel; (2) to prevent the unauthorized access to equipment, a facility (or installation or a portion thereof), audit materials, and information—either documents or electronic data; and (3) to safeguard all these items against espionage, sabotage, damage, and/or theft."[1] Physical security is a front-line defense and includes any of the

(*Source:* United Media.)

tangible tools put in place to help meet the overall security objective identified for a target environment.

As with all concepts relevant to the security industry, efforts to shape and explore the idea of physical security are ongoing. Ultimately, assisting emerging security professionals in their efforts to provide adequate protection for their clients is the goal of the entire security profession. In this chapter, an introductory presentation of physical security is provided. Attention will be given to the process of identifying vulnerable aspects of a space. Overall the emphasis is on the ways in which physical security measures can be used to enhance security within a target environment.

EARLY ACADEMIC EFFORTS: CRIME PREVENTION THROUGH ENVIRONMENTAL DESIGN

Early crime control efforts produced a vast amount of information on **crime prevention through environmental design** (CPTED [pronounced "septed"]). These early efforts to understand how the threat of crime could be prevented or reduced resulted in a focused effort to study how giving special attention to environmental conditions can reduce criminal activity. The application expanded to include architecture and environmental design. For this reason the discussion of physical security begins with a brief history of CPTED.

CPTED is based on criminological theories focused on the assumption that criminal activity can be reduced by the way a space is designed. The term *CPTED* was developed by C. Ray Jeffery in the mid-1970s. A related term, **environmental criminology,** refers to research focused on studying the relationship between physical space and criminal activity.[2] These theories have been applied with some documented success in various environments and have been incorporated into the activities of not only security professionals but also city managers, park planners, business consultants, and other professionals.

One of the most sustained applications of CPTED has been efforts to decrease convenience store robberies.[3] Industry officials, working with researchers, have identified four preventive measures that have been endorsed by the greatest numbers of studies.[4] (7-Eleven in particular was a leader in this field, using early research by Crow and Bull on changes that might reduce crime.) The four preventive measures are (1) having two or more clerks on duty, especially at night; (2) using specific cash-handling techniques (referring, for example, to the number of large bills kept in the register and how the employee is expected to respond when asked to break a large bill); (3) controlling access (making sure only the people who belong in a specific area have access to that area); and (4) using natural surveillance (the ability to keep an eye on an area without the use of surveillance devices).[5]

CPTED and related theories have been applied successfully to a wide variety of settings. Some examples are quite famous, such as the Disney theme parks. Researchers have documented the important role that environmental design plays in maintaining control over vacationers while also providing a sense of wonder and "magic."[6] Consider the following passage:

> For example, virtually every pool, fountain, and flower garden serves both as an aesthetic object and to direct visitors away from, or towards, particular locations. Similarly, every Disney Production employee, while visibly and primarily engaged in other functions, is also engaged in the maintenance of order. This integration of functions is real and not simply an appearance: beauty is created, safety is protected, employees are helpful. The effect is, however, to embed the control function into the "woodwork" where its presence is unnoticed but its effects are ever present.[7]

The authors are clear about presenting the features of this security plan as "an exemplar of modern private corporate policing."[8] Remember, *security* means establishing a stable and predictable environment. With fairly good precision, the physical layout of Disney theme parks provides subtle guidelines for how visitors should behave on park property.

One of the latest and most popular versions of CPTED is referred to as the "broken windows" theory of crime prevention/reduction.[9] Actually, this application of the theories is so new that the controversies about its related benefits are still largely unresolved.[10] The **"broken windows" theory** suggests that "just as a broken window left untended is a sign that nobody cares and leads to more damage and vandalism, so disorderly behavior left unattended is a sign that nobody cares and leads to more serious crime."[11] When the occurrence of minor crimes such as graffiti is reduced, the number of more serious crimes also decreases. Putting the theory into practice in a New York City subway produced a 75 percent drop in overall crime.[12] The preliminary results seem to suggest that a good way to prevent crime is to keep the physical environment clean and well tended.

Current evidence suggests that environmental conditions play an important role in the development of an appropriate physical security plan for a target environment. Developing a physical security plan, like developing other parts of a security plan, involves a process. Three of the most common approaches for outlining a physical security plan are discussed next.

THREE MODELS FOR DISCUSSING PHYSICAL SECURITY

What should a physical security system do? Depending on a security professional's overall security objectives, the objectives for the physical security system might be quite simple. At least three well-known models have been used to help security professionals explore the physical security needs in a target environment: (1) the dynamic Ds, (2) lines of defense, and (3) internal/external threat identification. While all of these approaches to physical security planning are viable, it is important to consider the environmental conditions, along with the security professionals' preferences, while deciding which model makes the most sense for a target environment. Note here that the physical structure is not the only place to enhance the physical security. Policies and procedures are another excellent example of a tangible measure to safeguard personnel, equipment, facilities, or information. Being clear about the objective for the physical security plan is an essential aspect of any physical security plan.

The Three, Four, and Five Ds: The D Is for Defense

Consider what I call the **dynamic Ds.** Various practitioners have developed three, four, and even five Ds to outline the physical security objectives. The three Ds include either deter, detect, and deny access or deter, deny access, and detect, depending on the priorities of the security professional. Using this model, and from a very pragmatic standpoint, the first priority of a physical security program is to deter a would-be criminal. Of related interest is the ability to detect an intruder who breaches protected areas. If such a breach occurs, the purpose of the physical security plan then becomes ensuring that access to the target area is denied. The interest in detecting the intruder may be to apprehend them, or it may just be to determine existing vulnerabilities. Whatever the overall security objective, physical security is intended to be one of the first lines of defense against a potential security threat.

Other introductory-level texts suggest that "the four Ds of protection are: 1. Deter the intruder, 2. Detect the intruder, 3. Delay the intruder, and 4. Deny the intruder access."[13] In yet another example, "the use of physical security is based on what is sometimes referred to as the five Ds."[14]

1. *deter:* to reduce or eliminate the likelihood that a potential violator will attempt entry
2. *detect:* to identify someone who has committed a breach in the security system so that person can be directed elsewhere or otherwise dealt with appropriately
3. *delay:* to restrict further movement so security can respond to the intrusion
4. *deny:* to thwart efforts of an intruder to reach a particular asset
5. *destroy:* in extreme circumstances, to remove the threat by the use of destructive force directed at either the asset being protected or the person causing the security threat

Being specific about selecting either three, four, or five Ds is less important than really thinking about what the physical security plan should do. For a security manager in a retail establishment, there would be no likely scenario that would warrant destructive force, the fifth of the five Ds. If destructive force is not appropriate in a target environment, destructive force should not be one of the security responses outlined for that environment.

It is important to be clear about the importance of the overall security objective for the target environment: It is a cornerstone for identifying potential security threats. For most security professionals, the objective is to reduce the risk levels of certain threats associated with doing business within a target environment. A good number of security professionals identify their primary, if not singular, objective as prevention. This means that security professionals will take **limited action.** They can take only those actions as defined by company policy and in accordance with the law. While it is unlikely that lethal force will be necessary for a large majority of these professionals, it is also true that some professionals within the security industry are trained to use deadly force if necessary. Physical security plans should be developed to include a clear understanding of the objectives of the overall security plan. Most security system plans will not include officers who are authorized to carry weapons, so agency policies and procedures are not likely to cover such scenarios.

Lines of Defense

After using the Ds to help identify the purposes of a physical security plan, the **lines of defense** concept could also be used in the assessment and implementation of the physical security plan.[15,16] Also referred to in the industry as the **"onion philosophy"** because security is provided in layers, the lines of defense concept invites the security professional to begin with the outer edges of the property/building/target area and then move inward toward the assets to be protected.[17] A traditional lines of defense graphic can be found in Figure 5–1. By beginning at the outside, the security professional can assess the specific sectors of the overall environment, one at a time. After considering the physi-

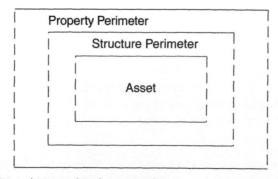

FIGURE 5–1   Traditional Lines of Defense Graphic

cal security vulnerabilities at each line of defense, the security professional is ready to think about countermeasures. Remember that countermeasures (discussed in Chapter 2) are any practice(s) put in place to reduce the risk level of an identified threat. Countermeasures include policies, procedures, and technological aids being discussed within the broader context of physical security.

The idea of lines of defense is commonly presented in graphic form as a rectangle or as a circle,* but either way the idea is the same. The graphic in Figure 5–2 demonstrates, at a very basic level, the idea that there are levels—or layers—of security (or access, depending on your point of view) surrounding important assets. First is the perimeter of the target environment (the property boundary—a parking lot, for example). Second, there is the perimeter of the building or other physical structure. At this second level, efforts are focused on securing and regulating access to and egress from the building, for example. Once the security issues have been met at that level, the next layer of security is inside that building or other structure. The third level is the heart of the target environment, or the specific area within the building (or other target environment) that requires focused attention because it holds assets (e.g., safes, computers, or other company assets identified for protection). For the physical security features to be effective in the building interior, the structure and function of the building must be considered.

The graphic in Figure 5–2 is somewhat elementary, however. Few target environments are structured so as to provide specific access and egress points, with only one centrally located asset in need of the most extensive protection. More likely, a target area will have various assets, of varying value, within each layer of security. For example, on the perimeter of the property, there may be a parking lot. Whether the lot is gated or open, people and property (their cars) will need to be secured. The security department will need to make efforts to reduce the likelihood of damage. If there have been reports of vandalism, the security protocol will need to be reassessed.

In theory, increasing the layers of security between the alleged perpetrator and the most important assets in the company enhances the security of the overall structure. In the perfect scenario, would-be thieves would be deterred or denied access because they would be unable to clear all of the layers of security. If people were to penetrate the layers of defense, their actions would be detected and their departure delayed to ensure the appropriate security response could be mounted. But security systems are never this simple. Once the grounds and property, even access to the building, are secured, there will still be a variety of security concerns within the building. It is likely that specific

---

*A version of this can be found in Don T. Cherry's *Total Facility Control* (Woburn, MA: Butterworth-Heinemann, 1986, p. 100) or as a circle (as demonstrated in Clifford Simonsen's *Private Security in America* [Upper Saddle River, NJ: Prentice Hall, 1998, p. 246]).

physical security plans can be incorporated at each layer to address each any (or all) of these security concerns.

So again, while the traditional graphic is useful for conveying the idea of layers of security, it should also be made clear to the aspiring practitioner that each of these lines of defense also has layers (e.g., there might be a five-story structure with four or five different security concerns on each floor). To illustrate this more fully, I have modified the traditional lines of defense graphic to provide a more realistic presentation of the multiple factors in each layer (Figure 5–2).

Consider the differences between Figures 5–1 and 5–2. The variety of security concerns in the second graphic is evident at first glance. Furthermore, there are some of the same concerns on the perimeter of the property as there are inside a given area of the building. Employees and customers might be the best example of these common concerns. Consider the placement of the people within the facility. Some are relatively contained within specific areas, but others are free to roam. The security needs of each of these groups are likely to be different. Therefore, a security professional must think about the multiple levels or layers of physical security that will be necessary at each line of defense. It is too simple to address these lines of defense without also developing an understanding of how these lines intersect with other aspects of the overall security plan.

Take a few minutes and think of various kinds of security settings where all of these lines of physical defense are applicable. How do these lines of defense present themselves at the regional airport? The local bank? A higher education campus? Your house? The local hospital? Although the Figure 5–1 graphic is

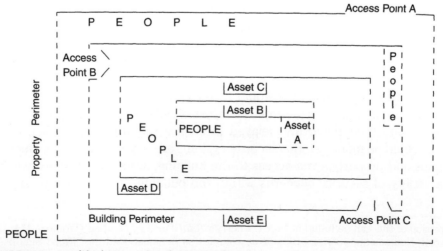

FIGURE 5–2   Modified Lines of Defense Graphic

overly simplistic, the physical security objective is clear: Implement physical security protocols or measures to deter, deny, delay, and detect intruders; then consider these objectives from the lines of defense based on the assets to be protected. Although access points and crowd control can be important basic elements of a physical security plan, various other elements of a physical security plan can be introduced at each line of defense to enhance the security protections provided.

External and Internal Threats

A final approach to considering the assessment and implementation of good physical security is discussed in the form of external and internal threats or external and internal security. This approach, a traditional one, allows the security professional to concentrate on either issues that originate from outside of the target environment or specific aspects of the environment where threats present themselves from within.[18] Pretty simple, right? Well, not necessarily. Security professionals have not been consistent about how they talk about or what they mean by *internal* and *external*. In one version of this model, security issues have been defined in general as "internal" and "external" security issues.[19] In *Security and Loss Prevention*, by Philip Purpura, specific chapters are focused toward internal and external loss prevention. **Internal loss prevention** focuses on threats that present themselves from *within* the organization.[20] **External loss prevention** focuses on threats from *outside* an organization.[21] Purpura also identifies internal and external relations and discusses them in the context of cooperative arrangements with other groups and individuals who may be useful for meeting loss prevention objectives.[22] Ricks, Tillett, and VanMeter also highlight the internal and external distinctions, but their focus is on threats. They mention internal threats such as employee problems (embezzlement, fraud, and pilferage), theft control strategies, alcoholism, and drug use; and external threats such as robbery, burglary, shoplifting, bad checks, credit card fraud, telecommunications fraud, bombs, terrorism, crisis management, espionage, and sabotage.[23] Again, we see similar objectives from the authors, but the language is used just a bit differently.

The internal/external scheme may seem simple and easy to follow on one level, because in this model, the threat is either inside or outside of the organization. You should note, though, that the orientation for this approach shifts our focus, to some degree. We went from looking at the physical environment to looking, instead, at a protocol for identifying potential threats that are either internal or external. This can muddy the waters a bit for those new to security, because these ideas are sometimes subsumed within a discussion about physical security, but the focus is initially on the threat rather than on the physical measures that by definition are, in fact, physical security. Physical security concerns are addressed after the threats are identified and evaluated as to their importance. One widely referenced introductory security textbook identifies "outer defenses" as the building and perimeter, and "interior defenses" as intrusion and access control.[24] Security textbooks also discuss physical security in terms of "internal security" and "external security."[25] So again, you can see that the internal and external references are varied. They are all interesting and offer good information, but it is important to make certain you are on the same page when referencing internal and external security issues.

The difficulty with internal and external references may not be helpful at all when the topic is practitioner response to a specific incident. Consider the act of espionage. Someone may hire on with a company and therefore be an employee, but that person's goal is only to get information and transfer that information back to the company that hired him or her. Crisis management is another good example. A crisis situation could begin within or outside the organization. This makes distinguishing between internal and external threats really difficult. In short, a bomb threat may come anonymously, from a disgruntled employee, or from an outsider. Therefore, calling bombs external threats could be somewhat misleading. What really matters is not the source of the bomb but whether the company has a plan for responding to any bomb threat no matter how it comes to the attention of the people present.

How you use language is important, and in some cases, people who use the terms will make it clear how they intend for the reader to understand their use of those terms. For example, the following issues should be addressed by the architect and engineering teams responsible for renovations on or new construction of any federal building (and recommended for state and local buildings):

- *Perimeter security* and *exterior security* focus the security professional on the parking area, closed-captioned television (CCTV) monitoring, lighting, and physical barriers.
- *Entry security* includes intrusion detection systems; upgrade to current life safety standards; screening of mail, persons, and packages; entry control with CCTV and electric door strikes; and high-security locks.
- *Interior security* includes employee identification, visitor control, access control, emergency power, and an evaluation of the placement of day care centers.[26]

Various measures can be discussed as a response to both interior and exterior security threats. Locks, windows, doors, and CCTV surveillance systems (e.g., where CCTV is used on the perimeter and in the entryways)[27] can be security technologies used to address either interior or exterior concerns, depending on the structure and/or layout of the target environment. Outer defenses, like exterior concerns, are likely to be focused first on the perimeter of the target environment and are likely to include fences, gates (with or without personnel), CCTV, identification of specified access points for people (both pedestrians and those in vehicles), and policies and procedures for determining which points are controlled at what times throughout the day and night. The second focal point while considering the exterior is the building. Consider issues like points of access into the building (windows, doors, and unusual access points such as roofs, skylights, tunnels, etc.). The third focal point is the building interior; while, as noted elsewhere in the book, security professionals often use the same terms in different ways, interior defenses are discussed in this model in terms of intrusion prevention and access control protocols.

THE ROLE OF PHYSICAL SECURITY IN THE OVERALL SECURITY OBJECTIVE

The International Foundation for Protection Officers (IFPO) suggests that good physical security planning consists of five steps: (1) Assets are identified, (2) loss events are exposed, (3) occurrence probability factors are assigned, (4) the impact of occurrence is assessed, and (5) countermeasures are selected.[28] While these five issues can provide a useful directive for helping security professionals focus on the process of installing a physical security response, it is not necessarily clear to the novice security professional how these five things relate directly to the identification and implementation of the overall security objective. Remember, physical security is the use of physical measures to safeguard people and things in any form, against espionage, sabotage, damage, and theft. What role does physical security play in the overall security objective? How is physical security different from other aspects of a comprehensive security program? These are good questions; people able to answer these questions are likely to be good at assessing and making decisions about various security-related options.

TOOLS FOR A BASICS PLAN: LOCKS, LIGHTS, ALARMS, AND ACCESS CONTROL

Although security professionals might disagree with specific aspects of what constitutes physical security, some of the most commonly discussed aspects of a physical security plan are locks, lights, alarms, and access control features. This section considers these essential physical security features in some detail.

Locking devices are one of the most common security devices used by both security professionals and people who are not security professionals. Whether on a car, a home, or a locker at the gym, locks convey a simple message to a potential thief: This property does not belong to you. People with keys are meant to have access. No key, no access.

Locks are common, it is true. A complete understanding of locks, however, is anything but common. Locksmiths are in business because they understand

Vanished . . .

The days of job security are vanishing, but it is not the kind of job security that keeps the paycheck coming in. An entrepreneur is trying to run a successful business while providing a secure workplace for employees. The entrepreneur installs the latest security devices that seem appropriate—adequate for meeting the company's needs. But how much is adequate? Surely, there will be a difference between the security needs of an office complex in a metropolitan area and those of a sporting goods store in a small town. What about a convenience store on the outskirts of a small town? What if the store sits alone, just a short distance from the interstate highway?

It was almost midnight on May 26, 1999, when a customer walked into the Conoco store, a convenience store near an interstate highway, just outside Moose Lake, Minnesota, a small town. The store was usually open all night, but on this night something was different. When a customer entered, the clerk was nowhere to be found. The customer called the police, and the search was on. With the mystery surrounding what happened, the police were thankful that the store had a video surveillance system. They went to the tape, and what they found out was horrendous. The clerk, Katie Poirier, who was working alone, was seen on the tape being forced out of the store at what appeared to be gunpoint. This happened at about 11:30 P.M. No money or merchandise was found missing from the store. The man walked around the empty store, up and down aisles for more than four minutes. Then he struck. The surveillance system did capture what happened, but the images were not clear enough to decipher. The video was sent to NASA's Marshall Space Flight Center, to the world's leading expert in videotape enhancement. Still no good information was discovered, and even more questions were raised. What if two people had been working together at the Conoco? What good is a video surveillance system when it cannot record something well enough to see images clearly? What needs to be done to prevent something like this from happening in the future? It is very rare in many places to see more than one person working the night shift at a convenience store.

There are a few different reasons for these one-person shifts. Outside of metro areas, most convenience stores do not make enough money to cover the cost of having a second person there. Some stores just cannot afford the extra help, nor can they afford to pay the overtime to have more current employees cover this shift. Also, there is usually no requirement that two employees work the night shift; only Florida requires this. The justification behind the Florida law is that clerks working alone at night are "exposed to a great danger of harm by crimes of violence."[1] The Federal Bureau of Investigation reports that convenience store robberies generally are down, and studies have shown that the presence of two clerks generally does not deter the robberies anyway. However, no data are available on the effect of having two clerks versus one with regard to kidnapping and sexual assault. In store after store, night clerks in Minnesota were found to be women.

The surveillance system at the Conoco was so poor that it could not even make out a clear image of what was going on. All that could be determined was that Katie was taken by force. No significant features of the assailant could be made out. The Department of Labor and Industry's Occupational Safety and Health Division, the Minnesota arm of the federal Occupational Safety and Health Administration, ordered the company that owns the Conoco where the abduction took place to have a "security inspection done by a qualified professional 'crime prevention practitioner.'"[2] The company was also fined $50,000 for failing to protect its workers from violent acts. The inspection was to focus on whether the store needed to "install a protective barrier around employees, keep two workers on duty after 11:00 P.M., or close the store earlier."[3] The agency conducting the inspection also needed to decide if the store had to install a better security camera system. Investigators believed that the company knowingly violated some of these security standards. Some of the equipment being used to secure places of employment is now obsolete. The nation is continually progressing technologically. These technologies must be used to heighten the security of facilities at a time when greater security is badly needed. Updating security systems in businesses around the country may bring back the job "security" that Katie did not have.

References

1. J. Van Pilsum, "Working the Night Shift—Alone," *http://www.channel4000.com/news/dimension/news-dimension-19991116-2000808.html*. November 16, 1999.
2. "State Fines Poirier's Employer," *St. Cloud Times*, September 29, 2000, 2B.
3. "State Fines Poirier's Employer," 2B.

Other Sources

Maxwell, J. Moose Lake abduction caught on tape. *http://www.wcco.com/news/stories/news-990527-140736.html*. May 27, 1999.
Oakes, L. Truck stop scoured after clerk disappears. *http://www.startribune.com*. May 28, 1999.
Reyelts, B. I-Team report: NASA scientist enhances Poirier abduction video. *http://www.kbjr.com/special*. July 19, 2000.

the intricacies of various locking devices. A locksmith can be an excellent resource for security professionals who need information about the kinds of locks most appropriate for certain tasks.

Lighting can be the most cost-effective physical security measure. Lighting is an essential element at each line of defense. As with just about every aspect of the security profession, an elite group of security professionals has emerged as experts in the use of lighting for specific security functions. Many homeowners will install floodlights, or what they call "security lights," as a means to deter and detect intruders. Some lights serving this purpose have motion detection triggers, so the intruder assumes that a light coming on means someone has detected the intruder. Remember, lighting can have a direct impact on all levels of physical security—whether the approach to physical security is in terms of exterior and interior threats, lines of defense, or the dynamic Ds.

Alarm systems and **intrusion detection systems** (IDSs) are another common facet of an overall physical security program. In short, an IDS alerts security personnel to an action that endangers (or may endanger) the "security of the facility, a portion thereof, specific areas within, and/or certain equipment and protected information within the facility area."[29] IDS devices can be used to detect a person within an area or provide surveillance to supplement the security of a particular area. For example, an IDS could be used when fewer officers are on security patrol, after normal business hours, or for specific areas within a particular structure or facility. In short, intrusion detection devices allow for more economical use of personnel, provide an additional layer of protection for sensitive or vital areas, and enhance security in areas that are difficult to regulate due to building design, layout, safety regulations, activity operating requirements, costs and budgeting factors, or other locally controlled factors.[30]

Perhaps one of the most common and most visible perimeter protective barriers is a **fence.** Fences with different purposes look different. In some highly secured areas, two or three fences may be built within five or six feet of each other, with razor wire or barbed wire added as an additional deterrent to those wishing to access (or exit) the secured environment. Because fences come in all shapes and sizes and related security needs are just as varied, it is important for the security professional to consider many issues, including the function of the fence, the amount of money available for the fence, and other situational factors when deciding what type of fence to buy and where to put the fence.

Access control points are a likely addition to a perimeter fence. In short, anytime there is a feature in place to control access to specific buildings or areas in buildings, this is an access control point. **Access control** is a straightforward concept; access control features are put in place to regulate or control who is allowed access into specific areas. Whether the access control points take the form of a guard booth, a key card–controlled mechanical arm for parking access, or a swipe card for interior controls, a strategically placed access control feature will restrict access to a facility, or parts of a facility, as security needs dictate. As is the case with lighting, various security professionals are experts in helping security management teams determine the best means for controlling access to various protected areas within a target environment.

OTHER ASPECTS OF A PHYSICAL SECURITY PLAN

As stated earlier, a physical security plan includes any physical measure designed to safeguard people, facilities (or any portion therein), and information against potential threats. Physical security is a fairly comprehensive component of any overall security system design. Within this objective are at least three features to consider: asset protection, the use of technology as/in physical security, and security procedures manuals.

Asset Protection

The concept of **asset protection** is linked to the early security-related efforts focused more specifically on the use of "guards" (although the profession is moving away from using that term and using "protection officers" or "security professionals") and physical security.[31] The IFPO identifies the following categories for assets common to most companies: land, heavy machinery, office equipment, vehicles, goodwill, raw materials, buildings, production equipment, office furniture, cash or other negotiable items, public image, finished product, and personnel.[32] The protection and conservation of assets is where security can make its greatest contribution to an employer.[33]

The Use of Technology as/in Physical Security

Advances in security technologies are making these products an irresistible commodity for many businesses. In his article "The ABC's of Security Technology," Michael Fickes suggests that one of the first things to do is to establish a clear understanding of how that security product fits into the crime prevention/security continuum for the target environment (Figure 5–3). The figure helps illustrate the idea that security and crime prevention objectives encompass various aspects. In short, while a security professional may seek to prevent a crime or deter a criminal, it may be that the crime or emergency happens anyway. In such cases, an alarm or mechanism to notify people of the incident is necessary. Consider a fire. While it is important to understand fire prevention, or to deter someone from maliciously setting a fire, once the fire breaks out an alarm needs to sound and warn people of the potential danger. Also, the target environment may need a mechanism in place to investigate the events leading up to the critical incident. This allows the "victim" to review prevention strategies and incorporate any necessary changes. Once we assess the existing structure, we can modify plans to enhance prevention; this is an ongoing process as illustrated in Figure 5–4. This shows the reader that the security process is an evolving process that emphasizes the prevention objective but also involves these other aspects. For school security, for example, he suggests that emergency communication devices, badging systems, access control and alarm systems, CCTV, metal detection systems, and X-ray screening systems are likely to be used to enhance physical security needs in a school environment.

A second factor involves assessing the technology against the related personnel issues. What technologies would require additional personnel to oversee the technologies? A final issue involves assessing the technology in terms of the additional functions it can perform for the target environment. An access control card could also be used by students as their identification card, their library card, and their meal card, for example.[34] As is the case with concepts of asset protection, technology must be seen as a piece of the overall security objective. It is likely that a significant portion of a security practitioner's time will be spent following technology trends and making assessments about how new technologies can be integrated within the existing security system design.

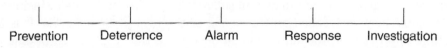

| Prevention | Deterrence | Alarm | Response | Investigation |

FIGURE 5–3   Crime Prevention/Security Continuum
(*Source:* Adapted from "The ABCs of Security Technology" in *American School & University,* Vol. 71, No. 11, July 1999. © 1999, Intertec Publishing, a PRIMEDIA company.)

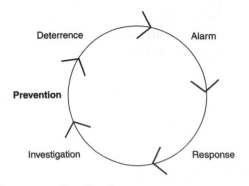

FIGURE 5–4 Technology Integration Continuum
(*Source:* Adapted from "The ABCs of Security Technology" in *American School & University,* Vol. 71, No. 11, July 1999. © 1999, Intertec Publishing, a PRIMEDIA company.)

Security Procedures Manuals

A final, essential element of the overall physical security plan that deserves more than a passing mention is the security procedure manual.[35] The inclusion of the security procedure manual as a physical security measure is debatable. Frankly, few security textbooks talk about it. In short, I consider the procedure manual the backbone of any aspect of the overall security plan. Many security professionals may never encounter circumstances for which they have been trained to respond. When a response is necessary, the security professional must have ready access to a clearly outlined protocol. This is found in the well-placed, clearly identifiable, centrally located security manual. It is not enough to have a sally port as an access control feature; there must be clear guidelines to follow if a breach of the security protocol occurs. As discussed in the introductory chapter, all aspects of the overall security plan should be outlined in some form of a security manual for reference purposes. The security manual, sometimes referred to as a training manual, will take different forms depending on the need of the target environment. As the company outlines its security objectives, and as the security professionals are used to assist the company with these objectives, it becomes critical for the security management team to explain the agreed-on security protocols to every member of the security team.

Because people change and problems occur with varying frequency, it is critical that security professionals make use of a documented reference manual that outlines all aspects of the overall security plan. The elements to include in the manual may vary based on the needs of the agency or business. It is important to provide a procedure manual describing the response to potentially disruptive actions involving employees, customers, or passersby. Furthermore, it is essential to highlight the specific aspects of the manual as they relate to a person's job function, for example.

CONCLUSION

How many lines of physical defense would one expect to find at an international airport? A university campus? A large retail store? A local dry-cleaning establishment? A local attorney's office that is a single office located on the top floor of a downtown skyscraper? A mall? A suburban apartment complex? A post office? Students should think about how physical security works in their community, looking closely at the properties they walk onto and the buildings they enter, taking note of physical security features and features that might impede a security response. Using the information presented in the chapter, students can evaluate the physical security (property, building, and building's inner design) of different environments and think about solutions to any security problems that are evident. Security practitioners need a keen eye for detail.

People who are new to the security industry may have trouble just getting a handle on what *physical security* means. Furthermore, it can be unclear how physical security is connected with other aspects of the overall security objective. Physical security includes all the tangible features of a security program that are implemented to assist the professional attempt to control a target environment. In short, the essential elements to be controlled are property, information, and people. Overall security is enhanced in all areas by an exceptionally well-placed physical security plan.

REVIEW QUESTIONS

1. What three things comprise the centerpoint for physical security concerns?
2. Describe the "onion philosophy" for providing security.
3. What modifications did the author make from the traditional lines of defense graphic (Figure 5–2)? Briefly outline the justifications for those modifications as they were presented by the author.
4. What is access control? Outline various places for access control use.
5. How is a procedure manual linked to physical security?

DISCUSSION QUESTIONS

1. How does CPTED relate to security concerns?
2. List the three different models of physical security outlined in this chapter. What distinction is the author trying to make between these models? Why do you think more than one model was presented?
3. Outline the five Ds. In what circumstance might it be appropriate to reach the fifth D (destroy)?
4. Why does the author suggest that the internal/external approach to security threats is awkward?

5. How would you outline the fundamental areas that must be included in a procedure manual? How would the different areas of the manual vary between target environments?

REFERENCES

1. C. A. Roper, *Physical Security and the Inspection Process* (Newton, MA: Butterworth-Heinemann: 1997), 1.
2. P. Brantingham and P. Brantingham, *Environmental Criminology* (Prospect Heights, IL: Waveland Press, 1981).
3. R. Hunter and C. R. Jeffery, "Preventing Convenience Store Robbery through Environmental Design," in *Situational Crime Prevention: Successful Case Studies,* ed. R. Clarke. (Albany, NY: Harrow and Heston, 1992), 194–204.
4. W. J. Crow and J. L. Bull, *Robbery Deterrence: An Applied Behavioral Science Demonstration—Final Report* (La Jolla, CA: Western Behavioral Sciences Institute, 1975).
5. Hunter and Jeffery, "Preventing Convenience Store Robbery," 195.
6. C. D. Shearing and P. C. Stenning, "Say 'Cheese!': The Disney Order That Is Not So Mickey Mouse," in *Private Policing,* ed. C. D. Shearing and P. P. Stenning (Newbury Park, CA: Sage Publications, 1984), 317–323.
7. Shearing and Stenning, "Say 'Cheese!' " 319.
8. Shearing and Stenning, "Say 'Cheese!' " 317.
9. G. Kelling and J. Q. Wilson, *Atlantic Monthly,* vol. 249, no. 3, pp. 29–38, March 1982.
10. C. Nifong, "One Man's Theory Is Cutting Crime in Urban Streets," *Christian Science Monitor,* February 18, 1997, 1, 10, 11.
11. Nifong, "One Man's Theory," 10.
12. Nifong, "One Man's Theory," 10.
13. R. Meadows, *Fundamentals of Protection and Safety for the Private Protection Officer* (Englewood Cliffs, NJ: Prentice Hall, 1995).
14. C. Simonsen, *Private Security in America: An Introduction* (Upper Saddle River, NJ: Prentice Hall, 1998), 244.
15. Meadows, *Fundamentals of Protection and Safety,* 93.
16. Simonsen, *Private Security in America,* 244.
17. R. Atlas, Site Security Planning and Design Criteria (paper presented at the American Society for Industrial Security International Conference, Las Vegas, NV, September 1999), 12.
18. T. Ricks et al., *Principles of Security,* 3rd ed. (Cincinnati, OH: Anderson Publishing Company, 1994), 247–299.
19. P. Purpura, *Security and Loss Prevention: An Introduction* (Woburn, MA: Butterworth-Heinemann, 1998), 77–96; 123–200.

20. Purpura, *Security and Loss Prevention,* 123.
21. Purpura, *Security and Loss Prevention,* 165.
22. Purpura, *Security and Loss Prevention,* 77.
23. Ricks et al., *Principles of Security,* 247–299.
24. Ricks et al., *Principles of Security,* 247–299.
25. Purpura, *Security and Loss Prevention,* 123–200; Ricks et al., 247–299.
26. Atlas, Site Security Planning and Design Criteria, 12.
27. R. Fischer and G. Green, *Introduction to Security,* 6th ed. (Woburn, MA: Butterworth-Heinneman, 1998).
28. D. O'Sullivan, "Physical Security Planning," in *Protection Officer Training Manual,* 6th ed. (Woburn, MA: Butterworth-Heinmann, 1998), 82.
29. Roper, *Physical Security,* 147.
30. Roper, *Physical Security,* 148.
31. Simonsen, *Private Security in America,* 187.
32. O'Sullivan, "Physical Security Planning," 82.
33. H. Burstein, *Introduction to Security* (Upper Saddle River, NJ: Prentice Hall, 1994), 5.
34. M. Fickes, "The ABC's of Security Technology," *American School and University,* 71(7), 21–25.
35. Roper, *Physical Security,* 195–206.

Information and Computer Security

KEY WORDS

Decrypt
Digital certificate
Encryption
Espionage
Firewall
Information technology

Intrusion and protection system
Password
Public key
Sabotage
Trade secrets

Recent conversations about protecting information have been directly related to computer databases. Information in the modern age has become very nearly inextricably linked to the technologies used for its organization and collection—primarily computer hardware and software. To discuss information security today is to discuss computer security. And to discuss computer security is to discuss how information is processed, organized, and recorded; how and when information is held privately; and how it can best be organized so that it is accessible to the people who need to use it while protected against invasion from people or actions that may harm the system.

This chapter focuses on information in its many forms. Some historical and some modern examples of efforts to maintain the secrecy of a corporate asset are reviewed. Sabotage and espionage are discussed in this context. Furthermore, the explosive impact of the computer age on security professionals and security management protocols is highlighted. Anyone who thinks that a security professional can be all things to a target environment may have a different opinion at the end of this discussion. Because computer technology in its various forms is still changing rapidly, computer security experts cannot seem to meet the security demand.

TRADE SECRETS: IMPORTANT INFORMATION IN A COMPETITIVE MARKETPLACE

In August 2000, Nielsen/NetRatings reported that 52 percent of U.S. homes, or 144 million Americans, have access to the Internet.[1] Forrester Research predicted that in 2004, 70.3 million households—close to 75 percent of all homes—would be online. In the United States, the number of people online in 1993 was estimated at 90,000[2] and went up to 68 million in 1998.[3] As the global community becomes more entrenched in the Information Age, the idea of **information security** has taken center stage in the process of identifying and exploring the overall security objective for any target environment. Information security can be defined as any series of protocols put in place for the protection of sensitive information.

Traditionally, discussions about information security related most directly to the issue of **trade secrets, espionage,** and **sabotage.** Trade secrets are highly sensitive pieces of information whose loss or theft is likely to result in huge losses to a company. Millions of dollars are lost by corporations due to industrial espionage,[4] including ethical, unethical, legal, and illegal means to gather information about a competitor or its product. Sabotage is the destruction of corporate property and is most likely to be of concern during times of company strife, such as during a strike or when layoffs are possible.

Sometimes doing business can seem almost like waging war, in that information is absolutely critical and must be protected. Philip Purpura outlines

Who Am I? Who Are You?

A person could be committing a crime and not even know it. That is, the person's name and personal information could be used in connection with criminal activity while the person is at home watching MTV. The problem: identity theft. All it takes is one mistake, one unguarded moment, and a person's identity can be stolen and ruined. Hundreds of thousands of people each year file complaints of identity theft, which has become one of the fastest-growing crimes in the nation. In March 2000, the Trans Union Credit Bureau reported 522,922 complaints of identity theft, up from 35,235 in 1992.[1]

Some people may believe getting personal, even confidential, information is almost impossible. Or they may think as long as it is not given to an individual with misguided intentions, what's the harm? However, getting the necessary information has become easier and easier. With the flood of telemarketing phone calls and direct mail offering amazing deals, it is seemingly impossible to live completely risk free. The Internet has been helpful to individuals seeking to gain by stealing someone's else's identity. Type "find Social Security numbers" into a search engine, and as many as 65 site links come up. The sites ask for a person's name and address and will locate the correct Social Security number for a small fee of $50 or less.[2]

More traditional methods for acquiring a person's vital information today include dumpster diving and shoulder surfing. When dumpster diving, a criminal goes through garbage cans or dumpsters to obtain copies of checks, credit card and bank statements, and other records that might contain personal information. When shoulder surfing, a criminal watches from a nearby location as a person enters numbers into a machine or listens as the person gives numbers and other information over the telephone.

Congress has decided to do what it can to hinder the actions of criminals in these types of situations. In 1998, the Identity Theft and Assumption Deterrence Act was passed. This act prohibits "knowingly transferring or using, without lawful authority, a means of identification of another person with the intent to commit, or to aid or abet, any unlawful activity that constitutes a violation of Federal law, or that constitutes a felony under any applicable State or local law" [18 USC 1028(a) (7)]. In most circumstances, this offense would carry a maximum term of 15 years imprisonment, a fine, and criminal forfeiture of all personal property that was used or intended to be used in committing the offense.[3] Congress also set restrictions on government and business use of Social Security numbers, which was the source of more than 30,000 reported complaints in 1999.[4]

The United States Department of Justice offers some basic steps people can take to combat identity theft or fraud. The agency says to remember the word "SCAM."

S—Be *stingy* about giving out your personal information to anyone, unless you known you can trust them.

C—*Check* your financial information regularly, looking for what should and should not be there.

A—*Ask* for a copy of your credit report periodically.

M—*Maintain* careful records of your banking and financial accounts.[5]

These steps will help reduce the risk of being a victim of this type of crime. To report this type of crime, people should contact the Federal Trade Commission.

Consumer Response Center, FTC
600 Pennsylvania Avenue NW
Washington, DC 20580
1-877-ID-THEFT (1-877-438-4338) or TDD at 202-326-2502[6]

Because it is so difficult to monitor what every business, school, and organization is requiring as identification, policing this type of activity is very difficult. It continues to be very important that people make efforts to protect themselves. They should shred all papers with important identification information on them, cancel all unused credit cards, carry only a few credit cards, and carry a Social Security card, birth certificate, or passport only when absolutely necessary. By taking a few precautionary measures and remembering the "SCAM" advice, people will be able to protect themselves to a greater extent than if they just relied on legislation.

References

1. Associated Press, "Identity Crisis," *http://moreabsnews.go.com/sections/us/dailynews/identitytheft000315.html*, created March 17, 2000; accessed October 15, 2000.
2. A. S. Marlin, "Online Identity Theft a Growing Concern," created August 16, 2000; accessed October 15, 2000.
3. U.S. Department of Justice, "What's the Department of Justice Doing About Identity Theft and Fraud?" *http://www.usdoj.gov/criminal/fraud/idtheft.html*
4. Marlin, "Online Identity Theft."
5. U.S. Department of Justice, "What Should I Do To Avoid Becoming a Victim of Identity Theft?" *http://www.usdoj.gov/criminal/fraud/idtheft.html*
6. U.S. Department of Justice, "What Should I Do If I've Become a Victim of Identity Theft?" *http://www.usdoj.gov/criminal/fraud/idtheft.html*

three sources of illegally acquired sensitive information: (1) internal sources, (2) external sources, and (3) a conspiracy that combines internal and external sources.[5] Many people may not be aware of the fact that during the Gulf War, there was a kind of war at home between two major chocolate manufacturers who were hoping to secure the government contract for the kind of chocolate to be included in the meals for U.S. soldiers.[6] But tough tactics are not only linked to modern warfare. Millions of dollars in sales go to people who are in the right place at the right time with the right information. Candy manufacturers who can capitalize on trends that are "in" stand to make huge amounts of money. Consider the following passages:

Ever wonder why candy trends seem to come and go all at the same time? A valid explanation, of course, is that popular candies quickly attract followers. But that doesn't explain how thirty different companies all introduced gummy worms, gummy bears, gummy fish, and gummy snakes all in the same year. Or why blue became the hot candy color virtually overnight, with hundreds of companies introducing blue foods at the 1992 national candy trade show in Washington, DC.[7]

"Anyone can read the ingredients on a Hershey bar," explains Hershey's Richard Zimmerman. "But to actually make a Hershey bar, you have to know a lot more than that." Like how the milk is processed to give the bar its distinct flavor. And which varieties of cocoa beans are used to develop the right chocolate liquor. And how long Hershey mixes and blends its chocolate to create that familiar consistency. Those are the real candy mysteries. And Hershey will do everything in its power to keep them mysterious.[8]

Candy companies have to be careful to protect themselves from outsiders—and their own employees.[9] No one discusses new products; marketing plans are disseminated to only a handful of people on a need-to-know basis; recipes are closely guarded in alarmed safes; and the manufacturing process itself is the biggest secret of all. According to a recent profile of two large chocolate manufacturing companies, the companies have been known to design and repair their own machines to reduce the need to bring outsiders in to the facility. Only a few people have been inside the Mars facility, for example, and those who go in must sign confidentiality agreements stating they will never share what they saw. "If Mars needs outside contractors to fix a particular problem, it insists on blindfolding the alien workers and escorting them through the plant to the area in question. Once the problem is resolved, the contractors are blindfolded again and politely removed from the premises."[10]

Large industries have large secrets that need protecting. Part of the role of a comprehensive security professional is to determine what information is of particular value to the company, and then the security professional must make realistic assessments of the amount of loss to the company should the information be stolen. Intellectual property (also referred to as proprietary information),[11] which includes information such as patents, copyrights, and trademarks, has long been protected under federal law. Trade secrets were protected under only state laws until Congress passed the Economic Espionage Act in 1996.[12] Intellectual property typically refers to a discovery, the construction of a product, or information developed during the course of one's work. In most cases, these discoveries become the property of the company that employs the worker and funds the project as proprietary information (although the specifics are explicitly legal and almost always controversial). A current example of an intellectual property controversy can be found in the education industry, most specifically including Internet courses. A raging debate exists in the academic community about whether—more specifically, what percentage of—the money for these courses should come to the university offering the course, the professor using the course, or the professor who originally designed the course.

The 1999 American Society for Industrial Security Intellectual Property Loss Survey Results suggest an estimate of $45 billion dollars in losses to the *Fortune* 1000 companies through various means.[13] The information at greatest risk, according to those companies responding, included

- customer lists
- financial data

- research and development information
- merger/acquisition information
- strategic plans
- unannounced product information
- second-party information
- prototype information
- manufacturing information

Various introductory-level security textbooks outline techniques for reducing company losses. I like, among others, Dennis Dalton's review, which includes various activities for identifying and outlining a company's "collateral value."[14] His approach includes a discussion about defining and assessing value, protecting proprietary property and confidential information, assessing and countering threats, and devising defensive strategies for defending assets.

COMPUTER CRIME ENFORCEMENT: A RETURN TO THE WILD WEST

Law enforcement and security-related professionals' attempts to "police" cyberspace today are somewhat akin to efforts at law enforcement and private security in the Wild West. As the United States expanded to the west, individuals and communities sometimes looked to less than honest and upright citizens for protection. These individuals were sometimes hired as "marshals" and became part of the "public law enforcement" effort.[15] Their connection to mainstream law enforcement may have been less than direct. Consider also the early "strikebreakers" who had the reputation for being "hired thugs."[16] The rogue player in today's game is the computer hacker.

One of the most interesting and perhaps disturbing aspects of the deficient market of computer security experts is the fact that after a company's security protocols have been breached, the company will often seek to hire rather than prosecute the offender. In one case, a 15-year-old student used his high school computer to hack into the computers of a software firm.[17] While the principal of the school tried to warn the student's parents to hire a lawyer, suggesting that the student was in real trouble, the student was completely unconcerned and made plans to get an agent—whose first client received "$1 million, a monster truck, and 'free agency,' meaning he can go work for a competitor at any time."[18] *Computer Insider*, a newsletter for hackers, estimated that about 900 recreational hackers have been hired in the last four years by companies they once targeted.[19]

Of course, the actions of these individuals taken against companies look a lot like protection rackets, but because the companies are refusing to prosecute, police have no recourse. The computer expert e-mails the head of a corporation and says, "I was just looking at your Web page, and wouldn't it be awful if something happened to it. I know a few things about computers, and for the right price, I can make sure that you are protected against outside attacks." Consider the case where a hacker broke into a regional department store's computer and instructed it to credit his Visa card approximately $500 per day. According to officials, "the boy racked up more than $32,000 in credit before he was caught—but the store wouldn't press charges. Not only did they let him keep the money, they threw in a $1,500 shopping spree—all in exchange for showing them how to improve their security."[20] It is pretty amazing that young kids are getting attention from software firms by breaking into their databases.

But businesses are not the only targets for computer security threats. Computer threats are finding their way into the mainstream in various forms. In late March 1999, the United States first learned about the Melissa virus, which ultimately clogged e-mail systems around the world. The virus was disguised as an e-mail marked "important message." Every time the mail was opened, the virus (a macro program) would tell the computer to send out 50 additional messages. David L. Smith, a former computer programmer, was arrested in April 1999 and allegedly admitted "to writing the 'Melissa' macro virus, illegally accessing America Online for the purposes of posting the virus onto cyberspace, and destroying the personal computers he used to post 'Melissa.' "[21]

In early February 2000, a hacker effectively shut down various Internet sites. The Federal Bureau of Investigation (FBI) was called in, and while the effects of the cyberattack were headline news for at least a week, the perpetrators went undetected for weeks. A 15-year-old Canadian teen, "Mafiaboy," who bragged about his exploits in chat rooms, and according to police made minimal efforts to cover his tracks, was eventually arrested in mid-April on two counts of mischief attacks against CNN, Yahoo!, eBay, and Amazon.com.[22,23] This "electronic assault" was described as "inconvenient" to users and "unnerving" to Wall Street.[24] Ironically, commentary in the early days of the "assault" suggested that the campaign waged by these hackers (initially, there were thought to be several hackers rather than one), referred to as a "denial of service" attack (where a barrage of messages is sent to computers that run Web sites), is a "crude and amateurish way of taking down a web site."[25] During this type of attack, legitimate Internet users encounter what would be comparable to a constant busy signal and therefore are denied access.[26]

In the wake of these highly publicized attacks, and even amidst calls for heightened high-tech security from businesses and the government, computer security experts admit there is no ironclad protection.[27] To add to the difficulty, it appeared after the initial attacks that third-party computers were being used. This means that the attack protocol could be placed in a computer whose operator is unaware of the protocol and be triggered from a remote location.

Smith, the author of the Melissa virus, was charged with interruption of public communications, conspiracy, and theft of computer service. The maximum penalty for the offense is 40 years in prison.[28,29] Penalties for Mafiaboy

and other individuals caught are unclear because of their age and the uncer-
tainties regarding the legal options available and a willingness to prosecute.
Penalties are speculated to be as much as five years in prison and a $250,000
fine. Computer security experts take opportunities like these to remind people
that the majority of companies have not really focused efforts on computer security.[30] The FBI began investigating after Yahoo! was made inaccessible for
several hours on February 7, 2000. On February 8, Buy.com, Amazon.com,
eBay, and CNN.com were attacked. After the February 10 attacks on the technology site ZDNet and the online trading site E*TRADE, it is believed that as
many as 13 Web sites suffered attacks. President Clinton responded by organizing a meeting of top computer security experts with his national security ad-
viser.[31] The investigation allegedly involved five FBI field offices and led the FBI
to at least four other countries, according to FBI director Louis Freeh.[32]

WHO NEEDS COMPUTER SECURITY?

Everyone—individuals, students, families, business professionals, and corporate executives—is scrambling to keep up with all of the advances in computer
technologies. As hardware and software are improved, people find themselves
using programs and equipment they do not fully understand. People everywhere are going online. In fact, the Bill and Melinda Gates Foundation has been
responsible for putting computers in public libraries across the country to ensure that everyone has access to the Internet. While this means that people
everywhere will have access to computers, it also means that people everywhere are vulnerable to computer threats. Even if a person believes that he or
she has nothing that anyone would want, plenty of unsuspecting people have
become "zombie" or third-party hosts.

Almost two years ago, it became clear to me that, even with my boring life
as a college professor, I would need to pay more attention to computer security. Through my university appointment, I am hooked up to the university network. Furthermore, I have a phone line at home dedicated to the computer,
with software that allows me to hook up to the university computer from my
home. At about 5 P.M. on a Sunday evening, someone called my home and identified himself as an employee of the phone company. He suggested that they
were running a check on the phone lines, then asked for the phone number to
the second phone line in my home. I was somewhat suspicious because there
was a lot of noise in the background while this individual was talking to me. I
told him that quite frankly I did not know the number. Then this person said,
"Yeah, whatever. I must have the wrong number," and hung up. I called the
phone company, then the police. Both agencies agreed the phone call was suspicious. The phone company told me that it does not do service checks on Sun-
days, although it does them on weekdays and sometimes Saturdays. I was sure

the phone company would want to get as much information as possible because it could stand to lose a lot of money should my number be fraudulently used for overseas calls, for example. But the phone company representative did not so much as ask a question. The police said they would file a report, but there "really wasn't anything they could do." Interestingly enough, I live in a small suburb of a central city. The police departments in my area are not hooked up to a central network, so the officer I spoke with could not tell me if other people in the area had reported calls like mine.

I was just really curious about what this unknown outsider wanted. I talked with people from the university computer network division, and they suggested that the caller might have been seeking remote access to the Internet using that second phone line. Being really new to the whole world of computer security, I said, "Well, they couldn't know I had a second line dedicated to my computer." The response: "First, you're a college professor, so it was a good guess; and second, he didn't have to know, you told him you did."

This served as my first lesson in computer security, and it certainly would not be my last. Even as I was outlining drafts of some of the first chapters in this book, I again had firsthand experience with computer security concerns. Within six months, I had two virus scares. First, several viruses were embedded in e-mail attachments from a colleague (yes, another security professional). Second, my e-mail address was listed in the address book of another colleague, a bright young woman who left the police department to go back to graduate school, and when she received a virus from a friend, the virus sent out e-mail to everyone in the young woman's address book. Luckily she was sharp enough to phone the affected people and warn them before they opened the e-mail.

I hope this illustrates the important fact that computer issues affect everyone. Even if people are not working in a network environment in which government secrets are being protected, one virus can wreak havoc in documents that are important in everyday life. In my case, I would have been more than annoyed to lose the almost eight months of work on this book project, not to mention grades for students, professional papers and research projects, and important correspondence from university committees and colleagues. Who needs computer security? Everyone does.

COMPUTER SECURITY OPERATIONS AND OCCUPATIONS

For the first three quarters of 1999, the Computer Emergency Response Team Coordinating Center logged 6844 intruder activity incidents or network security attacks that it investigated or issued advisories on. This included virus attacks, network probes, password hacking, and the use of break-in scanning tools.[33] With such a rapidly changing industry, **information technology** (IT) managers have a hard job. They are responsible for organizing computer systems and developing useful programs and procedures for people to use this information as it is intended; however, they also must be sure to protect those same systems from improper use. According to the 1998 Computer Crime and Security Survey (conducted by the Computer Security Institute and the FBI), security managers said that almost as many unauthorized attempts to get at sensitive information came from inside the enterprise as from the outside.[34] Consider the example of "City of Hope."[35]

> City of Hope National Medical Center (and Beckman Research Institute) is one of the world's leading research and treatment centers for cancer and other catastrophic diseases, including diabetes and HIV/AIDS. The work conducted at City of Hope is shared with medical centers worldwide. It is one of the largest providers of bone marrow transplantation services in the U.S. and is open 24 hours a day, seven days a week. They see an average of 16,000 people as outpatients, and 4,000 as inpatients per year. Among their 3,000 employees are more than 100 full-time physicians and 180 basic research scientists. Because it is a research facility AND a medical facility, all the research requires documentation—all of which is classified information stored on electronic files throughout the Center. Researchers need access to the information 24/7, while other medical staff have additional requirements to access the system anytime, anywhere. The environment requires a balance between the need to protect internal data while allowing researchers and physicians access to the information. Furthermore, City of Hope needed a secure way to send medical records to partners, such as insurance companies.[36]

Questions about whether an organization needs assistance with its computer security planning are best left to those who know the most about the information in the target environment and its value to the company. In most settings, even security professionals are likely to seek an outside contract with a respected computer security professional. Personal or business computers, Internet connections, and network environments are technical enough to warrant attention from specialized security professionals.

LAW ENFORCEMENT AND INDUSTRY RESPOND

Computer systems are rapidly becoming the predominant arena for crime.[37] In January 1999, the Kroll O'Gara Company, a private security and investigation company in New York, acquired Securify Inc., a Silicon Valley computer security firm, for $55.2 million in stocks. Such big-dollar acquisitions in the computer security industry suggest that computer professionals anticipate an era in which fighting computer crime will be as big a business as Internet commerce.[38]

After 9/11, President Bush created a position titled "Special Advisor to the President for Cyberspace Security," suggesting the need to protect against the

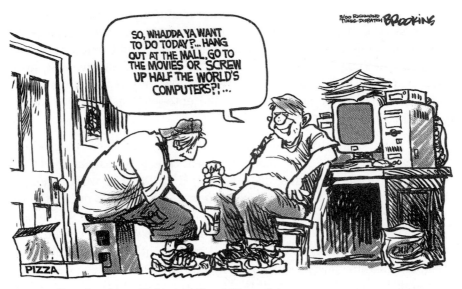

(*Source:* Gary Brookins, *Richmond Times-Dispatch.*)

possibility of an attack on the computer infrastructure that affects how business is conducted, how the government does its work, and how national defense is coordinated.*

Broader efforts to determine the impact of computer crimes on the public combine with attempts to determine an appropriate law enforcement response to computer crimes. Law enforcement has long been identified with policing, patrolling, arresting, servicing citizen complaints, and investigating crimes that have already happened. The explosion of crime on the Internet and in the computer industry has law enforcement divided between determining how relevant traditional law enforcement responses are and playing catchup in places where the public response is not as sophisticated as private business efforts. Although the crimes are technologically based, law enforcement officers are still dealing with people. Consequently, basic police investigation techniques can be implemented to provide a guide for adapting basic investigative skills to computer-related incidents, whether the criminal activities involve physical damage to equipment, manipulation of programming code, or simply using a computer as a means to an illegal end.[39]

Companies deal with threats from the outside and from within. The complexities of Internet-based financial systems leave many companies unable to adequately assess the risks they face. For example, a company may create a

---

*"Fact Sheet on New Counter-Terrorism and CyberSpace Positions." Office of the Press Secretary, The White House. *http://www.whitehouse.gov/news/release/2001/10/20011009.html.* Site constructed October 9, 2001. Last visited August 15, 2002.

"virtual private network" that allows people in different branches of the company to communicate on the Internet. But this may leave the company vulnerable to insider fraud, the most prevalent type of computer crime.[40]

Another difficulty in enforcing computer crime issues involves the response to these activities by private businesses, as discussed previously. Law enforcement officials complain that deals between companies and their online predators have made prosecution of online security breaches impossible. "We are basically paralyzed right now," explains Jim Ghort, who directs the Center for Interstate Online Investigations, a joint police project of 18 states. "We can't arrest or prosecute most hackers, because corporate victims are refusing to come forward. This is a huge problem."[41]

Computer Security: A Scarce Resource

Perhaps one of the most difficult jobs an IT manager has is to convince upper management that computer security protections are necessary. While reasons for hacking and other security breaches are being debated, breaches of programs like Microsoft Excel and Hotmail stress the fact that such breaches could happen in almost any given target environment.[42]

Efforts to protect computer systems are particularly difficult, complicated in part because skilled professionals who understand computer operations are hard to find. Related to this is the fact that computer technicians who do help provide oversight of existing computer security do not come cheap.[43] "Security vendors estimate that the IT industry will need 500,000 new computer security consultants over the next three years. As of the end of the century, only about eight American universities have programs specifically for computer security."[44] Consequently, security vendors have had to develop their own security training programs (Exhibit 6–1).

Exhibit 6–1 Computer Security Training Program Offered by Axent, of Rockville, Maryland

Level 1 Certification (enterprise security practitioner):	Level 2 Certification (enterprise security architect):
Network and operating systems skills	Completion of Level 1 certification
One information security topics course	Four security-related courses
Three product certification courses	Two advanced topics courses
Written and practical exam	Written and practical exam

Note: This program is structured to take 9 to 12 months to complete.
Source: J. Kersletter, "Wanted: Security Help; IT Labor Skills Shortage Extends to Encryption, Firewall Experts," *PC Week 16,* no. 4 (1999): 15.

Further evidence suggests that computer security is not being invested in as heavily as it should be. At a recent public conference, Scott Charney, chief of the Computer Crime and Intellectual Property Section for the Department of Justice's Criminal Division, said that "most organizations, including the federal agencies, should be spending 10 to 15 percent of their total information technology budget on security, but most organizations are barely spending 1 or 2 percent."[45] In part, this reality is connected to the complexities of a computer system or network, but it is also due in large part to a gap in communication between computer security practitioners and the personnel working within the company. Basic elements of the most common security breaches must be relayed to personnel. They too have a role to play in the overall security objective for the company's computer security. For instance, companies need to make sure to have separate systems for public access networks and internal networks; many companies do not. Some of the most common tricks for getting private information needed to gain access are not relayed to employees; therefore, employees may unsuspectingly give out relevant information to individuals posing as company officials to get enough information to hack into the system.[46] So, while it is essential to understand the importance of having a strong computer security program, it is also important to communicate well with employees about the ways in which that system might be breached.

Security Countermeasures

David Thompson, writing in *PC Week,* suggests that the list for "knitting a tight security blanket" include at least the following:

1. "Smart" people: Preferably security engineers.
2. A good look at security needs versus normal business operations: A restrictive security system can reduce a competitive business edge.
3. Firewalls: Control the types of traffic that come into and leave your network
4. Virtual private networks: Use encryption—encode or decode.
5. Virus protections: Software that scans documents for viruses.
6. Intrusion detection software: Tells you if anyone has been in your system.
7. Limited exposure: Make sure people on the inside do not have access to important company information.[47]

Security experts suggest that appropriate computer security technologies are out there; people just have to use them. In the case of the "denial of service" attack where hackers attempt to jam or block access to a particular internet location, computer security professionals say that existing software can protect Web sites from this kind of attack, but the sites do not want to use it because it makes their pages load more slowly.[48] And voice recognition software, al-

Mega-Bytes

- The capacity of the Internet backbone to carry information is doubling every 100 days.
- In just the last 24 hours, the Web has added 3,180,000 new pages, 59,200,000,000 new bytes of text, 716,000 new images, and 11,900,000,000 new bytes of image data.
- The average life span of a Web page is about 44 days.
- The Web now contains over one billion unique, indexable documents.
- Sixty-nine percent of all adults use a computer at home, work, or some other location (up 19 percent from 1995).
- The number of electronic mailboxes worldwide jumped 84 percent to almost 570 million in 1999 and should reach one billion by the end of 2001.
- Analysts forecast that netizens will spend 5.3 percent of their lives on the Internet.
- More than 5 million Americans joined the online world in the first quarter of 2000, which averages out to roughly 55,000 new users each day, 2,289 new users each hour, or 38 new users each minute.
- On average, the American worker spends 35 percent of his/her workday on the computer and 23 percent of his/her workday on the Internet.
- 61.5 million Americans will be using wireless devices to access the Internet in 2003, up from 7.4 million in the United States today (728 percent increase).
- The U.S. Postal Service delivered 101 billion pieces of paper mail in 1998. Estimates for e-mail messages sent in 1998 range from 618 billion to 4 trillion.

HOW LONG TO REACH 30% PENETRATION?

- Internet—7 years
- Television—17 years
- Telephone—38 years
- Electricity—46 years
- 332.73 million people worldwide have Internet access.
- There will be 830 million wireless Internet access devices deployed worldwide by 2005, with more people accessing the Internet by mobile phones than by PCs.
- By year-end 2000 there will be 375 million Internet users, up 100 million since 1999.
- There are 435 million electronic mailboxes worldwide, serving an estimated 200 million email users worldwide (up 66 percent since September 1998).
- Inner-city dwellers with access to computers and the Internet are as active online, if not more so, than the general U.S. user population (30 percent of these users buy goods online, compared with 27 percent of the general user population).
- Over 50 percent of U.S. college students now surf the Net from their dorm room, while 84 percent access the Net from another campus location.
- This summer 82 percent of college graduates will search for career and employment information online.
- Ninety-two percent of CEOs, CFOs, and CIOs had Net access in 1998, up from 90 percent in 1997, with 83 percent going online at least once a week, up from 71 percent the previous year.[1]

References

1. Cisco Systems Government Affairs—Facts & Stats *http://www.ieng.com/warp/public/779/govtaff/facts/factsNStats/Internet_Usage.html.*

though not perfect, is an option.[49] A report in *PC Magazine* concluded that efforts to subvert face recognition technologies were more successful than efforts to crack fingerprint or voice recognition systems.[50]

Penetration analysis, or "ethical hacking," is one way for businesses to find and fill holes in their computer networks.[51] Issues related to security breaches on the Internet are another logical focal point for IT security managers.[52] In 1997, SATAN (Security Analysis Tool for Auditing Networks) developer Dan Farmer raised questions when he used SATAN to "surreptitiously probe more than 2,000 Internet hosts."[53] While his tactics were questionable, he reported that nearly two-thirds were vulnerable to penetration by hackers.

Clearly, various articles and speakers have focused on outlining methods for enhancing computer security needs.[54–57] The number of resources is likely to continue to increase. Yet industry has another option if computer security is not up to par. New York insurance consultant Marsh U.S.A. Inc. has put forward a new insurance program to help companies cover e-business exposures.[58] Currently, only about six companies exist nationwide that carry the insurance, however, because the risks are so high. The program, NetSecure, is designed to help businesses facing lawsuits or other fallout attributed to Internet-related risks.

In a short review of computer security essentials, it should be clear that, as in other types of security, security professionals must consider the context in which the system is being used. They must have a clear sense of the business operations, the way in which the computer system is to be used within those business operations, and the costs—or difficulties for the business operations—associated with the various computer security options. The National Institute of Standards and Technology (NIST) recommends six ways to augment computer security:

1. Develop and implement security policies and architectures.
2. Embrace obvious solutions: password, virus detection tools, intrusion detection tools, digital certificates, public keys and firewalls.
3. Test systems continuously.
4. Configure systems with security in mind.
5. Buy independently evaluated and tested security tools.
6. Add support for security despite limited information technology budgets.[59]

Let us look briefly at some of the standard computer security options mentioned, in item 2, as "obvious solutions" for computer security. Most of us are familiar with the use of passwords. A **password** is a program that allows the user to identify a word that then must be provided to gain access to the computer terminal. The use of personal identification numbers at ATMs, for example, involves the same idea.[60] A **firewall** is a standard means of protecting a network system against attacks from the Internet. Intrusion detection systems are also a means to protect the network from outside access, but an **intrusion and protection system** shuts down access to networked computers when a breach is detected. BlackICE is a popular example of this type of program. This technology takes firewalls one step further because it logs evidence of attempted break-ins. The software is "aware" of over 200 intrusion techniques, so when an attack is executed against the system, BlackICE detects it and blocks all access from the intruder's IP address.[61] Depending on the level of security required for a system, this intrusion program could be recommended as a second level of protection, in addition to a firewall. A **digital certificate** works like a user identification card. It is a unique certificate, stored and processed on a central server and issued to each employee or business affiliate. Specific users can then be given access to specific applications. **Encryption** programs are used to scramble the data. In short, the person must receive the "**public key**," or the code necessary to **decrypt**—or translate—to retrieve the requested information.

Various technological advancements focused on computer security are emerging as interest in computer security—and, more important, threats to computer security—increases. Spending on Internet infrastructure is expected to quadruple to $1.5 trillion by the year 2003, surpassing the $1.3 trillion that will be spent on e-commerce in that same year.[62] Ensuring the protection of these investments is an emerging security essential.

CONCLUSION

Security professionals attempting to protect computer systems are learning some hard lessons about making sure their computers are protected from violation. In large part, computer security is an emerging area of concentration. Efforts to protect trade secrets are likely to involve some form of computer security. Security measures to protect against computer hackers, or any other misdirected individuals seeking access to a system, can be put in place to protect information that is important to the company, whether that be a trade secret or client information in a confidential file. Companies seeking to protect their systems have been known to request assistance and guidance from the very people who were able to hack into the companies' systems. These activities are proving disturbing to law enforcement officers, who are seeking legislation, such as the Uniform Computer Security Act of 1994, to assist with efforts to prosecute these people.

As activity increases on the Internet, more difficulties are likely. E-commerce is an emerging area, and the difficulties with such a system are virtually unknown. The capabilities to integrate and store information are seemingly endless. Computers afford people the ability to have access to information 24 hours a day, seven days a week. Information security, overshadowed by computer security because most information these days is stored on computers, is

Kids Will Be . . . Ph.D.s?

While most 16-year-old high school students are excited about getting their driver's license, Sarah Flannery, a 16-year-old girl from Ireland, is excited about something a lot more remarkable. She has devised a method of encoding important information, such as credit card numbers, as they are transmitted via the Internet. Using a method of two-by-two matrices-based multiplication,[1] her new encryption is praised as being just as secure but between 10 and 30 times as fast as the one currently in use, designed by three students from the Massachusetts Institute of Technology.

This new technology is making such a splash because estimates claim that by 2002, approximately "$426 billion worth of commerce will be done on the Internet, and all deals will be signed and documented using an encryption system."[2] This new encryption system could put Internet commerce skeptics at ease, for it makes it nearly impossible for outsiders to unscramble confidential information that is transmitted via computer.[2]

How did Sarah make her discovery? In March of 1998, Sarah spent two weeks getting work experience at Baltimore Technologies, based in Dublin, Ireland. There she met Michael Purser, who had written a paper about the new mathematics of encryption. He left it on his desk while he was on a holiday leave, and it was then that Sarah saw his idea and decided to give it a go. She did the programming in three days.[3] Sarah has named her new method of encryption the "Cayley-Purser Algorithm," after Arthur Cayley, a nineteenth-century Cambridge expert on matrices, and Purser.[4]

Sarah Flannery gives credit to her father, David, a mathematics professor at Cork Institute of Technology. She says that he used to drag her to night classes, where she fell in love with the subject.[5] According to Baltimore Technologies' senior cryptographer, Sarah "mastered the graduate level mathematics needed for the project in about three days" and could easily hold her own with the top mathematicians in the company.[6]

Even with its grand reception, Sarah's encryption program will have to stand the test of time. These kinds of "new algorithms are only accepted by the crypto community after years of detailed public analysis by world experts," added Ian Goldberg, a researcher in Computer Security and Cryptography at the University of California at Berkeley.[7] Despite all this, her project has garnered her numerous awards, including first prize at the Irish Young Scientists and Technology Exhibition, awards from the Intel and the American Mathematics Association, many scholarship and employment offers, and Esat Telecom's Young Scientist of the Year award. So what does the media-dubbed "genius" plan to do with her award-winning project, which has the potential to make her a very large amount of money? She said that she intends to publish her findings rather than patent them, because making a profit would go against the spirit of science. "I certainly didn't set out on this project to make money. I set out to have some fun with it," she claimed.[8] For now, Sarah Flannery will go back to being her school soccer team's star midfielder, back to her karate lessons, and most important, back to being a teenager.

References

1. R. Lemos, *http://www.zdnet.com/zdnn/stories/news/0,4586,2189301,00.html*, January 18, 1999.
2. Irish Independent Online, *http://www.independent.ie/1999/19/d14a.shtml*, January 20, 1999.
3. Irish Independent Online.
4. N. McKay, "Teen Devices New Crypto Ciphers," *http://www.wired.com/news/technology/0,1282,17330-2,00.html*, January 14, 1999.
5. Irish Independent Online.

6. McKay, "Teen Devises New Crypto Cipher."
7. McKay, "Teen Devises New Crypto Cipher."
8. CNN.com, "Irish Teen's E-mail Code Could Transform Internet Commerce," *http://www.cnn.com/TECH/computing/9901/14/e-mail.genius/index.html,* January 14, 1999.

Sources

ABCNEWS.com, "Irish Teens Invents New Code," *http://abcnews.go.com/sections/tech/DailyNews/encryption990113.html,* January 13, 1999.

still an essential security-related concept because companies must assess what information is the most critical to their operation and then take security-related measures in response to that assessment.

While the information may be the important piece, the computer security practices are likely to be responsible for protecting the information. The two seem to be inextricably intertwined, to a large degree, for the foreseeable future.

REVIEW QUESTIONS

1. What is the biggest problem with law enforcement's response to computer hackers and other computer crimes?
2. Does intellectual property usually belong to the person who created or invented something or the company he or she works for?
3. What makes Sarah Flannery's method of computer encoding so interesting?
4. How is a SCAM useful to protect yourself against identity theft?

DISCUSSION QUESTIONS

1. What elements of the information about corporate secrets and the candy industry were particularly interesting or even surprising to you?
2. How is computer crime compared to the Wild West?
3. What computer security devices do you use on your computer at work, school, or home? How could your computer system be made more secure?
4. Do businesses help or hinder law enforcement efforts to arrest computer criminals? Explain.

REFERENCES

1. B. Charny, "More U.S. Households On Line Than Not: Cheaper Computers, Free ISPs Are Shrinking the Digital Divide, Separate Studies Show," *http://*

www.zdnet.com/zdnn/stories/news/0,4586,2616761,00.html, August 17, 2000, accessed November 7, 2000.

2. Cisco Systems Facts and Stats, Government Affairs Facts and Stats, "United States: Number of Americans Online—Historical," *http://www. ieng.com/warp/public/779/govtaff/factsNStats/Internet_Usage.html,* accessed November 7, 2000.

3. Cisco Systems Facts and Stats, "United States: Number of Americans Online—Historical."

4. M. Nalla and G. Newman, *A Primer in Private Security* (New York: Harrow and Heston, 1990), 2–3.

5. P. Purpura, *Security and Loss Prevention: An Introduction,* 3rd ed. (Woburn, MA: Butterworth-Heinemann, 1998), 418.

6. J. G. Brenner, *The Emperors of Chocolate: Inside the Secret World of Hershey and Mars* (New York: Broadway Books, 2000), 3–18.

7. Brenner, *The Emperors of Chocolate,* 26.

8. Brenner, *The Emperors of Chocolate,* 27.

9. Brenner, *The Emperors of Chocolate,* 26–29.

10. Brenner, *The Emperors of Chocolate,* 28.

11. D. Dalton, *The Art of Successful Security Management* (Woburn, MA: Butterworth-Heinemann, 1998), 273.

12. E. Fraumann and J. Koletar, "Trade Secret Safeguards," *Security Management,* March 1999, 63–66.

13. D. Smartwood, 1999 ASIS Intellectual Property Loss Survey Results (ASIS International Security Conference, Las Vegas, NV, September 1999).

14. Dalton, *The Art of Successful Security Management,* 273.

15. C. B. Little and C. Sheffield, "Frontiers and Criminal Justice: English Private Prosecution Societies and American Vigilantism in the Eighteenth and Nineteenth Centuries," *American Sociological Review* 48 (1983): 796–808.

16. N. J. Smelser, *Social Change in the Industrial Revolution* (Chicago: University of Chicago Press, 1959), 13.

17. S. Glass, "Hack Heaven," *New Republic 218,* no. 20 (1998): 11–12.

18. Glass, "Hack Heaven," 11.

19. Glass, "Hack Heaven,"11.

20. Glass, "Hack Heaven," 12.

21. Associated Press, "Man Admits Virus Creation? Prosecutor Says Suspect Reveals Melissa Origin," *http://abcnews.go.com/sections/tech/DailyNews/ virus_melissa990825.html,* August 25, 1999; accessed November 7, 2000.

22. S. Segan, "Tracking 'Mafiaboy's' Steps," *http://abcnews.go.com/sections/ tech/DailyNews/webattacks000420.html,* April 20, 2000; accessed November 7, 2000.

23. J. Dube, "'Mafiaboy' Suspected: FBI Has Evidence That He and Others Launched Web Attacks, Expert Says," *http://abcnews.go.com/sections/tech/DailyNews/webattacks000216.html*, February 16, 2000; accessed November 7, 2000.

24. "Hackers Hit More Web Sites; Attacks Felt on Wall Street," *St. Cloud Times,* February 10, 2000, 1A; accessed November 7, 2000.

25. M. J. Martinez, "Hackers Call Web Attacks Amateurish," *http://wire.ap.org/APnews/center_story.thml?FRONTID+TECHNOLOGY&STORYID=APIS7 2HDF680*, February 10, 2000; accessed November 7, 2000.

26. Martinez, "Hackers Call Web Attacks Amateurish."

27. D. E. Kalish, "Companies Urged to Boost Cyber Security," *http://wire.ap.org/APnews/center_story.thml?FRONTID+TECHNOLOGY&STORYID=APIS7 2HDF680*, February 10, 2000; accessed November 7, 2000.

28. Associated Press, "Man Admits Virus Creation?"

29. Associated Press, "Feds Plan Penalties for Hackers," *http://wire.ap.org/APnews/center_story.thml?FRONTID+TECHNOLOGY&STORYID=APIS7 2HDF680*, February 20, 2000; accessed November 7, 2000.

30. Segan, "Tracking 'Mafiaboy's' Steps."

31. Segan, "Tracking 'Mafiaboy's' Steps."

32. Segan, "Tracking 'Mafiaboy's' Steps."

33. M. J. Miller, "PC Magazine's Technical Excellence Awards: Utilities," *PC Magazine,* 14 December 1999, 101.

34. S. Neil, "Arming the Network with Digital IDs," *PC Week,* March 1, 1999, 123.

35. "City of Hope Establishes Security Strategy To Enable E-Business," *Health Management Technology* 20, no. 7 (1999): 44.

36. "City of Hope," 44.

37. R. Mendell, "Matching Wits against Bits," *Security Management,* May 1999, 36–43.

38. J. Markoff, "New York Investigation Firm Plans To Buy Internet Consultant," *New York Times,* January 4, 1999, A13.

39. Mendell, "Matching Wits against Bits," 36.

40. Markoff, "New York Investigation Firm," A13.

41. Glass, "Hack Heaven," 12.

42. "It Could've Been You," *PC Week,* September 13, 1999: 72.

43. J. Kerstetter, "Wanted: Security Help; IT Labor Skills Shortage Extends to Encryption, Firewall Experts," *PC Week 16,* no. 4 (1999): 15.

44. Kerstetter, "Wanted: Security Help," 15.

45. Kerstetter, "Wanted: Security Help," 15.

46. C. J. Dorobek, "Justice Official Says Agencies Spend Way Too Little on Systems Security," *Government Computer News 18,* no. 20 (1999): 44.

47. Dorobek, "Justice Official," 44.

48. D. Thompson, "Knitting a Tight Security Blanket," *PC Week,* November 15, 1999, 140.

49. Martinez, "Hackers Call Web Attacks Amateurish."

50. "Breaking In: Voice Authentication," *PC Magazine,* February 23, 1999, 174.

51. "Breaking In: Face Recognition," *PC Magazine,* February 23, 1999, 174.

52. N. Nicolaisen, "Hackers Go Pro," *Computer Shopper 19,* no. 2 (1999): 400.

53. J. Rapoza, "Government Hacks Should Spur IT Security Sweep," *PC Week 16,* no. 23 (1999): 1.

54. G. Anhes, "The Work of SATAN," *Computerworld 31,* no. 2 (1997): 53.

55. S. Ricciardi, "In Pursuit of Internet Intruders," *PC Magazine,* June 7, 1999, 247.

56. R. P. Lipschutz, "Firewall: Guard Your Perimeter," *PC Magazine 18,* no. 15 (1999): 151.

57. B. Brown, "Effective Security," *PC Magazine,* 16 November, 1999, 213.

58. E. Gonzalez, "Latest Insurance Protects Businesses from Web Problems," *http://www.insidedenver.com/business/0210mars().html,* February 10, 2000; accessed November 7, 2000.

59. F. Tiboni, "Feds Make Security Recommendations to Hill," *Government Computer News 18,* no. 20 (1999): 45.

60. C. J. Dorobek, "CIOs Tell Agencies To Prepare for Post-2000 Security Push," *Government Computer News 18,* no. 7 (1999): 8.

61. National Institute of Standards and Technology, "Guide for Developing Security Plans for Information Technology Systems," *http://csrc.nist.gov/publications/nistpubs/index.html,* created July 15, 2000; accessed January 18, 2001.

62. Miller, "PC Magazine's Technical Excellence Awards: Utilities," 101.

Personnel and Security Management

CHAPTER HIGHLIGHTS

Personnel management (and related issues)
  1. Employees
  2. Customers
  3. Visitors
Models of security management
  1. Resident managers
  2. Contract provider as security man-
    ager

  3. Nonsecurity security manager
Policies and procedures
*Review of issues that affect safety and
  security in the target environment*
Involving personnel in asset protection
*Security personnel versus personnel
  and security*

KEY WORDS

Contract provider as security manager
Contract security services
Development

Education
Human resources departments
Interrogations

Interviews   Security management
Nonsecurity security manager   Security personnel
Personnel security   Shrinkage
Private corporate justice   Training
Resident manager   Workplace violence

Efforts to create a stable, predictable environment can be impeded anytime the security equation includes the human factor. This is particularly tricky because, at this point, all forms of security management strategies require some level of human involvement. When working with people, one must learn to expect the unexpected. People who need assistance finding their destination, changing a flat tire in the parking lot, or any number of more serious issues (having a medical emergency, being the victim of a crime) look to security professionals for leadership and support.

This chapter discusses security practices directed toward managing personnel, including employees, customers, and visitors (vendors, employee family members, or others). The security team's responsibility to provide protection for personnel within the larger target environment is discussed. Security management models are discussed, and the importance of developing policies and procedures and putting them together in a policy and procedure manual is also discussed as an essential part of any overall security plan. Issues of importance for organizing and managing a security division are considered. Common examples to be discussed include applicant screening, outside contracting, investigations, and responsibilities to existing employees.

To ensure adequate protection for personnel within a target environment, attention should be focused on maintaining a stable, predictable environment that is safe for all people, which involves preventing employee theft, workplace violence, sexual (or other types of) harassment, and drug use and abuse among employees. Readers should keep in mind a familiar target environment as they consider the information presented in this chapter.

THE ROLE OF SECURITY IN PERSONNEL MATTERS

As noted earlier in the text, it is important to define the security terms being employed because many security terms are used differently by different people. When talking about security personnel, this is particularly important because the term **security personnel** has been used to identify various types of private security professionals in many different security-related occupations.[1] References to security personnel are focused almost exclusively on security features or departmental characteristics important for ensuring the integrity of the security divisions, including oversight of security personnel. Now, of course, security personnel are not the only people working in a business setting. **Personnel security** has been used with broader application and has typically referred to preventative measures of protection put in place to provide security to all personnel within a target environment. I plan to focus on both areas, first focusing on the concept of security management as an overarching guideline and then looking more directly at security department staff and strategies for protecting the company and its employees. Let us first take a look at some common security management models, then emphasize the importance of policy and procedure manuals.

Security Management

Clifford Simonsen reminds those interested in security management to remember that the security leader must contend with a split objective: The first part of the objective is a concern for security and order, the second is a concern with programs and personnel relations.[2] **Security management** is defined generally as an attempt to identify, address, and manage security issues as an integrated part of the overall environment. Dennis Dalton outlines three models of security management: the resident manager, the contract provider as security manager, and the nonsecurity security manager.[3] The **resident manager** is someone on staff serving as the security manager. The resident manager's responsibilities include having a plan for every aspect of the overall security operation. This includes physical security, operations, management, security policies, loss prevention, employee protection, protection from liability issues, protection of information, investigations, and coordination of internal and external resources as they impact the security management strategy.

Dalton outlines four reasons for adding a full-time security professional. First, administrative accountability affords the opportunity to provide ongoing reviews of policy development (and compliance issues), staffing, and system (including technology) management. Second, establishing employee awareness and responsibility invites the employees to become involved in and assume a greater responsibility for both their personal safety and the protection of company assets. Third, systems management includes the development, administration, and oversight of security devices such as access control, photo identification badges, and other established security protocols. The final important benefit of a resident security manager is the opportunity for that person to take a central role in establishing external liaisons. This will include, for example, local law enforcement officers as well as other security consultants and contractors.

Heck No, They Wouldn't Go!

National Autonomous University of Mexico (UNAM) is one of the largest universities in the Western Hemisphere, providing an education to approximately 275,000 students. With a student body the size of a large city, security is a big concern at UNAM. There are so many issues brought forth on a college campus that a security response that is not well planned could pose a threat to the security of students, the faculty, or the facilities. When the administration raised the idea of increasing tuition from what is equivalent to $0.04 per year to what is equivalent to $145 per year, the students reacted.

Guaranteed to free higher education by Mexico's constitution, the students at UNAM shut down the school when they learned of the proposed tuition increase. "The institution wants students to serve the multinational companies. They are refocusing the curriculum for the capitalists," one student striker exclaimed. A group of a few thousand students barricaded themselves inside the campus on April 20, 1999. The strike caused the administration to abandon the tuition proposal, but the striking students were not satisfied. Some of the strikers devised a new list of demands, which would give students more power. The dean proposed meeting most of the demands of the students, and he had the support of nearly 90 percent of the students, faculty, and university employees. However, the strikers refused the offer. They knew that they had one advantage in this situation: The administration was very reluctant to use force because of an incident that occurred in 1968. That year, a demonstration was held in a downtown Mexico City plaza. Soldiers were called in to break up the assembly and ended up killing hundreds of UNAM students. Because of this, the 1999 striking students' security was seen to be guaranteed. At least they would be safe from violent counterattacks.

On February 6, 2000, nearly 2700 unarmed federal police entered the main campus of UNAM in Mexico City. They arrested 745 students and staff who were still holding their ground inside the buildings, some 292 days after the incident began. A couple of days later, some of the worst violence of the entire strike occurred within a university-affiliated high school. Antistrike students and university security forced the strikers out of the school, but they returned later that day and regained control of the building. In the second overtaking, 37 security guards were injured. A week after the arrests, 579 of the 745 students arrested were released due to lack of evidence.

It is not uncommon to see situations get out of control on college and university campuses. However, security must be maintained at all times. Security can be difficult to ensure in these situations because no one knows what might happen.

References

J. Barrios, "Our Sixty Annual Roundup of Campus Activism," *Mother Jones 24,* no. 5 (1999): 20.

Comtex, "Mexican Police Occupied University Campus," *Xinhua News Agency,* February 10, 2000.

Comtex, "Mexico Releases Arrested Students," *Xinhua News Agency,* February 14, 2000.

J. Preston, "Big Majority Votes To End Strike at Mexican University," *New York Times,* January 22, 2000, A5.

"Unoccupied," *Economist 354,* no. 8157 (2000): 34.

A. Zarembo and P. Bierma, "Strike and Struggle: Radical Students Wage a War They've Already Lost," *Newsweek International,* September 13, 1999, 39.

The second security management model, the **contract provider as security manager,** has three types: the buyer-seller relationship, the preferred vendor relationship, and the strategic partnership. The buyer-seller relationship is a one-way relationship where the client assumes responsibility for nearly all the decisions.

The preferred vendor relationship is a middle ground, where the supplier is given some say in major decisions but typically the client still has the final say. In the strategic partnership, there is interagency cooperation. The security supplier becomes the managing operation for the security function, but the client still has a significant role to play in setting the parameters for what is expected. The security provider, or supplier, is then responsible for carrying out those operational decisions. Again, there are benefits and costs to contracting with an outside security vendor. Typically, security costs are reduced when the company contracts with someone outside the company. Furthermore, because of the nature of the business, the security contractor will assume the lion's share of liability concerns that arise for the company. While this clearly does not alleviate the company's legal liability, it is likely to reduce its legal responsibility. Finally, a contracted security response provides the company with the benefit of not having to deal with the personnel issues related to a security division. Training, evaluations, promotions/demotions, hiring, and firing are all done by the contract security company, leaving the business operations personnel free to worry about business.

The final model outlined originally by Dennis Dalton, and presented for discussion here, is the **nonsecurity security manager.** While it may not be the ideal, it is not unheard of to take a middle manager and ask him or her to assume the responsibility for security. Any small business operation will likely fall into this model; the operator of a small business, who is primarily interested in the management of that small business, also has to assume responsibility for making decisions about any targeted security concerns. For someone who is not dealing with security issues full time, attempts to deal with security issues are likely to be left until a problem arises.

As suggested by Dalton and others, security professionals are increasingly called on to work in tandem with business professionals to ensure that adequate security concerns can be integrated with a company's business objectives. Businesses are beginning to acknowledge that they are well served when an accomplished security professional is provided with enough resources and information to get the job done. In the business of protecting assets and personnel, security professionals are proving to be essential resources within an overall business management plan. Let us take a look at some of the issues related to developing a security division within a target environment.

Policies and Procedures: Enhancing Security from Within

To make personnel security a priority, a company needs to develop clear policies and procedures related to personnel security. Policies are management tools that control employee decision making; they reflect the goals and objectives of management.[4] Procedures are management tools that point out a particular way of doing something; they are used to guide action.[5] One such series of procedures dictates appropriate activities for hiring new security professionals. In addition, guidelines for responding to unanticipated circumstances, including accidents or emergencies, can provide an all-important checklist to ensure adequate security response. Accidents and disaster management are discussed in more detail in Chapter 12.

Guidelines for Preemployment Screening

Security professionals identify preemployment screening as one of the most effective tools they have to protect the target environment from employee theft and other potential losses.[6] Without clear guidelines for how the screening should be conducted, the company can leave itself vulnerable to bad hires. This section begins at the beginning, with the hiring process, and presents information about hiring, training, and ongoing evaluation of employee behaviors. Because employees working within the target environment are the group most likely to steal from the company, early attention to detail can reduce the need for damage control later.

The use of policies and procedures in the hiring process means that **human resources departments** are a first line of defense against internal security threats.[7] Furthermore, human resources departments can assist security personnel with employee orientation and training. Adequate protections, via policies and procedures, put in place to identify the appropriate process for employee screening can assist a company by decreasing the number of employees who are not serious about the job or do not have the company's best interests at heart. If strong preemployment screening policies can screen out candidates who might cause problems for the company, it is also true that poor hiring policies increase the likelihood of insider fraud.[8] Examples of restrictions on employers with regard to the guidelines for screening must be noted. As outlined in Exhibit 7–1, legislation has been passed at the federal level to protect people's rights during the hiring process.

One piece of legislation relevant to the hiring process is the Americans with Disabilities Act (ADA). In short, the ADA divides employment into three time periods: before the job offer, after the job offer, and while employed.[9] In the time before the job offer has been made, certain questions are not allowed if it is thought the response to these questions might reveal the person has a disability. In the time period between when the offer was made and when the per-

Exhibit 7–1   Federal Legislation Relevant for Hiring and Guiding Employee Relations

Age Discrimination in Employment Act
Americans with Disabilities Act
Consolidated Omnibus Budget Reconciliation Act of 1985
EEOC Sexual Harassment Guidelines
Employee Polygraph Protection Act of 1988
Fair Credit Reporting Act
Fair Labor Standards Act of 1938
Federal Wage Garnishment Law
Immigration Reform and Control Act of 1986
National Labor Relations Act
Occupational Safety and Health Act of 1970
Pregnancy Discrimination Act of 1978
Rehabilitation Act of 1973
Title VII of the Civil Rights Act of 1964
Vietnam Era Veterans' Readjustment Assistance Act of 1974
Whistleblower Legislation
Worker Adjustment and Retraining Notification Act

son begins working, it is permissible for an employer to ask any type of medical question or require any medical tests. At this time, the job offer is considered provisional, but the offer can be retracted under only two conditions: if the test reveals that the applicant cannot perform the essential functions of the job, and if placing the candidate in the job, given the applicant's medical condition, would pose a direct threat to the health or safety of the applicant or other employees.[10]

Various articles have been written on the liability concerns related to workplace hiring, performance evaluation, and firing conditions. For the purposes of preemployment screening, drug tests are not considered medical tests, although some states have legislation that restricts the conditions or circumstances under which an employer can test for drugs.[11] Information used to assess employee responsibility should be thoroughly reviewed to make certain it is consistent with the law, protects both the employee and the employer, and meets the needs of the target environment.

At a minimum, effective employee screening should include information on dependability, honesty, initiative, judgment, personal appearance, ability to be courteous, and integrity.[12-14] A more thorough screening might include (as permitted by law in the area) educational requirements, reference checks, verification of job history and/or job stability, arrest or conviction information, indications of drug use, indications of poor interpersonal relationships or emotional well-being, credit history information, unexplained gaps in employment history, indicators of improper use or abuse of authority or force, the ability to meet designated physical requirements (where appropriate), and demonstrated ability to communicate well in both oral and written formats. Although controversial and legal in only some states, three main categories of integrity and lie detection tests are also used for employee screening purposes: polygraph tests, the Psychological Stress Evaluator, and the Personal Security Inventory.[15]

When hiring security professionals, companies should expand efforts to ensure that applicants are truly interested in the security profession and are a good fit for the job; these screening efforts reduce turnover. Whether the new hire decided to leave because he or she did not like the position or whether the company was unhappy with the new hire's initial performance, money and time can be saved by using an adequate screening process.

Other Uses for Policy and Procedure Guidelines

As stated earlier, employee theft will be one of the more common issues a security management team will confront. Efforts to control internal theft can be undertaken by enhancing the policy and procedure manual within the company. Perhaps the single greatest weapon to prevent fraud is a set of detailed policies that strictly regulate all behaviors that can lead to fraud.[16] Policies and procedures can also lay out the protocol for admitting visitors. It is not uncommon to have a visitor badge issued to someone who has an appointment with someone in the target environment. In many companies, the visitor signs in, takes the badge, and is escorted to the appropriate location in the building. Should the visitor, at any time, not comply with the policy for visitors, then procedures will outline the appropriate security response. Policies and procedures can also provide guidance on responses to bomb threats, fire alarm checks, personnel evaluation and termination guidelines, complaint procedures, and training requirements. Just about every aspect of a business's operations can be directed and controlled by the use of policies and procedures.

The Role of Technology in Personnel Security Concerns

Security experts advise information technology (IT) managers to have a clear understanding of the likely threats to their system and to have a risk analysis conducted that outlines what is at stake for their agency should something unexpected happen.[17] As discussed in Chapter 6, computer security issues cut both ways. Technology can enhance the job being done by professionals in an industry, but it can also increase their vulnerability to both internal and external dangers. Furthermore, security professionals are likely to use computers and other technologies in their routine operations. Problems such as electrical outages can cause huge delays and damage to the overall business operations. Also, should security-related data be stored on computers, it is important to think about a backup system in case of damage to the hard drive or a virus that ruins the computer hardware. If valuable reports necessary for presentation in a controversial court case, for example, are stored on a computer, then it will be important to ensure that adequate protection for that security system is in place.

Adequate protection will need to be in place for all technological systems, including cameras, alarms, access control features, and other security-related technologies. Sometimes it becomes the job of the security director to solicit funding allocations to enhance the security objective, for the overall security system and particularly to address computer vulnerabilities. Exhibit 7–2 lists some well-supported justifications to present to management when information and computer security enhancements are necessary.

MAINTAINING SAFE WORKING CONDITIONS FOR EMPLOYEES

All personnel within a target environment, not just security personnel, need to be safe in the work environment. Shootings at schools and businesses have compelled people to review the risk levels for such an event in their target environment. This section simply highlights several common themes which affect personnel management, which include workplace violence, harassment and discrimination, drug use, disruptive behavior, and the need to promote ethical conduct. Yes, there are more, but this will get you started.

Workplace Violence

It is important to remember that safety and security issues in the workplace take various forms. Sometimes striking workers incite violence. In more highly publicized cases, the violence has come from a disgruntled employee or a dis-

Exhibit 7–2   Steps to Help IT Managers Develop a Solid Case
for Enhancing Security Resources

Perform a risk analysis on your site to determine the value of assets and risks to designated areas.

Demonstrate that the threat from intruders is too high to ignore. Set up a passive network sniffer on your network backbone to show the high frequency of remote access attempts and probes.

Discuss the potential impact to organizational reputation and efficiency in the case of widespread reports that you have been hacked.

Discuss the potential impact to organizational efficiency that widespread denial of services could create.

Provide information on the frequency of Internet attacks, who was attacked, and the damage inflicted.

Source: "Justifying Security," Government Computer News, 18, no. 13 (1999): 6.

turbed citizen. It is true an employer cannot guarantee absolute safety, but companies that have not taken adequate measures to counter a threat have been found liable in court. A business has a legal and moral responsibility to provide a good faith effort to make the workplace as safe as possible.

Johnson and colleagues divide **workplace violence** incidents into four categories:

1. robbery and other commercial crimes
2. domestic and misdirected affection cases
3. employer-directed actions
4. terrorism and hate crimes[18]

Additional violence may occur during strikes and other demonstrations, although they were not discussed by Johnson's research. Strikes are typically thought of as organized protests by blue-collar or line workers who believe they are not getting paid what they deserve. But the idea that strikes are for the "working class" only is outdated. In Seattle, Washington, in February 2000, well-paid Boeing engineers went on strike.[19] And unions of pilots and flight attendants seem to battle regularly over working conditions.

Recommendations to reduce employees' risk of being a victim of workplace violence include (1) preemployment screening, (2) drug screening, (3) zero tolerance for all forms of violence, (4) training for managers to identify high-risk employees, and (5) establishment of a threat and incident management team.[20,21] Schools across the country are confronting the issue of workplace safety and coordinating efforts to prevent violence in school. Several recommendations, many of which are easily applicable to other settings, might prove instructive.

1. Establish parameters for acceptable behavior. Be fair and consistent in responding to violations.
2. Demonstrate sincerity in your concern for a safe school.
3. Emphasize conflict resolution.
4. Reinforce the idea that the school is there to benefit students, and invite them to report crimes and suspicious incidents.
5. When you become aware of possible threats, take immediate action.
6. Do not condone bullying or harassment by students.
7. Become involved in the community.
8. Bring parents and guardians into the school's response to incidents.
9. Have a plan in place in the event of a dangerous situation.
10. Be a role model for positive behavior.[22]

One of the things that school safety and security response in schools has taught us is that sometimes the most significant security measure one can put in place is a structured effort to increase communication and trust. Some schools with extremely effective security programs in response to specific threats involve the implementation of programs to increase trust between students, teachers and parents, and *not* the installation of metal detectors and CCTV cameras.

Sexual Harassment and Discrimination

Other forms of criminal activity can impact workers within a given environment. Security departments are an appropriate arena to address personnel's concerns about their safety. In the few traditional security textbooks that include a discussion about sexual or other types of harassment (e.g., stalking, behavior that is perceived to be threatening), harassment is presented as "a new challenge."[23] It is perhaps more accurate to say that harassment is a *newly acknowledged* challenge for business owners. Internal investigations are often necessary in cases of alleged harassment. Security personnel must help to actively address harassment complaints within legal guidelines. This is likely to require the collection of additional information.

Diversity issues in the workplace include issues related to preferential treatment or discrimination based on race, age, gender, religion, disability, sexual orientation, and national origin. Some agencies have had great success dealing with diversity issues in the workplace. But diversity can also cause divisiveness and distress within a setting. Putting aside the issue of corporate objectives, which include internal cooperation and a harmonious working environment, failure to address both harassment and discrimination issues can be legally devastating to a company. An employer must take immediate and appropriate corrective action when addressing either of these issues. For this reason, and for the safety and security of all employees, it is essential for company officials to know the law and establish appropriate policies and procedures for reporting and investigating claims of harassment or discrimination.

(*Source:* United Media and Clay Bennett.)

Drug Use and Abuse

Illegal drugs have proven to be a formidable foe in the United States and other countries. The impact of drugs in the workplace reflects this overall social concern. Although Exhibit 7–3 outlines several effects associated with drug use in the workplace, the use of drug testing is controversial. Concern is raised about the privacy issues involved with drug testing in the workplace. However, computer-generated performance tests could be used to measure skills believed to be impaired by drug use (e.g., hand-eye coordination, response time) while being less controversial than drug tests. Types of drug tests include urinalysis, hair follicle tests, sweat patch tests, chromatography tests (sophisticated but quite expensive), saliva tests, and blood tests. Workplace drug testing takes several forms: preemployment screening, postaccident screening or for-cause testing, scheduled testing, random testing, and treatment follow-up drug testing. Decisions about whether to establish a drug-free workplace require decisions about how to ensure that an environment is drug free, and these decisions can be controversial.

Disruptive Employee Behavior

Historically, people have assumed that certain areas within a community and certain parts of the country would not be touched by violence. That sense of security was shaken by the events of 9/11. Even before the terrorist acts, newspaper headlines reminded us that violent outbursts and the subsequent loss of life can be a possibility in just about any setting.

Mike Hannigan outlines five major causes of disruptive behavior (Exhibit 7–4).[24] Professionals from many disciplines have not been able to predict with certainty who will commit violent assaultive behavior or what might motivate a person to act in such a way. Security professionals are integral in planning for and, if necessary, responding to aggressive behavior. Security personnel are perfectly placed to assist in assessing issues that may be impacting the health and welfare of people they come in contact with throughout their daily routines.

Exhibit 7–3   Effects of Drug Use on the Workplace

Decreased productivity
Greater number of accidents
Increased absenteeism
Increased theft
Greater number of workers' compensation claims
Increased health care costs
More morale problems
Greater training and replacement costs

Exhibit 7–4   Causes of Disruptive Behavior

Illness or injury
Emotional problems or mental illness
Substance misuse or abuse
Stress
Anger/frustration

Source: Michael A. Hannigan, "Crisis Intervention," in *Protection Officer Training Manual,* 6th ed., ed. International Foundation for Protection Officers (Woburn, MA: Butterworth-Heinemann, 1998), 172.

Promoting Ethical Conduct

Security practitioners have moved from being a group of professionals who did not discuss ethical behavior within the field to being professionals who give direct, focused attention to the role of ethics in various aspects of their jobs, including training, professionalism, customer relations, and security responses. The particular difficulties with discussions about security professionals and ethical behavior have to do largely with the fact that security practitioner breaches of appropriate conduct are typically high profile. While most people in any organization will prove to be ethical and moral, operating within the unwritten rules of appropriate interpersonal relations can almost ensure that there will be those whose actions prove challenging, and as a result fly in the face of efforts to maintain a stable, predictable work environment.

Simonsen reminds us that attitudes about behavior and conduct in general are not constant but change over time, at different times, and are different in different societies.[25] The International Foundation for Protection Officers defines "ethics" as the study of "good" and "bad" behavior within a profession.[26] See Appendix C for IFPO and ASIS Code of Ethics. Furthermore, ethics is said to deal with an

> examination of moral philosophy combined with the duties and obligations within a certain profession. Ethical behavior results when the correct ethical decisions have been made and carried out.[27]

Yet, again, Simonsen reminds security practitioners that they, like other professionals, are likely to find themselves weighing different ethical angles that may conflict. In fact, he refers to what he identifies as a conflict between organizational ethics, professional ethics, and situational ethics.[28] The terms are in bold in his text, indicating that they are important to the discussion, but he does not define the terms to assist the reader with their interpretation. A significant point he makes rests with a rather simple notion that security professionals might be encouraged by unethical colleagues to "go along to get along."

While it might be easy to rationalize such behavior with thoughts that "everyone does it," security professionals must provide a positive example to all other employees about what is appropriate conduct.

Ethics have been discussed as "good" and "bad" and behavior as "correct" and "incorrect," but there are many gray areas. Burnstein[29] provides an excellent example of this when he discusses the Fourth Amendment and searches in the workplace. While the courts have ruled that searches of employee belongings are permissible, the discretion used when conducting searches of an employee's handbag, briefcase, or backpack or a customer's shopping bag might be suspect. If people are targeted for a more thorough inspection because of certain characteristics, such as race or class, this can be clearly identified as unethical behavior. If all employees are stopped, and a more thorough search is conducted on every fifth person through the door, that would be a policy that makes sense. If a customer was seen on camera doing something that suggested the possibility of shoplifting, that too might warrant a more thorough search, depending on company policy and procedural guidelines for investigating shoplifting. This kind of issue is, in fact, related to ethical practices. But decisions about whether this type of behavior is "right" or "wrong" have varied over time and in different settings. The practice of targeting someone because of his or her gender or race is unethical. Many security practitioners and police departments across the country, however, continue to teach that using a profile of a "likely criminal" is a useful tool for "catching crooks." Recent high profile concerns about profiling highlight the controversy surrounding this idea.

In fact, some companies to this day incorporate various forms of discriminatory practices into their security or staff training. Many students I work with do security-related internships or hold security positions and they often tell stories about their work-related security experiences. In one case, a student relayed a story in which he was instructed to be very alert any time an African American came into the store where he worked. This "training" suggested that "those people" are known for their criminal activity, so to prevent theft this student was instructed to "watch them closely." Lawsuits have resulted in damage awards being served to the victims of such practices. Yet the practice persists. In some cases, people who are behaving "unethically" and who might even be in violation of the law may be unaware of this violation and believe their behavior to be totally justified.

Here is another example. A security colleague I know relayed a story to me about rejecting a security contract because the two women who had solicited his services were known to be lesbians. He said while the money was good, he could not in good conscience take the contract because he judged the moral behavior of these women (in his assessment) as questionable. His company declined the contract. Another example: A security company has a written code of ethics that outlines as a priority the company's desire to help every person, business, or public organization interested in enhancing its security. The company mentions just one condition: The person, business, or organization seeking security expertise must be engaged in legal activities. Compare these two examples. The second company's priority is to service people with legal requests for security, while the first company's priority seems to be servicing people with specific personal attributes.

If I have established a professional, ethical standard for my security business that highlights the importance of making people feel secure in any setting, I will need to think about how this issue will play itself out if I am contacted for a security consultation. Consider clinics where abortions are performed, or scientific labs where animals are used for experimentation. In both of these cases, a security professional might need to check his or her own ethical framework before choosing to provide security services. While it is important to be attentive to the legal guidelines, the ethical framework guiding the security business (in a small security company) or corporate philosophy (for security departments in large organizations) should provide guidance when outlining security response priorities.

Decisions outlining appropriate or inappropriate behavior within a given setting will be determined in large part by managers, owners, and (sometimes) workers. The organization will establish a collective ethical vision. Security professionals will be expected to understand those community standards and reflect them in their highest form. At a minimum, decisions should be in accordance with the law, outlined in policy and procedure guidelines, and afford dignity and respect to every person.

PROTECTING ASSETS IN THE TARGET ENVIRONMENT

Creating a safe work environment for employees is critical, and anyone working in a corporate or business environment knows that one of the biggest threats to the environment is likely to come from an employee. Therefore, one of the primary responsibilities of the security management staff is to ensure that policies and procedures are in place to do at least two things: (1) to protect the employee from harm while on the property, and (2) to protect the company (any company assets) from dishonest employees. Whether the target environment is a private business or a government agency, employees can be a security professional's biggest vulnerability.

Shrinkage is the term used to refer to losses due to employee theft, misplacing of goods, shoplifting, and vendor/supplier theft.[30] A report by the Association of Certified Fraud Examiners (CFE) suggests that small companies (companies with fewer than 100 employees) suffer the most extensive losses.[31] Costs to employers as a result of fraud and other employee crimes are estimated at more than $400 billion a year.[32] Employee screening practices and

(*Source:* Reprinted with special permission of North America Syndicate.)

various internal controls are a means to reduce the employee theft problem. In fact, the CFE report suggests that most people are caught because of tips from fellow employees.[33] Even as employers begin to get a handle on methods to prevent employees from stealing, an increasing reliance on computers adds another potentially devastating aspect to the overall security objective.

Richard L. Johnston, Director of the National White Collar Crime Center, says that "95% of criminals today are not computer literate" but "90% will achieve computer literacy within the next decade."[34]

Efforts to deal with employee theft have been referred to as **private corporate justice** because companies choose not to involve public law enforcement agencies for a variety of reasons. The issue of private corporate justice suggests the company hands out "justice" privately, and away from public scrutiny.[35] A corporate executive might embezzle hundreds of thousands of dollars, and the company fires the employee rather than informing the police and charging the person with theft. While these issues have not been studied extensively, the number of research studies on the topic is increasing, and in the future, more focused attention on the formal versus informal justice systems in place is likely.

MANAGING SECURITY PERSONNEL

As has been indicated up to this point, many security considerations go into the everyday operations of a security department. Acknowledging that the top priority when thinking about personnel security is keeping workers and assets

Crackdown on Corporate Corruption?

On July 9, 2002, President George W. Bush signed into law H.R. 3763, "the Sarbanes-Oxley Act of 2002."[1] After a summer rife with high profile corporate scandals and criminal investigations, on the heels of the Enron Scandal, and in the wake of a predicted record number of corporate bankruptcies for 2002,[2] the political climate was ready for such an action out of the White House. Add to the mix the potential for huge losses in individual retirement accounts, and it seems all eyes are on corporate America and Wall street.

Enron Corporation, an energy trading company, filed for Chapter 11 bankruptcy in December of 2001 and since then several controversial business actions have become high profile over the summer of 2002. In the Enron case, the bankruptcy is said to be the tip of the iceberg, with investigations under way by the Securities and Exchange Commission (SEC), the Department of Justice (DOJ) and Congress.[3] Lawsuits have been filed by the shareholders and employees, seeking payment for their stock losses amid accusations of accounting manipulations, to conceal debt from investors, and claims that while executives unloaded stock before the share price plummeted, employees' ability to sell their shares was restricted.

On June 13, the Arthur Andersen accounting firm was found guilty of obstructing justice for destroying Enron documents after being notified of a federal investigation. The Arthur Andersen firm and its branches located around the globe are being forced to close as businesses pull their accounts from the company.[4]

June also saw Xerox go public with a public announcement, in the works for years, acknowledging a $2 billion dollar accounting error over a five-year period.[5] The firm has been accused of improperly posting revenues before they were actually earned and defrauding investors. Xerox paid a $10 million dollar fine.[6] Global Crossing, a telecom giant, is also under investigation by the SEC and FBI for improper accounting practices.[7] On June 3, the CEO of Tyco, International Company resigned as a federal investigation progressed, and on June 12 the SEC announced a formal investigation of the CEO and may pursue criminal charges.[8] The former CEO is accused to tampering with evidence, using corporate cash to buy art and a home, and more than $1 million in sales tax evasion.[9]

On June 12, former CEO of ImClone was arrested on charges of insider trading and perjury after he allegedly tipped off friends and family members about the Food and Drug Administration's rejection of that company's application to produce a cancer drug. The Securities and Exchange Commission is considering civil action against ImClone for improper disclosure of information about the drug. The actions of ImClone former CEO were linked with Martha Stewart, Inc. because of a sale of 4000 shares of ImClone Systems, Inc. stock the day before the information about the FDA's decision about the cancer drug was announced.[10]

On June 24 the 37-count indictment of four Rite Aid top executives, including the CFO, went public.[11] Their actions have made it necessary for Rite Aid to cut stated earnings by $1.6 billion. Three of the executives falsified contracts to give themselves millions of dollars in extra severance pay. 2 are accused of perjury and witness tampering.[12]

In many of these cases, Enron's case being one of the most high profile, workers have lost their entire life savings because their 401 (k) plans were largely invested in Enron stocks. About 60 lawsuits so far have been brought in Houston state and federal courts but are likely to be frozen until the bankruptcy issue has been closed.[13]

Interesting questions arise about the role of any security management team to protect intangible corporate assets. Worldcom or Enron may have had excellent security organized to protect their facilities, but this still did not protect the corporate assets from alleged criminal and/or questionable business practices that resulted in fraud, and then

(continued)

bankruptcy—a potential loss of all corporate assets. The role of a security management team works outside of typical security objectives for a large corporation where matters of finance are concerned. How is theft of a computer or other asset different from the theft of financial assets and why does the government treat these penalties so differently, particularly when loses of huge sums of money may be involved? What responsibility does a security management team, working within a corporation, have to ensure that the financial stability of that company is maintained along with security of the tangible assets of that corporation? If it is the job of security management teams to protect the company assets, isn't it a good idea to ask how security personnel identify the potential thieves from which the company needs to be protected? Is there any role security professionals could play in assuring the financial integrity of a corporation for stockholders when usually it is the upper management within that corporation who oversees the role of security within that agency? How does this security and crime prevention structure insulate high level executives from prosecution? How does it highlight more potentially insignificant offenses, like misuse of a company's internet or e-mail policy, not because they threaten the corporate structure, but simply because these kinds of offenses may be easier to take action against? Consider how these questions and issues relate to the idea of "private justice" discussed in the text.

References

1. The White House Web page. "A New Ethic of Corporate Responsibility." *http://www. whitehouse.gov/infocus/corporateresponsibility/*. Posted July 9, 2002. Last visited August 15, 2002.
2. Harbrect, Douglas. "A record for corporate bankruptcies." BusinessWeek online. *http://www.businessweek.com:/bwdaily/dnflash/mar2002/nf20020319_2038.html*. Posted on March 19, 2002. Last viewed August 15, 2002.
3. Flood, Mary. "Bankruptcy tip of the iceberg in forums seeking redress." Houston-Chronicle.com. *http://www.chron.com/sc/CDA/printstory.hts/special/enron/dec01/1166721*. Printed on January 17, 2002. Last viewed August 15, 2002.
4. "President Takes Wall Street to Task: Former Worldcom Execs Take 5th on Capital Hill." CNN.com, *http://www.cnn.com/2002/ALLPOLITICS/07/08/bush.corporate.abuse*. Posted July 9, 2002. Last viewed August 15, 2002.
5. CBC Online staff. "Xerox forced to restate revenues." CBC News. *http://www.cbc.ca/stories/2002/06/28/xerox_02-628*. Posted on June 28, 2002. Last visited August 15, 2002.
6. Ibid.
7. Kennedy, Siobhan. "Global Crossing Says Shredding Claim Under Investigation." *http://asia.news.yahoo.com/020704/reuters/asia-113562.html*. Posted July 4, 2002. Last viewed August 18, 2002.
8. Webber, Harry. Associated Press. "Investigation of Tyco's Ex-CEO leads to SEC Probe." The Nando Times. *http://nandotime.com/business/story/432619p-3459166c.html*. Posted on June 12, 2002. Last visited August 15, 2002.
9. Ibid.
10. Meeks, Brock. "Ex-Worldcom CFO indicated." msnbc.com. *http://www.msnbc.com/news/800/73.asp*. Posted August 28, 2002. Last visited August 28, 2002.
11. Taub, Stephen. "Cash and Apothecary?" CFO.com. *http://www.cfo.com/Article?article=7362*. Posted June 24, 2002. Last visited August 15, 2002.
12. "President Takes Wall Street to Task: Former Worldcom Execs Take 5th on Capitol Hill." CNN.com, *http://www.cnn.com/2002/ALLPOLITICS/07/08/bush.corporate.abuse*. Posted July 9, 2002. Last viewed August 15, 2002.
13. Flood, Mary. "Bankruptcy tip of the iceberg in forums seeking redress." HoustonChronicle.com. *http://www.chron.com/sc/CDA/printstory.hts/special/enron/dec01/1166721*. Printed on January 17, 2002. Last viewed August 15, 2002.

protected, the security professional is left with the responsibility for making critical decisions about how to do just that. Consideration is given here to the structure and appropriate size of the security operation, the professional transformation from security guard to protection officer or security professional, adequate qualifications, hiring and training issues, equipment, tactics, and uniform decisions (including the patrol function, report writing, investigation and interrogations, use of force). Throughout these discussions, the reader will notice that all of the areas include a discussion about the importance of good communication.

Determining the Structure of a Security Department

Discussions about security personnel have been linked to organizational resources, such as human relations departments, in an overall business management plan. As suggested earlier, one of the initial decisions will be whether the security personnel will be part of a division within the corporate structure, or whether these personnel will come from an outside contract. Harvey Burnstein[13] outlines clearly several specific considerations that must be given attention by a developing (or even existing) security department. These issues will include determining an adequate size for the security department; assessing specific qualifications for the hiring of security personnel; and making decisions about uniforms and equipment, training exercises, supervision, recordkeeping, and communication.

As noted earlier, a decision must be made about whether to place the security professionals within the company structure, to contract for their services with outside security vendors, or to have some combination of these approaches. External providers are typically referred to as **contract security services**.[36] These professionals are in the business of providing supplemental and/or targeted security services as the managers within the target environment deem appropriate. This request could be coming from the security managers within a given environment, or from professionals within the company who are seeking enhancements or evaluation of their current security needs. Exhibit 7–5 lists 10 ways for security professionals who provide contract services to highlight the value they bring to a client seeking additional security services.

A Guard No Longer

When most people think of security professionals, they think of security guards. Within the last decade, professional security organizations have worked to eliminate the use of the term *guard* from the professional vocabulary. Chris Hertig and other members of the International Foundation of Protection Offi-

Exhibit 7–5   Benefits of Contract Services

1. Promote the fact that you are an industry leader—a subscriber to world-class standards and principles.
2. Let it be known that you have access to other markets because of your business relationships.
3. No one can do everything themselves, so as a manager or executive be clear that your value is in operations, policy setting, consulting, investigations, and so forth.
4. Since your clients have access to your money and resources, by offering them monthly invoicing or alternative pricing strategies you can give them the edge.
5. Security is your core competency, not theirs. By trying to handle security matters, they are diverting valuable resources away from their core competency and therefore operating less efficiently than they could be. You can offset this imbalance through your efforts.
6. Using you as a strategic partner, the company stands to gain more than they will lose. As your strategic partner, they can transfer some—though certainly not all—of their risk to you.
7. Work that may be temporary or cyclical can be better managed by you. For example, systems design work, special investigations, executive protection, and so forth.
8. By creating strategic alliances with other synergistic service providers, you can achieve economic synergies for the company.
9. You can guarantee that greater management flexibility will be achieved relative to assignments of personnel, training costs, and so forth.
10. Because you believe in continuous quality improvement, your performance is not tied to profit alone. Thus the end users gain higher performance from your staff than they will from others.

Source: D. Dalton, *The Art of Successful Severity Management* (Woburn, MA: Butterworth-Heinemann, 1998), 24.

cers have been among the leaders in this charge. A security colleague of mine often describes the popular attitude toward security guards: If they are "upright with a pulse," they qualify for the job. Although the term *guard* is still used, the security profession as a whole is pursuing a collective effort to upgrade the general perception people have about security professionals.

Identifying Qualifications for Security Personnel

Most managers and professionals would agree that the process of hiring security professionals should be tedious. Good security personnel are the backbone of an exceptional security plan. Recommendations for an appropriate hiring protocol include a screening interview, an honesty test, and a background investigation.[37] The qualifications, of course, will be dependent on the job the security professional is hired to perform. As society increases its reliance on security professionals, as the use of security technologies increase, and as the explosion in computer use continues without hesitation, more and more professionals in various disciplines find themselves involved in some aspect of the security objective.

In 1991, then-Senator Al Gore introduced legislation to establish screening and training standards for security officers hired by the federal government or government contractors (the legislation was introduced in the 102nd Congress, 1st Session, as Senate Bill 1258).[38] After a decade with little action, some security watchers suggest the role of the federal government in determining security-related professional standards will change as a result of September 11. Certainly, only time will tell. Changes have already been seen in at least one area. Airport security personnel are now federal employees.*

The requirements to become employed within the security industry, if there are any, vary in the United States from state to state. And the reality a security professional is confronted with may in fact be quite a bit different from the ideal they are looking to achieve. I hear from students all the time who are hired as security directors for regional business operations before they finish their college degree. Standards for the profession are varied, but right now experience is the key for entrance into most security departments.

Training and Supervising

Chris Hertig outlines distinct differences among training, education, and development, suggesting that **training** refers to an instructional setting that is "designed to improve human performance on the job the employee is currently doing, or is being hired to do."[39] **Education,** in contrast, is designed to improve the overall competence of the employee beyond the job held. **Development** refers to any necessary "retooling" of employees or their skills so that they can move or change with the company. There is nothing sacred about the distinctions made here, but they remind security professionals to spend some time thinking about their objectives for the learning they want to have happen within their targeted group of security professionals.

Training sessions have been the typical learning approach, although there are other creative alternatives for teaching future security professionals. The Social Security Administration, which must train many employees, has implemented Interactive Television (ITV) training at 830 field sites and is planning to expand by approximately 700 more.[40] The training originates in five studios (two in Baltimore and one each in Atlanta, Dallas, and Kansas City, Missouri). The two-way audio and viewer response keypads, which operate over telephone lines, provide real-time voice and data communications between the teachers and the students.

---

*Jon Doughherty, "Experts: Federal Airport Security No Better." WorldNetDaily.com Posted 02.27.02. Last visited 08.18.02. *http://www.worldnetdaily.com/news/*

A format like this has been said to make sense for security practitioners, many of whom are working professionals who seek out additional educational opportunities while also working full time. Michigan State University's School of Criminal Justice has established an online security education graduate program as part of its "virtual university." Successful students graduate with a master's degree in security management.[41] The options for security education continue to grow,[42] although there is an ongoing debate about whether these academic programs are best suited to a criminal justice curriculum or a business or management program. Dr. Jim Calder at the University of Texas, San Antonio, has done some excellent work in this area.

Equipment, Tactics, and Uniforms

Security professionals do a difficult job. But part of the difficulty of the job comes in not knowing what to expect and in having to be prepared for anything. Exhibit 7–6 lists important topics to be covered in a security training program. The list should provide readers with a clear understanding of the breadth of security training topics.

When making contact with people is an essential part of the everyday operation, professional presentation is important. They must dress well, look neat, and behave professionally. A professional appearance is essential because active protection professionals need to look like they have authority to act in that role, particularly in times of crisis; however, what that uniform should look like is an open debate. Some companies want the security staff to blend in a bit better, so they prefer their officers to wear something less intimidating. Others want a high-profile officer whose uniform is obvious.

Exhibit 7–6   On-the-Job Training Topics for Security Professionals

corporate philosophy
corporate structure and environmental conditions
policies and procedures
liability issues
report writing
self-defense
communication issues
public relations issues
investigation procedures
interrogation procedures
first aid response
search and seizure issues
equipment
observation and documentation

Typical equipment issued to security professionals includes a two-way radio, a pen and pad, handcuffs, gear for bad weather, and a flashlight. Agencies deciding to provide weapons (e.g., nightstick, pepper spray, firearm) for their officers need to think carefully about their organizational needs. For some security professionals, carrying weapons will not be seen as appropriate. Using a firearm in a security position is extremely controversial. Again, decisions about uniforms, appropriate security practices or tactics, and equipment to be issued to security personnel must be considered within the overall objective for the security team. The following are a few more issues to consider.

The Patrol Function

Security professionals are responsible for noticing things that seem out of place, so they need to get out into the target environment and make sure things are as they should be. There are three primary ways security officers patrol: on foot, on bikes, and in a car. Depending on the environment, it may make sense to use more than one approach. The purpose of the patrol will also be dictated in large part by the needs of the environment. Examples of uses for patrols include

- detecting unauthorized activity
- preventing and deterring unauthorized activity
- ensuring compliance with policies
- looking for unusual conditions
- asking targeted questions or initiating discussions
- monitoring the physical security system
- responding to emergencies

Several actions can be taken to enhance security professionals' effectiveness in monitoring operations, one of their responsibilities. It makes sense, for example, for security professionals to know the people in the various divisions or departments in the agency. Having some idea of what their job entails and how they do that job can also be useful. Because of the job the security professional is there to do, it is important for security professionals to maintain a professional relationship with employees and customers and not encourage personal relationships. Security professionals also need to be informed about all aspects of the building and business operations. Therefore, security professionals should know the maintenance people and understand well any maintenance concerns.

Christopher Vail outlines three principles of patrols.[43] First, patrols should be conducted in a random fashion. Second, the frequency of patrols should also be random. Finally, good communication, both oral and written, is essential. Constant radio communication with the other security professionals is essential throughout routine patrol. Furthermore, it is important to document any unusual events or circumstances and report them to a supervisor. Appropriate documentation is also essential.

Report Writing and Recordkeeping

Security reports are the last line of defense when a company needs to protect itself against unwelcome accusations. For this reason, the reports must be well organized, comprehensive, and trackable. Interestingly, computers afford the opportunity to capture a great deal of written information, but people still must be able to find the relevant material when they need it. Organization is key. Security documentation is prepared by an officer to share information with any concerned individuals who may not have been present at the time of the event. For instance, corporate executives who receive a complaint about someone being injured on the company property are probably going to be interested in reading the security officers' report of the incident. The report must be clear, concise, accurate, and complete.[44]

Investigation and Interrogation

If security professionals are dealing with an incident that requires police involvement, such as shoplifting or some type of personal injury on the property, then they need to think about the information they can put together to assist the law enforcement officer with collection of evidence to assist with future determinations about possible criminal prosecution. Upon initial contact with an injured person, for example, a security officer must request an emergency medical response. Assuming the injuries are not life threatening, it might be reasonable for the security officer to ask the victim what happened. If additional people were involved, then the security officer might need to interview each person, attempting to understand the sequence of events that led to the injury. The security officer may need to search for witnesses to the event, to get a more well-rounded presentation of these events. This investigative process, collecting information and interrogating the people involved, is a routine part of the security professional's responsibilities. The importance of the documentation of these events and the fact that there are right ways and wrong ways to conduct investigations and interrogations cannot be overstated.

Christopher Hertig outlines some basic rules of interviewing: (1) being pleasant; (2) thanking people for their help; (3) trying to avoid asking yes or no questions and instead asking questions that require some explanation from the responding person; (4) not feeling compelled to speak for people and listening well, even if this means pausing for long periods; (5) picking a quiet, calm setting for the interview; (6) taking notes in a way that records key information without being disruptive; (7) trying to make people comfortable while talking with them; and (8) giving people a card with information telling them how to contact the interviewer if they think of anything else.

It is essential to remember that employee fraud can occur at any level of an organization and the motivations can be wide ranging. It could be a clerical worker or senior executive who is making off with company assets.[45] While **interviews** are conducted to collect additional information about an event or occurrence, **interrogations** are conducted when focusing on an individual as a suspect. Interrogations are ultimately focused on seeking a confession from the accused.[46] For this reason, it is essential to involve a security professional who is experienced in interrogations. Remember, the law has guidelines for appropriate ways to get information from a suspect. Typically, the use of threats, force, and intimidation is not allowed. It is important to advise a suspect of his or her Miranda rights, but security professionals (who have no police powers) are not bound by the same legal standard.

Use of Force Issues

Security professionals are ultimately charged with preventing damage or harm. Most security professionals avoid using force.[47] Injuries and death can result when security officers are confronted with an individual who is resisting being detained but who has a medical condition, for example, not immediately obvious to the security officers. Situations where force is used can result in significant liability for a company, even if deadly force was not the objective. More about use of force issues is included in the chapter on legal liability (Chapter 11).

CONCLUSION

Security departments have a significant role to play in overseeing personnel matters in various business and professional settings. Also, security professionals have a number of considerations to make when organizing the management of a security department or security business. Attention is given here to the essential role of policies and procedures for enhancing security from within the organizational structure. In an adequately prepared management division, whether it be a security management division or human resources management personnel, attention is given to the roles and responsibilities of the security professionals as well as the roles and responsibilities of other personnel working in that target environment.

Good hiring practices can help to produce the best-qualified, most thoroughly screened applicants. Guidelines for preemployment screening should be outlined in a policy and procedure manual to ensure that a rigorous, legal hiring process is followed exactly. This can be one way to protect against the aggravations (and liabilities) that come from hiring employees who are either not particularly interested in the job or whose employment history or experiences suggest a questionable fit.

In addition to assisting with hires, security professionals are also largely responsible for overseeing the working conditions and ensuring that the personnel remain safe and secure while at work. In some cases this can be done with the assistance of technological devices, but appropriate guidelines are also necessary to provide direction in cases of workplace violence, harassment or discrimination claims, disruptive employee behavior, investigations of employee (or other) theft cases, and any other questionable practices within the target environment. In the end, the security department will be responsible for monitoring just about any measure put in place to protect people, property, and assets.

Officials making decisions governing the overall security management objectives must acknowledge the vulnerability gaps that result from a decision made to protect one area of the company that may have a negative effect in another area of the system. Ideally, the security department will work directly with the human resources department to identify the kind of security-related criteria important enough for the company to outline it in a policy and procedure manual. Once those guidelines have been established, they must be enforced. Deviation from selected personnel standards can leave the company vulnerable to lawsuits.

The final sections of the chapter include a discussion of general issues within security departments. Attention is given to the structure of the security department, whether contract or proprietary. Training issues such as equipment, patrols, report writing, recordkeeping, use of force, and uniforms are also discussed. A good security plan can be an effective means for maintaining a stable and predictable environment within any given setting. Personnel issues and security management strategies can be integrated into aspects of physical security, asset protection, and computer and information security to create an even more comprehensive security plan. The issue of integration is discussed more fully in Chapter 8.

REVIEW QUESTIONS

1. Outline briefly the personnel issues involved in keeping a safe workplace outlined in the text. What other issues can you think of that were not presented for consideration?
2. Outline the three models for security management as described by D. Dalton.
3. Discuss the critical issues one might want to check when screening employees.

4. What four categories of workplace violence issues are outlined in the text?
5. Outline the significance of private corporate justice within the context of the overall criminal justice system mission and objectives.
6. Outline briefly the primary responsibilities of a security professional as presented in the chapter.

Discussion Questions

1. Discuss the importance of a policy and procedure manual for matters involving employees.
2. What role does technology play in coordinating personnel security concerns?
3. Why would the issue of sexual harassment be important to include in a personnel policy and procedure manual?
4. What difference does it make whether security officers are referred to as guards? Be prepared to justify your position.
5. What training standards should be established for security professionals? Should those standards be state or national level in their implementation? Please justify your response.

References

1. T. A. Ricks et al., *Principles of Security*, 3rd ed. (Cincinnati, OH: Anderson Publishing Company, 1994), 203–224.
2. C. Simonsen, *Private Security in America: An Introduction* (Upper Saddle River, NJ: Prentice Hall, 1998), 80.
3. D. Dalton, *The Art of Successful Security Management* (Woburn, MA: Butterworth-Heinemann, 1998), 117–134.
4. P. Purpura, *Security and Loss Prevention: An Introduction*, 3rd ed. (Woburn, MA: Butterworth-Heinemann, 1998), 54.
5. Purpura, *Security and Loss Prevention*, 55.
6. R. Fischer and G. Green, *Introduction to Security*, 6th ed. (Woburn, MA: Butterworth-Heinneman, 1998), 325.
7. Fischer and Green, *Introduction to Security*, 325.
8. K. Riddle, "Unbuttoning White Collar Crime," *Security Management*, January 1999, 57.
9. T. Anderson, "Treading Lightly through the Hiring Thicket," *Security Management*, June 1999, 35.
10. Anderson, "Treading Lightly," 35.
11. Anderson, "Treading Lightly," 36.
12. Ricks et al., *Principles of Security*, 203–224.
13. H. Burnstein, *Introduction to Security* (Englewood Cliffs, NJ: Prentice Hall, 1994), 118.
14. Fischer and Green, *Introduction to Security*, 335–347.

15. Fischer and Green, *Introduction to Security,* 336.
16. Riddle, "Unbuttoning White Collar Crime," 57.
17. "Justifying Security," *Government Computer News 18,* no. 13 (1999): 6.
18. D. L. Johnson et al., "Break the Cycle of Violence," *Security Management,* February 1994, 24–28.
19. D. Paton, "Strike Echoes in White Collar World," *Christian Science Monitor,* 24 February 2000, 2, 4.
20. J. Jones, "Steps That Reduce Workplace Violence," (1995): 1, 27.
21. R. Olmost, "Is the Workplace No Longer Safe?" *Security Concepts,* April 1994, 9.
22. M. Dunn, "Critical Elements in School Security," *American School and University 71,* no. 11 (1999): 13–16.
23. Simonsen, *Private Security in America,* 347.
24. M. A. Hannigan, "Crisis Intervention," in *Protection Officer Training Manual,* 6th ed., ed. International Foundation for Protection Officers (Woburn, MA: Butterworth-Heinemann, 1998), 172–175.
25. Simonsen, *Private Security in America,* 31.
26. C. Hertig, "Ethics and Professionalism," in *Protection Officer Training Manual,* 6th ed., ed. International Foundation for Protection Officers (Woburn, MA: Butterworth-Heinemann, 1998), 274–279.
27. Hertig, "Ethics and Professionalism," 274.
28. Simonsen, *Private Security in America,* 33.
29. H. Burnstein, *Introduction to Security* (Englewood Cliffs, NJ: Prentice Hall, 1994), 108.
30. S. Traub, "Battling Employee Crime: A Review of Corporate Strategies and Programs," *Crime and Delinquency 42,* no. 2 (1996): 246.
31. R. T. Gray, "Clamping Down on Worker Crime," *Nation's Business 85,* no. 4 (1997): 44.
32. Gray, "Clamping Down," 44.
33. Gray, "Clamping Down," 44.
34. Gray, "Clamping Down," 44.
35. Traub, "Battling Employee Crime," 244–256.
36. Dalton, *The Art of Successful Security Management,* 24.
37. Ricks, *Principles of Security,* 209–210.
38. "News from U.S. Senator Al Gore," press release (Washington, DC: June 11, 1991).
39. C. Hertig, *Avoiding Pitfalls in the Training Process* (Bellingham, WA: International Foundation for Protection Officers, 1993), 3.
40. F. Tiboni, "SSA Reaps Benefits of Video Training for Employees," *Government Computer News 18,* no. 25 (1999): 20.
41. P. P. Miller and R. Jones, "Online Options Extend Classroom," *Security Management,* May 1999, 45–50.

42. C. Hertig, "Academic Programs Continue to Grow," *Protection News*, Fall 1998, 3–4.

43. C. Vail, "Patrol Techniques," in *Protection Officer Training Manual*, 6th ed., ed. International Foundation for Protection Officers (Woburn, MA: Butterworth-Heinemann, 1998), 58–60.

44. M. Fawcett, "Field Notes and Report Writing," in *Protection Officer Training Manual*, 6th ed., ed. International Foundation for Protection Officers (Woburn, MA: Butterworth-Heincmann, 1998), 39–43.

45. Riddle, "Unbuttoning White-Collar Crime," 57–63.

46. C. Thibodeau and C. Hertig, "Security and Loss Prevention Investigations," in *Protection Officer Training Manual*, 6th ed., ed. International Foundation for Protection Officers (Woburn, MA: Butterworth-Heinemann, 1998), 253.
C. Hertig, "Considerations Regarding the Use of Force," *Protection News 13*, no. 1 (1997): 1.

47. C. Thibodeau and C. Hertig, "Security and Loss Prevention Investigations," in *Protection Officer Training Manual*, 6th ed., ed. International Foundation for Protection Officers (Woburn, MA: Butterworth-Heinemann, 1998), 250–258.

48. Thibodeau and Hertig, "Security and Loss Prevention Investigations," 252–253.

CHAPTER

Integration as
the Centerpiece
Meeting Overall
Security Objectives

CHAPTER OUTLINE

One-Dimensional Thinking: Restrictions
  No One Can Afford
The Essence of Integration
  Know the Environment
  Know the Security Field
  Rely on Other Security Experts
The Importance of an Integrated
  Security Design

Integrating to Move Outside of the
  Box
A Model for Integration: It Is Magic
Conclusion
  Review Questions
  Discussion Questions

CHAPTER HIGHLIGHTS

*Integration: The Importance of
  Integrating Fundamental Security-
  Related Functions*
*Emphasizing Again the Importance
  of Setting*

*Outsourcing and Contracting for
  Security Resources*
*Examples of Integration Ideas
  Applied to Various Settings*
Review of Disney's Integrated Design

KEY WORDS

Integration

Outsourcing

The preceding chapters have introduced what I have been calling security essentials, fundamental areas for inclusion in any security plan. Collectively, the focus of Chapters 5–7 was to highlight six fundamental aspects of an overall security management strategy: physical security, asset protection, information security, computer security, personnel security, and security management. In the world of security textbooks, reality can be easily chopped up, mixed together, and simplified to fit neatly predetermined categories. The real world is not so easily contained or categorized. In truth, security objectives should stress **integration,** or the interconnections *between* as well as *within* each of these six areas. Ideally, the overall security objective is a seamless integration of all of the previously identified security objectives outlined in the various sectors of the target environment. Readers take note: *Any action, however small, taken to meet any component of a security objective within a target environment should be considered part of the overall security strategy.* An integrated security design optimizes resources and readily allows for a systematic review of existing security protocol. For a security professional, life doesn't get better than that.

ONE-DIMENSIONAL THINKING: RESTRICTIONS NO ONE CAN AFFORD

In the more than 10 years I have been teaching security-related topics within criminal justice departments at institutions of higher education, I have listened to students who demonstrate a myopic, one-dimensional conception of the security function. One student, discussing the new lighting equipment implemented across campus, argued that the technology was a waste of resources. In a bid to save money, the university had installed motion-sensitive lighting. If no motion was detected, the lights would go out. I mentioned that the lights were also a useful security feature. The minute a person stepped into a hallway, for example, the lights came on. The lights lessen the risk of falling over a chair or other object left in the hallway. Students who left late after night classes said they felt safer because the areas would illuminate as they entered the areas. Furthermore, I pointed out, if a light was on in a building that should be empty and locked, university security might want to take a closer look. Lighting of any kind is relevant to security concerns. But because the primary purpose of the light was not security (it was to save electricity), the student didn't make that essential connection.

Another student was bothered by my suggesting that certain shipping techniques could be easily integrated into a security management strategy. We were talking about the plastic wrap used to secure skids of products before shipping. Depending on how the shipping process was organized, this wrap could be used to reduce internal theft. He remained unconvinced. We talked about how a bad process, whether it be for shipping or receiving or production, can create "holes" that can be easily exploited by employees. This he agreed with thoroughly. When the company makes decisions about how it is going to prepare its product for shipping, the ease with which employees can exploit a hole in the system must be considered. As that product is transported to its destination, how secure is it against pilfering from outside? Several opportunities to pilfer product this may exist, and as a company you are smart to think about this as you decide how you plan to ship the product to its final destination.

The tendency toward dualism—either/or thinking suggesting something is *either* related to security *or* it is not related to security—is powerfully restrictive. You have security issues, and you have everything else. As discussed in the prelude to this book, some people see a target setting as either secure or not secure. This either/or mentality does not serve security professionals well, but it is pervasive.

Security is a dynamic enterprise and does not lend itself well to dualisms. For those new to security, it is important to see some level of security everywhere. It is more accurate to think about an area having security ranging somewhere between "really good" to "really bad." Consider the highlight box about the revised U.S. currency. Readers who focus on the fact that the government was responsible for these security-enhancing currency changes will miss the more important point. If a business accepts bad money, typically, those losses come out of their bottom line. For example, it becomes important to think about how to ensure that workers in a retail setting do not accept counterfeit money.

When a student has difficulty seeing the multiple layers of security within a target setting, I ask a simple question: "Does the practice we are discussing assist in any way with either the safety and/or security of the people or property in the target environment we are considering?" If the answer is yes, it is related to security. These students start seeing layers of security everywhere. Most important, they start to notice when security features outlined to meet one objective might in reality impede or actually increase existing risk levels.

Consider the story of the chicken plant fire discussed in the second highlight box. The management made decisions to padlock eight out of nine fire exit doors, from the outside, in an effort to reduce vandalism and theft. As a result, 25 people died and 56 more were injured when an explosion in a fryer vat started a huge fire. Certainly, management will want to work with security if vandalism and theft is a problem within the target environment. Security professionals and management must respond if they want to reduce the risk levels associated with these threats. The countermeasure must be reviewed to ensure that it does not compromise the overall security objective.

To overlook how the essential elements of a basic security design (presented in Chapters 5–7) are brought together is to miss the point for developing a seamlessly integrated security design. It is essential to see the existing security protocol as a work in progress. If the members of the security management team spend too much time responding to incidents, they need to step back and take a look at the overall system. Responding to incidents rather

Show Me the Money!

With more than $400 billion in U.S. currency in circulation, the task of protecting against counterfeiting is enormous. According to estimates provided by the U.S. Secret Service, there is more than $400 million in imitation currency circulation in the United States. Personal computers, laser and inkjet printers, scanners, and copiers are becoming more sophisticated and are being used in the production of about 40 percent of this phony money.[1] This was before the Series 1996 currency was introduced.

The New Currency Design Task Force conducted a $765,000 revamping of the national currency.[2] The Task Force included representatives from the U.S. Treasury Department, the Federal Reserve System, the U.S. Secret Service, and the Bureau of Engraving and Printing.[3] The National Academy of Sciences conducted tests on more than 120 security features, including those that have proven reliable, those that are relatively easy to manufacture, and those that are durable over time. The Design Task Force was to include as many security features as it deemed justifiable; it just wanted to make sure the new features were compatible with the traditional design of U.S. currency.

The most prominent change in the new currency is a larger portrait, which is set slightly off center. This portrait allows for the incorporation of greater detail, and its position provides more room for the watermark. The watermark is created during the production of the paper, depicts the same historical figure as the portrait, and is visible when the currency is held up to a light. Color-shifting ink is used in the numeral in the lower right-hand corner on the front of the bill. This ink looks green when viewed straight on but appears black when viewed at an angle. Microprinting has also been incorporated into the new currency. This printing is not legible to the naked eye, but it can be read with a low-power magnifier (such as a standard magnifying glass). For example, in the $20 note, microprinting is found in the border of the portrait and within the number in the lower left corner of the front side. The backgrounds of the portrait and picture on the reverse side use the techniques of concentric fine-line printing, which makes it difficult to accurately replicate the new currency because it does not copy well.

Not all has been changed, however. The currency is still being printed on the same paper. Chosen for its durability and distinct feel, the paper is made of cotton and linen rag with tiny red and blue fibers embedded in it to give it a more distinguished appearance. The size of the currency has not changed since 1929, with dimensions of 6.14 inches by 2.61 inches. The motto "In God We Trust" first appeared on U.S. money in 1864 (on a two-cent coin), and the new currency will continue to display these words.[4]

This attempt to bolster the security of U.S. currency while still preserving its heritage has lead to a decline in counterfeiting. According to Treasury Secretary Robert E. Rubin, "We have seen in the first year of circulation alone significantly less counterfeiting of the new note compared to the older series."[5] Federal Reserve Chairman Alan Greenspan added, "Our currency is trusted and accepted by people throughout the world. Because of this special status, the protection of our currency from counterfeiting has long been a priority."[6]

The protections put in place by the Treasury are also focused on protecting the business's bottom line. The ability to spot counterfeit money is important because incidents where fake money is accepted by a retail establishment lead to losses for the business. Particularly because computer reproduction and color printers are quite common, loss prevention efforts should incorporate training on spotting counterfeits.

(continued)

References

1. M. A. Saadi, "Developments to Watch," *Business Week,* August 14, 2000, 79.
2. Technical Background Security Features, Currency Facts, Bureau of Engraving and Printing. *www.bep.treas.gov/welcomehtm#top,* accessed January 26, 2001.
3. Ibid.
4. "U.S. Treasury and Federal Reserve Introduce New $50 Bill," *http://www.treas.gov/press/releases/pr1746.htm,* accessed on January 26, 2001.
5. "Redesigned U.S. $50 Bill Debuts Today," *http://www.treas.gov/press/releases/pr2010.htm,* October 27, 1997.
6. "Redesigned U.S. $50 Bill Debuts Today."

than monitoring prevention efforts suggests some room for improving the security management system. When all of the essential components are put together and the overlap is assessed, the process of integration has begun.

THE ESSENCE OF INTEGRATION

To develop an effective, successful security protocol, security professionals must obey at least three fundamental truths: (1) They must know every aspect of the target environment, (2) they must stay abreast of the trends and activities in the security field as they relate to their environment and their security objectives, and (3) they must feel free to utilize other qualified security professionals as resources when introducing specialized security functions into the target environment.

Know the Environment

Security issues for a local amusement park will be different from security issues for a bank. Yes, aspects of the operations in each of those environments are similar and a general understanding of security essentials will prove useful for people in either setting. We understand that site-specific nuances, environmental issues, and other factors make each environment unique. But let's say a security professional is working at that local amusement park. Perhaps this is his fourth year working there. How much can he *not* know about that target environment? What else could there possible be to learn or think about that has not already been addressed or considered? Let's see.

Because he has worked there for so many years, he knows the operation fairly well. Perhaps he has even been promoted and is now the security coordinator of personnel issues for the upcoming season. While his experience with the organization helps him know the environment, it is also true that his new responsibilities require additional understanding. In this case the focus is on personnel issues. Further, critical elements within that environment can change quickly. Perhaps the company changed owners, and new policies are being introduced. How might this change the target environment? How might

Imperial Chicken, Not So Noble

Business owners are required to provide a safe working environment for all of their employees. It may not be possible to eliminate the risk of disasters such as storms and fires, but minimizing the reverberations of these disasters is important, and it can be simple. Storm shelters, fire exits and extinguishing equipment, and proper procedural training can lead to a significant decrease in fatalities and injuries. However, what happens when one of the basic elements in employee security is violated? Imperial Foods found out the answer when it took away some employee protection to increase the security of its facility from outside threats.

Around 8:30 A.M. on September 3, 1991,[1] workers in the Imperial Foods chicken processing plant in Hamlet, North Carolina, smelled something burning. Suddenly, they were engulfed in thick, yellow smoke, a pungent mixture of melting insulation and burning soybean oil and chicken parts,[2] a fire that was started (according to witnesses) in a 25-foot-long fryer vat.[1] As the employees tried to flee the burning facility, many met an obstacle: getting through the fire exit doors. Of the nine fire exits in the facility, all but one were locked. Employees tried tirelessly to break through, screaming, "Let me out! Let me out!"[1] Indentations of footprints were found on at least one of the exit doors, which was locked from the outside. When the smoke cleared, 25 workers were found dead, with about 50 more injured, with severe burns, blindness, respiratory disease, neurological and brain damage, and posttraumatic stress syndrome.[2]

How could Imperial Foods get away with having eight out of nine fire exit doors locked? It had not had a safety inspection in 11 years.[1] At the time of the fire, there was a shortage of safety inspectors in North Carolina, so the Department of Labor inspected only facilities for which there had been complaints. However, the plant was visited daily by the poultry inspector; he was aware that the fire exits were locked (in violation of safety codes) but never reported it.[2] The plant also did not have any sprinklers and contained a lot of asbestos. Only two oxygen tanks were seen by witnesses. Given that the plant had experienced three fire flare-ups earlier in the year, precautions should have been taken to reduce the imminent danger.

One of the workers summed up the situation best by saying, "It was like being locked up in hell."[2] As trapped workers screamed for help and fought to get out, they had to witness coworkers dying and suffering severe injuries. Emergency response expert Clark Staten of the Emergency Response & Research Institute in Chicago, Illinois, said, "It's hard to believe, in today's day and age that any business owner or manager would be so insensitive to fire safety as to allow this sort of incident to happen."

Liability issues are always a major concern in businesses. There is no question that the plant owner was responsible for what happened. He was aware that the doors were being locked; it may have been a policy that he implemented. The owner agreed and pleaded guilty to 25 counts of manslaughter. Sadly, this ruling will not bring back the loved ones that were lost in this tragic fire. But hopefully it will lead to stricter fire safety codes and prevent future tragedies like this one.

References

1. Emergency Response & Research Institute, "Fire Violations Kill Twenty-Five in Chicken Plant," http://www.emergency.com/nc-fire.htm, September 4, 1991, accessed January 23, 2001.
2. N. Riley, "Hamlet: The Untold Tragedy," http://www.organicanenews.com/news/article.cfm?story_id=103, accessed January 23, 2001.

that affect issues involving personnel? Consider what the impact would be if management ran a "Senior Week Supersale" for all graduating high school seniors who come to the park in groups of five or more. How would that impact the security objectives within the park? What about a heat wave? What about a news report about the abduction of two small children from an amusement park in a neighboring state? What about the chance that one of those college students hired on as seasonal help is a "bad apple"?

All of these factors will impact how security professionals think about and decide to implement the security essentials. As they review the system in place, security professionals may not need to add any physical security features, but perhaps they choose instead to use the existing features differently. They may already have an employee screening process, but if they suffered after an exceptionally bad hire, it will make sense to revisit this protocol.

If the security management team at the amusement park expects an additional 500 to 1500 high school seniors to visit the park the week of graduation, it makes sense to think about whether they want to add additional staff and revisit the policy for handling disruptive people and responding to uncooperative groups. It makes sense to remind park staff about the no-alcohol policy in the park and how to respond if there is a violation. As you can see, the list of things to consider can get pretty long.

Certainly, the more familiar you are with the environment, the better. It is not enough, however, for security personnel to think that just because they have been working in a given setting for a number of years, they know all they need to know. Part of knowing about an environment is paying attention to the different layers of activity necessary for making the whole park system run smoothly. A variety of things can change any given day.

It is not uncommon to have a well-known speaker or even a nationally known figure on a university campus. Bill Cosby recently performed at the campus where I teach. While these events are normal within the university setting, each event has specific needs and security-related concerns unique to that event. What changes in the event preparation if the guest is not Bill Cosby, but Gloria Steinem, or the rapper Eminem?

Knowing an environment means constantly researching to learn more about issues that might affect the environment. The more security professionals know about an environment, its threats, and the related risk levels, the more comprehensive their overall security response will be.

Know the Security Field

It might be somewhat obvious to say that part of the job of a security professional is to keep up with crime trends, technology trends, and any other security-related trends. Security professionals always need to be learning. Security practitioners are often quite open when it comes to providing information about their experiences, and the professional organizations can prove to be an excellent resource for networking with other security professionals working in the same business or on the same issue. Trade journals and security-related magazines profile different security settings and report their experiences with security in those settings.

As you become more familiar with security as a discipline, it will become apparent that various issues outside of your environment will also affect how you do business. Experienced security professionals, for example, understand how changes in legislation or technological advances can dramatically affect how they are able to provide security in your environment. Security management teams must be given the ability to brainstorm concerns and possibilities and explore how any emerging issues might affect the existing security system. If the chief executive officer of a company begins to travel internationally, the security team needs to be aware of the threats and risk levels associated with international travel.

Technologies are changing and improving at a tremendous pace. This is good, because security professionals in various environments can improve security for less money than they could before. However, the rapid technological advances, especially in computers, mean that security professionals may confront a system need they do not have the expertise to address. It makes sense to touch base with a security professional who does have expertise in the area where you need support. You don't have to know everything about every security item ever made to be an excellent security professional. Sometimes it simply takes a willingness to learn. Maybe you won't have the kind of mastery of information technology that your security colleague has, but you know how the system works within your system and what the computer system is designed to accomplish. You can rely on the knowledge gained from the professional's specialized security knowledge and maintain the integrity of your security management system. This requires you to build and maintain essential connections with other security professionals.

Rely on Other Security Experts

Every time I go to the American Society for Industrial Security (ASIS) international conference, I am amazed by the variety of specialization areas within the security field. This is Security Professional A, and she is an expert on threat assessment and workplace violence. This is Security Professional B, and he is an expert on security lighting. The list of specialties goes on: school security, the banking industry, nuclear facilities, health care organizations, terrorism, and so forth. Much of what is done within the security profession is accomplished by networking with other security professionals and incorporating their knowledge and expertise.

As a researcher and industry observer, I wonder if the industry growth rates serve as more evidence of **outsourcing** various security responsibilities.

Free as a Bird?

December 8, 1980 is a date that is etched in the minds of many people, especially three members of the legendary rock group the Beatles. It was on that treacherous winter day in New York City that John Lennon was shot and killed outside his apartment by an obsessed fan. That month had been very distressing for the Beatles because they had received more threats than they ever had before. Lennon's murder forever changed the way at least one former Beatle, George Harrison, lived his life.

"After what happened to John, I am absolutely terrified," admitted Harrison.[2] He lived for years with the dread that he too will fall prey to some crazed fan. Fanatical about preventing this, and facing a wave of death threats, in 1990 Harrison overhauled the security system at the 120-room nunnery-turned-mansion where he lived—at a cost of 250,000 pounds[2] (equivalent to about $364,000). Neighbors refered to Harrison's mansion as "Fort Knox." The mansion was set on 34 acres, surrounded by a 10-foot-high wall that is topped with razor wire.[1] The system also incorporates powerful lighting, videocameras, and electronically controlled gates.[2] There used to be a team of security guards patrolling the wall and posted at the gates, but Harrison now uses them only when he has VIP guests. There is also a sophisticated alarm system on the house that is directly linked to the Henley police station, which sits just 400 yards away.[2] Another alarm system, similar to that used by the British Army in Northern Ireland, was installed over the 34-acre estate.[2] These alarms are so sophisticated that they can detect any movement taking place on the grounds.[2]

Security consultants agree that even the most advanced security systems are never foolproof. It turns out that the system at Harrison's mansion does have a flaw. The 10-foot-high fencing around the iron gates is only a small obstacle to someone who is intent on getting onto the property. This vulnerability was once accounted for when the hired guards and dogs were patrolling the area. Why would a man who is so afraid for his own safety decrease his security force and rely solely on technological instruments?

Celebrities bring more security issues to the table than common people do. They seem to be targeted and put under the microscope for everything they do. With a life that is so public, it is difficult to hide from people intent on inflicting some type of harm. As the Harrison example makes clear, security comes in many forms, but no matter what people spend to protect themselves, they are still going to be vulnerable.

References

1. M. Baltierra, Associated Press, and Reuters, "Ex-Beatle Stabbed in His Home," *http://abcnews.go.com/sections/entertainment/DailyNews/harrison991230.html*, December 30, 1999.
2. I. Gallagher, "How Did Intruder Breach the Fanatical Security System?" *http://www.lineone.net/express/99/12/31/news/n0420how-d.html*, December 31, 1999.

Additional Resources

"Harrison Attack 'Deliberate,' " *http://news:bbc.co.uk/hi/english/uk/newsid_583000/583403.stm*, December 30, 1999.

S. Lyall, "George Harrison Stabbed in Chest by an Intruder," *New York Times*, December 31, 1999, A1.

J. F. O. McAllister, "Bad Day's Night," *http://www.time.com/time/magazine/articles/0,3266,36762,00.html*, January 1, 2000.

D. McGrory, "Woken by the Sound of His Worst Nightmare," *http://www.Sunday-times.co.uk/news/pages/tim/1999/12/31/timnwsnws01002.html?1996766*, December 31, 1999.

Also known as contract outsourcing, this is the decision to contract with an outside agency to provide a specific security-related service. Even within a security department or private business offering security services, there may be a need for outside expertise. Rely on security practitioners whose professional reputation and personal integrity has been clearly demonstrated and whose actions will not unexpectedly add to your existing list of security concerns.

THE IMPORTANCE OF AN INTEGRATED SECURITY DESIGN

Resources for security professionals are everywhere. In addition to the various professional organizations, many areas of academic study can provide useful information. Leadership theory, management theory, conflict resolution, human relations, crime prevention through environmental design (CPTED), technology development, engineering, law enforcement, computer engineering, and other topics can be easily applied to specific security-related issues. In more traditional interpretations of security, as both a concept and an area of study, security was considered entirely separate from jobs done by other people within an agency or environment. Today the erroneous logic of this dualism is being realized. A company's organizational structure can easily reflect the company's interest in integrating multitude of security objectives (see Figure 8–1).

Although the company's management (e.g., the board of directors, the vice president) often dictates the structural components of the formal organiza-

FIGURE 8–1   Organizational Possibilities: Security as the Centerpoint

tional structure, it is important to recognize the central role security plays in that environment. Security personnel must interact in and work cooperatively with people in each division. For example, security will work closely with the human resources department to provide adequate support for preemployment screening. Also, security will work with persons who handle computer services throughout the company. As they make sure that any vulnerability gaps in the computer system are identified and secured, security professionals should re-member that computer technology experts have quickly taken center stage in many settings. Working with qualified, trustworthy employees in the computer division can aid security practitioners as they attempt to provide essential buffers to ensure that the computer systems are adequately protected.

If an employee is suspected of embezzling funds, for example, and is under investigation, it will be important for security personnel to have a good com-munication with the people responsible for maintaining any related records as the investigation proceeds. This can be tricky, particularly if the person under suspicion has access to these records. Discretion is as important as healthy communication with others in the division.

Security professionals must work hard to maintain strong communication with people in all divisions of the target environment. Office managers will typ-ically contact outside vendors to repair copy machines, for example, and un-known outside vendors can be a security threat. Building maintenance profes-sionals must stay on top of repairs; a door-locking mechanism could be malfunctioning, leaving an area open that is intended to be secured. Custodians asked to routinely check locks, lights, entryways, and windows to ensure that the building is adequately maintained are contributing to overall security man-agement. In fact, people in many of the areas listed in Figure 8–1 perform du-ties that affect the overall security of the environment.

People throughout a target environment, not just security professionals, can be used as the "eyes and ears" of that environment. Consider the role non-security employees play in helping to maintain a secure setting. Security man-agers and security teams benefit when employees are brought in on various as-pects of the overall security objective. Increasingly, security professionals are discussing ways to improve communication within the agency or organization, especially to enhance employees' sense of security in the workplace. To create a well-integrated security response, the security team must interact well (and regularly) with people from each division in the organizational structure.

Aspiring security professionals are likely to find it interesting that the in-centive for applying CPTED techniques to the convenience store environment, discussed in more detail in Chapter 5, had little to do with the financial losses from robberies and much to do with employee and customer relations.[1] A crit-ical factor for industry officials was the loss of business from customers, who were afraid to shop in the stores; the loss of qualified employees, who were afraid to work in the stores; and successful litigation by individuals who were harmed during convenience store robberies.[2] It is good business to work in conjunction with employees, customers, and industry officials to ensure that people feel safe and secure while they work or shop.

Workplaces are also educating workers about taking an active role in their own protection and the security of the environment.[3,4] Examples include personal security training strategies, presented to workers, to outline how the company can be a resource for employees if they have security concerns or witness things that are suspicious and should be brought to the attention of the security department. Education or training programs about sexual harassment, diversity education, computer security, and other topics help incorporate individuals into the security plan.

The role of the security professional is pivotal here. Security professionals must be trusted and responsible if other employees are to respect them. Attention has been given to interactions with aspiring security professionals from the initial contact through hiring, training, assessment of job responsibilities, and ongoing performance evaluations to see what characteristics make a good security professional.[5] Yet efforts to ensure that good security professionals are hired can be undermined if there is no effort to ensure that all employees, not just security professionals, hired meet specific standards identified as important by the company. In addition to careful training of employees, companies report the use of magazines, newsletters, videos, posters, daily meetings, public address announcements, and interactive workshops to spread the word that security is everyone's responsibility. Nonsecurity personnel can be trained about security issues and then used to assist in identifying any potential problems before they become big problems.[6,7] Employees become the "eyes" and "ears" of the security management team.[8–10]

An excellent example is found in some of the discussions about computer security. If an outsider can call into the company and get certain information from the company's receptionist that will allow the caller to hack into the computer's system, the receptionist becomes an unwitting accomplice. If a security professional learns about new ways that people are hacking into systems, he or she can organize a training session and help prevent these hacker attacks.

Creating a seamless, integrated security design requires a thorough review of existing resources and security objectives from within the individual divisions and across the organization. The integration theme is becoming so popular that *Security Management* (the industry's trade magazine) runs a regular section titled "Focus on Integration." Just about everything, from customer service to employee relations, can be enhanced to provide better security.[11] System integration has been described as both an art and a science.[12] The term *integration* has been used to describe the need to coordinate existing technology and equipment with new technology and equipment.[13] Integration can also involve making sure that the human security response and the technological security response are coordinated.[14] The lesson here for security professionals is to think about how security needs overlap and how security objectives can be considered as a whole.

Integrating to Move outside of the Box

Consider school security. The shootings at Columbine High School in Littleton, Colorado on April 20, 1999 made headlines around the world.[15] School administrators around the country were wondering what they could do to make sure that such an event does not materialize on their school grounds. In New Hampshire, acting on a tip (from a student) that a student in the school was making a list of people to kill, administrators at a high school decided to get involved and broke into a boy's locker. They found a .22 caliber revolver and 400 bullets in the locker. This principal elected to use an active response, encouraging students to notify an adult if there was trouble, rather than installing guards, surveillance cameras, or metal detectors.

Many security experts say this works. Effective communication between teachers and students is an important aspect of reducing school violence, but it is often overlooked. While some schools have opted for enhancing security with technology, security professionals are quick to remind people that if that is all they do, they'll "fail abysmally."[16] In the area of school security, experts have elected to focus on early intervention. This includes using role-play techniques to teach empathy and impulse control and watching for signs that students are in trouble, including excessive feelings of rejection, expressions of violence in writing and drawings, and serious direct threats.[17]

Or consider a sample security concern of one of the world's largest pharmaceutical operations, Glaxo Wellcome. The pharmaceutical giant has operations all over the globe and built a breeding farm in the English countryside. The breeding farm produces animals for government-mandated testing of new medicines conducted by the company. Breeding farms are often sites for animal rights groups to hold protests and demonstrations with various objectives. Sometimes they seek to disrupt work, heckle employees, or free the animals being used for the experiments. So, while they may be bothersome, the company must often simply work around their presence. Glaxo Wellcome's U.K. breeding farm is protected by many of the same physical security safeguards and security policies in place at other large international operations, including physical security and access control features, proprietary information safeguards, bomb threat response, personal protection, and insider theft prevention response.[18] Consideration of the overall security objective was incorporated into the design of the breeding farm, incorporating a seven-foot-tall fence around the perimeter of the property. From a secure gatehouse, on-site security personnel monitor the property around the clock. The gatehouse doubles as the control room, from which intruder alarms, closed-captioned television, and the fire alarm system can be handled. Because no police stations are nearby, security personnel from another operation 12 miles away are used for backup. To minimize the risk of intruders, the company purchased the property adjacent to the farm.

While the layers of protection put in place at the breeding farm are interesting, the different security operations at the different facilities run by Glaxo
Wellcome are also worthy of note. The building that is the most in need of protection is where the research is conducted.[19] At that location cameras are
mounted on the fence line about every 75 yards or so, so that every inch of the
perimeter is covered. Cameras work in tandem with video motion detection and
infrared technologies (for better night vision) and are always recording. The
camera system is sophisticated enough to meet the needs of the operations.
When motion is detected, the real-time transmission of the camera covering
that part of the fence line automatically appears on a designated monitor in the
control room. A freeze-frame of the cause of the alarm is also displayed, providing further information. This setup not only facilitates tracking of an intruder but also lets monitoring personnel quickly determine whether the alarm
was triggered by animals, blowing leaves, or other "nuisances."

The system integrates security-related ideas with the objectives for each of
the various sites owned by the company. It is not uncommon for activists to infiltrate a site in an attempt to expose what they perceive to be animal abuses
within the testing setting.[20] Another part of the overall security plan is to increase communications between the company and the local community. Company representatives attend forums and workshops, even school functions, in
an attempt to explain why animals are used in medical research and how these
animals are cared for in the facility. The outreach program affords members of
the community the opportunity to ask questions and voice their concerns. On
a final note, the company emphasized the fact that the public relations program
could be jeopardized if the company was found to be misrepresenting its practices, particularly with the animals. Therefore, two internal committees perform spot checks to make sure employees are following the strict procedures
for animal treatment that are used to ensure the animals' protection.[21]

Consider the role of security professionals at a local mall. The responsibilities include dealing with the various retailers, addressing employee concerns
and questions, and interacting with the public in a very high-profile, uniformed
position. The public relations function can be important to the overall security
objective because the security staff are the front-line response to a variety of
citizen concerns. This may include requests for directions to a specific store,
assistance with a flat tire or dead car battery, the unlocking of an office door,
late-night or off-hour escort services, traffic control, help with health concerns,
assistance finding a lost child, and any of a number of "walk-up" complaints.
Imagine a scenario where a man with two small children approaches a security
officer. He reports that he has lost his keys somewhere in the mall while he and
his children were shopping. A security officer could offer two extremely opposite responses. First, the security officer could act professionally, respectfully,
and immediately (as his or her responsibilities dictate), perhaps taking some

basic information and then contacting dispatch to coordinate an appropriate response. Second, the security officer could shake his or her head and half-laugh, saying, "Well, what do you think I can do about it?" The man with the two children might feel desperate because his toddler needs a diaper change and the diapers are in the car. Perhaps the man has no one to call to bring him a second set of keys. Perhaps he is thinking that without his house key, he will not be able to get into his house, even though it is naptime and the children are getting cranky. The security officer's response to this man's circumstances is likely to affect how this man perceives the mall in general, on this day and in the future. The security officer's ability to help this person and not add to an already frustrating situation is likely to be remembered for a long time. If the experience is positive, this person's perception of the mall will be positive. If the experience is negative, not only will this person's reaction to the situation be negative but he is likely to tell everyone he knows about his negative encounter at the mall.

Imagine another situation. After driving three hours, a woman is late for a day-long conference at a downtown hotel. After parking quickly in a garage, she walks out onto the street. Getting directions from several people along the way, she finally makes it to the hotel. After the workshop is over, she attempts to retrace her steps back to the parking garage but realizes that she was in such a hurry to get to the workshop that she did not pay close attention to the location of the garage. Furthermore, she left the ticket she got at the gate in the car, so she has no way of knowing which parking garage she parked in. It is getting close to 5:30 P.M., and one thing she does remember is that the parking garage closes at 6 P.M. Imagine the first security professional this person encounters after searching in vain for the parking garage. Imagine how a single comment like "Don't you worry about a thing; this happens more than you would think. Let me get some information about your car, and I will make some calls to the local lots" would ease the woman's stress. A professional, helpful security officer is an asset to the overall operation.

A MODEL FOR INTEGRATION: IT IS "MAGIC"

In March 1999, Disney's security department provided a tour of the grounds and offered the opportunity for a group of criminal justice practitioners to take a tour and ask questions about Disney's security operations in Orlando, Florida. The Florida operation includes approximately 50,000 "cast members" (employees) at any given time. There are over 2000 alarms and approximately 200 cameras across the 44 acres.[22] Thirteen hundred security professionals are used across the five parks (Animal Kingdom, Downtown Disney, Epcot, Universal Studios, and the Magic Kingdom).

Several books and articles have been written about the Disney operation, with some of them focusing more specifically on the security of the facility. The comments from very prominent security professionals[23] suggest the strength of the Disney security operation is linked directly to the integration of the security function with all other aspects of the overall Disney operation.[24] Disney employees use passive confrontation as a means to control their park visitors. "Security may not be ever apparent at the park, but it is ever present. It makes its presence felt only when necessary."[25]

Disney tries to make the security presence inconspicuous. Disney's employees are told to be polite to everyone, but to act decisively when and if the park's tranquility is threatened. "When officers first approach suspects, they must be conciliatory, even friendly. 'It's better to grin 'em to death than to start fighting,' said one officer."[26] Like most organizations, Disney must remain vigilant in monitoring employees. The security director in Florida suggested that 70 percent of the theft there is internal.[27] He described Disney's security response in terms of a pyramid structure (Figure 8–2). The pyramid refers to the overall operations. Because Disney focuses the overall park operations on keeping people safe, that provides the base of the pyramid. Everyone on the Disney team is involved in the responsibility of creating a safe and secure setting. When problems arise, the security response involves investigating the suspicious circumstances. This comprises the second level, or layer of protection efforts. Loss prevention is the third largest level and involves prevention efforts. The next largest layers of security response come from the community centers where security issues are centralized within the operation. These security efforts are less visible and involve less officers. The top two layers of security response involve canines and access control systems.

One of the biggest inside jobs ever to take place in the California park involved a supervisor who had worked at Disneyland for 19 years without incident. "For three-and-a-half years, a warehouse supervisor had been stealing videotapes, stuffed animals, toys, stationery, clothing, and other memorabilia and reselling them to local shops. He said he had a special deal with the park.

FIGURE 8–2 Disney: An Example of Security Pyramid Structure

He stole $500,000 to $800,000 worth of souvenirs, and his half share of the sales profits netted him an estimated $170,000."[28]

Particular attention is given to guest relations, to ensure that all visitors have an excellent experience while on the Disney property. The security officers' job is described as 85 percent public relations.[29] In fact, the Disney Corporation has created a motto that each of its employees recites when asked: "We create happiness by providing the finest entertainment to people of all ages, everywhere."[30] The company philosophy is always on the minds of employees, who seek to maintain this objective while performing their responsibilities in the park.

Security experts have held Disney's operation up as a model for security planning, primarily because security-related concerns are integrated into every aspect of the overall business operations.[31] The control strategies are embedded in both environmental features and structural relations. "Opportunities for disorder are minimized by constant instruction, by physical barriers which severely limit the choice of action available and by the surveillance of omnipresent employees who detect and rectify the slightest deviation."[32] The California operation is reported to have security people in costumes.[33] Similar statements about the Florida operation have been made, but the Florida Disney representative who led the tour said that all Disney employees are instructed to be aware of potential security concerns but that security personnel were all in casual security attire or plainclothes.[34]

One of my favorite Disney prevention tactics has to do with the maze of lines where people wait—sometimes for hours, sometimes in hot temperatures—to go on their favorite park rides. The planning of these mazes is not accidental.[35] Waiting in lines can be aggravating and stressful, especially with young children. For this reason Disney planners created areas within the lines that offer a good view of the ride, so that people will forget that they are waiting and focus on the fact that they are getting closer to the head of the line. After moving along a waiting line for the Log Ride for approximately 35–40 minutes, for instance, people get to an area in the line with an excellent view of the ride. They may even get splashed by the water from the ride. This is a friendly reminder that they will be duly rewarded for their wait—even if it is long.

The fact that most of the excellent security features are invisible to park visitors is one of the primary reasons this integrated system is of such interest to, and has achieved such high regard among, security professionals. Instead of the tight controls, the visitors notice the cleanliness, the well-organized paths and walkways, and a sense of security that comes from a well-ordered operation. The multitude of smiling, helpful Disney employees completes the picture.

Disney employees from all areas of the park are included in the security response. There is a toll-free number for reporting any suspicious activities of other cast members. The organization uses "shadow" programs for training new cast members. Background checks and drug tests are used to screen future employees. In fact, employees are taught that safety always comes first. "Workers are taught that safety is everyone's responsibility, and they must follow a comprehensive safety policy and complete mandatory accident reports."[36] Disney employees are said to be so adept at handling various little hitches that few guests notice when something unexpected takes place.

Clearly, Disney has an interest in making sure details about the organization's operations are not made public. Of the books about the Disney operation, a few have been published without support from the Disney establishment. Even though the details are less than apparent to the general public, someone with a working knowledge of security can begin to see how these safety and protection systems work well with the security systems put in place to protect workers and visitors. Although claims have been made that Disney, like any other organization, has violated Occupational Safety and Health Administration guidelines,[37] the objective for the Disney enterprise is to make certain people who come to Disney have a great time and leave with a smile on their face. This is not always easy if people are smuggling in drugs, alcohol, and weapons; if teenagers celebrating graduation are trying to jump from car to car on a moving ride; or if a guest has a medical emergency, such as a heart attack. Some examples of security response involve investigation of fraud in various form (including credit card, travelers checks, personal checks, and efforts to exchange counterfeit money) and dishonest employees. At Disney, security efforts are coupled with employee training efforts to ensure that any security response is inconspicuous and effective, meeting the overall security and safety objectives for the park.

CONCLUSION

Security professionals have a monumental task before them. Identifying the essential elements of a security plan, researching particular security options, and finding the resources necessary for putting the security system in place in the designated target environment are only the beginning of an ongoing security strategic planning process. The security practitioner must also determine how well the security strategies focused on targeted security concerns work within the system in place to meet the overall security objectives. Policies put in place to direct employees and assist employers with the sometimes overwhelming task of training and overseeing these employees cannot be dismissed because the target environment has a plan for managing security concerns. The personnel within the security management team are critical players in designing and revising the overall security objectives of a target environment. The need to revise security objectives as an ongoing element within an overall security plan is as essential in a small "mom and pop" business as it is to a chief executive officer and board members of a major corporation. Computer concerns are an excellent example of this. Although the sophistication of the security needs will be different, a modern business will require computer security regardless of size.

Security must be an integral part of the overall objectives within a target environment. This means integrating all aspects of security into the overall operations within a target environment. Decisions about physical security features, asset protection protocols, the handling of sensitive corporate information, computer security practices, and personnel issues must all be made with consideration for the overall security-related needs of the target environment. It is not enough to have a security plan for issues identified as security concerns. That security plan must touch every aspect of the overall operations. Anything less than that is inadequate. As the Disney example indicates, an excellent security response can be quite sophisticated and involve the expertise and resources of many capable security professionals. If yours is a small operation, it makes sense to use security professionals who have expertise in specific areas to assist you with your own security needs.

The examples of various settings allow students to apply their new knowledge and build confidence in their own analytical skills. I want students to think about their unique environments, their own needs, and their own (perhaps even preexisting) expectations about security. Then I want them to question existing practice, calling into question what they think they know. Why have they decided that one security standard is acceptable for a particular environment? If the environment were different, would the same standard be appropriate? Are there other standards that also make sense for the target environment? Have they conducted any research? Do they have a thorough understanding of new findings in the field of security? How do they begin to think about introducing new ideas into a traditionally static environment? What opposition might they encounter, even from their own security colleagues?

This profession is about identifying a plan, putting it in place, and then asking questions about the plan's effectiveness, with the goal being the development of a better plan. Nothing is static in the field of security. It is the layering of these ideas, as much as it is the context in which these ideas are put into practice, that warrants more instructional and intellectual exploration from both students and practitioners. There are many resources discussing how, for example, the Americans with Disabilities Act affects hiring practices. But because laws change and details may be rearranged, efforts to pile on too much information too quickly can overwhelm aspiring security professionals. The ability to memorize facts and information is only one ingredient of becoming an excellent security practitioner.

REVIEW QUESTIONS

1. Explain the concept of integration as it is applied to the six areas discussed in the preceding chapters: 1) asset protection, 2) physical security, 3) in-

formation security, 4) computer security, 5) personnel security, 6) security management.

2. The author talks about "one-dimensional thinking," Why is this concept important in a security context?
3. How is counterfeit money related to security issues in business?
4. Outline the justifications for needing to know about the target environment, the trends in the security field, and using other security professionals as a resource for meeting your own security objectives.
5. Identify the aspects of Disney security that reflect a model for integration.
6. Why is it inappropriate to link security function with common sense? Justify your response.

DISCUSSION QUESTIONS

1. Consider an example where a security management team is responding to a significant number of incidents. What might this suggest? How might you go about fixing it?
2. What elements presented in the Disney discussion do you find particularly interesting? Be prepared to justify your response.
3. Identify a target environment of your choosing. Review the six areas presented in Chapters 5, 6, and 7, and then decide what additional steps (if any) might be required to integrate the overall security measures put in place.
4. If you were the owner of a security business that provided alarm equipment, what responses might you be interested in outsourcing to another security company?

REFERENCES

1. R. Hunter and C. R. Jeffery, "Preventing Convenience Store Robbery through Environmental Design," in *Situational Crime Prevention: Successful Case Studies,* ed. R. Clarke (Albany, NY: Harrow and Heston, 1992), 194–204.
2. Hunter and Jeffery, "Preventing Convenience Store Robbery," 195.
3. W. J. McShane, "Raising Security Awareness," *Security Management,* April 1999, 29–30.
4. T. Wilson and M. Bielec, "Security's Human Resourcefulness," *Security Management,* March 1999, 97–104.
5. T. A. Ricks et al., *Principles of Security,* 3rd ed. (Cincinnati, OH: Anderson Publishing Company, 1994), 203–224.
6. S. Traub, "Battling Employee Crime: A Review of Corporate Strategies and Programs," *Crime and Delinquency 42,* no. 2 (1996): 244–350.
7. McShane, "Raising Security Awareness," 29–30.
8. Traub, "Battling Employee Crime," 251.

9. Marx, G. Sherizen, S. and Westin, A. F., Do Monitoring Technologies Threaten Employee Privacy Rights?" *Editorial Research Reports,* vol. 2, no. 12, September 30, 1988, p. 489.
10. Reichman (1987).
11. R. Abrams, "The Customer Comes First," *IFPO Protection News 14,* no. 1 (1998): 4.
12. R. Pearson, "An Artful Approach to Integration," *Security Management,* December 1999, 74–75.
13. Pearson, "An Artful Approach to Integration," 74–79.
14. Wilson and Bielec, "Security's Human Resourcefulness," 97–103.
15. D. L. Marcus, "Metal Detectors Alone Can't Guarantee," *U.S. News & World Report 126,* no. 17 (1999): 26.
16. Marcus, "Metal Detectors Alone Can't Guarantee," 26.
17. Marcus, "Metal Detectors Alone Can't Guarantee," 26.
18. M. Gips, "A Pharmacopoeia of Protection," *Security Management,* March 1999, 42–50.
19. Gips, "A Pharmacopoeia of Protection," 44.
20. M. Gips, "Protecting Endangered Humans," *Security Management,* March 1999, 48.
21. Gips, "Protecting Endangered Humans," 48.
22. Disney Security Tour. March 10, 1999. Academy of Criminal Justice Sciences. Orlando, FL.
23. C. D. Shearing and P. P. Stenning, "Say 'Cheese!': The Disney Order That Is Not So Mickey Mouse," in *Private Policing,* ed. C. D. Shearing and P. P. Stenning (Beverly Hills, CA: Sage Publications, 1987), 317–323.
24. Shearing and Stenning, "Say 'Cheese!'", 317.
25. D. Koenig, *Mouse Tales: A Behind-the-Ears Look at Disneyland* (Irvine, CA: Bonaventure Press, 1995), 147.
26. Koenig, *Mouse Tales,* 147–148.
27. Disney Security Tour.
28. Koenig, *Mouse Tales,* 168.
29. P. Ohlhausen, "Silver Screen Security," *Security Management,* September 1991, 146–152.
30. D. Dalton, *The Art of Security Management* (Woburn, MA: Butterworth-Heinemann, 1998), 61–62.
31. Shearing and Stenning, "Say 'Cheese!'"
32. Shearing and Stenning, "Say 'Cheese!,'" 319.
33. Koenig, *Mouse Tales,* 148.
34. Disney Security Tour.
35. Shearing and Stenning, "Say 'Cheese!,'" 319.
36. Koenig, *Mouse Tales,* 169.
37. Koenig, *Mouse Tales,* 183.

CHAPTER 9

A Sampling of Settings

After reviewing the basics in Part I and then taking a look at the multiple layers of security that can be applied to any target environment outlined in Part II, readers will begin to see how ideas about security and the process for identifying security objectives begins to take shape. Chapter 3 provided a series of snapshot scenarios to use to consider how some of the basic threat and risk related security concepts from Part I could be discussed in various settings.

Those new to the security industry may have difficulty in their initial efforts to apply these concepts in different environments. This is an acquired skill and takes some practice. So practice. This chapter provides an opportunity to play with the ideas presented in the text so far, and will allow you to play with these ideas more fully by offering the chance to consider these ideas in four fairly comprehensive, yet totally fabricated, target environments. In class we call this "target practice."

The target environments include a bank, an airport, a school, a hospital, and a convenience store. Think about the security issues you are likely to encounter and then plan a security response for each of these settings. Consider an abbreviated list of the topics discussed in the book so far: threat identification, assessment of risk levels, physical security, asset protection, information security, computer security, personnel issues, and security management. Your goal is to take this information and develop a clear set of security objectives. Maybe you even want to provide an integrated system. Maybe you want to identify the threats to the environment. How would your evaluation differ if you do it by yourself, or if you do it with two other students? How much research can you do to help you make decisions about the threat list and possible countermeasure responses?

Certainly, there is no way to provide information about any environment in such a short scenario. Consider the information provided in this chapter to be only general background information. Get to know the setting by looking at the relevant sample floor plan, and then begin the process of identifying and exploring information about securing that particular environment. Even with the floor plans provided, you will have to make some assumptions about the settings. If you get stuck, make a note about the information you think you need in order to move forward with a decision and then move on to other things. These exercises are appropriate for individuals, groups, or for the entire class, if you have one. They are always fascinating, loads of fun, and, without exception, informative.

USING THE STRUCTURE OF THE TEXT AS A GUIDE

One approach to using this chapter might be to do a security evaluation for each setting, based on the information presented in the previous chapters. For each setting, review the basics from Part I, including environmental conditions, threats, risk levels, and countermeasures, and then expand on those to include the internal security issues presented in Part II. Again, these are physical security and asset protection, information and computer security, and personnel and security management. Think about how these distinct elements of the security response could be integrated and connected into an overarching security plan. No two readers will develop exactly the same plan, and that is fine.

The objective here is to take time to think through the layers of security and spend time considering the breadth and depth of their importance in a specific target environment. Security must be seen as being bigger than just buying cameras and contracting with an alarm company. Attention must be given to the concepts, the essential pieces of the larger security system. I teach my students that specific information may not always be useful, but if you understand the concepts and general principles behind the specifics you can take that information anywhere and make it work for you.

Consider using the plan in Exhibit 9–1 as a guide to the chapter. Note that public law enforcement, legal liability, and disaster responses (including accidents and emergencies) are involved in an overall security management strategy, but they are discussed in Part III as external connections. After spending time with Chapters 10, 11, and 12, revisit these scenarios with an eye toward linking your existing security objectives with these external connections.

The Selected Settings

Each case study begins with a sample floor plan that I made up. Information collected from recent journal articles and trade publications about that type of target environment follows. This information is not exhaustive. Just as in real-life target environments, security professionals get to know what else they need to know by going beyond the information provided. Readers may choose to look beyond this information and bring in additional resources. It is not the job of the people working within the environment to provide a security professional with everything he or she needs to know about security in that setting. Security professionals must research both their environment and environments with similar security-related concerns, in an effort to better serve the needs of the target setting. Such is the task you now have before you.

Exhibit 9–1   Proposed Plan for Reading about Each Setting

1. Draft a list of individual security objectives for areas within the target environment.
2. Draft a statement detailing the overall security objectives for the target environment.
3. Identify a list of likely threats and assign related risk levels.
4. Consider the physical security concerns.
   - Using the "layer of defense" process or the "interior/exterior" threat identification process, discuss physical security options.
   - Identify technologies that would be useful in the setting to ensure physical security.
5. Consider asset protection.
   - What areas in the environment include assets important to the company?
   - What actions should be taken to enhance security for these targeted areas?
   - What assets are going to be particularly troublesome to protect?
   - What specific conditions may make providing adequate security difficult?
   - What technologies would be useful in the setting to protect the assets?
6. Consider the information and computer security needs.
   - What information in the target environment needs securing?
   - What would a policy and procedure manual for that environment contain?
   - What computer system (networks, etc.) are at work in the environment?
   - What vulnerabilities are likely to exist in the computer systems?
7. Consider the personnel issues.
   - Is it better to use contract or proprietary security personnel in the environment?
   - How should hiring and employee selection be handled in the environment?
   - What groups of people will spend time in the environment?
   - What responsibilities will nonsecurity personnel within the environment have for security?
8. Consider the security management concerns.
   - What role do different divisions of the company plan in security?
   - What is the structure of the group of security professionals within the target environment?
   - What authority do the security professionals have?
   - What coordinating efforts are necessary for addressing a threat?
9. Consider the goal of integrating security objectives.
   - How do agencies and divisions within the target environment relay information to each other?
   - How do agencies and divisions relate to each other?
   - How do agencies and divisions relate to the overall security objective?
10. Think about the generalizations you have been forced to make during this exercise. Which of your responses might change as a result of adding additional information about the site-specific conditions in a given target environment?

Another thing readers may want to keep in mind is the fact that many large environments (e.g., hospitals, airports) will have different people in charge of different aspects of their security and/or management operation. Most security professionals do rely on other security professionals. For purposes of this chapter, however, readers should imagine that they are the security manager charged with directing the development of the overall security plan in each setting.

TARGET ENVIRONMENT: HOSPITAL

Hospitals (Figure 9–1) must be prepared for everything. If there is an accident involving multiple victims, the hospital must be prepared to address the needs of a large number of people—sometimes without much notice. Most hospitals have many different parts, including maternity wards, operating rooms, recovery rooms, intensive care areas, emergency rooms, patient waiting areas, pharmacies, gift shops, and food service areas. There are different security concerns for each division.

Specific threats in the hospital will differ, depending on the area of the hospital. Risk levels associated with those threats may also differ. Consider the following issues as they relate to the security needs of a hospital:

- Most hospitals are shifting paper medical records to computer databases that contain electronic medical records.[1] Hospitals, like other organizations in other industries, are moving toward an organized information system, with a chief information officer coordinating this effort.[2] How can patient information be protected yet still readily available to medical personnel?
- Between 1983 and 1998, 103 babies under six months of age were abducted from health care facilities by nonfamily members.[3] Newborns were taken from the mother's hospital room, the nursery, the pediatrics

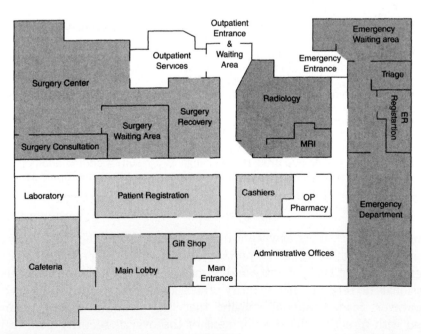

FIGURE 9–1 Sample Target Environment: Hospital

unit, or elsewhere on the facility property. Most of the babies have been recovered; six remain missing.[4]

- Hospitals with psychiatric wards face additional threats and risks.[5,6]
- Various steps must be taken by hospital personnel to prevent the transmission of disease. One of the most prominent occupational risks to health care workers is exposure to blood-borne viruses. While disease transmission to workers can take place in various ways, much research has been done on the process of taking blood from the patient.[7]
- Hospital emergency departments experience many security problems. People who are under stress, either as a patient or as the family member of a patient in a life-threatening situation, can be extremely demanding—so much so that hospital staff may require security resources to get their job done. Often understaffed due to budget cuts and overflowing with patients who use the emergency department as a "walk-in clinic," emergency departments must deal with people who yell and get irate because they are not being attended to as quickly as they think they should be.[8]
- With cuts in social assistance, more people are coming in with more social problems. "You get a lot of street people, a lot of psychiatric patients and drunks."[9]
- The implementation of managed care systems (including health maintenance organizations) has health care professionals frustrated with the frantic pace they must keep, which they blame on the change toward managed care coverage.[10] Jobs are being cut, and people are nervous about losing their jobs.
- Hospitals are introducing computer-controlled drug vending machines, like the Pyxis Med Station System 2000. One hospital reported that the new system jammed two times in one hectic weekend, making the drug supply unavailable.[11]
- Hospitals that provide acute care and operate at bed occupancy levels of 90 percent or more face regular bed crises, which place patients at risk.[12]
- It is recommended that medical equipment or utility system components that are deemed "critical to patient safety" have emergency procedures including backup systems in the event of malfunction or failure. "Critical to patient safety" means that the equipment or component includes life-supporting, life-sustaining, or other critical equipment whose malfunction would result in an "adverse patient outcome."[13]
- Hospitals are deciding how to best provide quick access to data and furnish referring physicians with relevant data while also maintaining patient privacy. Some hospitals use a computer program that provides access to information electronically from any Web browser on the hospital's computer network.[14]

- Certain types of protective clothing are more effective at filtering infectious agents and, therefore, can help health care workers reduce exposure to several pathogens that are borne in blood and body fluids.[15]
- A California-based health care association estimates that 1500 of the 2700 hospital buildings in the state could collapse during a serious earthquake.[16]

TARGET ENVIRONMENT: AIRPORT

Airport (Figure 9–2) security is increasingly a feature of national and international news. As the airline industry expands, as people increasingly travel for business and pleasure to all parts of the globe, the industry is forced to confront some new challenges. Aviation disasters create disturbances for the industry and the traveling public. Within the next decade, the number of annual U.S. aircraft passengers is expected to be 1 billion.[17] Threats of terrorism result in increased security efforts, which can lead to flight delays and unhappy passengers. The causes of some aviation disasters may never be determined. After four years of investigation and recovery of more than 95 percent of the wreckage, the cause of the crash of TWA flight 800 is not known.[18] The federal government's response to this tragic crash included the implementation of heightened security measures at all airports and the creation of a White House

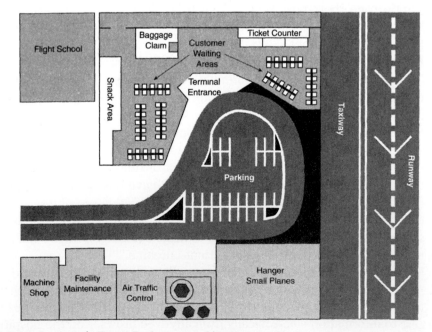

FIGURE 9–2   Sample Target Environment: Airport

Commission on Aviation Safety and Security. Reducing unknown risks in air travel comes with direct tradeoffs. "Each measure to improve safety and security can have an impact on the direct costs to travelers, delays, convenience, civil liberties, fatalities, and taxpayer costs."[19] Consider the following issues being discussed in the aviation industry:

Considerations Identified Prior to 9/11

- In 1998, the National Transportation Safety Board received 2210 reports of commuter and private aircraft accidents within the United States, and these accidents resulted in 641 fatalities.[20]
- Thieves in airports are targeting laptop computer owners. By employing distraction techniques, the thieves are making away with the computers.[21]
- Enhanced security precautions allowing only ticketed passengers into gate areas do not permit entry for persons traveling with the new electronic ticket, or e-ticket.
- An airport in southwest Florida has been using a dog to scare away birds; collisions between birds and jets last year cost the U.S. civil aviation industry an estimated $300 million in damages.[22]
- In August 1999, a sting operation at Miami International Airport highlighted security concerns about airport employees. The relaxed nature of checks on prospective employees has been a real problem.[23]
- Strikes or sickouts by air traffic controllers, flight attendants, and pilots have disrupted airline services to passengers.
- Airport security managers can implement a new technology, called threat image projection, to test the alertness of the security screeners. The technology projects a simulated threat into an actual bag, for example.[24] The system projects simulated objects, such as a handgun, into a bag as it moves through the X-ray machine to see if guards make the observation.
- The Coalition for Airport and Airplane Passenger Safety (a group of labor unions representing firefighters, airline pilots, flight attendants, and workers in a number of airline trades) prepared a report titled "Surviving the Crash: The Need to Improve Lifesaving Measures at Our Nation's Airports."[25] The report suggests that passengers and workers at U.S. airports are not adequately protected from a variety of life-threatening conditions.[26] (The Federal Aviation Administration [FAA] disagrees with the findings presented in this report.)
- Outdated FAA regulations are to blame for firefighter and rescue units not being properly staffed, equipped, or trained to respond to crashes and other emergencies. In addition to being unprepared for aviation disasters, airports are woefully unprepared to address terrorism threats, accidents involving hazardous materials, medical emergencies, and problems that

might result from such a heavy concentration of passengers in the airline terminals.[27] (The FAA disagrees with the findings in this report.)

- Traveler fatigue and frustration are becoming increasingly evident, with high-profile incidents resulting in the need for security intervention.[28]

- There is concern about the state of explosive detection technologies, their lack of reliability, the frequency of false alarms, and the delays in processing passenger baggage. The FAA has certified only one explosives detection machine (the CTX 5000) for checked baggage screening. The certified machine has an actual "throughput rate" that is much less than the designed rate of 500 bags per hour; thus, two units are necessary to meet the FAA's throughput requirement. Even with two machines, there is significant potential for operator error. It seems likely, for example, that in the press of rush hour, operators will start ignoring "positives" to reduce the ire of busy travelers. Estimates are that it would cost $2.2 billion to put these detection machines in the 75 busiest airports in the United States.[29]

- Proposed programs to match passengers with bags by checking claim tickets, for example, could add an estimated $2 billion annually, compounded by the need to find additional personnel and additional time to implement the programs.[30]

- The Computer-Assisted Passenger Screening program, developed by Northwest Airlines, is being used in over 240 cities to screen passengers in an effort to prevent terrorism. Customer information is matched against undisclosed criteria to determine whether the passenger's luggage should be subjected to additional screenings. The passengers are not informed that the additional screening is taking place.[31]

- Surface capacity at airports is increasing, and existing ground control efforts are argued to be insufficient to prevent collisions on the ground.[32]

- In bad weather, both pilots and air traffic controllers require critical information on airport conditions and relevant traffic.[33]

- Personal identification and verification of airport personnel is essential.

- Most airports deal with cargo and freight transport as well as passenger transport, although this usually happens in a different section of the airport.

- Investigators from the FAA conducted a battery of 170 tests at eight U.S. airports. They gained access to restricted areas in 117 cases. Of particular interest is the fact that once they had entered secure areas, they were able to board aircraft operated by 35 different aircraft carriers. Violations that allowed access to restricted areas included an absence of personnel assigned to the task or lack of awareness and willingness to enforce the existing procedures.[34]

- Questions have been raised about the role of vendors and other airport tenants (fast food vendors, newsstands, mall shops, etc.) in meeting security objectives.[35]

Considerations After 9/11

- There are additional security checks of carry-on luggage.
- Vehicle check points are in place at many large airports.
- Increased numbers of Federal Air Marshals are on board commercial aircraft.
- There is strong support for pilots to carry guns in the cockpits on a voluntary basis.
- Armed National Guard officers are posted throughout airports to increase security.
- Some security experts say that an invisible wall of security, like that set up in casinos, could help alleviate anxiety and inconvenience. This would mean relying heavily on surveillance cameras and undercover security officers. The possibility of profiling is expected to increase.
- The Transportation Security Administration (TSA), which oversees airport security, recently conducted tests and found that privately contracted screeners missed fake weapons smuggled by undercover agents in a quarter of the trials.
- The TSA has deployed federal screeners to 82 airports.
- The TSA has announced 145 Federal Security Directors, who are responsible for 380 airports.
- The TSA is accepting applications for positions in 420 airports and has received over 1.1 million applications to fill some 52,000–54,000 federal passenger and baggage screener positions.
- The Aviation and Transportation Security Act mandates that a sampling of all checked luggage must be scanned for explosives after December 31, 2002.

SCHOOL SECURITY

Incidents of school violence (Figure 9–3) have been prominent in the media in the last 5 to 10 years. Technological devices for enhancing security are becoming fixtures in schools across the country. The most likely products used by school security professionals include emergency communications devices, badging systems, access control and alarm systems, closed-captioned television (CCTV) systems, and metal detection or X-ray screening.[36-38] Judging by the incidents reported in the last decade, students could be facing various threats that might require expanded emergency response plans. If evacuation is or-

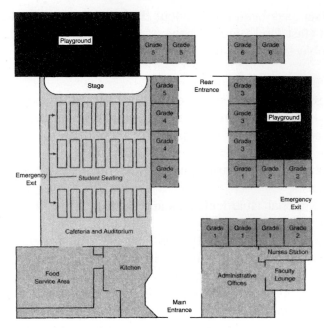

FIGURE 9–3 Sample Target Environment: School

dered, it is possible that students could be sent into the line of fire if snipers wait outside the school. On the other hand, if a classroom lockdown is ordered in an attempt to isolate students from attackers but the attackers used explosive devices, students, faculty, and other staff may become victims. School security professionals (such as Curtis Lavarello, executive director of the National Association of School Resource Officers) argue that much of the concern about security in schools is directly linked to access to guns. While many people are concerned about what they identify as an increase in violent crime in schools, experts are constantly reminding people that "schools are still among the safest places for children."[39,40] Some school officials argue that what is done in schools to provide a safe learning environment will not ever be the same after the Columbine High School shootings in Littleton, Colorado.[41] Consider the following information about school crimes and crime prevention efforts:

- Safe School Crime Stoppers set up an anonymous hotline for parents and students to call and report suspicious or unlawful behavior.[42]
- Most of the alleged killers in recent school shootings actually told other people about their plans before they acted.[43]
- Violence occurs at greater levels in schools where minor infractions of school policy are ignored.[44]

- School resource officers are used for security but go beyond the traditional role of security guard to developing relationships with students as a proactive measure to prevent crimes.[45]
- Schools can enhance physical safety by taking the following steps:
  1. supervising access to buildings and grounds
  2. reducing class size and school size
  3. adjusting scheduling to minimize students' time in hallways or in potentially dangerous locations
  4. conducting a building safety audit
  5. arranging supervision at critical times
  6. having adults visibly present throughout the school facility
  7. staggering dismissal times and lunch periods
  8. monitoring the school grounds
  9. coordinating with local police to ensure that there are safe routes for students going to and from school[46]
- Creating a positive school environment by increasing positive encounters in the classroom and school community is proving to be one of the most effective ways to address potentially violent or disruptive behavior. Clear expectations, consistent treatment, and just actions can go a long way in addressing classroom fears.[47]
- Although windows are also vulnerable, doors are the usual access point for intruders in schools. Choosing the right locks for entryways can be critical.[48]
- Each year, on average, 9 children die in school bus crashes; another 26 die when hit by either the bus or a passing car.[49]
- "Peer mediation" is being added to school programs to help students resolve conflict.[50,51]
- Some school programs are rejecting metal detectors and bomb-sniffing dogs in favor of programs focused on prevention and early detection. One example is the Principal's Student Leadership Group, in which kids who are selected to help monitor incidents.[52]
- Signs that a student is troubled include excessive feelings of rejection, expression of violence in writings and drawings, and overt threats.[53] Other warning signs are a history of drug abuse, talk about suicide, a lack of coping skills, a precipitating event, and no apparent emotional support system.[54] Schools must have a plan in place to help these students when warning signs are displayed.
- One of the most troubling trends in schools is the increasing incidence of bomb threats.[55]
- Arson, theft, and vandalism can be recurring problems for any school.
- A "war on drugs" is being waged in the nation's public schools.[56]

- Requiring students to wear uniforms is argued to reduce "acting out" behaviors.[57]

BANK SECURITY

Clearly, banks (Figure 9–4) are one of the most notorious targets for theft. These days, however, in addition to their traditional banking services, banks have added automated teller machines (ATMs) and are expanding to include banking services online. Banks are increasingly layering access control throughout their facilities rather than just having perimeter security.[58] Furthermore, various techniques are argued to be excellent weapons against counterfeit checks. These techniques include transaction reports, fingerprint signatures, a training and award program for bank personnel, and the issuance of security alerts. Consider the information in the following lists.

Banks in General

- The greatest financial losses to banks result from external check fraud and internal embezzlement.[59]
- The prime time for bank robberies is from 10 A.M. to 3 P.M. with Friday being the day of choice.[60]
- One type of secure entry that is being explored in various banks is a series of double-locking, bullet-resistant doors. A customer comes in

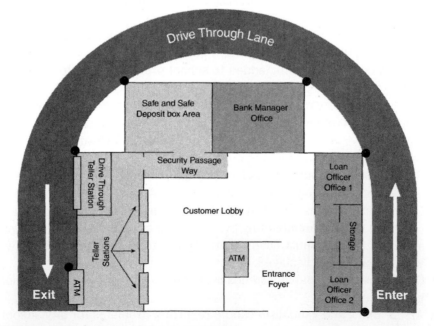

FIGURE 9–4 Sample Target Environment: Bank

through one door and must go through selected security devices (e.g., CCTV, metal detector) before proceeding through a second entry door. As the exterior (or first) door locks, the interior (or second) door unlocks so the person may proceed through. The system resets itself when the interior door is shut.[61] These systems are more common in European and South American banks and, at $40,000–$50,000, are quite expensive.[62,63]

- Today, sophisticated computer programs allow criminals to create corporate payroll checks that are nearly indistinguishable from the real thing.[64]
- One type of fraud that appears in banking institutions is the use of a legitimate customer's information by an illegitimate user. The legitimate customer's full name, address, Social Security number, and account information is used by the perpetrator, who then acquires a fake ID and comes to the bank claiming to be that customer. In one bank, this happened three times in a year, to the tune of just over $50,000 in losses for the bank.[65]
- Although the number of bank robberies is down, according to the Federal Bureau of Investigation (FBI), the number of incidents involving a weapon and the number of cases that involve violence are up.[66]
- Some of the best information about robbery prevention comes from analysis of the robberies that have happened across a chain of banks over time. This allows the banking institution to zero in on vulnerabilities.[67]
- Title 12 of the U.S. Code, also known as the Bank Protection Act of 1968, outlines minimum standards for the installation, operation, and maintenance of security devices and procedures at financial institutions.[68] It requires all federally insured banks, savings and loan institutions, and credit unions to designate a security officer, cooperate with and seek advice from the FBI and other law enforcement agencies, develop comprehensive security programs and implement protective measures to meet (or exceed) federal standards, keep "bait money" (or money for which numbers have been recorded), periodically remove excess cash from the tellers' windows and bank premises, and finally, develop stringent opening and closing procedures.[69]
- Security cameras installed at a six-foot height can easily be covered over with spray paint or disabled during a robbery.
- Computerized signature and photo records are a much more effective means by which to verify signatures than the signature cards that have traditionally been used.[70]
- Poor-quality security cameras can result in a picture whose resolution is so bad that the picture taken is useless.
- The open design of banks often leaves tellers accessible and overexposed.[71]

- Client information is as important as the money clients deposit. If clients do not believe the bank will keep their information confidential, they might take their money somewhere else.[72]
- The theft of data (e.g., customer accounts, customer profiles, credit records, loan records) has compelled many banks to invest in access control systems.[73]
- Banks are reported to be interested in security systems that are convenient, able to be networked throughout their entire system of bank branches, sophisticated, and integrated.[74]
- Financial institutions want access control databases that can automatically communicate with all other databases so that information can be exchanged almost instantaneously.[75]
- Bank management wants access control features that are integrated with other features (like CCTV and ID badging systems) to provide, for example, visual confirmation in addition to the access record kept by the access control system.[76]
- Online services are said to "save you hours of standing in lines, punching a calculator, and juggling paperwork." An increasing number of banks now offer custom Web sites that let people pay bills and download bank and credit card statements. Even better, the sites help people research mortgage refinancing, find the best credit cards, and analyze their investments.[77]
- In 1998, approximately 1200 banks contracted for Web-based banking designs. In 1999, over 7200 were estimated, with more projected to come in the following years.[78]

ATMs

- In 1992, there were 70 ATM burglaries and attempted burglaries. By 1997, there were an estimated 200.[79]
- With the growing need for convenient access to cash, ATMs are more common and less fortified. In 1985, there were approximately 44,000 ATMs; in 1997, that number had increased to approximately 165,000.[80]
- ATMs hold anywhere from $15,000 to $250,000 depending on the size of the machine.[81]
- Satellite tracking systems are being used in ATMs as a means of retrieving the equipment if it is taken.[82]
- Various ATMs in the United States and abroad are testing the use of iris scan technology. A photo of the iris is taken and then converted into a computer pattern. The pattern is compared to data on file. The process takes about two seconds.[83]
- Fraudulent use of ATM cards costs banks up to $150 million a year.[84]

- Bank cards with magnetic tape are being replaced by "smart cards" that store cardholder data. Smart cards are said to be infinitely more durable and secure.[85] From the moment smart cards appeared on the market-place, hackers have been trying to crack the code.[86,87]
- Lighting is seen as an integral security feature for ATMs, but there are no national guidelines about this lighting. In some places (e.g., New York City) a city ordinance dictates the lighting standards required for ATMs.[88]

CONVENIENCE STORE SECURITY

When looking at information about the incidence of robbery at convenience stores (Figure 9–5), readers must be discerning. For example, a 1991 report put out by the National Association of Convenience Stores (NACS) said that during the 10-year period from 1976 to 1986 the number of convenience stores doubled while the number of convenience store robberies remained relatively constant, suggesting that the robbery rate per store was cut in half over that 10-year period, due in large part to the implementation of several deterrence measures.[89] These measures include (1) cash control techniques, (2) clear sight lines in the stores, (3) prominent position of the cash register, (4) lack of

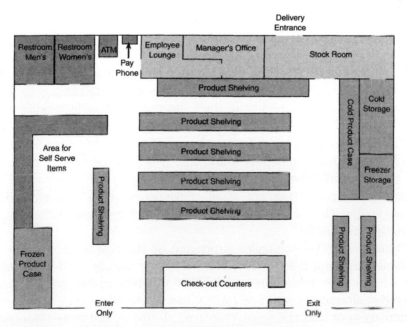

FIGURE 9–5   Sample Target Environment: Convenience Store

escape routes, (5) balanced exterior and interior lighting on the premises, and (6) employee training programs. Furthermore, the industry study took issue with FBI data reported in 1990.[90] It may not be surprising that the industry projected numbers that were lower than the FBI's. In 1989, the NACS study projected 23,311 convenience store robberies compared with the FBI report of 36,435.[91] For 1990, the NACS findings suggest 22,935 compared to the FBI-reported 38,435 convenience store robberies.[92]

In 1992, Ron Hunter and C. Ray Jeffery outlined in their research that the preventive measures endorsed by the greatest number of studies include (1) having two or more clerks on duty, especially at night (a form of employee surveillance); (2) cash handling techniques; (3) access control features; and (4) natural surveillance.[93] Hunter and Jeffery highlight elements of the Sessions report (the FBI data) suggesting that between 1985 and 1989 robbery in convenience stores increased 28 percent, representing the most rapid growth within all categories of robbery during that period.[94] While the NACS study suggests crime rates were "cut in half," the Hunter and Jeffery article suggests the "dramatic increase in convenience store robberies is of major concern to public officials and the convenience store industry."[95]

The industry also disagrees with the FBI regarding the dollars lost at these robberies. According to the NACS survey, register robbery in 1989 averaged $173, compared to the FBI's average of $364. As mentioned briefly in Chapter 8, the losses from theft are minimal when compared to the loss of business from customers, who are afraid to shop in the stores; the loss of qualified employees, who are afraid to work there; and successful litigation by individuals who have been harmed because of convenience store robberies.[96]

In one of the earliest studies of convenience store robberies (1975), Crow and Bull found that the "results support the concept that robbers select their targets and that physical and behavioral changes at the site can significantly reduce robberies."[97] Consider some of the following points of interest:

- The peak robbery period for convenience stores is between 9:00 P.M. and 11:00 P.M. That same study found that nearly 35 percent of robberies in Florida occurred between 11 P.M. and 6 A.M.[98]
- Approximately 94 percent of all convenience store robberies had only one victim. The robbery success rate does not increase as the number of victims increases.[99]
- Crime prevention strategies supported by the NACS include the use of signs indicating that the clerks have access to only limited funds, good cash handling procedures, enhanced visibility inside and outside the stores, alteration of escape routes, use of security devices, encouraging activity in or near the store, employee alertness, and store cleanliness.[100] NACS argues that if these recommended practices are followed, it will be

unnecessary to have multiple clerks on duty, use security enclosures, and limit store hours (close stores at midnight).[101]

- Florida has some of the most stringent, mandated prevention strategies in the nation. The prevention techniques recommended by the Florida Department of Legal Affairs include silent robbery alarms, security cameras capable of identifying robbery suspects, drop safes or other cash management devices, well-lighted parking areas, posted signs indicating that there is less than $50 cash on hand, clear and unobstructed windows, height markers at entrances, no concealed access or escape areas, cash handling policies to limit available cash at any given time, employees trained in robbery deterrence and safety, and two clerks on night shifts.[102]

- Handguns were used in 71 percent of the reported homicide cases in convenience stores.[103] Sixty-five percent of the homicides involved no resistance or provocation from the clerk and were therefore labeled as "random/senseless" violence.[104]

- Two-thirds of the reported rapes in convenience stores were unrelated to a robbery.[105] Eighty-nine percent of the rapes reported occurred at night.[106]

- No conclusive findings could be reached about the effectiveness of bullet-resistant barriers in convenience stores.[107]

- Gasoline driveoffs accounted for 48 percent of all police calls from convenience stores.[108]

REFERENCES

1. M. Hagland, "Confidence and Confidentiality," *Health Management Technology 18*, no. 12 (1997): 20–25.
2. S. Pelton, "Authentication Captures Security of Hardware, Convenience of Software," *Health Management Technology 20*, no. 10 (1999): 50.
3. T. Eskreis Nelson, "Safeguarding Newborns: Managing the Risk," *RN 62*, no. 3 (1999): 67–70.
4. Eskreis Nelson, "Safeguarding Newborns."
5. C. Leliopoulou, H. Waterman, and S. Chakrabarty, "Nurses' Failure To Appreciate the Risks of Infection Due to Needle Stick Accidents: A Hospital-Based Survey," *Journal of Hospital Infection*, May 1999, vol. 42, no. 1, 53–59.
6. R. L. Calvin, "Evaluation of the Protective Value of Hospital Gowns against Blood Strikethrough and Methicillin-Resistant Staphylococcus Aureus Penetration," *Association of Operating Room Nurses Journal 69*, no. 6 (1999): 1264.

7. C. Leliopoulou et al., "Nurses' Failure."

8. M. McDonald, "Overstretched in Emergency: On Both Sides of the Border, Hospital ERs Feel the Pinch," *Maclean's 109,* no. 49 (1996): 74(4).

9. McDonald, "Overstretched in Emergency."

10. McDonald, "Overstretched in Emergency."

11. McDonald, "Overstretched in Emergency."

12. A. Bagust, "Dynamics of Bed Use in Accommodating Emergency Admissions: Stochastic Simulation Model," *British Medical Journal 319,* no. 7203 (1996): 155.

13. G. Mills, "Issues in Health Care Construction," *Heating, Piping, Air Conditioning 70,* no. 7 (1998): 28(4).

14. Pelton, "Authentication Captures Security of Hardware, Convenience of Software," 50.

15. Calvin, "Evaluation of the Protective Value of Hospital Gowns," 1264.

16. C. Vanchieri, "Badly Braced for the Big One," *Hospitals and Health Networks 72,* no. 20 (1999): 42.

17. M. Lease and T. Burke, "Law Enforcement's Response to Small Aircraft Accidents," *FBI Law Enforcement Bulletin,* February 2000, 14.

18. R. W. Hahn, "The Cost of Airport Security Measures," *Consumer's Research Magazine 80,* no. 7 (1997): 15(5).

19. Hahn, "The Cost of Airport Security Measures."

20. National Transportation Safety Board, "1998 Aviation Accidents," *http://www.ntsb.gov/aviation/9801.htm,* accessed February 2000.

21. "Laptop Theft: A Variation on an Old Trick," *Maclean's 109,* no. 20 (1996): 17.

22. "Feather Buster: A Florida Airport Unleashes a Weapon in Its Battle against Birds: Border Collie Jet," *People Weekly 52,* no. 7 (1999): 85.

23. J. Dettmer, "FBI Has Grounded Airport Security," *Insight on the News 15,* no. 35 (1999): 48.

24. M. Lavitt, "New Technology Tests Alertness of Airport Security Screeners," *Aviation Week and Space Technology 150,* no. 13 (1999): 88(2).

25. M. Bradford, "U.S. Airport Safety Criticized," *Business Insurance 3* (1999): 1.

26. Bradford, "U.S. Airport Safety Criticized," 1.

27. Bradford, "U.S. Airport Safety Criticized," 1.

28. "Diana Ross Released and Given Warning," *Jet,* vol. 96, no. 19, p. 54.

29. Hahn, "The Cost of Airport Security Measures."

30. Hahn, "The Cost of Airport Security Measures."

31. P. G. Chronis, "Airlines Have New Security 'Screen': Secret System Raises Discrimination Questions," *Denver Post,* 1 January 1998, B-01.

32. S. Young et al., "Safely Improving Airport Surface Capacity," *Aerospace America 36,* no. 5 (1999): 22.

33. Young et al., "Safely Improving Airport Surface Capacity," 22.
34. T. Anderson, "Airport Security Fails Tests," *Security Management*, February 2000, 73–74.
35. Anderson, "Airport Security Fails Tests," 74.
36. M. Fickes, "The AVS's of Security Technology," *American School & University 71*, no. 11 (1999): SS21 (4).
37. M. Kennedy, "The Changing Face of School Violence," *American School & University 71*, no. 11 (1999): ss6(3).
38. Kennedy, "The Changing Face of School Violence."
39. J. Agron, "Lessons Learned," *American School & University 71*, no. 11.
40. Kennedy, "The Changing Face of School Violence."
41. Agron, "Lessons Learned."
42. Agron, "Lessons Learned."
43. M. Simpson, "Taking Threats Seriously," *NEA Today 17*, no. 1 (1998): 27.
44. M. Dunn, "Critical Elements in School Security," *American School & University 71*, no. 11 (1999).
45. C. Mulqueen, "School Resource Officers More Than Security Guards," *American School & University 71*, no. 11 (1999): p. 17(1).
46. Dunn, "Critical Elements in School Security."
47. J. N. Lederhouse, "You Will Be Safe Here: Realizing a Positive School Climate," *Educational Leadership 56*, no. 1 (1998): 51(4).
48. J. D. King, "Locking in on Safety," *American School & University 70*, no. 2 (1997): 36.
49. A. Spake, "Tussling over Buses," *U.S. News & World Report 127*, no. 13 (1999): 62.
50. P. Welsh, "The Price of Protection," *U.S. News & World Report 126*, no. 17 (1999): 28.
51. "NEA Affiliates at Work for Safety," *NEA Today 18*, no. 1 (1999): 14.
52. D. Goodgame, "7:10am School Security: Always on the Lookout for Signs of Trouble," *Time 154*, no. 17 (1999): 74+.
53. D. Marcus, "Metal Detectors Alone Can't Guarantee Safety," *U.S. News & World Report 126*, no. 17 (1999): 26.
54. S. Band, "School Violence: Lessons Learned." *FBI Law Enforcement Bulletin 68*, no. 9 (1999): 9.
55. J. Agron, "Safe Havens: Preventing Violence and Crime in Schools," *American School & University 71*, no. 6, (1999): 18(5).
56. B. Dority, "Big Brother Goes to High School," *Humanist 57*, no. 2 (1997): 37(2).
57. M. Gips, "Securing the Schoolyard," *Security Management*, March 1996, 47–53.
58. J. Kirch, "Investing in Better Controls," *Security Management*, May 1999, 83.

59. R. E. Anderson, "Bank Security," in *Handbook of Loss Prevention and Crime Prevention*, ed. L. Fennely (Woburn, MA: Butterworth-Heinemann, 1982).

60. P. Carroll, "The Chicago Bank Robbery Initiative," *FBI Law Enforcement Bulletin 66*, no. 4 (1997): 9–15.

61. J. Konicek and K. Little, *Security, ID Systems and Locks: The Book on Electronic Access Control* (Newton, MA: Butterworth-Heinemann, 1997), 76.

62. Konicek and Little, *Security, ID Systems and Locks*, 76.

63. T. Mann, "Policies That Pay Off: Although Robberies Are Down, They Are Becoming More Costly and Violent," *Security Management*, February 2000, 42–46.

64. K. Null, "One Bank's Fraud Fight: Security Doesn't Have To Sit by Helplessly in the Fight against Financial Services Fraud," *Security Management*, February 2000, 37–41.

65. K. Null, "One Bank's Fraud Fight," 38.

66. T. Mann, "Policies That Pay Off," 45.

67. Mann, "Policies That Pay Off," 45.

68. Anderson, "Bank Security," 740.

69. K. Hess and H. Wrobleski. *Introduction to Private Security* (Minneapolis, MN: West Publishing Company, 1996), 526.

70. R. Bordes, "Security Measures That Earn Interest," *Security Management*, June 1994, 71–72.

71. Bordes, "Security Measures," 71–72.

72. J. Kirch, "Investing in Better Controls," *Security Management*, May 1999, 82–88.

73. Kirch, "Investing in Better Controls," 84.

74. Kirch, "Investing in Better Controls," 85.

75. Kirch, "Investing in Better Controls," 84.

76. Kirch, "Investing in Better Controls," 84.

77. M. Hogan, "Easy Money Meets the Web," *PC/Computing 10*, no. 10 (1997): 129.

78. B. Orr, "A Service Bureau for Next Generation E-banking," *ABA Banking Journal 91*, no. 4 (1999): 68.

79. Gannett News Service, "ATMs Proving Convenient to Robbers as Well as Users," *St. Cloud Times*, 6c.

80. Gannett News Service, "ATMs Proving Convenient," 6c.

81. Gannett News Service, "ATMs Proving Convenient," 6c.

82. Gannett News Service, "ATMs Proving Convenient," 6c.

83. P. Davidson, "ATMs That ID Consumers by Eye To Get Test." *USA Today*, March 18, 1998, p. A1.

84. Davidson, "ATMs That ID Consumers," A1.

85. J. Kutler, "Even Abundant Security Features Don't Spur Smart Card Buy-In," *American Banker 163,* no. 221 (1988); 1–3.

86. Kutler, "Even Abundant Security Features," 1–3.

87. P. Wayner, "Code Breaker Cracks Smart Cards' Digital Safe," *New York Times,* 22 June, 1998, D1.

88. R. Goetzke, "Shedding New Light on ATM Security," *Security Management,* September 1994, 57–60.

89. National Association of Convenience Stores, *Convenience Store Security: Report and Recommendations* (Alexandria, VA: 1991), 4.

90. W. B. Sessions, *Crime in the United States: 1989 Annual Report* (Washington, DC: Federal Bureau of Investigation), 1990.

91. National Association of Convenience Stores, *Convenience Store Security,* 13.

92. National Association of Convenience Stores, *Convenience Store Security,* 13.

93. R. Clarke, ed., *Situational Crime Prevention: Successful Case Studies* (New York: Harrow and Heston, 1992), 195.

94. W. B. Sessions, *Crime in the United States: 1989 Annual Report* (Washington, DC: Federal Bureau of Investigation, 1990), 21.

95. Hunter and Jeffrey, "Preventing Convenience Store Robbery Through Environmental Design," in *Situational Crime Prevention: Successful Case Studies,* ed. R. Clarke. (Albany, NY: Harrow and Heston, 1992).

96. Clarke, *Situational Crime Prevention,* 195.

97. Crow and Bull, *Robbery Deterence: An Applied Behavioral Science Demonstration—Final Report* (La Jolla, CA: Western Behavioral Sciences Institute, 1975), ii.

98. R. Degner et al., *Food Store Robberies in Florida: Detailed Crime Statistics* (Gainesville, FL: Florida Agricultural Market Research Center, 1983), 26, 27.

99. Degner et al., *Food Store Robberies in Florida,* 18–19.

100. Clarke, *Situational Crime Prevention,* 204.

101. Clarke, *Situational Crime Prevention,* 204.

102. R. Butterworth, *Study of Safety and Security Requirements for "At-Risk Businesses"* (Tallahassee, FL: Florida Department of Legal Affairs, 1991).

103. National Association of Convenience Stores, *Convenience Store Security,* 17.

104. National Association of Convenience Stores, *Convenience Store Security,* 17.

105. National Association of Convenience Stores, *Convenience Store Security,* 17.

106. National Association of Convenience Stores, *Convenience Store Security,* 17.
107. National Association of Convenience Stores, *Convenience Store Security,* 22.
108. N. LaVigne, "Gasoline Drive-Offs: Designing a Less Convenient Environment," in *Crime Prevention Studies,* Vol. II, ed. R. Clarke (Monsey, NY: Criminal Justice Press, 1994), 91–114.

III

Exploring Essential External Connections

Great spirits have always found violent opposition from mediocre minds. The latter cannot understand it when a man does not thoughtlessly submit to hereditary prejudices but honestly and courageously uses his intellect.

—Albert Einstein

The security profession depends on people who are intelligent, capable of critical thinking, and prepared to spend the better part of their career educating themselves, learning more and more about the security objectives and needs within a target environment. Whatever the setting, security professionals must constantly think over and rethink their security-related needs and ways to meet those needs. Sometimes that may mean breaking with an old tradition and opening up to new possibilities.

Although the security profession has built its reputation on the renegade enforcers and big, burly strike-busters, good security professionals today are nothing like these predecessors. Today's security practitioners must have a tremendous amount of knowledge, and they must know when to share that knowledge and when to hold that knowledge in confidence. In reality, this is a profession for people who work well both alone and in groups. Security professionals rely on other security or public safety professionals to do their job well. When security practitioners are in situations that require them to take action, they will probably need to consult with other security professionals, law enforcement officers, legal counsel, or emergency response crews. Part III introduces readers to these topics.

Chapter 10 discusses the long-standing, often hostile, relations between law enforcement officers and security professionals. In short, arguments about security professionals being "bought and paid for" and responsible only to the company are countered by law enforcement professionals who suggest that the Constitution of the United States is their "boss." Law enforcement officers are proud of the training and educational standards required of them. Some law enforcement officers suggest that there are not the same standards for becoming a security professional, implying that security professionals have an inferior status. In some cases, security professionals have behaved in such a way that reinforces this inferior status and the stories about how easy it is to become a security professional and abuse the power and authority that come with a security job. Leaders in the security profession should think about establishing some professional standards that will enhance the profession's image.

Whether law enforcement officers or security professionals are better prepared to do the job is only one question. How these two groups should interact and cooperate is also a critical question. Law enforcement officers have a particular responsibility to the public, and security practitioners are showing that they can bring a level of professionalism to public police objectives and provide necessary services at competitive prices. It is true that law enforcement agencies are using security professionals more often to supplement aspects of their overall public safety function. But there are critical, often heated debates about the role of each group of professionals in the overall public safety objective for communities.

Chapter 11 is focused exclusively on legal aspects of the security profession and how a business might be exposed, or vulnerable, to these security-related liability issues. In short, legal liability concerns can necessitate an earnest, and sometimes lively, association with legal counsel. Some security professionals have found themselves in situations where someone they have detained for shoplifting later files a claim saying he or she was abused in some way during the "detention." Security professionals can find themselves the targets of legal action and must be prepared with an adequate response. Several current legal issues are identified for consideration, and the chapter discusses recent legal cases involving security professionals.

Chapter 12 is focused on preparation for a disaster response. Emergency response is never the preferred security response. There are circumstances, however, where unanticipated activities result in a catastrophic event and security will be required to respond. Various accident and emergency situations are discussed, and the chapter closes with a series of exercises about emergency situations.

Chapter 13 looks at persistent security issues and identifies tomorrow's security trends. This book has only briefly discussed issues of national security, domestic terrorism, and international terrorism. Clearly these are security issues. And with examples like the bombing of the World Trade Center and the Murrah Building in Oklahoma City, it becomes clear that these are issues that some businesses—public and private—cannot ignore. Various issues related to the notion of security actions taken as a form of "private justice" will require academics in the criminal justice and security arenas to consider more fully how they talk about theories of crime and criminal enforcement. Furthermore, concerns about genetically altered food and poverty across the globe suggest that traditional areas such as air, food, and water might be factors in a security conversation of the future.

Chapter 14 invites readers to revisit Chapter 9 and think about these settings once again, with an eye toward external security-related resources.

CHAPTER 10

Public and Private Police Interactions

CHAPTER OUTLINE

CHAPTER HIGHLIGHTS

- Understand the history of public and private police relations
- Understand how public and private police responsibilities are similar and different
- Understand the importance of excellent interagency cooperation

- Begin to think about the future of public/private police relations
- Begin to identify critical areas for public/private interaction and integration

KEY WORDS

Black Panther Party for Self-Defense
Community policing
Contract outsourcing
Displacement effect
Ethics

Gated communities
Global positioning system (GPS)
Mass private property
Self-help security

With the establishment of the Metropolitan Police in London in the mid-1840s, policing became an organized agency of public servants, paid for with public money and accountable to governments.[1] Yet as is demonstrated throughout history, both organized and disorganized groups of private citizens have been involved in efforts to instill a sense of public safety in communities. While it is easy to focus on public law enforcement as the primary social control mechanism for the state, other groups and individuals have identified specific security concerns they believe are not being adequately addressed by local police and then have subsequently taken intervening action.

While the ongoing association between public police and more privatized security-related groups has been rocky at times, there may in fact be room for an integrated focus on public safety issues involving both public and private police groups. Earlier in the book, I have talked about loosely organized groups, such as neighborhood watch groups, and more formally organized groups, such as the Guardian Angels. Although public safety concerns are primarily addressed by public law enforcement officers, various formal and informal groups in society have assumed a leadership role in the responsibility for public safety. The growth of security has been identified as an indicator that people (and organizations) are increasingly relying less on public law enforcement and seeking to establish a form of "self-help" security.[2,3] *Self-help security* refers to actions taken by individuals and/or groups to protect their person or a group to which they belong.

This chapter focuses on exploring, in more detail, the relationship between public and private protection agencies. After a brief orientation to the ongoing debate among academics, police, and security professionals about the role of policing in society, attention is given to the most recent calls from both public and private police professionals to integrate efforts with an eye toward the collective goal of enhancing community safety and security. Several efforts to combine law enforcement resources with private security resources will be profiled. Furthermore, as more departments move toward community-oriented policing, several indicators suggest that an increase in cooperation between public and private law enforcement is to be expected.

PUBLIC AND PRIVATE POLICE RELATIONS: A DYNAMIC INTERACTION

Transformations in formal and informal police responses throughout history have been related to overall social change. Although Sir Robert Peel is said to have moved to formalize the system of public police in response to increasing crime rates associated with industrialization, current trends suggest that the shift of policing services back onto the private sector may be in large part a response to specialized security needs emerging in industry as society continues to shift into a global, electronic marketplace fully entrenched in the Information Age.[4] Other theories proposed explain the rise in private security as only a recent trend connected to a larger, systemic ebb and flow of community resources.

In nineteenth-century England, security services were provided only by private measures. Small localities could not afford the high cost of public security. As the urbanization process became more pronounced in the twentieth century, there was a shift from private protection to public security, as the economies of scale favored public security. In the late twentieth and early twenty-first centuries, with metropolitan regions dominating the developed world, there has been a shift back to private protection and a decline in the share of public security inputs. Furthermore, in large cities there seems to be little cooperation between public and private security.[5]

The tradition of Peel and his efforts to formalize policing have been well documented and discussed throughout criminal justice programs nationally. While there is also considerable documentation of Allan Pinkerton, the security services he provided were for heads of state (including President Lincoln) and heads of industry. More informal security practices have not typically been presented for discussion, nor are they well documented.

How public and private police will assume (or divide) responsibility for providing services to representatives of both public and private interests is a controversial topic, but not a new one. An emphasis on both differences and similarities between public and private policing objectives has been highlighted in dramatically different ways. Because the growth of security as an industry has been considerable, people sometimes talk about security enterprise as if it is a relatively new concept. In reality, the history of private security law enforcement happened right alongside the history of private security. The services assumed by the security profession have changed, and many would argue that these changes resulted in large part from action, or inaction, on the part of law enforcement agencies. There are reminders of the intense levels of discomfort between public and private policing agencies in the ongoing conversations about not only what constitutes a private security force but what role private security is destined to play both within the community and within traditional law enforcement.

Unhappy Associations from the Past

In a recent visit, I asked a local city police chief about his experiences with public and private police issues. He defiantly pronounced, "The U.S. Constitution is my boss. I do not make myself accountable to anyone or anything else." It seems I had touched on a sore subject, one to which he had a well-rehearsed response. Perhaps he articulates the feelings of many law enforcement officers, who see themselves as custodians of the legally outlined rights granted to each

The Hallcrest Report and Hallcrest II

Perhaps the most well-known information collected to date on the private security industry is linked to two studies, both presented by Hallcrest Systems, Incorporated and sponsored by the National Institute of Justice (NIJ). In the early 1980s, Hallcrest Systems, Inc. was asked by the NIJ to conduct what was believed to be one of the first in-depth studies of the security industry.[1] Their task had three primary elements:

1. Gather information on the general character of the private security industry in the United States, updating previous research completed on the subject.
2. Describe the contribution private security makes to the overall problem of crime control and order maintenance and identify opportunities for improvement.
3. Describe the working relationships between private security and public law enforcement agencies and develop recommendations for improving these operating relationships.[2]

Known in the industry as *The Hallcrest Report,* the final report was published in 1985 and produced an immediate reaction from both the law enforcement community and the private security industry. In 1990 a second version of the Hallcrest Report, known as *Hallcrest II,* was also supported by the National Institute of Justice and was intended to

- profile trends and issues in private security over the past two decades
- provide relevant projections to the year 2000
- consolidate and compare the various findings of earlier private security research efforts.[3]

In sum, the findings were focused on describing the relationship between law enforcement and private industry, presenting an updated profile of the security industry, and exploring progress in the area of professionalizing the security industry. Hallcrest II suggested an explosive growth in the security industry well into the twenty-first century. The figures and statistics are heavily reproduced and used by the security industry to demonstrate its own value in the objective to meet public safety concerns. The figures have come to represent the Hallcrest II findings, showing the relative changes in employment in both public police and private security sectors from 1970 and projected into the year 2000,[4] suggesting that the cost in dollars spent by security and law enforcement crossed over in 1977 (with private security steadily increasing expenditures while the increase in law enforcement spending was much slower[5]).

References

1. National Advisory Commission on Criminal Justice Standards and Goals, Report of the Task Force on Private Security (Washington, DC: U.S. Government Printing Office, 1976).
2. National Advisory Commission on Criminal Justice Standards and Goals, Report of the Task Force on Private Security (Washington, DC: U.S. Government Printing Office, 1976), p. 205.
3. W. C. Cunningham, J. Strauchs, and C. VanMeter. *The Hallcrest Report II: Private Security Trends* (Newton, MA: Butterworth-Heinemann, 1990), p. 4.
4. Ibid., p. 237.
5. Ibid., p. 239.

individual under the law. But clearly, as security and law enforcement experts who have studied this agree, the existing policing structure is changing.

Conflict Surrounding the Definition of Public and Private Space

The growth of **mass private property,** large areas that invite the public to utilize their service, whether it be a mega mall or theme park, is evident.[6] Consider the example of large shopping malls, gated communities, or large recreation centers such as Disney World. Although large venues for the public, these areas are almost exclusively under the protection of private police agents. Such environments highlight areas where the roles of public and private policing objectives become blurred.

The specific functions of private and public police agents are becoming more interactive and interdependent. Community policing efforts have further expanded the idea that police agencies are not the only bodies within a given community who perform policing functions.

Individuals are increasingly electing to take more of a role in addressing security matters for themselves and their families. Fortified, walled housing developments, often called **gated communities,** have been identified as the fastest-growing residential communities in the nation.[7,8] These gated communities are privatized community living spaces with a host of privatized services, including a security detail; they are private worlds that share little with their neighbors or the larger political system.[9] People seem to be so worried about their personal safety that in increasing numbers they are seeking refuge in heavily reinforced, walled housing developments.

The popularity of gated communities is increasingly referred to as a high-profile indicator that people do not want to be afraid in their own homes. Discussions about people's fear of crime have become a mainstay in political discourse. Media accounts suggest people may have good reason to be afraid. Whether the fear is based in overall attitudes about crime, perceived increases in violence, juvenile crimes, gangs, drug activity, or newly emerging cybercrimes such as identify theft, fear has become a part of mainstream conversations about social reality. Hugely popular books suggest that fear can also be good and advise people to rely on their "gut instinct" to better protect themselves.[10]

While the relationship between public fear and gated communities has not been well documented, people are making comparisons between the explosion in gated communities and the growth in the security industry.[11] No one contests that there has been explosive growth in the number of private security professionals. Bruce Benson, using U. S. Census data, indicates that from 1964 to 1991 employment by private firms specializing in protective and detective services increased by 746.8 percent, and the number of firms offering these services grew by 543 percent.[12] It might surprise some people to know that wealthy communities are not the only communities looking for the protection afforded by a gated, privately policed community. Inner-city residents are also fortifying their communities. In Los Angeles, for example, dozens of neighborhoods—black, white, and Latino, and rich, poor, and middle class—petitioned the city to privatize their streets since the 1992 riots, and about half a dozen have done so.[13] Furthermore, the demands for a security response are often linked to the idea that the public law enforcement response is not adequate, particularly in lower class, minority communities.[14,15]

People are afraid, and they are willing to pay to feel safer. Whether they actually *are* safer or whether they just *feel* safer is an open question. Even the designers of gated communities suggest they are selling the *perception* of security rather than a more secure reality.[16] Whatever they are selling, it is clear that people are buying it. Not much research has been done connecting perceptions of fear about crime, gated communities, and crime victimization particularly, with attention given to issues of class, race, and the role the access control features (such as a gated community) might have on crime in lower income areas. Research suggests a person's behavior is not necessarily predictable when he or she is fearful.[17] Various criminological theories talk about the likelihood of unstable social conditions when communities and community groups are in a state of transition. Many possible connections to criminological theory deserve exploration regarding the effects of fear of crime and the introduction of a security response. The full implications for both rational and irrational fear have simply not been fully explored.

Securing Public Places: Who Provides Security?

Citizen involvement in the public law enforcement function is not new to the American scene.[18] The existence of **self-help security** groups (also referred to as "self-defense groups"), or groups organized for purposes of individual or community protection, provides an interesting area for consideration among those interested in either security or law enforcement issues. The role of citizen participation in the planning, control, and delivery of the security-related services that affect them can be both positive and negative. In some ways, the organization of these groups is threatening to the established law enforcement order.[19] In other ways, they may also be viewed as a rather loud statement of the need to increase security services in certain areas—usually poor, minority areas. With the performance of conventional police identified as least effective and most controversial in black neighborhoods, the emergence of alternate security organizations in those areas should not be surprising.[20]

While the specifics in the discussion about what constitutes a security response are currently being debated in academic circles, many argue that private security operations in private companies are no different than the local neighborhood groups that have elected to organize citizens to serve in a security capacity within their own neighborhoods, for example. Such groups come prepared with a training protocol and patrol operations for the group to pursue. It is likely that the idea of citizens assuming responsibility for their own security will bring various debatable elements into an already expansive discussion; it also highlights the importance of understanding the objective of security-related enterprises that operate outside local law enforcement departments.

Researchers and police professionals have introduced the idea that local citizen groups are, in fact, a form of private security.[21] Indeed, the integration and overlap of public and private police functions have taken on several surprising forms.[22] In general, there are four forms: (1) Public and private police run joint operations, (2) the police hire private firms, (3) private firms hire the police, and (4) there is hybrid policing.[23]

The demand for public safety and security services is seemingly endless and rapidly changing. Security needs come in many forms, whether designed for businesses, to keep customers safe while in a given environment, or to meet individual protection concerns. As discussed in Chapter 2, during the time the policing objective and the organizational structures for police response were becoming formalized in the United States, aspects of the Wild West were still present. With the advent of computers and other technology, there is a kind of Wild West atmosphere again. The growth in computers, for example, has made it difficult to regulate the activities associated with the computer industry. As discussed in Chapter 6, sometimes the rogue players in the computer arena end up being hired to provide security for the very companies whose systems they were once hacking.

But industries are not the only areas where enhanced security efforts outside of law enforcement are emerging. Anticrime informational newsletters, databases, and interactive Web sites are increasingly used by concerned citizens to play a role in securing their own communities.[24] Historically, some of these organizations have worked with local law enforcement, while others have worked around law enforcement.[25]

A high-profile example of a more confrontational group is the **Black Panther Party for Self-Defense,** which was organized in November 1966 in Oakland, California, to address the issue of police brutality. "The city's black community was beleaguered by a systematic problem of police abuse and citizens had no powers of redress whatsoever. [The founders of the Black Panther Party] decided to form an organization of armed volunteers to directly confront abusive police."[26] *Eyes on the Prize II: America at the Racial Crossroads,* a PBS video from 1989, discusses a predawn assault on a Black Panther chapter in Chicago after questionable uses of police surveillance and allegations of police harassment at both the local and federal levels. Two people were killed, and the Chicago Police Department became embroiled in race-based scandal as a result.[27] The Panther party was also focused on reading and intellectual work, and the Panthers' commitment to serve their community resulted in some of the first student breakfast programs and health clinics in minority communities.[28,29] Certainly, there was controversy within the Black Panther organization about its role. Furthermore, members were often in conflict about the fact that certain group members would recklessly provoke the police. Former Federal Bureau of Investigation (FBI) Director J. Edgar Hoover called the Black Panther Party the greatest threat to the internal security of the United States and developed a counterintelligence organization to "neutralize" the group.[30] The police response to the Black Panther Party was controversial and included police infiltrating the groups, killing several Panther leaders, destroying some chapter offices, and locking up scores of members on trumped-up charges.[31–33]

The points of connection between the role of law enforcement and the need for security services may eventually be defined within a community that has been seeking security but does not feel adequate police protection has been provided. Consequently, these citizens form their own groups in an effort to better protect themselves from known threats. In some cases, the threat itself has been thought to come from law enforcement. The issues raised by the Black Panthers, for example, seem to persist today, given the fact that young, unmarried, low-income nonwhite males are the people most likely to file a complaint against the police (based on an 1998 FBI study conducted in Chicago, St. Louis, and Philadelphia).[34] Even today, there are well-organized, professional efforts to protect minority communities from an absence of police response, at best, and a negative police response, at worst. According to social scientists, there are two primary reasons for the persistent distrust of law enforcement: historical experience and present-day practice.[35]

The United States has a history of difficulty with regard to race relations. People in all races, and from all classes, seek to feel safe in their homes and communities. In a 1995 Gallup poll, more than half of black Americans said that the justice system was biased against them; two-thirds of black Americans in that same Gallup poll said that police racism against blacks is common across the country, and a majority of white Americans agreed.[36] Even among police officers, black officers agreed that whites get better treatment than blacks and that police officers are more likely to use physical force against blacks and other minorities than against whites in similar situations. Security professionals are likely to play an important role in meeting the safety and security needs of this group of citizens. An excellent example is the development of District Security Investigation, Inc., in Cincinnati, Ohio. These security practitioners expanded their company to include community policing, because they viewed public police enforcement in their community to be woefully inadequate.[37] Various other community groups, such as SOSAD (Save Our Sons and Daughters), which was organized to address deaths of children and random violence in the local community, are determined simply to make their communities safe, whether protecting themselves or hiring private security professionals.

As this book has discussed, private industry is not the only group to use security professionals. In some public buildings, private security professionals are used to perform security-related functions. Certainly, public agencies are susceptible to security-related breaches. But the importance of a security management plan within a public agency setting is too often forgotten. A typical security breach, whether related to a public or private setting, is likely to involve someone with inside information. A woman was accused of embezzling over $419,000 (over 3.5 years) from the Department of Human Resources.[38] The woman created fraudulent claims and then had the claim checks sent to a post office box that she rented. Her plan was not very sophisticated, but her knowledge of the system—most specifically the security protocols—allowed her to escape detection.[39] She was one of the people in the office who was responsible for training other employees on the use of a new computer system.[40] The county may be forced to pay back the money the woman embezzled.[41] With several layers of "financial safeguards" in place county officials said that even after the losses were detected, the supervisor assumed the loss was nothing more than a computer error.[42] The woman accused was "a well-liked team player who was considered knowledgeable in program areas and systems and was always willing to help out."[43] In this case, the accused was caught, charged, and eventually sentenced to 10 years in prison.[44] In spite of the fact that crimes occur in a public agency, questions about how best to oversee the security features clearly remain. It should be clear that this woman's security breach will have a significant impact on the county because it may be held responsible for the monetary loss and be forced to pay back the money. The people, as taxpayers, may be responsible for paying for the loss, leaving less money for city and county services. These kinds of examples certainly make plain the fact that public and private security interests are not as easily distinguished as some might think.

WHO IS QUALIFIED TO PROVIDE SECURITY?

As indicated, professionals in criminal justice, business, management, and related fields suggest that security professionals serve an essential need in spite of the fact that they do not have the authority of local law enforcement. Interestingly enough, the interactions between private and public police are often ignored. A number of police tasks (e.g., public building security, parking enforcement, court security) have been assigned to security professionals in an effort to save public police agencies money.[45] Public and private law enforcement identify their responsibilities as dramatically different, and in some cases members of one group hold contempt for members of the other group.

This blurring of the responsibilities of public police and private security professionals is important to remember when identifying and exploring security objectives within a given target environment. There are concerns about the authority private citizens have to provide what could be called anticrime activities. Significant questions arise about a citizen's authority to arrest, search, carry weapons, interrogate, and detain persons suspected of certain crimes.[46] A significant issue has been raised around the "state action" doctrine, which suggests that "prearranged plans and joint activity between the public and private sector can lead to a finding that the entire activity is regulated by constitutional norms, such as the Fourth Amendment's prohibition against searches and seizures."[47] It is argued that the only way to protect both citizens involved in crime prevention efforts, and law enforcement agencies actively working with these citizen groups, is to legislate appropriate roles and responsibilities for both groups.

It Really Is SOSAD

In 1986, Detroit documented 43 young people who were killed and 365 who had been wounded in street violence.[1] Such violence was attributed to the invention of crack cocaine in the mid-1980; neighborhoods began looking like war zones and children walking to and from school risked being shot and killed.[2]

In January 1987, in response to this crisis in their community, Clementine Barfield (together with other mothers whose children had been killed in street violence) founded SOSAD—Save Our Sons and Daughters. Through SOSAD, Barfield and others have helped over 1500 families overcome the loss of a child to violence. One mother recalls dropping her 16-year-old daughter off at a party, only to receive a phone call from police saying her daughter had been shot and killed at random by someone who crashed that party.[3] Parents who have lost children to random violence help others in the same situation cope with the feelings of guilt, anger, helplessness, and frustration that are common. Another parent described how his son, while on the way to football practice, was shot and killed by a gang member who was aiming at someone else.[4] It is important that any feelings of guilt and revenge are validated in order to limit the destructive effects on the people left behind.

Making Peace (St. Paul, Minn.: Independent Television Service) is a four-part documentary that aired on PBS. The first program, titled "Soul Survivors," profiles Clementine Barfield. Save our Sons and Daugthers can by contacted in Detroit, Michigan at (313) 361–5200.

References

1. Grace Lee Boggs, "Empower young people to reduce violence." Synapse. Winter 1995, number 34. *www.nrec.org/synapse34/boggs.html*. Last accessed January 25, 2001.
2. Ibid.
3. Mark Puls, "Grief-stricken help others cope: SOSAD marks decade of comforting families of kids lost to violence." The Detroit News. November 12, 1997. Last accessed January 25, 2001 by electronic format. *http://detnews.com/1997'metro/9711/12/11120104.htm*.
4. Ibid.

Efforts to understand the discord between public and private police have been long standing. Since 1971, at least three significant studies have been conducted in an effort to determine what, if any, measures can be taken to improve the strained relations between law enforcement officers and security professionals.[48] The first was conducted in 1971 by the Rand Corporation, the second by the Private Security Advisory Council in 1976, and the third by Hallcrest Systems, Inc. in 1985. Researchers like Harvey Morley have been following studies that outline the relations between public police and security professionals. Morley notes little positive effect and is currently working on a project that promises to propose several reasons why little change in communication has materialized.[49] One of the primary barriers to improving the strained relationship between public and private law enforcement is the lack of training expected or required of security professionals.[50] While the well-known Certified Protection Professional (CPP) certification process offered by the American Society for Industrial Security (ASIS) discussed earlier is well known and well respected among security professionals, research suggests that police are aware of the modern private security profession and have had "strong, often quite negative" views of this growth. Findings suggest that much of the animosity that exists between public and private police can be linked to the fact that police officers are measuring the job performance of the security professional by the law enforcement standard. This supports other security researchers, who have suggested that strained relations continue because law enforcement officers do not have a clear understanding of the role and function of security professionals.[51]

In short, law enforcement officers see security professionals as "law enforcement wanna-bes" rather than serious professionals with a particular job responsibility that is separate from the law enforcement function. Because the training and responsibility to the state of both groups are markedly different, these comparisons made by public police are considered unrealistic.[52] Finally, it is also true that communication between the agencies is minimal, and cooperative efforts are not pursued with much enthusiasm.

Mistrust of Police—In Whatever Form

Throughout the history of policing, both private and public police agencies have found themselves at the center of controversies. It takes only a glance at the local newspaper headlines to confirm the fact that neither form of policing is without its measured difficulties, including charges of racism and other diversity issues, internal corruption, and excessive use of force. Security and criminal justice professionals speculate that the growth currently seen in the security industry reflects an indictment of public police abilities to meet the changing needs of the community—whether that be corporations or low-income families.

Security professionals who offer protection services to African American communities suggest that "the traditional means of policing African American neighborhoods doesn't work. The police tend not to be from the community and don't understand [our] needs."[53] For members of these communities, security groups organized to work with neighborhood watch groups are often the preferred protection format.[54] Furthermore, members of these communities may not trust law enforcement sufficiently. Security professionals were hired in public housing areas in Texas to profile potential problem areas, and this then became information used in crime prevention.[55] Rules for residents were outlined, which allowed the security professionals working in the area to establish guidelines for maintaining order and "reduce the occurrence of situations conductive to criminal activity."[56] But there are people who question the use of public (and private) police resources to aggressively pursue crime in specific areas rather than others. Interestingly enough, the rule-making process was followed by a phase involving an undercover operation where the security professionals worked in conjunction with police to identify community members involved in criminal activity. The undercover operation was in place with the objective of collecting enough information to secure arrest warrants for those residents. A "shock team" was then sent in to do a "massive cleanup campaign," where everyone who was identified was then arrested in one great sweep.[57]

According to initial reports conducted to assess the effectiveness of the program, the number of calls for police service to that neighborhood decreased from 170 during the four months before the program was implemented to 50 during the four months after the program was implemented. This program is listed as a community crime prevention effort, but critics of police misuse of power might have a different interpretation. While on the surface security and law enforcement practitioners might see this as a success story, questions exist about how appropriate it is to infiltrate an area undercover, with the intention of making arrests. Certainly this is the purpose of undercover law enforcement operations. A classroom discussion about what might happen if this type of activity were moved to a different setting would be interesting. Several scandals involving politicians have been brought to public attention, or, more specifically, to the attention of police; so imagine, for example, that law enforcement officers in Washington, D.C., worked with private security professionals to organize a campaign to "reduce the occurrence of situations conducive to criminal activity" (as was the objective identified for the Texas program). Law enforcement operatives would be sent in, undercover, to meetings of politicians with industry officials, or meetings of politicians with political action committee representatives, or any other activities to look for anything "conductive to criminal activity." Then, at the end of a designated time period, or after enough information had been collected to secure arrests, a massive cleanup would be scheduled. Would that be an acceptable practice? What differences are there in the two communities where the cleanup is taking place, other than the obvious lack of power people in minority communities have compared to politicians? Does this kind of an undercover operation represent effective or appropriate use of either public police or security professionals? Are social conditions such that certain groups of people are targeted for "cleanup campaigns" and other communities are not "policed" with the same diligence? Would there be support for having such a cleanup campaign in areas other than the public housing example presented previously? What would happen, for example, if such a cleanup was implemented to target underage drinking activity on college campuses and private security officers went undercover to collect information about violators to later make a series of arrests? What about the use of undercover security in a private setting to investigate employee theft? Clearly, matters of ethics, matters of privacy, and matters of law must be discussed fully and openly when people are trying to answer these and other important questions.

When police efforts (whether public or private) are seen to target "powerless" communities to the exclusion of enforcement and prosecution of other equally vexing social ills—such as white-collar crimes—trust for the enforcement process seems to grow shaky. Yet at the same time, private security agencies have not been openly identified as community resources. Even after trends to professionalize public law enforcement have been under way for almost 30 years, questions about police practices are seemingly continuously under fire. The popular media has highlighted extensive claims of abuse by law enforcement officers, including tampering with evidence, drug dealing, and various claims of discrimination and unequal treatment of alleged violators. Various articles and government reports have pointed to the significant absence of the private security industry in community efforts to organize crime prevention protocols.[58] In fact, the more recent mentions of the term *private policing* are linked to the early 1970s and with industry.[59] The dramatic increase in the numbers of people working in security-related professions and the increasing overlap between public and private police functions create a scenario that opens up questions, and in some cases makes people increasingly nervous, about how public safety will be ensured.

Demand for Public Safety

In the modern era, police response and other public safety functions (such as the 911 service) have come to be seen as essential public safety features in just about every city across the country. Groups of citizens argue that they are involved with security issues because they must be if they are to ensure a reasonable degree of security within their own blocks.[60] Yet not all communities are comfortable with the level of security and safety afforded by law enforcement. It becomes clear that the affluence of a community can affect the extent

(*Source:* Reprinted courtesy *The Detroit News* and Larry Wright.)

of these services. One affluent community in Texas is experimenting with the practice of providing a pocket-sized 911 emergency call button to every citizen so that a person could contact emergency personnel from any place at any time, thus enhancing personal security.[61] Another wireless location device is the **global positioning system (GPS),** technology that allows tracking of vehicles, people, and even pets and has become an attractive security feature for those who can afford it. A high-priced new car might come with a GPS option marketed as a security feature because people in the car have the ability to push a button and receive assistance anywhere, anytime. For people envisioning getting lost in a snowstorm or having a heart attack while driving, such a security feature is attractive.

The use of technology has been influential in determining how policing services are delivered to the public, yet the transformation associated with integrating technology into the broader society is proving to be a significant challenge, and protection and enforcement agencies are at the forefront of that technological revolution. New technology is clearly a double-edged sword. Even with the advanced numbers of home security systems being installed, which suggest that people are assuming responsibility for their own protection, the public police have identified this one technology as accounting for a critically high number of false alarm calls (these alarms are often set off by homeowners). The large number of false alarms has created quite a bit of difficulty, because public police are required to respond to these false alarms. So, in another example of cooperation, law enforcement agencies have incorporated security professionals into efforts to address this false alarm problem.

But changes within the security industry are going to impact how police do their job as well. For example, Pinkerton's, a large private security organization, says security-related technology has replaced many security guards.[62] So it seems the technological advances will have a direct role to play in coordinating the police and security response. With interactive, integrated security system designs, audio and video systems can be used to relay live video and audio to a remote command center, where experienced security intervention teams act as remote security personnel for all kinds of businesses.[63] Experts in law enforcement agree that whatever role private security will play in public safety issues, cooperative efforts between sworn law enforcement officers and private security must be nurtured.[64]

If there is a specific security need, chances are really good that there is a company that can provide that service for the right price. While public police balk at offering "protection for a price," private security professionals have become so diversified and specialized that they are able to provide protection services that some public law enforcement agencies have not fully developed. Simply stated, private security professionals, in large part, make their own rules for providing services. They are entrepreneurs motivated by market demands, personal expertise, and the need to provide a service in order to get paid. This singular objective, in the minds of many public police, makes the security professional an unreliable resource if the objective is to protect all of society—not just the highest bidders. While the expansion and development of specialized security areas may be a response to public fear, it is precisely this business-oriented, capitalistic, competitive market strategy that has resulted in questions about the need to regulate the security industry.

MARKET DEMANDS REQUIRE COMPETITIVE MARKET RESPONSES

As a discipline, the security industry can be spoken of in general terms. A person might say something like "I work in the security industry," for example. As the security profession expands and the industry becomes more competitive, however, there is increasing specialization. At one time, security companies were sought out to provide a range of security needs. Today, however, it is more likely that someone interested in meeting specific security needs will contract with multiple security professionals who have each developed an expertise in a particular aspect of security.

Some practitioners argue that it is simply not possible for public police agencies to compete with private industry. The security industry itself (as the name of the largest professional security organization, American Society for *Industrial* Security, indicates) is in part responsible for the persistent, but perhaps false, identification of security-related activities as issues that are exclusive to "big" business.[65] Private security forces are said to operate in areas of private space "to which the public police do not have routine access."[66] Furthermore, people have raised concerns about what goes on behind the corporate veil. This relates back to the idea of private corporate justice, discussed in Chapter 7. But does this notion of private security include the kinds of neighborhood watch being discussed as security functions?

People close to the industry argue, as a rule, that elements of the public police are "fragmenting into forms designed to deal with the problems of *policing different* **places** or to provide *policing of different functions* [italics in the original; bold added]."[67] A related consideration on the opposite end of the spectrum is the fact that public police are increasingly expected to focus on the specific concerns identified as priorities within the private sector, and in this way are "increasingly being required to imitate aspects of private business concerns."[68] Consider the crime of computer hacking or the crime of money laundering. While private policing bodies are defined as profit-making bodies selling services in a competitive market, there are specific examples where private companies are providing services for public purchasers because the private company has the people with the expertise.

There are also the routine police services that do not require specialized training or skills, where public agencies have chosen to replace their offering of specific services by contracting with private agencies, through a **contract outsourcing** process.[69] Private security professionals are used both within and outside of structured parameters typically thought to be exclusive to law enforcement. They are also utilized only as they are determined to be needed. This "need" could be determined by a corporate official, a private person, or a public organization that seeks to enhance security for a large upcoming community event.

In short, the specific responsibilities of a private security professional are dependent on the job, more specifically the needs outlined by the client. It has been more common than most people understand to have public law enforcement agencies contract with private security firms to perform specific security-related functions. Having said this, however, security professionals still do not have the powers granted by the state to police officers.

To ensure the safety and security of society, a public police officer must make sure people comply with the laws that are put in place to protect citizens. This is one clear distinction between public and private police responsibilities. Security professionals, as Chapter 11 discusses more specifically, have responsibilities that do not include powers of arrest. The private security officer is above all a private citizen. Private security professionals have no more legal authority than the average citizen. When on company property, security professionals have the directives provided by the company and are likely to have the benefit of training on local ordinances and laws that apply to their security function within that environment. How this matches up with the responsibilities of local police will depend on the situation.

A Shift from Past Policing Practice

It is clear that community attitudes about police —either public or private— have varied over time and are often dependent on the community. Until the 1950s, most departments prohibited any private employment of off-duty police "that required officers to work in uniform for a private employer or to exercise police powers on that employer's behalf."[70] Articles from the late 1960s and the 1970s highlight the animosity felt between law enforcement officers and private security professionals.[71,72] In the 1980s the United States saw proactive policing efforts come into vogue, while beginning in the late 1980s and extending throughout the 1990s, policing agencies moved toward wholesale adoption of the concept of **community policing,** a policing philosophy that stresses the importance of active community involvement in identifying issues of importance within the community. Innovative, nontraditional approaches to address a range of problems that were not previously considered by the police to be within their domain of responsibility are being collectively discussed under the heading of community policing.[73] Consequently, the issues identified under a community policing format for a small town may in fact be quite different from those for a big urban center, because the people within those communities set the policing priority.

The historically grounded rejection of private security personnel as unprofessional and poorly trained is being replaced by an increasing willingness to view them as "colleagues, and assist private security companies with special training and technical assistance."[74] Furthermore, support for community policing within law enforcement expands the responsibility of public police to include the need to make essential connections with community members. More recent research suggests various cooperative programs between public law enforcement agencies and private enterprises are emerging. In fact, public law enforcement agencies are contracting more frequently for private security services. In 1971, some 5000 federal police provided security at government buildings around the country. Today most of that work is handled privately.[75]

Everyone Has a Role to Play in Personal Protection

One aspect of the security profession that often gets lost is the need to address community questions and issues surrounding personal protection. This is an ongoing educational process for people of all ages- an educational process with connections to both public and private police agencies. Security professionals, public law enforcement officers, and other public safety officials can be a valuable resource for community members. Communication among these people is essential for a comprehensive program to meet general community security concerns. Agencies such as the National Crime Prevention Council, in cooperation with private agencies such as ADT Security Systems,[76,77] have put together information for citizens about how to protect themselves against common types of street crime and cons.

So many of the criminal activities individuals are likely to confront cut across all groups. Fraud, for example, comes in numerous forms and may be committed by anyone, from a highly regarded professional to a fly-by-night con artist. According to the Insurance Information Institute, a nonprofit group in New York, fraud cost all sectors of the insurance industry as much as $120 billion in 1995.[78] So while police are sometimes utilized as an informational resource, and almost always are involved when a crime happens, much of the security practitioner's response will involve prevention. People need to educate themselves and take charge of their own protection. And, as is the case with just about all aspects of security, different groups face different personal security threats. Consider, for example, a recent report suggesting that older people are particularly susceptible to being taken advantage of by bogus get-rich-quick schemes, fabricated charity organizations, and substandard service contractors, for instance. The totals involving fraudulent misrepresentation to the elderly are reported to exceed $40 billion per year.[79]

In many cases people will assume the primary responsibility for securing their person and their property—their house and car, for example. When crimes takes place, public law enforcement officers are usually called in. If a person's car is broken into, it makes sense for him or her to either purchase a security device or talk to a police officer about better ways to make the vehicle safe. It is not uncommon for public law enforcement officers to educate people on crime prevention.

Although part of the police function is to assist in crime prevention, in some departments this happens on a very limited basis, so security professionals might be used. Furthermore, people may turn to private security professionals when dealing with particularly difficult situations such as identity theft, discussed in Chapter 6.

High-Profile Protection

Another area of clear overlap between public police and private security functions can be found in the case of executive protection. Minnesota has been making national news since its citizens elected a Reform Party candidate to the state's highest office. As the highlight box indicates, Jesse "The Body" Ventura is a flamboyant politician who is praised for his direct, fearless approach to governing. The citizens of Minnesota are finding that providing security for such a high-profile individual can be expensive. Whether the security professional is contracted as a state employee or is a private protection professional, the objective is the same: to protect the high-profile client from every threat. Consider the following excerpt:

> The chief executive . . . is obsessed with anonymity. All details of his personal life are a carefully guarded secret. He is loath to appear in public, resisting requests even to address his own workers at closed company gatherings. He has not been photographed since [his] college yearbook photo . . . and according to those who work closely with him, he is apt to wear disguises when conducting business with corporate outsiders. . . . His travel plans are strictly classified . . . and he often changes his schedule at the last minute to avoid would-be followers. He has never signed a hotel registry and owns nothing in his own name. He shuns the media, and except for one brief interview . . . in 1991, he has never talked to the press.[80]

I Ain't Got Time to Worry About Costs

In November of 1998, Jesse Ventura shocked the nation and much of the state of Minnesota when he was elected governor. With this victory, the ex–Navy Seal and professional wrestler became the highest ranked member of the Reform Party.

A very high-profile individual is subjected to significant public scrutiny. Consequently, Governor Ventura cannot seem to keep himself out of the media spotlight, with just about every move making headline news. Ventura's celebrity draws large crowds wherever he goes, so considerable attention must be given to providing an adequate security response. When Governor Ventura was on a book tour in early summer 1999, headlines and top news stories read "Taxpayers Will Pay for Ventura Security" and "Ventura's Book Tour Cost Us . . . about $16,000."

The cost of security for Governor Ventura is said to be higher than the cost of security for his predecessors, although this is hard to confirm. Many governors can get away with having no security at their homes; however, Governor Ventura has higher security demands because of his celebrity and perhaps too because of all the controversy that has surrounded him in his days as governor. "I can't imagine a scenario with this governor where the law wouldn't require security," said the state's public safety commissioner, Charlie Weaver.[1] So, when the security force was sent with him on his promotional tour for *I Ain't Got Time to Bleed: Reworking the Body Politic from the Bottom Up*, the people demanded a breakdown of how much was paid for by the public and how much was paid for privately. He was provided with three Minnesota state troopers and one staff member on his trip. Media reports indicate that taxpayers were outraged because citizens of the state were required to foot the bill for those traveling with the governor. Governor Ventura's publisher paid for his other expenses. The trip cost taxpayers about $16,000.[2]

Many people within the state government were also upset at the actions and expectations of the governor. The chairwoman of the House Transportation Finance Committee, Carol Molnau, said that the governor should consider reimbursing the state for at least part of the expenses for those traveling with him because he was

(continued)

profiting personally from the trip.[3] However, the attorney general's office said that "ensuring the governor's safety during the promotional tour is consistent with the over-arching public purpose of protecting the governor at all times."[4] These sentiments were echoed by State Patrol Chief Anne Beers, who said, "We're not going to compromise the security for the governor. We're providing the security that's necessary."[5] Ventura was seemingly irritated that people did not want to provide the security necessary to keep him safe on his tour. He noted that the state provided security for Vice President Al Gore and Texas Governor George W. Bush when they were in Minnesota. He said that they were "two political figures . . . looking to personal achievement and gain, yet we provide security for them."[6] He said that it seemed as if people were saying that it was fine to go on a crusade for personal gain if you were a Democrat or a Republican but not if you were a member of the Reform Party. Other governors were provided security when they were on vacation, which is what Governor Ventura called his trip. But Molnau said this was security for his personal business, which she defined as being different from a vacation.

"The state of Minnesota must protect me 24 hours a day because I'm the governor,"[7] Governor Ventura told Regis Philbin and Kathie Lee Gifford when he visited their show on his book tour. Whether people love him or hate him, he was still the governor, and a higher-profile governor means a higher-profile security response. If adequate security were not provided, the results could be devastating. Governor Ventura summed it up best: "If something happens to me, who's responsible then?"[8]

References

1. "A.G.: Taxpayer Money OK for Book Tour," *http://www.channel4000.com/news/ventura/news-ventura-990603-163841.html*, June 3, 1999.
2. "Ventura's Book Tour Cost Us . . ." *http://www.channel4000.com/news/ventura/news-ventura-990621-204827.html*, June 21, 1999.
3. R. Whereatt, "Attorney General Says State Can Pay for Ventura's Security," *http://www.startribune.com*, June 4, 1999.
4. "A.G.: Taxpayer Money OK for Book Tour."
5. "Taxpayers Will Pay for Ventura Security," *http://www.channel4000.com/news/ventura/news-ventura-990526-184958.html*, May 26, 1999.
6. P. Lopez-Baden, "Ventura Blames Partisanship for Security Costs Flap," *http://www.startribune.com*, July 31, 1999.
7. "A. G.: Taxpayer Money OK for Book Tour."
8. "Taxpayers Will Pay for Ventura Security."

Much more detailed information about this individual was presented in a national news article, from that "one brief interview" mentioned previously. After the story broke, people from the company, particularly the chief executive, were outraged, suggesting that the vivid description of them in their daily environment was a "violation of their privacy—a threat to their lives."[81] To ensure that the pictures included with the newspaper story were never reprinted, the company paid the freelance photographer $20,000 for the rights to the photos.[82] Furthermore, these individuals indicated that their ability to keep their lives private is "a key to healthy, normal living."[83]

People who are high profile can find themselves the target of misdirected attention. How someone decides to provide protection to either his or her person or property varies with the individual, but it is not rare for a high-profile person to require a collective public and private police response to his or her personal protection issues. The circumstances surrounding Martin Luther King, Jr.'s assassination are identified as an extremely poignant example of a series of missteps involving interaction between public police and private security. The official version of the assassination has been contested, and a series of unexplained activities documented in various publications are said to suggest that the handling of the King visit to Memphis was less than responsible.[84] It is argued that "the Memphis police department handled the King assassination with the efficiency of the Keystone Cops."[85] King had his own security detail, and Memphis police officers were also assigned to him. Some of the unexplained activities include a reduction in the public police assigned to King; a charge that two black firefighters stationed across the street from the Lorraine Hotel (where King was shot) were told to report to other stations that day; claims that the Memphis public safety director's office was filled with military personnel two hours before the assassination; an "aide" to King was doing undercover work for the Memphis Police Department; and, when a private ambulance arrived after the shooting, the police insisted on waiting for the city ambulance and would not allow them to drive King to the hospital. It has been documented that over 50 death threats against King had been reported. In short, people today still believe that the FBI had targeted King for surveillance, harassment, and sabotage just as they had with Malcolm X and countless other black activists.[86] Although extremely controversial and contentious, certainly the case is a model for how not to integrate public and private security protection efforts for a high-profile person. In the case of King, of course, the outcome was the worst one possible.

ACKNOWLEDGING ESSENTIAL CONNECTIONS: DEVELOPING RESPECT AMONG PROFESSIONALS

The provisions of policing services by public and private police are in some ways similar, but the objectives of the public police are different from those of private security professionals. The primary differences between public and private police as outlined in the law are left for Chapter 11. Throughout the remainder of this chapter, and after highlighting several common themes that exist between public and private law enforcement objectives, attention is given to the issue of interagency interdependence. The problems confronting both public and private policing agencies are used to highlight the possibility of complementary relations. Several of the essential elements for success in offering security-related services in a public format are discussed next.

Ethics

One of the critical issues related to both public and private police response is ethics. **Ethics** is an area of interest focused on questions of appropriate and inappropriate activity. Ethical behavior is behavior that is considered acceptable or appropriate, while unethical behavior is behavior that is not considered appropriate. The difficulty with studying ethical behavior is that it varies from setting to setting: from individual to individual, from group to group, and from country to country, as is referenced in several other introductory-level security textbooks.[87-89]

The Importance of Public Relations

Of the many roles a security professional must assume, one that appeals to many students is the ability to work with people in a service role. This feature of the job requires (at a minimum) leadership skills, interpersonal communication skills, and a genuine interest in providing assistance. Security professionals must be prepared to respond to emergency situations, make effective decisions, observe things ordinary and unusual, and be a good role model for others. People often look to security officers if they need information, have problems or questions, or need assistance with a task. In this way, security officers are often the connecting point between a particular business and the people in a particular area.

A Professional Presence and Order Maintenance

"The Pinkerton's bureau may have taken up the phrase. 'The eye that never sleeps' to describe its private detective agents, but at least ideally the phrase describes the function of the security [officer] more accurately."[90] The security officer is supposed to keep an eye out for any and all potential security problems. As the security profession seeks to enhance its image with customers and contracting agencies, it is essential that its workers be polite, self-assured, respectful, and responsible. Furthermore, security professionals are actively involved with individuals in their area. As they interact with individuals, security professionals learn about their own individual needs and are therefore better prepared to identify easily and quickly the kinds of concerns or needs other individuals may have. A security professional working in a local school, for example, is well advised to keep abreast of the issues that confront specific teachers and specific kids. This kind of constant information gathering can prove useful in identifying a problem before it gets out of hand. While security professionals are often thought to be people who are passively uninvolved until an emergency arises, this could not be further from the truth. Good security professionals get involved right from the start.

Random and/or Structured Patrols

Perhaps one of the most important jobs the security professional has is that of routine patrol. Routine patrols are part prevention and part public relations. During routine patrols, a security professional has the opportunity to make connections with the company's personnel. This assists with efforts to meet employee needs and helps employees feel secure within their work environment.

Community Resource Officers

Security professionals are considered resource people—people to go to who can take necessary action. Because security professionals are on the front line, interacting with various people (workers, customers, visitors, family members, etc.), security professionals must be skilled in interpersonal communication. Security professionals are likely to help customers when they lock the keys in their car or lose personal belongings such as purses or glasses. They may help older people who have Alzheimer's and become lost. Or they may help people with temporary or long-term disabilities, including hearing or visual impairments.

Structured Emergency Response Coordination

Should an emergency arise, it is essential to organize the response to this threat in an orderly, well-rehearsed fashion. Because potential emergencies and accidents vary according to the setting, more detail on the variety of accidents and emergencies is discussed in Chapter 12. For example, if a small girl wanders away from her parents at a mall, both the distressed parents and the helpful citizen assisting the girl are likely to seek out security professionals in the mall to assist them with the reunion of this girl with her parents. In such encounters, parties are in need of a professional who is competent, knows the resources at his or her disposal, and can provide the required service. In an emergency, a protocol will outline the emergency services to be contacted and how to do so. Emergency response is a critical piece of the overall safety and security function for both public and private police organizations.

Targeting Areas of Public Concern

Concern about the "changes in both the incidence and distribution of street crime and disorder" in urban centers has produced several innovative cooperative efforts. "The relative immunity of these problems to conventional police tactics is a driving force behind the community policing initiatives and the development of nontraditional policing strategies as urban police organizations search for more effective ways to deal with these challenges."[91] Community policing problem solving requires interagency coordination.[92] Furthermore, the community response to public police involvement will vary, based in large part on associations from the past between private agencies and community groups.

SOME QUESTIONS REMAIN

Citizen involvement in law enforcement, "particularly when it involves autonomous groups, is unlike other forms of citizen participation. The stakes are higher; the risk of miscarriage is great and the consequences of abuse or error appear more serious."[93] Often citizens can be enthusiastic yet lack professional training. Law enforcement may not be working closely with these groups as they develop, and the relations between the two groups may be strained. With the emergence of community policing and efforts on the part of various local police departments to get out into the community and build cooperative relationships with citizen groups, it is also likely that these citizen groups will lobby police departments to respond to the concerns that affect specific neighborhoods rather than leave the police departments to attend to the overall needs of the community.

Some critics suggest that private security enterprises are not in business to serve the public good and lead to a **displacement effect,** which means that those less able to pay for additional security become more vulnerable to victimization.[94] In fact, various members of minority communities have argued publicly for years that their communities are not adequately protected by the existing public police structure. Perhaps not as visible or as controversial as the Black Panther Party, these groups and the questions they raise need to be addressed.

Too Poor to Pay for Police Protection? You May Have an Option

The borough of Sussex, New Jersey, a small municipality of about 2500 residents, experimented with privatizing its police department and as a result, became what may be the first modern American community to privatize its municipal law enforcement.[1] Residents sought a more constant uniformed presence ... [while] political leaders considered a police department an expense the municipality could no longer afford.[2]

The Sussex Borough had been considering closing the department for several years, even though the four-member department patrolled only on a part-time basis and had little or no modern equipment, because of its cost and the financial difficulties being experienced by the borough. In 1992, in the wake of a drug scandal that culminated in the indictment of the police chief and another department officer, the borough's law enforcement operations were taken over by the Sussex County Prosecutor's office for several months.

In time, the borough, for primarily economic reasons, elected to abolish the police department and rely on the state police for law enforcement services. Slow response times and limited resources suggested that this option would not provide a permanent solution. Consequently, borough leaders developed a plan to hire a private security company to provide a more constant uniformed presence within the borough.

While the security company's initial mission was simply to supplement the state police, it soon became clear that the "true mission of the company was to function as a fully independent municipal police department."[3] Reports surfaced that a number of the guards had minor criminal records, primarily for assault. Furthermore, the security officers were said to have returned a knife, after an incident, to a person suspected of assault. As a result, an injunction was obtained by the New Jersey attorney general's office "on the basis that the Sussex Borough could not create a private police department without complying with existing state statutes relating to the creation of a police force."[4]

In sum, the Sussex County Prosecutor argued that "the hiring of a private security firm in lieu of a municipal police department not only circumvented a longstanding statutory framework, it also constituted a giant step backward in terms of law enforcement professionalism."[5] Structural changes involving a cooperative effort between law enforcement and security firms could likely provide significant financial savings, which would be attractive, particularly to small police departments. The drawbacks would include a significant cost to hire and train qualified security personnel. Additional concern was expressed about the effect of contracting with a corporate agency rather than local community members.

Remember, as discussed in Chapter 2, the privatization of police services is not a new idea. Groups of citizens, railroad police, and individual citizens have organized and provided police services. Furthermore, security professionals are increasingly targeted for providing supplemental resources to local law enforcement agencies. New York City allocated $28 million in 1992 to increase private security at public schools.[6] In Kansas City, Kansas, the chief of police would like to contract with private firms to provide 22 tasks currently performed by his law enforcement officers.[7]

References

1. This information is presented from the article by D. O'Leary, "Reflections on Police Privatization," *FBI Law Enforcement Bulletin,* vol. 63, issue 9, September 1994. pp. 21–25. Quote from p. 21.
2. Ibid., p. 22.
3. Ibid., p. 22.
4. Ibid., p. 23.
5. Ibid., p. 24.
6. Ira Lipman, "Thugs with Badges: We Need Federal Regulation of Security Guards," *The New York Times,* July 3, 1993, Section 1, page 19.
7. Ibid.

If the public police response to public safety needs is called into question, then the use of private security forces to meet public safety needs will certainly raise some eyebrows. Private security does not fit neatly within the cultural image of "protector." The fact that private security officers are often viewed negatively, even in the mainstream, means that people may not feel confident about security professionals who are hired to act in the public interest. But as discussed in the highlight box "Too Poor to Pay for Police Protection?", significant critical commentary has been sparked by "a disturbing trend toward the privatization of entire city police departments."[95] Furthermore, people see the contract professionals as guardians of someone else's interest.[96] Private security is seen as a "biased" and "selective" system of "policing."[97] The impact of an indiscriminate administration of justice and law enforcement will be felt by

You Can Run, But You Can't Hide

Movies often show someone being watched but not knowing it. Sometimes the FBI or the Central Intelligence Agency is doing the tracking. And sometimes it is criminals who are watching. In real life, one of the more common methods for tracking people involves the use of bounty hunters. In the Wild West, bounty hunters would walk into a sheriff's office and tear "wanted" posters off the wall. The bounty hunters would then hunt the wanted people, find them, and drag them back to the sheriff (sometimes using any means necessary) to collect the reward. Though many of the methods used to locate and capture an individual have changed, the image of bounty hunters as physical enforcers remains. Bounty hunters seek individuals who have violated their contracts with the companies that bailed them out of jail. The company, fearing a loss of hundreds or thousands of dollars, hires a bounty hunter to track down these people and bring them back to jail. The company pays for this service, usually an amount equal to 10 or 15 percent of the bond amount. The company issuing the bond and the hired enforcement agent enter into a contractual agreement with one another regarding the rights and responsibilities given to the enforcer for the capture of wanted person.

Bounty hunters are regulated to some degree with laws that attempt to restrict some of the methods used to make an apprehension. The smart bounty hunter is able to use stealth, seduction, trickery, and surprise. The skippers are usually coaxed into releasing their whereabouts and identity to bounty hunters, who prey on them by appealing to their greed and taking advantage of their gullibility. One bounty hunter has posed as a radio disk jockey, offering free tickets to a concert. Many try to stay invisible and wait for fugitives to reveal themselves. Some bounty hunters track people when they make a credit card transaction, rent an apartment, place a call to their mother, or even just order a pizza. Having Social Security numbers and driver's licenses required for identification makes tracking much simpler. Also, mailing lists can be bought from companies and can reveal people's whereabouts. "If you're breathing, there's no way to stay private," explains Buck Buchanan, cofounder of U.S. Fugitive Task Force, Inc. "If you've got a girlfriend who hates you, I'll find you. If you've got a mother who loves you, I'll find you," he adds.[1]

Although laws have been established to limit the use of force by bounty hunters, many still resort to force. Bounty hunters that are employed by the federal government are carefully trained in the proper use of force. Bail bond companies and the enforcers they hire have the right to break down doors and use force to haul bail jumpers back. Bounty hunters are protected against kidnapping charges but can be charged with aggravated assault if they use more force than deemed reasonable. But sometimes the situation gets terribly out of hand. In September of 1997, five bounty hunters dressed in black clothing, ski masks, and body armor broke down the door of an Arizona resident's home at 4 A.M. They were in search of a California man who skipped out on a $25,000 bail. The people in the room, including children, were tied up and held at gunpoint. The homeowner opened fire, and the bounty hunters returned fire. In the end, the homeowner and his girlfriend were dead, and one bounty hunter was wounded. Thirty-five states do not regulate bounty hunters. No background checks and no training are required,[2] which allows even convicted criminals to call themselves bounty hunters.

Bounty hunters prove to be a necessary cog in the law enforcement machine, making around 30,000 arrests each year.[3] Although they provide a contracted service, bounty hunters are not typically considered security practitioners. But how does society protect innocent people who are mistaken for fugitives? Should individuals be allowed to protect themselves from these low-ranking professionals? In many instances, bounty hunters invade innocent people's personal space. And yet bounty hunters are providing a security service to society. Attempting to apprehend fugitives, bounty hunters sometimes rob, beat, manhandle, and even murder innocent people. Who will protect innocent people from the people who "protect" security?

References

1. D. Tofig, "Relentless Pursuit of Quarry Has Few Rules for the Chase," http://www. accessatlanta.com/partners/ajc/newsatlanta/bounty0407.html, April 7, 2000.
2. J. Walker, "Is Anyone Watching?", http://abcnews.go.com/onair/DailyNews/ wnt990127_walker_story.html, July 27, 1999.
3. B. Serafin, "Renegade Lawmen Scrutinized," http://more.abcnews.go.com/sections/ us/dailynews/bountyhunters/0312.html, March 12, 1998.
4. Associated Press, "Critics Seek Tighter Rules for Bounty Hunters after Fatal Mistake," Minneapolis Star Tribune, September 3, 1997, A4.
5. The Washington Post, no author listed. Nov. 1, 1998, "Bounty Hunter Guilty of Murder in AZ: Man Said He Was Seeking Fugitive," accessed January 25, 2001.

all, regardless of the specific application of the private policing establishment. "A secondary system of policing that provides unequal protection to different groups in society is in itself socially divisive but it also has a direct influence on the operational priorities of the public police and perhaps affects people's attitudes toward policing in general."[98] Caution has been expressed about a public environment where even public agencies contract for police services—with no distinction being given to whether those services are public or private, as these terms have traditionally been used.[99]

CONCLUSION

This chapter outlines several ways the private security professional can be used to enhance the inner workings of a target environment while also enhancing the feeling of safety of employees, customers, and citizens. The connections between public police activity and private responsibilities of security professionals for providing public safety are considered. Attention is given to the interactive relationships with local law enforcement, ethics, public relations, patrols, emergency response, and the need to target specific areas of concern within the target environment.

The chapter also discusses the historic discord between public and private police professionals. Some of the discord concerns who can be considered a security professional and how security organizations work in connection with public law enforcement operations. Clearly, the specifics of this debate will change as the security industry itself changes. The security objective is changing, partly due to new technology.

It is essential for the security professional to establish a secure environment, make certain that customers and other visitors feel safe while on the property, respond to media inquiries responsibly, and assist individuals with inquiries. It should be clear that dialogue about the current standing of the field of security continues. Strong support for the role of the security professional can be found among critics of citizens' efforts to supplement their own security-related needs, who suggest that these groups are untrained and should not be acting in a public safety capacity. In an effort to address these concerns among others, public and private policing agencies are being forced to interact and discuss matters more than they ever have before. The discussion of community policing objectives within neighborhoods may help move these issues beyond public versus private—to "public safety."

REVIEW QUESTIONS

1. Describe an example of self-help security.
2. How does the definition of public and private space impact the role of law enforcement?
3. How does a mistrust of police in certain community areas impact the role of private security officers?
4. Based on information presented in the chapter, who is qualified to provide security?
5. How does protection of a high-profile person involve both public and private police needs?
6. Explain the importance of public relations for both public police and private security professionals.
7. How do community policing initiatives fit into the efforts to meet public safety concerns in specific communities?

DISCUSSION QUESTIONS

1. What issues might people have about discussing the Black Panther Party as a group of people organized to provide security within their own community?
2. Throughout this chapter we have discussed the fact that the distinctions between public and private police are not as clearly delineated as previously thought. Outline the points that you find the most interesting.
3. Does a demand for public safety involve protection from computer crimes? Please explain your response.
4. After spending some time in the library, what issues can you uncover about the assassination of Martin Luther King, Jr. that might cause you to wonder about the protection provided by both the public law enforcement and private security detail?

IN-CLASS PROJECT

1. Each student should list the responsibilities he or she attributes to local law enforcement. What elements of public safety do public law enforcement officers fill? Each student should then make a second list, outlining the responsibilities that private security professionals have. As a class, discuss these lists. As a group, have students share their lists and critically reflect on whether the function attributed to either profession is unique to that profession. Afterward, see how many responsibilities remain exclusively on one list.

REFERENCES

1. "Welcome to the New World of Private Security," *Economist 342,* no. 8013 (1997): 21(4).
2. D. Smith and C. D. Uchida, "The Social Organization of Self-Help: A Study of Defensive Weapon Ownership," *American Sociological Review* 53 (1998): 95.
3. L. Sherman, "Watching and Crime Prevention: New Directions for Police," *Journal of Contemporary Studies* 80 (1982): 87–96.
4. "Welcome to the New World of Private Security."
5. J. Friedman et al., "The Effects of Community Size on the Mix of Private and Public Use of Security Services," *Journal of Urban Economics* 22 (1987): 230–241.
6. T. Jones and T. Newburn, *Private Security and Public Policing* (Oxford, U.K.: Clarendon Press, 1998), 46.
7. T. Egan, "Many Seek Security in Private Communities," *New York Times,* September 3, 1995, A1.
8. J. B. Owens, "Westec Story: Gated Communities and the Fourth Amendment," *American Criminal Law Review 34,* no. 3 (1997): 1127–1160.
9. E. J. Blakely and M. G Snyder, *Fortress America: Gated and Walled Communities in the United States* (Lincoln Institute of Land Policy No. WP95EB1, 1995), discussed in Owens, "Westec Story," 1129.
10. G. DeBecker, *The Gift of Fear* (New York: Dell Books, 1987).
11. Owens, "Westec Story," 1129.
12. B. L. Benson, "Crime Control through Private Enterprise," *Independent Review 2,* no. 3 (1998): 341–372.
13. Blakely and Snyder, *Fortress America,* as discussed in Owens, "Westec Story," 1129.
14. C. Oliver, "Private Sector Crime Control: More Firms, States Think Government Efforts Wanting," *Investors Business Daily,* May 12, 1994, 1.
15. T. Carlson, "Safety Inc.: Private Cops Are There When You Need Them," *Heritage Policy Review 7,* no. 73 (1995): 66.

16. J. B. Owens, "Westec Story: Gated Communities and the Fourth Amendment," *American Criminal Law Review 34,* no. 3 (1997): 1127–1160.

17. C. Keane, "Evaluating the Influence of Fear of Crime as an Environmental Mobility Restrictor on Women's Routine Activities," *Environment and Behavior 30,* no. 1 (1990): 60–74.

18. G. Marx and D. Archer, "Special Issue on Decentralization and Citizen Participation," *American Behavioral Scientist 15,* no. 1 (1971): 52–72.

19. R. Smith, "Private Policing—No Way," in *Private Sector and Community Involvement in the Criminal Justice System,"* ed. D. Biles and J. Vernon (Canberra, Australia: Australian Institute of Criminology, 1994).

20. G. T. Marx and D. Archer, "Citizen Involvement in the Law Enforcement Process: The Case of Coummunity Police Patrols," *American Behavioral Scientist 15,* no. 1 (1971): 52–72.

21. Marx and Archer.

22. "Welcome to the New World of Private Security."

23. "Welcome to the New World of Private Security."

24. S. Laporte, "Download Your Local Sheriff," *Policy Review* no. 82 (1997): 16(3).

25. Laporte, "Download Your Local Sheriff."

26. S. Muwakkil, "Black Panthers Reconsidered," *Chicago Tribune,* February 28, 2000, 11.

27. *Eyes on the Prize II: America at the Racial Crossroads: A Nation of Law?* (Public Broadcasting Service, 1990, videocassette), Alexandria, VA.

28. Muwakkil, "Black Panthers Reconsidered," 11.

29. *Eyes on the Prize II: America at the Racial Crossroads: A Nation of Law?* (Public Broadcasting Service, 1990, videocassette), Alexandria, VA.

30. Muwakkil, "Black Panthers Reconsidered," 11

31. Muwakkil, "Black Panthers Reconsidered," 11.

32. *Eyes on the Prize II: America at the Racial Crossroads.*

33. S. Acoli, "A Brief History of the Black Panther Party and Its Place in the Black Liberation Movement," *http://www.ask.com/main/metaanswer.asp? metaEngine=directhit&origin=o&Meta1URL=,* April 2, 1985, accessed November 17, 2000.

34. R. Johnson, "Citizen Complaints: What the Police Should Know," *FBI Law Enforcement Bulletin 67,* no. 12 (1998): 1–6.

35. C. Stone, "Race, Crime, and the Administration of Justice," *National Institute of Justice Journal,* April 1999, 26–34.

36. Stone, "Race, Crime, and the Administration of Justice," 27.

37. A. Brown, "Community Policing: DSI Investigation Firm Markets in Safety," *Black Enterprise 27,* no. 6 (1997): 30–31.

38. L. Rood, "Missing Funds Amount Climbs," *St. Cloud Times,* May 18, 1996, A1.

39. K. Johnson, "Board Blames Trust in Loss of $419,000," *St. Cloud Times,* May 29, 1996, A8.

40. Johnson, "Board Blames Trust," A8.

41. K. Johnson, "Woman Accused of Embezzling Money Quits Stearns County Job," *St. Cloud Times,* May 28, 1996, A1.

42. Johnson, "Board Blames Trust," A8.

43. Johnson, "Board Blames Trust," A8.

44. T. Cooper, "Ex-Stearns Worker Gets 10-Year Sentence," *St. Cloud Times,* December 11, 1996, A1.

45. N. South, *Policing for Profit: The Private Security Sector* (Beverly Hills, CA: Sage Publications, 1988), 158.

46. S. Puro and R. Goldman, *Legal Authority and Liability in Anti-Crime Activities: Citizens, Community Groups, Police and Private Security* (Rockville, MD: U.S. Department of Justice, National Institute of Justice, 1993).

47. Puro and Goldman, *Legal Authority and Liability.*

48. H. N. Morley and R. S. Fong, "Can We All Get Along? A Study of Why Strained Relations Continue to Exist between Sworn Law Enforcement and Private Security," *Security Journal* 6 (1995): 85–92.

49. H. Morley, telephone conversation with author, November 3, 2000.

50. C. Shearing, P. C. Stenning, and S. M. Addarlo, "Police Perceptions of Private Security," *Canadian Police College Journal 9,* no. 2 (1985): 127–153.

51. M. Nalla and G. Newman, *Primer in Private Security* (New York: Harrow and Heston, 1990).

52. Shearing et al., "Police Perceptions of Private Security," 129.

53. A. Brown, "Community Policing: DSI Investigation Firm Markets in Safety," *Black Enterprise 27,* no. 6 (1997): 30.

54. Brown, "Community Policing," 30.

55. G. Carson and D. A. Armstrong, "Use of Private Security in Public Housing: A Case Study," *Journal of Security Administration 17,* no. 1 (1994): 53–74.

56. Carson and Armstrong, "Use of Private Security," 53.

57. Carson and Armstrong, "Use of Private Security," 53.

58. W. Cunningham and T. Taylor, *Private Security and Police in America: The Hallcrest Report.* (Portland, OR: Chancellor Press, 1985).

59. "Welcome to the New World of Private Security."

60. J. Blyskal, "Drugbusters," *New York,* March 13, 1995, 43–48.

61. S. Baldauf, "Tiny Texas Town Gets a Pocket Sized Crime Fighter," *Christian Science Monitor,* January 20, 1999, 2.

62. S. Lubove, "High-Tech Cops," *Forbes,* September 25, 1995, 44–45.

63. M. Foote, "Interactive Security: Police and Private Security Join Forces," *Police Chief,* June 1999, 57–61.

64. Morley and Fong, "Can We All Get Along?" 86.
65. Jones and Newburn, *Private Security and Public Policing,* 266.
66. C. Shearing and P. Stenning in *Crime and Justice 3,* eds. M. Tonry and N. Morris (Chicago: University of Cheicago Press, 1981), 213.
67. Jones and Newburn, *Private Security and Public Policing,* 266.
68. Jones and Newburn, *Private Security and Public Policing,* 210.
69. Jones and Newburn, *Private Security and Public Policing,* 213.
70. A. J. Reiss, Jr., *Private Employment of Public Police,* National Institute of Justice: Research in Brief, (Washington, DC: 1988), 1–8.
71. J. Henderson, "Public Law Enforcement, Private Security, and Citizen Crime Prevention: Competition or Cooperation?" *Police Journal 60,* no. 1 (1987): 48–57.
72. J. E. Lance, *Privatization of Law Enforcement: Are We Prepared?* (Rockville, MD: National Institute of Justice, 1986), folder A1.
73. E. J. Williams, "Enforcing Social Responsibility and the Expanding Domain of the Police: Notes from the Portland Experiences," *Crime and Delinquency 42,* no. 2 (1996): 309–323.
74. Williams, "Enforcing Social Responsibility," 317–318.
75. G. Hanson, "Private Protection Is a Secure Industry," *Insight on the News 13,* no. 36 (1997): 19.
76. National Crime Prevention Council, the Federal Bureau of Investigation, the National Citizen's Crime Prevention Campaign, and ADT Security Systems, *Use Common Sense To Spot a Con* (Washington, DC: U.S. Department of Justice, 1998).
77. National Crime Prevention Council, the Federal Bureau of Investigation, the National Citizen's Crime Prevention Campaign, and ADT Security Systems, *Street Sense* (Washington, DC: U.S. Department of Justice, 1998).
78. C. Coward, "Battling Insurance Fraud: These Scams Cost the Insurance Industry $200 Billion a Year—Don't Be a Victim," *Black Enterprise 28,* no. 8 (1998): 101.
79. Gannett News Service, "Program Helps Elderly Avoid Being Scammed: Criminals Swindle More Than $40 Billion Every Year From Consumers," *St. Cloud Times,* February 21, 2000, 4C.
80. J. G. Brenner, *Emperors of Chocolate* (New York: Random House, 1999), 34.
81. Brenner, *Emperors of Chocolate,* 35.
82. Brenner, *Emperors of Chocolate,* 36.
83. Brenner, *Emperors of Chocolate,* 37.
84. D. Gregory and M. Lane, *Murder in Memphis: The FBI and the Assassination of Martin Luther King* (New York: Thunder's Mouth Press, 1993).
85. C. Overbeck, "The Assassination of Dr. Martin Luther King, Jr.: An Overview/Section 5: Strange Goings-on at the Memphis P.D.," *http://www.parascope.com/articles/0197/m1k5.htm,* 1996.

86. "The Assassination of Dr. Martin Luther King, Jr.," accessed January 25, 2001.
87. Wrobleski and K. Hoss, *Introduction to Private Security* (Minneapolis, MN: West Publishing Company, 1996), 651.
88. C. Simonsen, *Private Security in America: An Introduction* (Upper Saddle River, NJ: Prentice Hall, 1998), 31–42.
89. R. Fischer and G. Green, *Introduction to Security,* 6th ed. (Woburn, MA: Butterworth-Heinemann, 1998), 20–21.
90. C. Shearing et al., *Contract Security in Ontario* (Toronto, Canada: Center of Criminology, University of Toronto, 1980), 168.
91. E. J. Williams, "Enforcing Social Responsibility and the Expanding Domain of the Police: Notes from the Portland Experience," *Crime and Delinquency* 42, no. 2 (1996): 309–323.
92. Williams, "Enforcing Social Responsibility," 312.
93. Marx and Archer, "Special Issue," 70.
94. South, *Policing for Profit,* 152.
95. M. Chaiken and J. Chaiken, *Public Policing—Privately Provided,* National Criminal Justice Resource Service, (Rockville, MD: National Institute of Justice/NCJRS, 1987), 4.
96. A. Reiss, "The Legitimacy of Intrusion into Private Space," in *Private Policing,* eds. C. Shearing and P. Stenning (Beverly Hills, CA: Sage Publications, 1987), 19–44.
97. South, *Policing for Profit,* 155.
98. W. Flavel, "Research into Security Organizations," unpublished paper, Second Briston Seminar on the Sociology of the Police, 1973, 8.
99. Chaiken and Chaiken, *Public Policing—Privately Provided.*

11
Legal Liability Issues

CHAPTER OUTLINE

Foundations of Law
  Basic Organization of Law: Criminal, Civil, and Administrative Functions
  Federal, State, and Local Regulation of the Security Industry
  Employee Rights Granted through Legal Protections
    Civil Rights Act of 1964
    Americans with Disabilities Act
  Primer in Basic Crime Classifications
Legal Authority of the Security Professional
Basics Concepts of Criminal Procedure and Their Application to Private Security
  Stop and Frisk

Arrest, Detention, and False Imprisonment
Search and Seizure/Probable Cause
Reasonable Expectation of Privacy
Use of Force
Tort Law
Miscellaneous Legal Issues
  Nondelegable Duty
  Color of Law
Conclusion
  Review Questions
  Discussion Questions

CHAPTER HIGHLIGHTS

- to develop a working knowledge of the basic legal issues affecting security professionals
- to understand the role of civil liability in a security management plan
- to be familiar with court cases that have impacted the security enterprise

- to be better prepared to identify liability issues relevant to a target environment
- to be better prepared to introduce the concept of liability protection into the overall security management strategy

KEY WORDS

Administrative law
Americans with Disabilities Act
Case law
Civil law
Civil Rights Act
Color of law
Common law (*mala en se/mala prohibita*)
Criminal law

Exclusionary rule
Felony
Foreseeability
Inevitable discovery
Intentional torts
Merchant's privilege statute
Misdemeanor
Negligence
Nondelegable duty

Precedent   Supremacy Clause
Probable cause   Tort law
Statutory law   Vicarious liability
Strict liability

People developing a security management plan should understand basic civil and criminal liability issues. Litigation can prove financially disastrous for any business. It often falls to the security professional, working with management, to ensure that the agency or business is protected, as much as is reasonably possible, against any circumstance that might result in legal trouble. The chapter highlights some foundations of law, then reviews tort law (negligence issues), and then examines common legal entanglements that security professionals face. Laws related to security vary from state to state. All security professionals should make themselves intimately familiar with legal resources available to them through security resources. For example, in Minnesota, various security professionals with an understanding of law are affiliated with the state chapter of the American Society for Industrial Security.

This chapter is focused on providing a basic understanding of the law as it relates to the security profession. Because laws change, sometimes rapidly and significantly, security professionals and the businesses or organizations they work for must have access to legal counsel. It is essential that security professionals remain up to date on security-related legislation and alter company policies and procedures when necessary.

FOUNDATIONS OF LAW

Society is regulated by policies and laws implemented by legislative bodies and interpreted by the courts. Simply stated, there are three sources of laws: (1) common law, (2) case law, and (3) statutory law. **Common law** is based in judicial decisions and laws that originated in England. Today, some of these laws have lost their significance. In some states, a couple not legally married but cohabitating as man and wife may meet the designation for "common law marriage." Not all states acknowledge the concept, however, and the length of cohabitation required to meet the standard may vary. **Case law** is based on the idea that a court should stand by decisions that have been previously handed down; these previous decisions are known as **precedent.** The applicability of another case can be determined by whether the facts and applicable law in the case are similar, whether the level of the court is higher or lower, and whether the court has the same legal jurisdiction.[1] **Statutory law** is codified law. These laws are drafted and approved by a governing body and often change, by amendment, repeal, or revision.

Basic Organization of Law: Criminal, Civil, and Administrative Functions

This chapter is not intended to act as a legal document or provide the kind of legal direction one would require of a lawyer. The objective is simply to review some of the essentials for security professionals. It is important that security professionals understand that law is organized into three basic parts: (1) criminal law, (2) civil law, and (3) administrative law. **Criminal law** protects order in the state. Criminal law has less to do with the protection of individual rights, because its primary role is ensuring the preservation of the state. **Civil law** protects private rights, whether those be an individual's rights or the rights of a corporation. **Administrative law** includes rules, regulations, orders, and decisions created by administrative agencies.[2]

Administrative law can be important to security professionals. Decisions of administrative agencies such as the Occupational Safety and Health Administration (OSHA) and the Equal Employment Opportunity Commission (EEOC), for instance, affect how security professionals do their jobs. In short, administrative agencies make certain that federal and state requirements are being followed.[3]

Civil litigation is an increasingly significant concern for security professionals because the amount of damages in court actions in security-related incidents has exploded.[4] Civil law is divided into a variety of different areas. These include (but are not limited to) contract law, warrants, agency, and torts.[5] It is true that a particular incident can be handled both as a criminal offense and as a civil offense. Interestingly enough, it is often the decision of the security professional, working with directions from management, as to whether police will be involved in an incident. In other words, specific practices must be outlined for the security professional who is likely to confront a situation where he or she is faced with a decision about whether to pursue criminal charges.

Such decisions come up regularly in retail settings. Consider the example of retail outlets that post "All shoplifters will be prosecuted" signs. While shoplifting is a problem, employee theft often results in more dollars being lost. So while security professionals have a critical role to play in protecting the company and its employees from various threats (including shoplifters), security professionals are also confronted with the reality that transgressions they investigate may involve employees of the company. Security professionals must be prepared for this possibility.

Because proceeding with criminal prosecution is often a less-than-perfect option, companies that discover people inside the company stealing from the company often simply seek remuneration and dismiss the people. Whether the actions taken by security professionals are directed toward customers or employees, the activities involve the potential for criminal or civil confrontations. This means that all the information that could be used at trial must be thorough, accurate, and well preserved. The involvement of police is typically required in criminal complaints, so the emphasis for security personnel is typically noncriminal legal actions between two parties, where one party has claimed a loss or grievance and seeks a private remedy. In short, perhaps the most significant legal challenge to security firms and security personnel involves the corporate need to be protected against liability in the form of tort law, or civil litigation.

Federal, State, and Local Regulation of the Security Industry

For security professionals, it is critical to make distinctions between levels of governance and determine how federal law, state law, and local community ordinances impact the delivery of security services in an area. This cannot be stressed enough. Authority to take action comes from very specific legal precedents; for security professionals employed to provide certain services to an organization or agency, this authority usually comes from administrative law or corporate policies and procedures. Such policies and procedures dictate how the organization expects a security professional to act under various circumstances. Laws governing state operations must comply with legal precedence should a controversial matter go to court. Laws based in statutes are binding, whereas legal precedence can only be associated with case law. Article VI of the U.S. Constitution defines the **Supremacy Clause,** which outlines the main foundation of the federal government's power over the states (technically, *Marbury v. Madison* implemented the Supremacy Clause). All legal requirements governing the security industry that were legislated by Congress must be followed as interpreted by the appropriate administrative agencies. The federal standard is established as a minimum standard. States or other lesser bodies of governance can only make the standard more stringent, not less so.

Even novice security professionals must be able to determine how laws govern any security-related activity. Furthermore, department or company policy should provide guidelines for security professionals. While these policies must be in compliance with federal, state, and local laws, different corporations and organizations are likely to interpret laws to suit their own needs. One company may be extremely concerned about employee drug use and therefore establish "no tolerance" policies. Other companies may establish policies focused on meeting drug-using employees' needs, perhaps by requiring counseling. Security professionals can refer to other companies' policies but must always tailor policies to their own environment, taking into account the enterprise to be secured, its geographic location, its size, its corporate mandates, and so forth.

Administrative agencies of the federal government that contract for private security services include

- the Federal Aviation Administration
- the Interstate Commerce Commission

The Wretched Face of Hate

Despite decades of struggles for civil rights, sad stories of hatred, discrimination, and oppression are still being told. Many individuals have to walk the streets of cities, the halls of schools and offices, and even the rooms of their own houses in fear. All over the nation people are still being attacked because of their race, their sex, or their religion. In this new millennium, is it going to be possible to create a safer environment for all people? Can the United States become the "Land of the Free," as the founders intended over 200 years ago? Sadly, individuals and groups that espouse hate are still active in the country.

The Aryan Nations is one of the most significant forces in the nation's white supremacist movement. Operating out of a compound at northern Idaho's Hayden Lake, the camp is known for its "whites only" sign, its barbed-wire fortifications, and its occasional cross burnings. The founder and leader, Richard Butler, began the operation as the Church of Jesus Christ–Christian/Aryan Nations. This "church" believes that whites are the true children of God, that Jews are Satan's offspring, and that minorities are inferior.[1]

On July 1, 1998, Victoria and Jason Keenan, a mother and son, were driving along a public road near the Aryan Nations complex. Jason accidentally dropped his wallet out of the window, and when they turned the car around to get the wallet, the car backfired. The security guards at the complex believed this to be a gunshot and decided to pursue the Keenans' vehicle. Chasing the car for two miles, the guards shot at the family with assault rifles, forced them into a ditch, and violently attacked them with the butt of a gun. The Aryan Nations claims that the guards violated the organization's rules by leaving the compound to chase the Keenans. It also claims that the guards were intoxicated and could not coherently react to the situation. In fact, many of the security guards working for Aryan Nations were known to be ex-convicts, some of whom had drug problems and often acted impulsively. Former Aryan Nations security chief Michael Teague said of the many members' prison records, "We are in the business of forgiving people. We try to help reform them."[2]

Yet mainstream America is unlikely to support these actions as "reform." Members of the community surrounding the Aryan Nations complex argue they are scared. How should Americans provide security for people who are threatened by hate groups? With chapters of various groups spread all over the nation and more than 450 hate Web sites on the Internet today, the job seems difficult and endless. But the Southern Poverty Law Center, which represented the Keenans, believes that bankrupting the groups will stifle the message a great deal, even though it may not eliminate them completely. The Aryan Nations was forced to pay a total award of $6.3 million dollars in compensatory and punitive damages to the Keenans.

The Aryan Nations' security system failed. The guards acted irrationally and harmed two innocent individuals. The legal consequences are steep. Aryan Nations most likely will lose its compound to pay for the damage award. Butler is not worried, however. "We have planted seeds," he proclaimed, using language from the Bible. The seeds of hate, it seems, are sprouting.

References

1. "Close That Sad Chapter," *http://more.abcnews.go.com/sections/us/dailynews/aryanverdict000908.html*, September 8, 2000.
2. J. K. Wiley, "Too Drunk To Remember," *http://more.abcnews.go.com/sections/us/daliynews/aryantrial000831.html*, August 31, 2000.

Christian Science Monitor, September 11, 2000, 20.

"Idaho Trial Aims To Shut Down Neo-Nazi Aryan Nations," *http://www.cnn.com/2000/LAW/08/27/crime.aryan.reut*, August 27, 2000.

N. Karlinsky, "Hate on Trial," *http://www.abcnews.go.com*, August 27, 2000.

J. K. Wiley, "Trial of Aryan Nations Begins," *http://more.abcnews.go.com/sections/us/dailynews/aryantrial000829.html*, August 29, 2000.

- the Nuclear Regulatory Commission
- the Securities and Exchange Commission
- the Food and Drug Administration
- the General Accounting Office[6]

Furthermore, these agencies have established standards (on age, experience, education, and character) for the security professionals they elect to employ.[7]

The federal government has also dictated standards for how polygraphs can be used. The Polygraph Protection Act of 1980 placed extensive restrictions on the role of polygraphs in preemployment screening, so it is important to look to state statutes to determine how this federal legislation has been applied.[8] In Minnesota, for example, state law prohibits the use of polygraphs in the hiring process. Another example where state laws differ dramatically is in how much information on past employment can be requested.

While the federal role in the security industry remains primarily isolated to government contracts with private industry, more than 45 states have also passed legislation governing the security industry.[9] Several of the qualification requirements outlined by states cover education and training, age, experience, licenses, and personal character.[10] This emphasizes how important it is for security professionals to be familiar with security-related legislation in the area where they work.

Finally, any local ordinances or company policies that relate to the role of the security professional in that community or within that company must be identified and introduced into the security operations. Actions taken by local law enforcement, for example, and how they are expected to work with the security professionals in private industry will be dictated in large part by city and county ordinances, police department policies and procedures, and corporate policies and procedures. Well-trained security professionals will be aware of how these laws, policies, and procedures are likely to impact their work responsibilities.

Employee Rights Granted through Legal Protections

Actions at the federal level do impact the job security professionals perform. Figure 11–1 highlights several pieces of legislation and the impact of that legislation on protected classes of citizens. Two other important pieces of federal legislation that impact the security professional are the Civil Rights Act of 1964 and the Americans with Disabilities Act.

Civil Rights Act of 1964

The **Civil Rights Act** of 1964 prohibits employment discrimination based on race, color, religion, sex, or national origin. Title VII of the Civil Rights Act prohibits discrimination with regard to any employment condition, including recruiting, screening, hiring, training, compensating, evaluating, promoting, disci-

Legislation	Race/Color	National Origin/ Ancestry	Sex	Religion	Age	Disabled	Union	Covered Employers	Federal Agency
Title VII Civil Rights Act	X	X	X	X				Employers with 15+ EEs; unions, employment agencies	EEOC
Equal Pay Act (EPA) as amended			X					Minimum wage law coverage ("administrative employees" not exempted)	EEOC
†Age Discrimination in Employment Act (ADEA)					X 40+			20+ EEs (union with 25+ members), employment agencies	EEOC
*Age Discrimination Act of 1975 (ADA)					X			Receives federal money	EEOC
*Executive Order 11235.11141	X	X	X	X	X			All federal contractors and subcontractors	OFCCP
*Title VI Civil Rights Act	X	X	X	X				Federally-assisted program or activity—public schools and colleges also covered by Title IX	Funding Agency and EEOC
*Rehabilitation Act of 1973						X		Receives federal money: federal contractor, $2,500+	OFCCP
National Labor Relations Act (NLRA)	X	X	X	X			X	ER in interstate commerce	NLRB
Civil Rights Act of 1866	X							All employers	Courts
Civil Rights Act of 1871	X	X	X					Private employers usually not covered	EEOC
Revenue Sharing Act of 1972	X	X	X	X	X	X		State and local governments that receive federal revenue sharing funds	OFCCP
Education Amendments of 1972 Title IX			X					Educational institutions receiving federal financial assistance	Dept. of Education
Vietnam Era Vets Readjustment Assistance Act—1974						X		Government contractors— $10,000+	OFCCP
Pregnancy Discrimination Act of 1978			X					All employers 15+ EEs	EEOC-OFCCP\
Fair Labor Standards Act *Rehabilitation Act of 1973								Includes minimum wage law and equal pay act with complex method of coverage	DOL
						X		Receives federal money: federal contractor, $2,500+	OFCCP
Americans with Disabilities Act of 1990						X		Covers employers with 15 or more employees	EEOC
Federal Privacy Act of 1974								Federal agencies only	
Freedom of Information Act								Federal agencies only	
Family Educational Rights and Privacy Act								Schools, colleges, and universities, federally assisted	
Immigration Reform and Control Act of 1986								All employers	INS

*Applies to federal agencies, contractors, or assisted programs only.

†Mandatory retirement eliminated except in special circumstances.

EE = Employee; ER = Employer; EEOC = Equal Employment Opportunity Commission
OFCCP = Office Federal Contract Compliance Programs; NLRB = National Labor Relations Board.

FIGURE 11–1 Federal Level Employee Protections

plining, and firing. The Equal Employment Opportunity Committee (EEOC) was established by Congress to implement Title VII. The legislation was updated in 1991 to permit women, persons with disabilities, and persons who are members of religious minorities to have a jury trial and sue if they can prove intentional hiring and workplace discrimination.[11]

Americans with Disability Act

The **Americans with Disability Act** (ADA) requires employers to provide persons with disabilities equal opportunity with regard to jobs and to make reasonable accommodations for disabled employees. Reasonable accommodations, according to the ADA, may include making existing facilities readily accessible to and usable by employees with disabilities, restructuring jobs, or modifying work schedules.[12] The legislation states that businesses are not expected to implement accommodations that impose an "undue hardship" on the businesses. The definition of "undue hardship," however, is unclear and therefore often a matter of litigation. Typically, undue hardships involve accommodations that are simply too costly for the company. Various accommodations may be implemented by the employer with little cost. The Job Accommodation Network (JAN) was established by the President's Commission on Employment of People with Disabilities in 1984. JAN provides information and consulting services for anyone who has questions about resources available to meet the needs of a disabled employee. JAN is located in Morgantown, West Virginia, and can be contacted at 1-800-ADA-WORK.

Primer in Basic Crime Classifications

To understand the criminal justice system, security professionals need to be familiar with several important concepts and legal principles. A **felony** is a serious crime—such as murder, rape, or burglary—that is punishable in most states by death or by incarceration for a period of longer than one year. A **misdemeanor** is a less serious crime; misdemeanors include petty offenses such as shoplifting, disturbing the peace, and violations of local ordinances and are usually punishable by fines or short jail terms.

Crimes are typically separated into two types: *mala en se* and *mala prohibita*. *Mala en se* crimes are acts that are considered by society to be inherently wrong. This includes crimes that are considered wrong even if there is no law prohibiting the activity. *Mala prohibita* crimes are acts that are made illegal by criminal statute but are not necessarily defined by society as inherently wrong. Clearly, these distinctions are problematic, as society's perspective changes. In a sense, all "legally defined or common law" offenses could be more accurately determined to be culturally specific. Many conditions must be met before someone who commits a violation of law will be tried in a court of law. Remember, though, a victim of a crime seeks redress in a civil proceeding. Criminal proceedings are brought by the state, which in fact makes the state the injured party.

LEGAL AUTHORITY OF THE SECURITY PROFESSIONAL

In most states, the security professional has no more legal rights than a private citizen. Common law provides authority to the private citizen for making an arrest in order to protect the safety of the public.[13] The private citizen is said to have a heavier burden than public officials of demonstrating actual knowledge, events, or other firsthand experience of the crime that led to the arrest.[14] Specific requirements regarding citizen's arrests may be dictated by state law. Furthermore, laws include restrictions on a citizen's right to arrest, which include (1) the time of the arrest, and (2) the arresting person's presence during commission of the crime.[15]

If security professionals are also accredited law enforcement officers or if security professionals work in states where they are required to be commissioned as peace officers, the rules will be different. In short, given the need for attention to state-specific protocol in the event of citizen's arrests, the actions of the security professional who is performing duties associated with his or her job will be established by the employer or client. *It is crucial for the benefit of the contracting agency and the security professional that the exact parameters of responsibility be documented in a policy and procedure manual so that the security professionals clearly understand the process they are to follow.* Should any concerns arise, the professionals can reference the policy and procedure manual to ensure company policy is being followed, or they can contact legal counsel. Following this basic rule may assist the company and the security professional in the event there are legal liability questions later.

BASIC CONCEPTS OF CRIMINAL PROCEDURE AND THEIR APPLICATION TO PRIVATE SECURITY

Various aspects of the law enforcement profession have been incorrectly associated with the security profession. A law enforcement officer has been granted specific authority by the state that a security professional simply does not have. Security professionals and commissioned law enforcement officers are not required to implement the same standards for various procedures. The most confusion exists around the following topic areas: (1) stop and frisk; (2) arrest, detention, and false imprisonment; (3) search and seizure/probable cause; (4) reasonable expectation of privacy; and (5) use of force. Consideration is given to each topic.

Stop and Frisk

Terry v. Ohio permits a police officer who believes criminal activity may be happening to conduct a pat down of a suspect. The objective is to allow the officer to find weapons, thus ensuring the safety of the officer and people nearby. Under certain circumstances, courts have upheld the right of security professionals to conduct a *Terry* stop and frisk, particularly when the search is conducted to protect persons and property. The courts have upheld that security guards, like any other citizens, are allowed to protect themselves and property, using a reasonable amount of force to do so. "Reasonable suspicion," not "probable cause," was said to be the relevant standard.

Arrest, Detention, and False Imprisonment

Security professionals do not often simply do a stop and frisk. But if a person is being detained, the concept of stop and frisk may be applicable. Most statutes agree that the merchant, employee, agent, private police, and peace officer are authorized to detain a suspect, but statutes typically do not mention that other citizens at large have such authority.[16] In some states, the **merchant's privilege statute** gives immunity, absent serious error or intentional tortious conduct, to merchants who detain a person suspected of shoplifting.[17] Consequently, security professionals are typically authorized to detain individuals to determine whether theft has occurred, but this authorization is predicated on the security professionals' intention to involve the police within a reasonable time after the detainment.

In what has been described as an unusual decision, the California Supreme Court ruled (in *People v. Zelinski*, 594 p.2d 1000 [1979]) that the constitutional prohibition against unreasonable search and seizure applied to private security personnel.[18] Critics argue that the application of the law enforcement standard to security professionals is inevitable as the scope of security increases.[19] Such decisions suggest that while precautions can be taken, ultimately controversial questions will result in legal involvement. An example of this is when a company makes decisions about the conditions for a search to protect proprietary information, for example, but does not have a response for the possibility that they might find other kinds of items (such as drugs). Particularly in the absence of a stated policy on drugs, if the outcome of the search (finding drugs) extends beyond the justification for the search (the need to protect company information), the rights of the employee and the responsibilities of the company can easily become entangled in ways that require legal resolution.

Law enforcement officers have the authority to arrest. Security personnel, depending on their function, may have the authority to detain. A person who is legally detained may be interrogated, depending on the circumstances.[20] This is, of course, the purpose of detaining someone, and the courts have supported this idea. The acceptability of the interrogation is based on the legality of the detention and the manner in which the interrogation is conducted.[21]

Search and Seizure/Probable Cause

With reasonable cause, law enforcement officers may stop individuals and require them to show identification and even search them without a search warrant. Without a search warrant, law enforcement officers may decide to make a reasonable search of a person, a vehicle, or some property, or all three, as a process leading up to arrest. If law enforcement officers have a search warrant, they may make a more detailed search of vehicles or property, as indicated in the warrant. **Probable cause** is the required legal standard that suggests that before an arrest, search, or seizure, a person must know of facts and circumstances that would cause a reasonable person to believe a crime had been committed.

A law enforcement officer making a lawful arrest has the authority to search the area within the immediate control of the suspect or to seize anything in plain view. As noted earlier, the stop and frisk guideline allows a law enforcement officer to pat down a person for weapons if the officer reasonably suspects that there has been criminal activity—for the officer's protection and for the protection of others in the area.[22] Furthermore, if something is taken from the person when the officer does not have a warrant, the evidence collected may be excluded from future court proceedings, as dictated by the **exclusionary rule** as a violation of the Fourth, Fifth, Sixth, and Fourteenth Amendments to the Constitution.[23] An exception to this might be in cases of **inevitable discovery,** which suggest that the information or evidence would inevitably have been discovered from lawful investigatory activities without regard to the violation.*

In most cases, security professionals do not possess legal authority to perform search and seizure. Security professionals should have consent of the individual involved before they are allowed to search the person or his or her property. But there are several methods that give security professionals the consent necessary to conduct searches; for example, at the time of hire, the conditions for a search are outlined or there are signs posted suggesting that packages, containers, and other similar objects may be searched upon entering or leaving the premises, or both. If there are employees who are also sworn officers or who are deputized or licensed, the Fourth Amendment standards for probable cause are likely to apply to them as well. Again, it is essential that security professionals develop a thorough knowledge of the state and local laws

---

*J. H. Israel and W. R. LaFave, "Criminal Procedure," *Constitutional Limitations in a Nutshell* series. (St. Paul, MN: West Publishing Company, 1998), p. 284.

dictating appropriate security responses. The laws will vary depending on industry, industry standards, and federal and state regulations. Specifically, if a security professional is also a licensed peace officer or police officer, the legal standards governing behavior while working in a particular setting need to be made clear.

Reasonable Expectation of Privacy

With the emergence of electronic activities, such as sending e-mail, offices are forced to reexamine employee privacy issues. Furthermore, because some aspects of the security profession can be covert by nature, such as an internal investigation to identify employee theft, there may be claims of violation of privacy. The issue of privacy also pertains to the hiring process. During the hiring process, certain information relating to the applicant may be protected. Personnel screening, background investigations, and other means by which agencies acquire personal information about current or future employees all relate to privacy. At the current time, it is not unusual for companies to require drug screening of all prospective employees. Drug screening, drug testing, and related monitoring programs have been challenged on privacy grounds, and at the present time the ability to use such tests has been upheld.[24]

Use of Force

Use of force refers to the actions private individuals must take to protect their person or their property. For security professionals, the use of force and the degree of force used must be justified in each particular instance. The multiple levels of force are outlined in Figure 11–2. For security practitioners, the use of force must be "reasonable." Consideration may be given to the severity of the situation, the danger present, and the kind and degree of threatened misconduct. Is the threat real, pressing, and imminent, and is it accompanied by the ability to carry it out?[25]

In short, the use of force and the amount of force used must be justified in relation to the person or property being protected. Note, finally, that various state statutes determine what are appropriate levels of force in different situations.

TORT LAW

Tort law deals with "private or civil wrongs (therefore a.k.a. civil law), other than contracts, and affects or controls relationships between people in any given situation."[26] **Negligence** and **intentional torts** are two areas of tort law that are of great concern to the private security professional.[27] Security officers have certain "duties" identified by law. A breach of these duties, either negli-

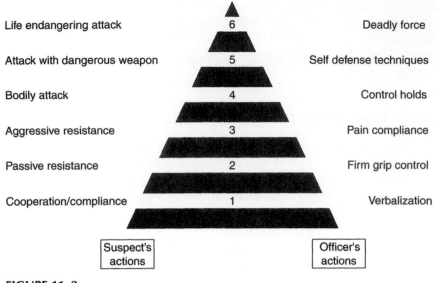

Life endangering attack	6	Deadly force
Attack with dangerous weapon	5	Self defense techniques
Bodily attack	4	Control holds
Aggressive resistance	3	Pain compliance
Passive resistance	2	Firm grip control
Cooperation/compliance	1	Verbalization

Suspect's actions | | Officer's actions

FIGURE 11–2

gently or intentionally, may result in legal action that concludes with a liability to the company.

Negligence is the failure to exercise a reasonable or ordinary amount of care in a situation that causes harm to someone or something. To prove a case of negligence, the claimant must demonstrate the following: (1) a duty, (2) a breach of duty, and (3) proximate causation.[28] **Foreseeability,** the ability to see or know of potential problems in advance, is a related concept. The concept of negligence could easily apply to liability of companies that do not adequately investigate, train, and oversee their security personnel.[29]

Intentional torts are acts committed by a person who made a decision to act. Intentional torts include (1) assault, (2) battery, (3) false arrest, (4) false imprisonment, (5) defamation of character, (6) malicious prosecution, (7) invasion of privacy, and (8) outrageous conduct.[30] Even though a tort is a civil wrong, a wrong between two private parties, it may also be a crime. One can be sued civilly for assault, for example, and also be prosecuted criminally for the same thing. Punishment for criminal prosecutions include fines, imprisonment, or death.

Defendants in cases of **strict liability** are held accountable regardless of their intentions. Elements of a strict liability case include the following: (1) There is a seller of a product or service, (2) the product is unreasonably dangerous to persons or property, (3) a user or a consumer suffers physical harm, and (4) there is causation.[31] For the security industry, this means (at a minimum) that a security company may be held liable for actions of employees if the acts were committed while the employees were on the job.

MISCELLANEOUS LEGAL ISSUES

Legal experts who have a clear understanding of the law as it applies to secu rity professionals are an exceptionally important resource for anyone in the se curity industry. The expanding role of security professionals and the potential exposures security companies have when dealing with hazardous conditions or dangerous people combine to put security personnel in situations where the legal waters have been untested. Two such situations are nondelegable duty and color of law.

Nondelegable Duty

Security professionals are responsible for reducing or eliminating the risk of certain threats in specific target environments. Security professionals find themselves on the front line when it comes to the possibility of litigation. The courts have repeatedly ruled that companies cannot reduce the amount of liability they incur by contracting with a private security agency. This principle is called **nondelegable duty.** Therefore, if security professionals are provided by a contractor, the company hiring the contractor, not the contractor, may still be liable for any harm a person receives while on the premises.

Of great concern to the security manager is the notion that the private company may have **vicarious liability** for the acts of its employees. Vicarious liability, present under the theory of *respondent superior,* is the indirect legal responsibility a supervisor has for the employees under his or her direction.[32]

Color of Law

Because of the interactive role of state or governmental agents and security professionals, combined with the possibility for assuming liability, "security managers should be knowledgeable about whether their employees are acting under the **color of law** by ordinance or statute, through joint action or significant involvement with governmental agents, as a public function, or because a nexus exists between the state and the challenged activity."[33] Color of law refers to the semblance, without substance, of a legal right: "Proof or demonstration that state action caused a personal loss, affront, or indignity under the auspices or *color* of state law."[34]

In other words, the circumstances are such that one might easily misinterpret the authority or power of the actor as being an agent of the state. A classic example might be the following: A county board decided to reject a licensing application from an African American man not on legal grounds but because of the applicant's race. The people on this board, employed by the state, were acting on behalf of the county and did not comply with the law. As a result of their action someone was harmed: Someone did not get a license for a business because of race, and the board provided some indefensible excuse. In this example, the county board acted under the color of law. This kind of case involves a related incident for security professionals when a state agency contracts for security professionals or when a private agency has chosen to employ an off-duty police officer. "For private security professionals, the 'color of state law' issues are applicable when a direct relationship between a public official and a private security agent has been established. The evidence must demonstrate the security professional is representing him or herself as a public professional, and as a result, directly cause injury."[35]

CONCLUSION

The importance of security professionals educating themselves about the legal liability issues likely to impact their operation cannot be stressed enough. Universities offer semester-long courses on criminal law and criminal procedure. The information presented here is intended only to highlight several areas of the law that affect security professionals. Poor training or negligent hiring can result in a lawsuit that can be financially devastating to a company. An everyday encounter with a customer or employee may lead to actions that are contested in a court of law. Is the company protected? Are the company's policies about conducting surveillance on a suspected shoplifter clear? What are the steps to follow if an employee is suspected of stealing? Should the approach to firing an employee change if the person is a member of a protected class? These and other important matters affect security plans, so security professionals will want to consult legal counsel and refer to some of the books in the references list.

REVIEW QUESTIONS
1. Which aspect of the law (criminal or civil) has the most direct connection with the security profession? Why? Be prepared to justify your response.
2. Outline two primary areas of federal law that dictate protocol for hiring practices in your workplace.
3. Outline the arrest powers of a security professional.
4. Discuss nondelegable duty. What duties can management delegate and what duties cannot be delegated?
5. Outline the issues involved in assessing the color of law. How does this most directly impact a security professional?

Discussion Questions

1. Discuss the role of liability in preparation of security responses in a given environment.
2. Discuss the important distinctions between arrest and detention of a customer suspected of shoplifting.
3. Discussions about the use of force also involve discussions of defense tactics. Discuss the most appropriate level of force for security professionals within a target environment. Be prepared to justify your response.
4. Based on information presented in the chapter, what does a security professional need to be concerned about when maintaining a reasonable expectation of privacy? How does this standard differ depending on the target environment?

References

1. D. Ray, "Legal Aspects of Security," in *Protection Officer Training Manual,* 6th edition, 208–210. ed. International Foundation for Protection Officers (Woburn, MA: Butterworth-Heinemann, 1998).
2. *Barron's Legal Dictionary.*
3. P. P. Purpurra. *Security and Loss Prevention: An Introduction,* 3rd ed. (Woburn, MA: Butterworth-Heinemann, 1998).
4. D. Ray, "Legal Aspects of Security," 208–210.
5. Ibid.
6. C. P. Nemeth, *Private Security and the Law,* 2nd ed. (Cincinnati, OH: Anderson Publishing Company, 1995).
7. Ibid.
8. *Congressional Record 131,* no. 148 (1988): S.1815.
9. Recent article reviewed for *Journal of Security Administration.*
10. Nemeth, *Private Security and the Law.*
11. P. P. Purpurra, *Security and Loss Prevention.*
12. J. E. Runyon. "Making the ADA Accessible," in *Mastering Security: Using Technology* (Dubuque, IA: ASIS Kendall/Hunt Publishing Company, 1998), 66.
13. Nemeth.
14. Ibid.
15. Ibid.
16. R. Fischer and G. Green, *Introduction to Security,* 6th ed. (Woburn, MA: Butterworth-Heinemann, 1998), 138.
17. Nemeth.
18. Ibid.

19. S. Euller, "Private Security in the Courtroom: The Exclusionary Rule Applies," *Security Management 24* (1980): 41.
20. L. Fennelly, *Handbook of Loss Prevention and Crime Prevention* (Stoneham, MA: Butterworth, 1982), 662.
21. Fennelly, *Handbook of Loss Prevention,* 662.
22. Nemeth.
23. Ibid.
24. Ibid.
25. Maxwell, 347.
26. Ibid., xxii.
27. Ibid.
28. Nemeth, *Private Security and the Law.*
29. For more information about the CPP program and materials, go online at *http://www.asisonline.org/cpp.html.*
30. Maxwell, xxiii.
31. Nemeth.
32. Maxwell.
33. Maxwell, 377.
34. Nemeth.
35. Ibid.

12

Preparing an Emergency Plan and a Disaster Response

CHAPTER HIGHLIGHTS

- Introduction to basic emergency preparation and planning
- Identifying distinctions between "safety" and "security"

- Consideration includes bomb, fire, hazardous material incident, severe weather, terrorism, workplace violence, and media relations

KEY WORDS

Disaster management
Flood warning

Flood watch

All security professionals consider prevention their primary objective. Yet security professionals also know no environment can ever be 100 percent free of threats. Safety and security response considerations often fall to security practitioners. A well-researched, well-respected safety and security response plan is one of the most effective means for protecting a target environment against accidents, emergencies, and any other threats with the potential to produce a disastrous outcome. A clear set of well-prepared guidelines for responding to likely problems will afford security professionals the opportunity to identify areas of concern before the issues get too big to handle.

As is the case with all security-related activities, emergency response planning must be done with attention to the needs of the target environment. A security-related response will depend on conditions in the setting to be protected. The type of emergency or disaster most likely to pose the greatest threat to a setting will depend on issues unique to the environment. In a simple example, if the work done within a target environment involves the use of hazardous chemicals, it will be important to have a plan to address the security department's response to an accident involving these chemicals, whether that be an explosion, a fire, or a hazardous spill.

This chapter introduces security professionals to basic emergency issues. As security professionals become more familiar with their target setting, and as they develop some confidence about their ability to assess the needs of that environment, they will also get a better sense of the accidents, emergencies, or disasters they should be prepared to address. While some aspects of emergency planning and disaster response are difficult to discuss in a general sense because environmental conditions are so different, it makes sense to think about threats that would have disastrous effects in just about any setting. Some common examples would include, but not be limited to, severe weather, fire, computer tampering and/or network shutdown, workplace safety issues, and workplace violence. **Disaster management** has become an entire discipline with national prominence, gaining significant attention among both academics and practitioners, and there is a growing body of research focused on disaster prevention and disaster response. This chapter is only an introduction to this vast topic.

Not surprisingly, emergency responses will be based in large part on the type of incident and the conditions immediately surrounding the incident. This chapter focuses on the importance of establishing emergency response plans as an essential part of the overall security objective outlined within the policy and procedure manual. The topics presented for consideration here are those emergencies common in multiple settings, structured with the relatively simple objective of helping readers begin to think about critical incidents, emergencies, and other disasters that might impact the environment they are hired to protect. Readers will then need to educate themselves about responding to the ac-

(*Source:* Bob Englehart, *The Hartford Courant.*)

cidents, emergencies, and disasters that might threaten their own target environment in particular.

Defining Safety and Security Issues

In the introduction to this book, I presented Mary Lynn Garcia's excellent distinction between safety issues and security issues. Garcia notes that safety and security issues are sometimes discussed as if they are the same thing. She cautions people to be aware of the critical distinction between the two: "safety" refers to "abnormal environments," while "security" refers to "malevolent human attacks."[1] Issues such as electrical outages, hurricanes, fires, chemical spills, and other kinds of accidents are safety issues, whereas workplace or school violence is a security issue. Both safety and security issues require response planning. As has been stated throughout this book, security responses should be integrated, and disaster response plans are no exception. The integrated emergency plan or disaster response should be structured and implemented to include everyone in the target environment. In addition to being well educated about a disaster response, people within a target environment need to understand what plan is in place and how they are expected to be involved—whether it be evacuating because of a fire alarm or determining who to contact in the unlikely event they find a suspicious package.

The Biggest Disaster Is Not Being Prepared

When outlining the emergency response to a disaster, security professionals must make sure all people in the environment know what their role will be if there is an emergency. When people working within a target environment every day are not involved in the response, problems can happen. Problems can be made worse when people are not aware of safety and security concerns, and people tend to make inappropriate decisions during a time of crisis.[2] Consider the following incident, in which an employee called the police after finding what appeared to be a pipe bomb in a gym bag in his office.[3] Most interesting from a safety and security standpoint is the fact that the bag was found outside the office building at the back door on a Sunday, but no one thought much about it. When rain was expected Monday and still no one had claimed the bag, someone brought it inside the office building. On Friday, after no one had returned for the bag, an employee opened the bag, hoping something inside would help him find out who was the owner of the bag. In short, he found what looked like a pipe bomb. Instead of evacuating the building, he carried the bag a block to City Hall, looking for a sheriff. When he did not find a sheriff, he carried the bag back to the office building. He said, "It probably wasn't the smartest thing to do, but I couldn't just leave it in City Hall either."[4] When he got back inside the office building, he called the police. The police dispatcher told him not to touch the bag and to evacuate the building. The bomb squad safely detonated the bomb in a parking lot across the street. The bomb squad supervisor said the bomb packed the punch of 1.5 to 2 sticks of dynamite. Employees suggested that there was much more controversy after the event than during it, once people started to think about how the event might have ended differently.[5] In spite of the uncertainty, the people involved in the events avoided a disastrous outcome. No one is immune from the effects of unforeseen events. For this reason, a plan should be completed well in advance of an emergency event, accessible to those who might need to reference it during the response to the crisis, and (where possible) rehearsed or practiced to determine its effectiveness.

A basic list of emergency equipment and supplies is included in Exhibit 12–1. While it is important to have a well-stocked cabinet of emergency supplies, these supplies will be more effective if used in conjunction with a well-considered emergency response plan. Here are some essential elements of an emergency response plan:

- *Facility warning system:* There should be a means for notifying employees in the setting of an impending emergency.
- *Communication protocol:* There should be a method for relaying information within the target environment and between the target environment and external emergency response crews.

Exhibit 12–1 Emergency Supplies for Offices and Departments

___ battery (specify types)	___ pliers, channel lock
___ blanket	___ putty knife, 1″
___ camera/film (specify type)	___ pry bar
___ candle and matches	___ radio, AM-FM
___ first aid handbook	___ rope (100-ft coil)
___ first aid kit	___ screwdriver (blade)
___ flashlight	___ screwdriver (Phillips)
___ food (2-day supply)	___ shovel
___ hammer	___ tape, duct (150 ft)
___ hand axe	___ tape, electrical (100 ft)
___ garbage bag (33 gal/50 ct)	___ tape, strapping (150 ft)
___ garbage bag (10 gal/100 ct)	___ tape, yellow caution
___ gloves, latex (100 ct)	___ vise grips
___ knife, Swiss army type	___ water (2-day supply)
___ pipe wrench	___ wire cutters

Source: American Business Resources, *Disaster Management Planning Manual* (Lakewood, CO: 1995).

- *Protocol to determine level of facility operations:* The plan should include delineation of responsibilities for shutting down equipment and operations, as is warranted, and a process for determining how those decisions will be made and who will make them.
- *Means to deploy facility security:* The plan should include a guideline for determining if security personnel are needed, where they are needed, and how to coordinate their activities.
- *Method for facility evacuation:* The plan should include a means for determining when it is appropriate to leave the building or the premises. Preferably this will be a well-practiced departure plan for getting everyone out of the affected area. Furthermore, it should have a means by which to verify all people have been evacuated.
- *Means for protecting company/agency property:* This will include personnel and essential documents. It makes sense to include in an emergency response the means by which certain aspects of the business operation will be addressed.
- *Method for contacting appropriate authorities:* Within the emergency response plan, a listing of specific persons and agencies that must be contacted should be clearly outlined (with full information) and someone (or several people, each responsible for a different area) should be designated to be responsible for making those calls.
- *Process for interacting with the media:* Media management is essential, and someone should be appointed who can accurately reflect the

Watch Out for Doomsday

It is frightening to sit back and think about how the world could come to an end. There are numerous theological predictions, fantasies of alien takeover, threats of global warfare, and so on. Technology has given people the ability to create weapons of mass destruction that could wipe out entire cities, countries—possibly all of humanity. Though total elimination from the planet does not appear likely anytime soon, some individuals are creating terror in many regions of the world. Situations like the Columbine High School shootings and the Oklahoma City bombing were horrifying but not the first of their kind. In 1995, however, something awful happened for the first time.

Thousands of people use the subway every day in large urban areas like New York City and Tokyo. The subway is meant to offer a safe, convenient method of travel for commuters who want to avoid hectic traffic. People's safety has often been violated on the subway, but never in a way so severe and terrifying as what took place during the morning rush hour on March 20, 1995, in Tokyo. As people filed into the subway trains thinking they were on their way to another typical day of work, they were struck by the overpowering force of the deadly nerve gas sarin, which was developed for use by the Nazis in World War II. The attack was launched by the Japanese doomsday cult Aum Shinri Kyo, or Supreme Truth. It killed 12 people and injured more than 5000 others. Labeled the worst act of terror in modern-day Japan, it was also the world's first mass chemical terrorist attack.[1]

The Aum Shinri Kyo cult was forced to disband, its commune at the foot of Mt. Fuji was seized, and more than 400 of the cult's 10,000 members in Japan were arrested. Yet sources claim that in 1998, the cult was attracting new members. One man noted, "Youth crime is on the rise and the economy is in bad shape. Our society is becoming very unstable. I think that's what's behind this resurgence."[2] There is some truth to what this man claimed. Difficult times tend to bring out the worst in people, but this is no excuse for what took place in that subway. There has to be a tighter lock on security controls in public venues where there are so many people.

Many people have already forgotten this messy ordeal. But those who experienced the attack firsthand find it impossible to forget. A survey of 285 victims conducted by St. Luke's International Hospital in Japan revealed that about half say they continue to suffer from fatigue.[3] "Thirty percent complained of chronic headaches, and more than 20 percent said they at times have dizziness, irregular breathing, nausea or loss of appetite."[4] A total of $2.6 million was spent by the labor Ministry on medical expenses for the victims. Families of the 18 people who died or were seriously injured received about $23,535 each in compensation, an amount that seems small when weighed against the loss of a loved one.[5]

Is the Japanese government at fault in any way for not providing enough security to protect passengers on the city's subway system? It is difficult to point a finger at the government, because this was the first attack of its kind in the world. Any city would have been surprised by such an attack. The hope is that, in some way, the world as a whole will be able to use this situation as a learning experience, developing improved methods for securing public and private spaces.

References

1. "Top World Stories in Review," *http://www.cnn.com/EVENTS/year_in_review/world/index2.html*, December 29, 1995.
2. "Japan Marks Subway Attack Anniversary, Worries about Cult," March 20, 1998.
3. "Japan Marks Subway Attack Anniversary."
4. "For Victims of Subway Nerve Gas Attack, the Nightmare Goes On," *http://www.infowar.com/WMD/wmd_040398a_j.html-ssi*, March 18, 1998.
5. "For Victims of Subway Nerve Gas Attack."

circumstances while also releasing factual information that has been confirmed, rather than speculating about possibilities.

The response plan should identify who should coordinate the response and then set up a system to educate people within the environment about their role in the security response. As noted in the preceding list, there must be a process for notifying employees of the incident. Serious consideration must be given to the mechanisms in place to protect people and property in various emergency response situations. Smooth evacuation of people is of primary importance. Remember the discussion of the chicken plant fire in Chapter 8. If the evacuation plan is not viable, lives could be lost.

After making certain everyone is out of danger, security professionals facing an emergency should turn to protecting property and important documents and other information. As appropriate, the proper authorities should be notified. A final issue involves the media. In emergency situations, and for purposes of preventing further problems, it is important to have a person appointed to deal with any media who might arrive on the scene. This issue, the media response, will be discussed in more detail later in the chapter. Exhibit 12–2 contains a list of basic safety and security events. Particular settings may face other threats.

Bomb Threat/Explosion

If a bomb threat is received, the information collected during the threat can be critical for developing an appropriate police response. Exhibit 12–3 contains a bomb threat form to guide the person who receives the bomb threat over the phone.

It may be the case that a bomb is discovered on site. Whether a bomb threat is phoned in or a bomb is found, a good response process should be set in motion. Ideally, the target environment will have a procedure in place for responding to bomb threats. After looking at the conditions within the target setting, security professionals should meet with local law enforcement officers to develop response procedures. It is important to identify people who will assume a leadership role and should be contacted immediately in the event of a bomb threat. After establishing a communication structure for notifying everyone who will play a central role in the response (including the person who will work with the media and address any questions), security professionals should think about the evacuation plan. How will people be removed from the target environment in an expeditious yet safe manner? If the bomb is found on site, it will be important to have a plan for how or whether the area should be secured.

An important part of the response plan is a training and education program to inform all the people in the target environment of the response plan. A form like the bomb threat response form in Exhibit 12–3 should be placed by all

Exhibit 12–2   Basic Safety and Security Events Requiring Consideration

Bomb threat/explosion
Fire
Hazardous materials incident
Severe weather: Floods and other natural disasters
Terrorist activities
Workplace violence

phones. It may make sense for the business to equip the phones with caller ID. With good training and education, anyone who might receive a threatening call will be prepared to respond appropriately.

Fire

Based on past trends, it is believed that businesses this year will lose more than $1.5 billion in property damage due to fire.[6] The Occupational Safety and Health Administration outlines what has become the general industry standard for emergency planning and fire prevention in 40 CFR 1910.38. All businesses must have an emergency action plan, but only businesses with more than 10 employees must have the plan written down.[7] It will be important to have a clear understanding of the fire codes and regulations in the business's industry. Equipment should be checked and maintained regularly to reduce the risk of fire. Attention must be given to important equipment and documents that should be filed or stored in a fire-resistant container.

A fire can be devastating, but the losses can be minimized by involving personnel in the response planning process and making use of local emergency response agencies. These agencies can not only provide good information but can be informed about where to find emergency information that might be of use to them in responding to the emergency.

A good training program for evacuation will be a key element of a successful emergency response. Security professionals should make an evacuation plan, and employees should practice it. Security professionals should show employees how to use fire extinguishers and remind them about critical issues, such as staying low to the floor. Employees should be educated about prevention, but they should also learn about classes of fire and appropriate responses to fire. (Fires are assigned to Classes A through D. Different types of extinguishers are required for different classes of fires.) Furthermore, employees should be well advised about reporting procedures. Target environments should have fire protection responses, which might include smoke detectors (which need to be checked regularly), sprinkler systems, and fire-resistant walls and doors. Insurance can be an option for replacing losses or rebuilding

Exhibit 12–3   Telephone Bomb Threat Check List

Date _____

_____ Time call begins.

_____ Any discernible identifying information?

Gender?	Male Female Unknown
Language?	English Spanish Other?
Age?	< 18 18–24 25–30 31–45 > 45 Unknown
The caller's voice is:	Slow Rapid Disguised
	Soft Loud Slurred
The caller is	Laughing Crying
	Calm Excited Angry

Essential questions   Additional notes:

_____ When is the bomb going to explode? _____

_____ Where is the bomb located? _____

_____ What does the bomb look like? _____

_____ What type of bomb is it? _____

_____ What causes the bomb to explode? _____

_____ Did you place the bomb here? _____

_____ If yes, why? _____

Other things to note if possible: Additional notes:

_____ Any background noises? _____

_____ Did the caller seem to know the area? _____

_____ Time call ends.

areas damaged by fire. It is not uncommon for insurance providers to offer advice about fire prevention and protection programs.

As with all safety and security emergency response plans, fire prevention and fire prevention plans should take into account industry standards, corporate policies, and other specific information. This section simply touches the tip of some of the critical issues to consider. Additional research will be necessary to make sure that a target environment's needs are being met.

Hazardous Materials Incident

It is important for security professionals in environments where hazardous materials are used to know about all hazardous materials, their amounts, and the areas of the environment where they are used or stored. This area of protection and prevention is particularly confusing because standards for certain chemicals change sometimes. It is important, therefore, to keep up with the changes. Furthermore, some chemicals are highly explosive or flammable, or both. External emergency response crews must know when fires involve hazardous materials. If the responding crews are unaware of these chemicals, they will not be able to fight the fire effectively and may put themselves in great danger.

Severe Weather: Floods and Other Natural Disasters

Natural disasters can produce a variety of negative consequences. Table 12–1 outlines the potential effects of natural disasters on workplaces. Many communities across the country will be impacted by flooding. Floods can develop slowly over days, giving people an opportunity to prepare, but a flash flood can erupt violently without warning. Security professionals must educate themselves about the local flood plains and the history of flooding in the target area. Warning and evacuation procedures will be important, as will listening to weather information and paying attention to flood watches and flood warnings. A **flood watch** is a circumstance where flooding is possible. A **flood warning** means the situation warrants taking precautions and moving to higher ground. Insurance companies provide flood insurance, which might be an excellent way to reduce the level of loss in a target environment if a flood does happen. Also, flood-proofing measures may be appropriate. Flood-proofing measures include establishing flood walls, putting in sandbags, or installing pumps.

Serious windstorms, whether on the coast in the form of hurricanes or inland in the form of streamlined winds or tornados, can be devastating. Both tornados and hurricanes typically come, especially with today's sophisticated weather tracking technologies, with some time for evacuation and planning. With hurricanes, storm surge can also be a problem, resulting in flood conditions. In all of these windstorms, wind pressure and flying objects cause damage.

Table 12–1   Impact of Natural Disasters on the Workplace

Natural Disaster	Potential Impact on the Workplace
Windstorm (hurricane, tornado)	Damage to structures and equipment; injury due to airborne projectiles, and related storm surge
Earthquake	Damage to structures and equipment; personal injury a hazard as floors and buildings crumble and debris and equipment fall; fire or explosions
Flood (flash flood, storm surge)	Disruption and danger to electrical wiring and gas lines if exposed to flood water; fires
Lightning	Tree falling on facility; fire; damage to equipment; electrocution of individuals
Winter storm	Travel hazards; power outages; roof collapse; frostbite, hypothermia, and death
Heat wave	Heat exhaustion, dehydration, and death

Source: Adapted from S. Wortham, "Expect the Unexpected: How To Protect Your Workers in a Natural Disaster," *Safety and Health* 156, no. 3 (1997): 48–53.

Winter storms can cause particular difficulty. Ice and snow can result in downed power lines, which may have significant impact on computer network systems. Furthermore, work settings may need to be prepared for the fact that some workers will not be able to travel to and from work safely in a serious winter storm.

In some areas of the country, security professionals must prepare for the possibility of earthquakes. Architectural changes and reinforcements have assisted in enhancing safety during earthquakes. Earthquakes cannot be predicted, which makes them more difficult to deal with than some other emergencies. Earthquakes may result in personal injury, and dislodged gas lines and other disruptions that result from an earthquake might lead to a compounded event, including explosions, fires, and hazardous waste spills.

Terrorist Activities

Terrorist activities include both domestic and international events. Terrorism involves threatening acts used to create fear for coercive purposes.[8] Typically motivated by political or economic reasons, terrorists are often affiliated with groups. Instances such as the World Trade Center bombing, the bombing of the Federal Building in Oklahoma City, and threats to research facilities by animal rights activists are all examples of terrorist activities. Threats against corporate executives are also increasingly faced by international firms.

Workplace Violence

Workplace violence is defined as "that which arises out of disputes or adverse personal relationships between employers and employees in and around the place of work."[9] Workplace violence can also involve domestic disputes in which a woman fears attack from a violent spouse who comes to find her at work. Workplace violence includes actions taken by disgruntled or disturbed employees and random violence. In short, workplace violence can be perpetrated by a stranger, a client, or an employee. In conclusion, although workplace violence and other emergency events may never affect a particular target environment, it is important to make plans in case they do. The degree of risk, including probability and criticality (discussed in Chapter 2), is an important consideration for determining how best to respond. Furthermore, vulnerability assessments (see Chapter 2) should take emergency events into account. Consideration of the type of emergency, the human impact, the impact on property, and the impact on the business will be important. It will also be important to assess the ability of the people in the setting to respond to each potential emergency. Careful consideration of conditions within the target environment will, as always, be critical.

Sixteen Strikes . . . You're Out!

The last 20 to 30 years have seen technological growth like no other period. Many people want everything to be faster, more powerful, smarter, more economical, easier to use, and so on. Some might wonder how anyone could be disappointed with the advancements. However, as with everything else in the world, the new technology has its enemies. Many people choose to live without modern advances; others choose to work at reversing the spread of technology. Some members of the latter group go to extreme measures to make their point.

Imagine striking terror in the minds of an entire country. Imaging doing it for 17 years. This is what Theodore Kaczynski did. Known as the "Unabomber," he went back and forth across the nation, planting bombs in various places. Most of his targets were individuals who were involved in areas of technology, such as engineering, airlines, and computers. Many of them did not know the danger they faced, as the bombs were often disguised as mail packages. Kaczynski was very straightforward about his distaste for technology. He wrote a 35,000-word antitechnology manifesto that was published by two newspapers. Bombs turned up all over the United States, but there was no apparent pattern of attacks, making it extremely difficult to track down the culprit. It would take 17 years, and 16 bomb strikes, before the Unabomber was found. Kaczynski's brother led authorities to a Montana cabin where Kaczynski had been hiding, ending the hunt that had lasted for so long.

In court, Kaczynski did not want to be labeled a "sickie," as he called it. He chose to admit that he was guilty, fully aware of the penalty that this admission might bring: death. He had kept a journal, proving that he proudly followed the fear and destruction that he brought to the streets of America. He wrote of his feelings about what he did, barely showing any remorse. He said of one victim, an aspiring astronaut, whose arm was mangled by a bomb, "Imagine, a grown man wanting to be an astronaut. I no longer regret what I did. His aspiration was so ignoble." Kaczynski sat expressionless as his journal was read aloud and as each bombing was detailed by prosecutors. He denied nothing, other than the idea that he might be a madman, even though a psychiatrist reported he suffered from paranoid schizophrenia. He was sentenced to life in prison without parole, but he took a plea bargain to save himself from the penalty. David Kaczynski, the brother who led authorities to the hideout, called the outcome "an appropriate, just, and civilized resolution to this tragedy."

Theodore Kaczynski knew what he was doing, and he was proud of it. He saw himself as some sort of soldier in the war against technological advancement. Was he sane? Well, probably not. It is frightening to think that one man, who wreaked havoc all over the nation, could escape the law for so long. It is likely that most people assessed their own security and that of their workplace while this prolonged attack was going on. This story illustrates the fact that security advancements must keep up with technological advancements. Mail bombs were thrust into the lives of everyone. Thirty or forty years ago, this was probably not an issue, much like computer security is still in its beginning stages. It only takes one time, one person to change something forever.

Sources

"Sixteen Strikes," *http://www.abcnews.go.com/sections/us/unabomber_timeline/index.html.*
B. Wolf, "Plea Ends Unabomber Saga," January 23, 1998.

A DOCUMENTED EMERGENCY PROTOCOL

One of the first lessons in an emergency response plan is to prepare for the real possibility that any response to an emergency will be implemented in an already chaotic set of circumstances. Therefore, having a response plan in writing, particularly in an easy-to-read checklist format, helps to make sure that essential elements of the plan are not overlooked unintentionally.

The security professional employed to establish and maintain a safe, secure target environment has a huge responsibility. Business owners, managers, and other parties responsible for establishing a safe environment can be held liable for injuries or losses suffered by the company, employees, customers, and members of the public. The first and most important step in ensuring a target environment is adequately protected is to develop the appropriate accident and emergency response plans. A second, equally critical step is to revisit the existing emergency response plans periodically (every six months or annually) and update them as necessary. Third, the plans should be "action plans." They should outline specific responsibilities of specific individuals. An organizational chart can be a helpful resource and is useful for attaching certain responsibilities to specific individuals or divisions within the organization.

A final issue, mentioned earlier, is media relations during emergencies. Consider the example of an incident in a school. These days, it is likely that parents of a child would hear about an incident at the child's school well before they get word from school officials. The media will want to cover the story, and parents will want to know what is going on and whether the children are safe. The potential for making an already bad situation worse is an additional concern for emergency response planners. For companies, this media coverage can be damaging if information is delayed or inaccurate.

Furthermore, consideration must be given to the flow of information about the incident within a company and to people outside of the company during the emergency event.[10] An emergency event is likely to result in an investigation of some kind, whether it be conducted by law enforcement or by the security division within the company. Throughout this investigation process, communication between employees and the people responsible for the investigation is important. The review of events must be conducted discreetly, and any information given to the media must be weighted against what is being shared with the employees. If they learn about events at their workplace from the media rather than from their security division, the confidence they have in the organization could be diminished. Consider an example where an employee is suspected of stealing company materials. The employees in that setting are likely to be the best source of information. If they sense that the investigation is being handled unfairly, they may hesitate to answer essential questions. Furthermore, they may question the validity of the investigation itself. These questions, if left unanswered, may cause significant barriers to the investigation.

Consider another example. If an employee has been accused of sexual harassment, the investigation of such a claim is essential. If the questions asked are offensive or disrespectful to either the person being interviewed or the person being accused, a negative environment may be created. Employees would be left to wonder if the charge was being taken seriously or if the determination of guilt had already been made. Either extreme can cause tensions and create the potential for future problems.

Consider the elements of another disaster and response plan that involves recovery. Issues about how a company moves through the disaster, from impact to protection to cleanup and recovery, can also be important for particular settings. The recovery of an operation, moving from the immediate disaster response to rebuilding after a disaster, is as important as the immediate reaction. Certainly resuming normal operations is an important part of recovery. For security professionals, the job is not over when the disaster has passed. Then it is time to rebuild, help get things back to normal, and reconsider the security plans in place. Exhibit 12–4 lists the essential elements of one disaster management and business recovery plan.

CONCLUSION

Safety and security issues are critical to any setting. Emergency response plans that include regular maintenance and weekly, monthly, or semiannual checks can be an important part of an emergency prevention plan. Several examples of forms appropriate for policies and procedures manuals are included in Appendix G. In addition, emergency response issues highlight the importance of an integrated security response. If the people in the target environment are not familiar with the protocol for an emergency, then chaos is likely. Furthermore, if you have an instruction guide for personnel who deal with important information and their responsibilities in the event of an impending disaster are outlined, then everyone can play a role in securing the facility and the company's assets. Certainly the personnel are the primary concern; however, depending on the circumstances (a hurricane, for example), the company may have time to plan for its own protection. This will minimize loss and ensure a quicker recovery from the disaster once it has passed. The response cannot be guesswork.

This chapter has highlighted several important pieces of an emergency response plan. Several safety- and security-related events that might require an emergency response are outlined here, but different settings will have additional threats. Industry-specific laws, corporate policies and procedures, and priorities (based on risk analysis) established by security departments will be incorporated into emergency response plans. As with all other areas of a well-considered security protocol, when it comes to emergencies and disasters, it is

Exhibit 12–4   Essential Components of a Disaster Management and Business Recovery Plan

---

- A statement of company philosophy, mission statement, and goals regarding disaster management and business recovery.
- Written and approved executive succession instructions.
- The appointment of a temporary Disaster Management Executive Committee for the term of the emergency, who may also act in the absence of the company's Board of Directors.
- Clearly defined guidelines and scope of all disaster management and business recovery efforts, based on a thorough risk-assessment exercise.
- Clearly defined duties, authority, and responsibilities for each employee classification, with designated primary and alternate department leaders and staff personnel to manage critical functions.
- A business recovery plan (operations manual) for each office, department, facility, and function within the company, and for essential service vendors.
- Designated and equipped sites for assembly of personnel for each phase of the disaster management and business recovery effort.
- A well-documented testing and evaluation process to be conducted at specified intervals, at least annually.
- A comprehensive training program for all employees.
- Written copies of the final Disaster Management Plan distributed to office and department leaders, including a complete list of all emergency response agencies and facilities.

Source: American Business Resources, *Disaster Management Planning Manual* (Lakewood, CO: 1995), 4.

---

essential for the security management team to be up to date on all of the guidelines and industry practices that affect the target environment.

Review Questions

1. Outline the difference between safety and security as discussed by Mary Lynn Garcia in the chapter.
2. What is a facility warning system?
3. Why is it important for environments to have a planned response to media inquiries?
4. What role should workers or employees play in an emergency response plan?
5. Should employees be involved in a bomb response plan? Please justify your response.

Discussion Questions

1. Is it important to differentiate between safety issues and security issues? Why or why not?

2. Discuss the meaning of integrated security response to disaster or emergency response planning.

3. Where are resources for disaster planning found?

4. Discuss ways that people can be assets and/or liabilities in an emergency response situation.

5. Outline specific disaster themes discussed in the chapter that could be applied to the setting in which you work. Compare your work setting concerns with those of your classmates.

REFERENCES

1. M. L. Garcia, "Coming to Terms with the Security Body of Knowledge" (paper presented at ASIS International Seminar, Las Vegas, NV, September 1999), tape 91, 12.

2. American Business Resources, *Disaster Management Planning Manual* (Lakewood, CO: 1995), 2.

3. M. E. Baca, "Pipe Bomb Lay Unnoticed at Waconia Newspaper for Five Dangerous Days," *Minneapolis Star Tribune,* October 12, 1996, B3.

4. Baca, "Pipe Bomb Lay Unnoticed," B3.

5. Ibid.

6. G. Joyce and L. Hurth, "Getting Out While the Getting Is Good," *Security Management,* May 1999, 71–75.

7. S. Wortham, "Expect the Unexpected: How To Protect Your Workers in a Natural Disaster," *Safety and Health,* September 1997, 50.

8. W. Cunningham and P. J. Gross, *Prevention of Terrorism: Security Guidelines for Business and Other Organizations* (McLean, VA: Hallcrest Press, 1978).

9. B. C. Morris, 1998, "Workplace Violence: Security's New Challenge," *IFPO Protection News 14,* no. 1: 7, 11.

10. D. Turner and R. Stephenson, "Managing Media Attention," *Security Management,* December 1994, 55–57.

CHAPTER

Securing Tomorrow
Drafting the Future
of Public Safety

CHAPTER OUTLINE

KEY WORDS

Compstat program
Corporate justice
Food security
Law enforcement industrial complex

Private justice
Queenswatch
TrafficStat

The U.S. Department of Labor estimates that security will be the fastest market of growth in the next decade.[1] These estimates came before 9/11, and security experts speculate that security job openings will be plentiful as the nation gears up to prevent future attacks. Market forecasts suggest that security-related technologies, particularly those used as physical security measures, will see consistent growth of between 15 and 20 percent per year.[2]

The security issues that will impact the United States and communities across the globe in the new millennium continue to emerge. Crime rates, international activities, and political and economic trends are only a few of the factors to be considered by U.S. security professionals as they prepare for the threats of the future. As discussed in Chapter 10, representatives from both the public police arena and the security profession agree that public and private police responsibilities will continue to overlap and the groups are likely to become even further integrated as public police continue to rely on specific types of expertise offered by private security organizations. While many experts argue that the relationships between public and private police have not changed in any notable way,[3] others suggest that policing initiatives, such as the current community policing efforts, reflect a trend toward integration and inclusion, especially in efforts focused on providing public safety.

MAKING A CASE FOR INTEGRATED EXTERNAL RESOURCES

Private security professionals are likely to be increasingly integrated into community public safety efforts—whether that community is defined as a neighborhood watch group, a corporate environment, or individual consultants who advise people about personal and home security. The future of security is arguably going to be more directly connected to a broader range of public safety issues, coordinated between public police and other public safety professionals. The future of security is arguably going to be linked more directly with a broad range of public safety issues, including fire, emergency response, police (particularly community policing issues), and community management organizations. Coordination between these groups will require targeted and focused attention between all concerned parties, yet some shining examples exist that suggest that such cooperation between agencies and organizations that have not typically worked directly together is possible. The case studies presented in this chapter provide examples of integrated, interactive agency and organizational cooperation.

CASE STUDY 1: COMPSTAT AND INTEGRATED
COMMUNITY-BASED APPLICATIONS

Criminal justice professionals argue that early prevention efforts both reduce crime and reduce the need for more prison buildings. "From within the system, many police chiefs, prosecutors, and corrections officials are speaking out about the need for more early prevention. For many years, the problem has been that few . . . state-level officials seem to recognize"[4] those other alternatives to reducing violence. Private companies have been able to aid local police departments in tracking and responding to crimes through the use of computer programs. These computer programs give police the ability to map crimes and plan responses.

Security professionals like William Bratton, former police commissioner of both the Boston and New York police departments and now a practitioner in the security industry, argue that growth of the private security industry is one of the keys to falling crime rates. Bratton was the founder of New York City's **Compstat program,** a computer comparison of statistics in a neighborhood-by-neighborhood analysis of where crimes occur.[5] A second aspect directly responsible for the decline in crime is community policing.[6] Community policing is said to be a better way of policing—a more positive way to address community crime concerns. The increased communication among different groups addressing various security-related or public safety features will make a considerable difference in how people think about and respond to crime.

Using Compstat, which cost $12 million and produces computer-generated geographic crime data, New York police can identify new crime hotspots and then focus resources in those areas.[7] Crimes factored into the comparison include even minor infractions such as subway turnstile jumping. Traditionally, these types of crime data were compiled monthly. With the use of the new computerized tool, the department can review this crime information within days.

Remember that computer issues are proving to be one of the most difficult emerging areas for law enforcement, and the security of sensitive information has emerged as a priority. "Criminal enterprises target law enforcement with an intelligence process similar to that used against a hostile force in wartime. This disturbing development demands that we rethink the way we define, handle, disseminate and protect information concerning the capabilities and intentions of law enforcement organizations."[8] Certainly, law enforcement organizations are prepared to deal with information security issues, because the protection of sensitive information (such as speaking about a case or information held in confidence about officers or activities under investigation within the department) has always been important. In the current scenario, however, access to police computer networks could provide information to outsiders planning a strategic response to police intervention. Information could include the size of the department, response times, routes to crime scenes, assignment of police department staff (including who will respond to what circumstances), and descriptions of unmarked vehicles. For this reason and others, policing organizations are having to ensure that their understanding of computer systems is much more sophisticated than it has been in years past. It is argued, too, that policing organizations will be more likely to contract with private computer security companies.

In addition to reviewing the crime data, the police department in New York City has developed a hard-line approach for police precinct commanders, who are expected to produce effective crime reduction results. If the crime rate does not go down in their areas, the commanders are replaced.[9]

The concept of teamwork has emerged as a central component in the Compstat process. Traditional ideas of community policing gave the responsibility of "all-purpose problem-solver" to the cop on the beat. Experience from the New York Police Department program suggests, however, that the best way to solve community problems is to give the bulk of the responsibility for critical issues to the precinct commander, because many patrol officers lack experience.[10] Centrally located authority has not proven effective in policing, but precinct commander authority is effective because a precinct commander, unlike a patrol officer, "has the experience, knowledge, authority, and resources required to build a multi-member team to successfully address a problem over the long term."[11] These objectives have been well met when the patrol officers make solid connections with citizens and security professionals in their precincts and report to precinct commanders, who utilize the resources available from the department. Responding to incidents in the community is important for patrol officers; they must know the community players as well as the environmental conditions and balance the informal collection of information they get by being out in the community against the use of the requisite authority to take effective action in that setting when it is necessary. Much of their job involves addressing community associations, senior groups, and other community organizations about ways people can protect themselves.[12]

New York has surveillance cameras watching city parks and housing projects. The cameras in the police headquarters are located in the Compstat room, so they can broadcast Compstat meetings where the data are reviewed. Furthermore, the cameras allow the department to get live feed of demonstrations if protesters are engaged in or about to engage in violence. Although some groups, like the American Civil Liberties Union, have raised concerns about what is seen as a problematic trend that might result in violations of basic civil rights associated with the "Police Department's zeal to monitor everything,"[13] others suggest that no one can argue with the success of the program in reducing crime. Even with the concerns, the Compstat program has been implemented in other cities across the country, in large part due to the success of the program in New York City.

New York City has also started a program similar to Compstat. The second program, known as **TrafficStat,** is focused on attacking the traffic problem in the city, and initial outcomes look impressive.[14] Traffic accidents and pedestrian fatalities, for example, have been reduced. Over 300 locations in the city were designated as accident prone. These trafficstat meetings are known for being "rough and tumble," and internal politics during the meetings can be complicated.[15] The commanding officer in the traffic division, Deputy Chief Henry Cronin, agrees that the meetings can be very intense. Leaders of precincts with high numbers are called to the podium and asked to outline what they are doing to prevent or reduce crime. Cronin suggests, however, that the tone is important so that everyone realizes how serious the department is about producing reductions in targeted areas.

Compstat is only one of several programs where police work with community organizations to lower crime rates in the city. Other types of crime-tracking computer-based programs are being used by police across the country to encourage residents to get involved in solving community problems.[16] Crimes are often committed in areas where community members have relinquished guardianship of their surroundings, so it makes sense to get residents involved in community improvement in those areas.[17] In another program, **Queenswatch,** participants in the program (who may come from a condominium or other community cooperative) report emergencies to a dedicated central base station, monitored by the New York Police Department around the clock.[18] Interested community participants must purchase a walkie-talkie at a cost of approximately $1100 and subscribe to the program at an annual fee of $365—$1 per day. Training is available for personnel interested in the program. Regular workshops are held where the coordinator of the community program and a New York Police Department detective discuss ways of enhancing the safety of particular buildings and the community generally.[19]

Ongoing debates exist about what are reasonable expectations of the police. While some police practitioners argue against the role of police as "social worker," other people highlight the importance of combining police and social services in a neighborhood setting. In Union City, California, two award-winning programs have been established that include police, city services, and community programs. Police are said to be able to respond proactively and provide resources to residents, including on-site counseling, educational tutoring, legal aid services and health care, domestic violence counseling, and after-school programs[20] While most costly technology-based solutions are being proposed in large areas like New York, smaller communities, such as Union City, with a smaller tax base rely on innovative programs utilizing all resources, including interested citizens and representatives from community-based organizations. Linked heavily with the community policing objectives, the program in Union City empowers citizens in the community to become largely responsible for their own security and protection. One of the most impressive programs is the after-school program for latchkey children, who are said to be prone to commit crimes between 3 P.M. and 6 P.M. Benefits from the community resource centers include reduction in policing costs because of active community service delivery, more encounters with citizens in nonconfrontational situations, and a heightened sense of security among community service providers. Most important, these programs have been examples of truly collaborative efforts between public and private services and have demonstrated that broad-based partnerships can help address community problems before they become police problems.[21]

Various interpretations of the community policing concept are being discussed and organized across the country with an eye toward assessing what private security and policing service providers bring to the table. Several examples of cooperative efforts suggest that community policing efforts are blurring the boundaries between public and private police responses. Other long-standing neighborhood watch programs organized in response to a community's internal assessment are finding cooperative climates in police departments that have traditionally played quite a different role within a community. Even with the advancement of community policing initiatives across the country, the cooperative interaction between police and private groups can vary dramatically. As the collective efforts focus more on common public safety needs, rather than separate private and public security-related needs, more blurring of traditional policing boundaries is likely to occur.

CASE STUDY 2: RIDGEDALE MALL, MINNETONKA, MINNESOTA*

As a faculty member in a department of criminal justice, I have the good fortune to work with various security and law enforcement professionals and study some innovative security-related programs. One such program was set up under the watchful eye of security coordinators, working with local police, at Ridgedale Mall in Minnetonka, Minnesota. Director of Ridgedale Security Don Olson oversees a private security office located in the mall, adjacent to a local office of the Minnetonka Police Department. The security office is an island to itself, with several layers of security access controls to secure entry. The police department has a fully equipped police division with holding areas and a National Crime Information Center (NCIC) computer terminal. Although the terminals are for the use of public law enforcement, not the mall security division, just about everything else is shared by the public and private police officers.

The Ridgedale Mall opened in 1974. The retail square footage for the Ridgedale Center is over 1 million square feet, with 334,000 square feet of mall space. In 1980, the deputy chief in Minnetonka approved opening the Ridgedale Police Department at the mall. Since the cooperative effort has been in place, there have been reductions in auto thefts, disorderly conduct,

---

*Most of this information was collected from an interview with Don Olsen on August 15, 2000, at the security department in Ridgedale Mall. The information presented was reviewed by Mr. Olsen for accuracy before it went to press. Additional information was collected from Dick Setter, adjunct faculty member at St. Cloud State University and retired chief of the Minnetonka Police Department.

thefts from stores in the mall, and break-ins on mall property. The security department can offer support to the police department in important ways, such as attending to details (paperwork, for example) so that the officers can get back to their other responsibilities. The security detail has two squad cars, bike patrol, and two officers in the building and two out of the building during prime hours of operation.

Two officers were originally assigned from the City of Minnetonka to share space in the department offices, and they also share the mall resources afforded to them because of their interactive work with the mall security department. In 1979 and 1980, when the mall put in the offices, the city split some of the $8000 cost with mall management. The police department paid for much of the equipment brought in. Costs for the recent renovations to the offices within the last two years were divided equally. The Security Plan for Ridgedale establishes the need to develop active relations with the local police department as an integral part of the program objectives.[22] There are separate responsibilities for the security professionals and the public police officers, however. In fact, the passage included in the Ridgedale Center security plan is quoted directly from the Minnetonka Department of Police Services Operations Manual. It describes in detail the operational guidelines of the Ridgedale Police Department in its relationship with Ridgedale Shopping Center.

Security and law enforcement officials who have been involved in this cooperative effort from the beginning like to talk about how much interest there has been in their pioneering cooperative public/private police effort. But some members of the media have expressed only moderate interest. In 1995, representatives of a high-profile national paper expressed interest in covering this "innovative" police initiative. After conducting interviews, the newspaper dropped the story. The reporter suggested that the paper expected to see more antagonism between the agencies and that people might not be interested in a police story with a happy ending.

Overall, this cooperative effort has benefited both the police and the mall. The security professionals in the mall have earned and maintain the respect of the personnel working in the police department. In some cases, the security professionals have such favorable associations with law enforcement that the people who come to work at the mall are exposed to important lessons about the distinct roles of law enforcement officers and private security professionals.

CASE STUDY 3: RETAILERS PROTECTION ASSOCIATION, ST. PAUL, MINNESOTA

Another excellent example of the effectiveness of public and private partnerships involves the Retailers Protection Association (RPA), based in St. Paul, Minnesota. Focusing in large part on the battle against check fraud, the Minnesota Retail Merchants Association (MRMA) created the RPA in an effort to open the lines of communication between bankers, merchants, and law enforcement officials.[23] The RPA is focused on producing effective prosecution of persons responsible for serious property crimes, by combining information collected from law enforcement, retailers, and banks across multiple jurisdictions.[24] RPA is composed of members from industry (including retail establishments, banks, and others), the MRMA, the Minnesota Bankers Association, the county attorney's office, sheriff's departments, and metropolitan law enforcement agencies.

Identifying a lack of communication as a significant obstacle, representatives of the MRMA were finding that repeat offenders would often go undetected because they could commit the same crime in different areas and there was no way to connect them to activities in multiple jurisdictions. Due to a lack of aggregate information, law enforcement efforts to arrest and then prosecute offenders were not very effective. By coordinating the sharing (between retailers, banks, and law enforcement) of information on fraudulent activity, the RPA is building a criminal history database that law enforcement officials can access 24 hours a day.

In Minnesota alone, check fraud is estimated at approximately $400 million in losses annually. TeleCheck Services, a Houston-based company, estimates that annual losses from check fraud are at least $6 billion nationwide.[25] In its most recent study, TeleCheck found the merchants hardest hit by check fraud are jewelry stores, general apparel stores, department stores, electronics stores, and specialty gift stores.[26] Several issues motivated the MRMA to start this coordination effort. The fact that these crimes happen in multiple jurisdictions makes it difficult for law enforcement to identify patterns of criminal activity. Furthermore, because of the cost associated with investigations and because there traditionally has been little return on resources invested in extensive investigations, check fraud has been a low priority for individual retailers. With the expansion of the database, the chance of convictions increases. Because the conviction typically involves more than one fraudulent act and because offenders typically commit other crimes in the community, retailers and law enforcement officials are seeing big results.

People working within the organized effort suggest that there are several critical components associated with the program's success. Collecting victim information from across jurisdictions is essential. Active policy-related support through legislative action and allocation of resources is also important for the program to be effective. Sometimes the coordination of individuals, groups, and agencies with diverse objectives can prove extremely challenging; there needs to be trust, patience, and cooperation.

Although the cooperative efforts originated in Minnesota, the program has had such great success that the programs are being replicated in Texas and California.[27] The success in Minnesota is being felt already, and some big names—including Dayton Hudson's Target stores, Kmart, and Wal-

Mart—are backing the effort. The objective is to work with RPA to get information from all of the stores into one database so the independent stores can network with other retailers. All participating retailers, like law enforcement, have access to the database. The cooperative effort has been taken even one step further through monthly meetings involving public police and private security for various local corporations to coordinate information in active fraud investigation cases.

EXPANDING AGENDAS FOR LAW ENFORCEMENT?

Future public police efforts, particularly as they are connected with the advancement of the community policing idea, are likely to focus on what produces the greatest amount of discomfort for community residents. This idea is not without its critics. Concern has been expressed about whether it is appropriate for residents, rather than law enforcement officers, to identify the enforcement priorities for a given community; the police, the argument goes, are supposed to provide service to the entire community, not only those members in the community who yell the loudest. Clearly, with the implementation and institutionalization of community policing, the appropriateness of an interactive assessment of community enforcement objectives will be explored more fully. Police departments must make decisions about how their resources will best be used to meet the needs of the community they are hired to protect. Community policing affords the opportunity for police agencies to focus directly on those issues that concern the community the most. The role the citizens play in determining police response is subject to ongoing discussion.

Furthermore, the debate over the appropriate role for citizens within the public policing process suggests varying attitudes among departments when considering the role of citizens and private industry and how those groups might appropriately influence—some might say dictate—community public safety efforts. Such efforts are particularly contentious when the topics for consideration involve race, class, and power.

To some degree, social reform has been the outcome of such discord and social unrest, but public police are criticized for not protecting and serving all people. Who decides who receives what level of security or protection, particularly in minority and low-income areas? To this day, public police efforts to establish and maintain public safety objectives within minority communities are not regarded with any significant levels of trust. Stories of ongoing controversy in Los Angeles and New York police departments certainly fuel the debates. Meanwhile, public police forces are left to maintain a coercive order within deteriorating inner cities.[28]

Businesses with transnational or multinational operations will require security responses appropriate to their industry and their geographic location in the world. Attention has always been given to particular types of crime identified as posing a threat to the security of the United States. This emphasis on enforcing "law and order," both within U.S. borders and abroad, is said to result in what is being called the **"law enforcement industrial complex,"** which has developed alongside the older and far more expansive "military industrial complex."[29]

To the extent that federal law enforcement efforts are increasingly focused on international issues, such as immigration, drug trafficking, organized crime, computer crime, and economic (white-collar) crime, police resources—and thus, the emphasis of crime control efforts within police departments—may be viewed very differently. Police resources may be distributed differently, either to include resources to combat these issues or leaving them to the federal agencies. These discussions about where to spend department resources impact decisions about crime control efforts within departments. At the present time, newspapers are covering the controversy associated with the Federal Bureau of Investigation's (FBI's) setting up headquarters in countries across the globe. The argument is about the priorities of the FBI, but these discussions trickle down to eventually impact decisions made in the local departments. Current leadership suggests that to protect the national borders, one must have access to information from all parts of the world. Others argue that international issues are the responsibility of the Central Intelligence Agency and that the FBI should stick to issues within this country's borders.

Questions about what role law enforcement is to play in the international community are coming up at the same time people are enlisting police as resources for enhancing safety and security within their own communities. Interestingly, in light of this expanded emphasis on the appropriateness of the law enforcement industrial complex, communities across the country are incorporating local citizens into community crime prevention efforts. So, in essence, law enforcement is being pulled from both directions: to take a larger role in both the international arena and local neighborhoods.

Furthermore, modern law enforcement agencies require sophisticated levels of expertise for dealing with a multitude of international and local issues, such as computer crime, organized crime, environmental crime, white-collar crime, gangs, and drugs. Law enforcement is being asked to lead the drug enforcement effort in both the international arena and local communities. While federal programs advance monies for more law enforcement assistance with interdiction efforts on the borders,[30] local law enforcement agencies are educating citizens about how to deal with drugs and gangs in their neighborhoods and communities.[31]

Efforts to address crime at federal, state, and local levels are not new by any means, but efforts to coordinate responses of public and private police are increasingly viewed as long overdue. Some citizens get involved with law enforcement efforts as a result of extreme frustration with the abilities of law enforcement. Forms of community protection that are less concerned about the public/private distinction and more focused on public safety are being hailed as success stories.

Given the idea that public police have historically been viewed as "tools of the powerful within the state" and the fact that private justice often means that many people who commit felonies in white-collar settings are not even prosecuted, it is clear that members of the criminal justice system will continue to be well served by adding focused research on the role of the police in society over time. It is hard to imagine that a person who shoplifts a bottle of aspirin from a local drugstore is likely to be arrested, prosecuted, and sentenced (even if to a diversion program), but if the same drugstore's accountant is caught embezzling money, the police might not even be called. It is difficult to imagine that children are shot and killed in inner-city America every day, but no action is taken to enhance their protection. These issues and others must be researched more fully by security and criminal justice professionals. It is the focused research attention on where these two areas connect, overlap, and interfere with the mission and objectives of the other group that should be more fully considered.

THE ROLE OF PRIVATE SECURITY WITHIN THE CRIMINAL JUSTICE COMMUNITY

More specific examination of law enforcement suggests that different police responses are needed for different types of criminal activities. For example, criminal justice professionals have argued for developing a dramatically different response for treating white-collar crimes (including no prison time) and crimes including violence (which, they argue, should include prison time).[32] Others might argue that this level of modified police response is already happening. Mr. South has argued that industry has elected to informally administer what he calls **corporate justice**.[33] Corporate justice refers to the internal decisions made by corporations or other private industries about whether they will proceed with addressing a given legal violation by pressing charges and involving the criminal justice system.[34] Corporate justice is also referred to as **private justice**.[35] Research has confirmed that an undetermined amount of economic crime is disposed of privately, within organizations, instead of being processed through the public criminal justice system.[36] It is argued that private industry has developed its own brand of private justice, in many cases letting felony violations go unreported, unprosecuted, and unpunished.

Are security professionals being asked to protect against this type of corporate violation, or are they willing participants in what seems to be an emerging trend that subverts criminal justice legal practices? Whose safety and security interests are served when these individuals are allowed to go to another company and perhaps do the same thing, with losses absorbed in large part by increasing cost to consumers? The criticism that private security professionals (and their managers) are subverting fundamental principles within the criminal justice community must be considered in conjunction with the ongoing criticisms of both private and public police. If security companies are choosing affiliation to the corporation or security customer over any sense of responsibility to the constitutional protections afforded all members of the community, questions arise about how these types of private guard forces are different from paramilitaries in Third World countries who are hired by the rich to defend their privileges and protect their security.

One of the most difficult issues for the future of public safety involves the attitude that the security industry is a "magnet for the socially dispossessed."[37] The minimal skill level required makes these jobs attractive to people who cannot get other jobs. Stories about inappropriate guard behavior are making headline news. The industry has critics working from within to paint a dismal picture of the industry. "The industry's greatest weakness . . . is the lack of rigorous background checks. [Security firms] do not even attempt to check applicants' criminal records, military service records, personal references, previous employers or educational claims. They don't test for literacy, they don't test for drug use, and they don't evaluate psychological fitness."[38]

The professionalism and role of security professionals in the criminal justice system must be considered more fully in order to strengthen the bridges between public and private police.

THE FUTURE OF SECURITY

As discussed elsewhere in this book, advances in technology are leading to crimes that are relatively new and often difficult to enforce. Computer crimes such as identity theft are obvious examples. Other security areas are clearly associated with international issues and are beyond the scope of this book.

Security students should at a minimum be mindful of the effects of the expansion of multinational corporations and the idea of the law enforcement industrial complex, and they should keep an eye toward various other international security issues that might impact the security responsibilities in their target environment. Some discussion and education about how international security issues might impact the security response from various security sectors in the United States makes sense. Issues like **food security** are not always in the forefront of security-related discussions, but questions are surfacing as interests in biotechnology and genetic alteration of food are accelerated. In fact, food security is defined as "access by all people at all times to enough food for an active and healthy life."[39] The recent recall of genetically engineered corn grown for animal feed but accidentally mixed with corn for human consumption has brought aspects of this conversation into the forefront of public discussion.

The United States has enjoyed unprecedented prosperity, so it is difficult for many to envision the flip side of prosperity. During the shift between 1999 and the year 2000, many people were concerned that computer malfunctions might cause devastating personal and community catastrophes. Those threats did not materialize, although to some these cautions served as a reasonable "check" that helped communities assess their readiness to address any catastrophic events, including threats to food, water, and community infrastructure—which more and more these days includes computer networks. The collective efforts of police and citizens are being referred to more and more often as essential to public safety in a community.[40]

CONCLUSION

Criminal justice professionals are continuing to offer critical assessments about law enforcement responses, and this includes efforts to address citizen and community concerns about local police activity. Clearly, police need to learn to share power and accept direction from others,[41] and this will increasingly include private security groups. Controversy will be expected to continue, however, until more consensus can be built around the idea of how to define a private security group. Are definitions of *private security* to include groups of volunteers organized within a community to "take back their neighborhoods" from drug dealers or random burglary threats, or must the definition link more directly with trained security professionals who get paid for their services? Furthermore, another critical issue is linked with the expansion of security forces and the question of how actions taken by security forces fit within the traditional criminal justice system.

REVIEW QUESTIONS

1. Based on the information presented in the chapter, outline what you see as the differences between Compstat, Traffic Stat, and Queenswatch.
2. Explain how the examples presented in the text speak to the issue of integrating external resources with your company's internal security needs.
3. In what way do you see programming, such as the cooperative program set up by the RPA in St. Paul, Minnesota, changing the way police officers and security professionals do their jobs? Please be specific with each and justify your response.
4. Outline the listed benefits presented by the cooperative police effort at Ridgedale Mall in Minnetonka, Minnesota.

5. Summarize the issues, presented by the author, that are likely to be future issues in the security field.

DISCUSSION QUESTIONS

1. Discuss the implications of private justice on the criminal justice system. How does this concept integrate the security profession into the study of the criminal justice system?
2. Discuss the role of community policing initiatives in the expanding agenda for law enforcement.
3. Based on your own knowledge, supplemented by information presented in the text, what effect will globalization have on the security industry?
4. Define the law enforcement industrial complex. How is this concept applicable to a discussion about security and globalization?
5. Discuss the relationships between the issues that will affect the decisions local law enforcement officers make with regard to the development of crime prevention strategies. How might private security professionals be integrated into these strategies?

REFERENCES

1. G. W. Bowman et al., *Privatizing the United States Justice System: Police, Adjudication, and Corrections Services from the Private Sector* (Jefferson, NC: McFarland & Company, 1992), 67.
2. E. J. Bowman, "Security Tools up for the Future," in *Mastering Security: Using Technology* (Dubuque, IA: Kendall/Hunt Publishing Company, 1996), American Society for Industrial Security reprint series, 3–6.
3. H. Morely, telephone conversation with author, November 1, 2000.
4. P. Greenwood, "Investing in Prisons or Prevention: The State Policy Makers' Dilemma," *Crime and Delinquency 44,* no. 1 (1998): 136–143.
5. J. Marzulli, "Bratton? Guest Not Safir: Invite Ax OK," *New York Daily News,* April 26, 1997, 7.
6. J. Rakawsky, "Bratton Lauds Community Policing," *Boston Globe,* October 19, 1996, G10.
7. T. Walker, "Taking a Bite out of Crime in the Big Apple: Oakland Officials Excited about Tough N.Y. Crackdown," *San Francisco Chronicle,* March 3, 1998, A13.
8. D. Cid, "Information Security in Law Enforcement," *Police Chief,* February 2000, 15–19.
9. Walker, "Taking a Bite out of Crime in the Big Apple," A13.
10. L. Anemone and F. E. Spandenberg, "Building on Success: TrafficStat Takes the NYPD's CompStat Method in New Direction," *Police Chief,* February 2000, 24.

11. Anemone and Spandenberg, "Building on Success," 24.
12. Anemone and Spandenberg, "Building on Success," 27.
13. J. Marzulli, "New Focus on Finest, via Camera Meetings Monitored," *New York Daily News,* April 27, 1998, 17.
14. J. Marzulli, "Cops Tackle Road Perils: Computer Helping to Identify Hot Spots," *New York Daily News,* July 19, 1998, 4.
15. Marzulli, "New Focus on Finest," 17.
16. C. Greenman, "Turning a Map into a Layer Cake of Information: Linking Geography and Data Can Help Fight Crime, Find Customers, and Protect Nature," *www.nytimes.com,* January 20, 2000; last accessed on February 2, 2001.
17. Greenman, "Turning a Map into a Layer Cake of Information."
18. Association for a Better New York, "Neighborhood Safety and Garbage Disposal Issues, Safe and Sound: Sidewalk Communication Enhances Neighborhood Safety," *http://www.cnyc.com/safesound.html,* 1998.
19. Association for a Better New York, "Neighborhood Safety and Garbage Disposal Issues."
20. M. Stephan, "Union City Community Resource Center," *Police Chief,* February 2000, 35–44.
21. Stephan, "Union City Community Resource Center," 44.
22. D. Olson, *Ridgedale Center Security Plan.* Minneapolis, MN: Ridgedale Mall (1995), 12.
23. "Payment Systems, Check Fraud: A New Bunco Squad," *Chain Store Age,* January 1, 1999, 154.
24. J. McCullough, "Public and Private Partnership: Successful Solutions to Check Fraud," Minneapolis, MN, 1999. Presentation made to MN chapter of ASIS. May 1999.
25. "Payment Systems," 154.
26. "Payment Systems," 154.
27. "Payment Systems," 154.
28. M. Zielinski, "Armed and Dangerous: Private Police on the March," *http://caq.com/CAQ/CAQ54p.police.html,* February 9, 1999, last accessed February 2, 2001.
29. P. Andreas, "The Rise of the American Crimefare State," *World Policy Journal 14,* no. 3 (1997): 37(9).
30. T. DeAngelis, "GIS: Answering the Why of Where?" *Police Chief,* February 2000, 12.
31. R. Landre et al., *Gangs: A Handbook for Community Awareness* (New York: Facts on File, 1997).
32. J. Gallo, "Effective Law Enforcement Techniques for Reducing Crime," *Journal of Criminal Law and Criminology 88,* no. 4 (1998): 1475.
33. N. South, *Policing for Profit: The Private Security Sector* (Beverly Hills, CA: Sage Publications, 1988).

34. South, p. 154.

35. C. E. Simonsen, *Private Security in America: An Introduction* (Upper Saddle River, NJ: Prentice Hall, 1998), 71.

36. J. Kakalik and S. Wildhorn, *Private Police in the United States* (Washington, DC: National Institute of Justice, 1971).

37. Zielinski, "Armed and Dangerous."

38. Ibid.

39. T. Franenberger and D. Goldstein, "The Long and the Short of It: Relationships between Coping Strategies, Food Security and Environmental Degradation in Africa," in *Growing Our Future: Food Security and the Environment,* ed. K. Smith and T. Yamamori (West Hartford, CT: Kumarian Press, 1992), 82–103.

40. J. Travers, "NIJ Director Emphasizes Community Policing in Keynote Address," *Corrections Today 58,* no. 4 (1996): 112–115.

41. G. Stephens, *Preventing Crime: The Promising Road Ahead* (Washington, DC: The Futurist, 1999).

CHAPTER 14

Review of the Target Environments

Part III, "Making Essential External Connections," highlights the need to think about resources for your target environment that exist outside your immediate control. It is essential to highlight the importance of the relationship between a security operation and law enforcement organizations, resources in the legal community, and emergency response organizations responsible for responding to your target environment in the event of a problem. While it is true that accidents and emergencies will happen within your target environment, I have included them in Part III because the resources needed to respond to a significant accident or emergency will usually come from outside the target environment.

Security professionals will need to make decisions about how their organizations work with these external groups, and they will need to think about whether other external organizations will be important to contact for meeting the target environment's security objectives.

After reading and thinking about making connections with law enforcement, reviewing legal issues, and preparing for accidents and emergencies, the reader may want to return to the target environments discussed in Chapter 9, to think about how relationships with external resources might be different in different settings.

Part II was focused on *internal* issues, or resources from within a target environment that can be used for assessing the essential elements of a security plan; Part III is focused on *external* resources. How do affiliations with local law enforcement affect security? Does employing off-duty public law enforcement officers as security professionals impact security procedures and how a business addresses questions of liability? What disaster management plans are in place? How should disasters be planned for, and, in the cases of several disasters occurring simultaneously (e.g., an earthquake that ruptures a gas line that might result in an explosion), which disasters should be addressed first?

Of course, how a security professional chooses to work with external resources depends on the objectives of the target environment. The security director of a large metropolitan airport will probably work regularly with a group of lawyers who specialize in aviation law, airport security, and related matters. A security director for a medium-sized university (25,000 students) may work with the university attorney, who may or may not be well informed about security-related issues in university settings. In both examples, the airport and the university, relationships with local police departments will probably already exist and will dictate when law enforcement should be called. Further, each setting has policies and procedures that dictate the security response. For example, protocol for an air disaster is fairly specific and is directed by the federal government in the form of FAA regulations, while decisions about how a security department might respond to a student rally or sit-in will be directed by state law and the policy and procedure manual.

So, once again, we see that every security decision must suit the target environment. You may be surprised to learn just how much more information you can fit into a comprehensive security plan. But remember, the process of expanding beyond physical security and asset protection (Chapter 5), information and computer security (Chapter 6), and personnel and security management (Chapter 7) brings us again to the issue of integration. It is possible that, once you have reviewed the areas for consideration in Part III, you might need to revisit the issue of integration in the larger environment.

This process of integrating external resources with internal considerations is critical to the development of a well-considered security protocol and a strong security plan. The difficulty for purposes of both discussion and application is the simple fact that individuals and management agencies in every environment will do things a little bit (or a lot) differently, even if the environments share the same objectives. Operations at Will Rogers International Airport in Oklahoma City are similar to operations at JFK International Airport in New York; for example, but security protocols will need to be tailored to each airport, and the airports are different. For instance, JFK International is a primary entry point for international flights, while Will Rogers International serves primarily domestic flights.

When you are ready to revisit Chapter 9, the following questions will get you started:

1. What agencies might be needed to respond to security problems in the target setting?
2. What type of a relationship exists between security officers in the setting and the individuals who work in the external agencies that might respond to a problem in the target environment?
3. What accidents and emergencies are likely in the target environment?
4. What legal liability issues might people in the target environment face?
5. What other external connections should be made outside the target environment?

Watching students use these application techniques is worth more than money. The conversation about security and security-related concepts expands dramatically because students can start to see how many attitudes we hold or decisions we make involve an idea about security or a security-related concern. When this happens, the field of security opens up for them. Security issues become important not just because students want a good grade in class but because the issues are relevant in students' everyday lives. They start seeing these issues in the world outside the classroom. As a result, they can make choices to enhance their safety and security in the world. Empowerment comes from understanding these simple ideas and using them for your personal and professional needs.

Basic Security Plan

Basic Security Survey

Preparing agency: _____

Name and address of facility surveyed: _____

Date of survey: _____ Date of report: _____

Date of previous report: _____

Name and title of person responsible for facility: _____

Name and title of security supervisor: _____

Number of security personnel: _____ Number of employees: _____

Number of acres: _____ Total square feet of building space: ____

Number of buildings: _____ Number of rooms: _____

Number of floors in tallest building: _____ Number of visitor parking spaces: _____

Number of miles of roadway: _____ Number of vendor parking spaces: _____

Number of registered vehicles: _____ Total number of parking spaces: _____

A brief history and description of the business carried on at the facility:

_____

_____

Name of person completing survey (typed): _____

Signature of person completing survey: _____

Name of person making report (typed): _____

Signature of person making report: _____

Notes: _____

_____

_____

_____

SECURITY SURVEY CHART

Part I: Facility Environment

	Yes	No	Remarks
1. Do employees feel secure at this location?			
2. What is the crime rate?			
3. Can local police observe approaches to the facility?			
4. Do other buildings and structures present security hazards?			
5. Does landscaping or shrubbery present a security hazard?			
6. Do trees, poles, or fences offer easy access to the roof?			
Comments:			

Part II: Perimeter

	Yes	No	Remarks
7. Is facility surrounded by a fence or other barrier?			
8. Are fences properly constructed with an outrigger top guard?			
9. Height of fence?			
10. Describe fence construction.			
11. Is selvage twisted at the top and bottom of fence?			
12. Is bottom of fence within two inches of solid ground?			
13. Is the fence other than chain link?			
14. If perimeter barrier is constructed of stone or other masonry, what is its height?			
15. If a wall, is it protected at the top by a proper guard or wire or broken glass?			
16. Are perimeter barriers increased in height at junctions with buildings and other critical points?			

Part II: Perimeter (continued)

	Yes	No	Remarks
17. Are barriers inspected for defects? If so, by whom and how often?			
18. Are openings (culverts, manholes) that are 96 square inches or larger protected by mesh or wire?			
19. Is mesh no greater than 2 square inches?			
20. How many gates and entrances are in the perimeter?			
21. Are all perimeter entrances secure with locking devices?			
22. Are all entrances closed and locked when not in use?			
23. Have all roof entrances, floor gates, and ventilation openings been secured?			
24. Are there any overpasses or subterranean passageways that could be used to gain access to the facility? Are they secured?			
25. Are perimeter openings inspected by guards for security?			
26. Are warning signs posted at all entrances at intervals of 100 feet?			
27. Are "No trespassing" signs posted and clearly visible for at least 50 yards?			
28. Are clear zones maintained on both sides of perimeter area?			
29. Is parking allowed against or close to perimeter barrier?			
30. Do guards patrol perimeter area?			
31. Are perimeter barriers protected by intrusion alarm devices?			

Comments:

Part III: Exterior Lighting

	Yes	No	Remarks
32. Does facility use municipal lighting? Is it dependable?			
33. What type of lighting is used?			
34. Are night lights activated automatically?			
35. How is lighting checked?			
36. What is the plan for replacing burned-out lights?			
37. Is there adequate lighting around buildings, company vehicles, and cargo?			
38. Are customer and employee parking lots lighted sufficiently?			
39. Are all doorways sufficiently lighted?			
40. Does the lighting provide adequate illumination over perimeter and entrances?			
41. Is lighting directed toward perimeter?			
42. Is there an auxiliary source of power for lighting?			
43. What is the plan for standby or emergency lighting?			
44. Does the emergency lighting activate automatically when needed?			
Comments:			

Part IV: Doors

	Yes	No	Remarks
45. Do all doors lock from both sides except for the main entrance door?			
46. Are all unlocked doors properly protected?			
47. Are the doors, locks, and hardware in good repair?			
48. Are the exterior doors strong?			
49. What types of lock is used on doors?			

Part IV: Doors (continued)

	Yes	No	Remarks
50. Are electrically operated overhead doors locked when not in use?			
51. Are overhead doors operated by rollers on tracks sufficiently strong?			
52. Are unnecessary doors bricked or permanently sealed?			
Comments:			

Part V: Windows

	Yes	No	Remarks
53. What type of glass is used in the windows?			
54. How are windows that are located less than 18 feet from the ground protected?			
55. Are the windows more than 14 feet from trees, poles, etc.?			
56. Is valuable merchandise visible through the windows?			
57. If windows are connected with an alarm system, what type?			
58. Are unnecessary windows bricked and sealed shut permanently?			
Comments:			

Part VI: Keying System

	Yes	No	Remarks
59. Is there a key control officer?			
60. Are all locks and keys supervised and controlled by the key control officer?			
61. Are personnel required to produce their keys periodically?			

Part VI: Keying System (continued)

	Yes	No	Remarks
62. Is a dependable person responsible for the master keys?			
63. Are key holders allowed to duplicate keys?			
64. Are keys marked "Do not duplicate"?			
65. Are keys issued to anyone other than installation personnel?			
66. Is the removal of keys from the premises prohibited?			
67. Are files kept on the buildings and entrances for which keys are issued?			
68. Are files kept on the number and identification of keys issued?			
69. Are files kept on the location and number of master keys?			
70. Are files kept on the location and number of duplicate keys?			
71. Are files kept on the location and number of keys held in reserve?			
72. Are files and keys kept in a locked, fireproof container?			
73. Is the fireproof container kept in an area of high security?			
74. Are losses and thefts of keys promptly investigated by the key control officer?			
75. Must requests for reproduction or duplication of keys be approved by the key control officer?			
76. Are locks changed when keys are lost or stolen?			
77. Are locks rotated within the facility at least annually?			
Comments:			

Part VII: Combinations

	Yes	No	Remarks
78. Total number of safes or other devices/locks that require combinations?			
79. When was the last time the combination(s) was changed?			
80. Is the combination(s) recorded? If so, where is it stored?			
81. How many employees possess the combination(s)?			
Comments:			

Part VIII: Proprietary Controls

	Yes	No	Remarks
82. What type of proprietary information is possessed at this facility?			
83. How is it protected?			
84. Is a "restricted" marking of some kind used?			
85. Are safeguards followed for the collection and destruction of paper waste?			
86. Are desk and cabinet tops cleared at the end of the day?			
87. Is management aware of the need to protect proprietary information?			
Comments:			

Part IX: Money Controls

	Yes	No	Remarks
88. How much cash is maintained on the premises?			
89. What is the location and type of repository?			
90. What protected measures are taken for money deliveries to the facility and to the bank?			
91. Is an armored car service used? If so, what company?			
92. Is there a procedure to control the cashing of personal checks?			
93. Are checks immediately stamped with restricted endorsement?			
94. Are employee payroll checks properly accounted for and stored in a locked container until distributed to the employee or the employee's supervisor?			
Comments:			

Part X: Record Controls

	Yes	No	Remarks
95. How and where are sensitive records stored when not in use?			
96. Is the location provided with adequate security to protect records (i.e., locks, passwords, etc.)?			
97. Are only certain people allowed to handle and distribute the records?			
98. How are sensitive records disposed of when no longer needed?			
Comments:			

Part XI: Computer System/File Control

	Yes	No	Remarks
99. Are computers located in areas that can be locked when not in use?			
100. Are they available to anyone who wants to use them?			
101. Are certain programs/applications available to only authorized persons to prevent alterations that could cause problems?			
102. Is each user given his or her own identification number and password?			
103. Is computer use monitored in any way?			
104. Are programmers/repair persons allowed unsupervised access?			
105. How are backup files stored?			
106. Is file usage controlled in any way? How?			
107. Is a log of all files kept up to date?			
Comments:			

Part XII: Storage Areas Outside Building

	Yes	No	Remarks
108. Are dangerous materials or chemicals stored outside the building area?			
109. Is the area protected by a fence?			
110. Are trespassing signs posted?			
111. Is the area adequate for the materials being stored?			
112. Is the area locked and secured?			
113. Is the area illuminated?			
114. Is the area patrolled?			
Comments:			

Part XIII: Employee Lockers

	Yes	No	Remarks
115. Are lockers provided to all employees?			
116. What type of lock is used on lockers?			
117. Does the company have a key to enter employee lockers?			
118. Does the company have written consent from employees to open their lockers at any time?			
119. Are the lockers located away from removable merchandise?			
120. Are regular and unscheduled inspections made of the lockers?			
121. What is the company policy if stolen merchandise is found in a locker?			
122. Do employees have access to each other's lockers?			
Comments:			

Part XIV: Outside Parking for Employees or Customers

	Yes	No	Remarks
123. Is parking in a designated area outside the perimeter?			
124. Are employees issued parking passes or decals?			
125. Are parking areas patrolled?			
126. Are parking areas well lighted?			
127. Is parking allowed near a loading dock?			
128. Is there any barrier between loading docks and parking area?			
129. Where are company vehicles parked? Are they in keeping with good security practices?			
130. Is an escort provided upon request at night?			
Comments:			

Part XV: Fire Protection

	Yes	No	Remarks
131. Has a fire department ever surveyed this facility?			
132. Were there any recommendations?			
133. Were these recommendations followed?			
134. Does the facility comply with fire regulations and ordinances?			
135. Are fire doors protected with panic bars and door alarms for emergency use?			
136. Does the facility have a fire safety program?			
137. Have employees been adequately trained and drilled on the fire procedures?			
138. Do employees know where fire equipment is located?			
139. Are fire extinguisher locations distinctly marked?			
140. Is the fire department number posted by all telephones?			
141. Is there a sprinkler system?			
142. Is the sprinkler system inspected regularly?			
143. What is the average response time for the fire department to arrive at the facility?			
144. Is there adequate water pressure at the facility?			
145. Are signs posted for procedures to follow in case of fire?			
146. Do employees know what to do in case of fire?			
Comments:			

Part XVI: Bomb Threat Protection

	Yes	No	Remarks
147. Is there a published plan that gives procedures for what to do in the case of a bomb threat?			
148. Has this plan been reviewed by all supervisors?			
149. Are employees aware of what to do in the event of a bomb threat?			
150. Is there a specific person in charge of telling everyone what to do in this type of emergency?			
151. Does the plan include how to handle the situation, depending on how the threat is received?			
152. Are appropriate authorities notified in these situations?			
153. Is the building monitored during the threat to prevent entry or exit of unauthorized persons?			
154. Is a danger area blocked off with a clear zone (at least 300 feet in all directions)?			
Comments:			

Part XVII: Guard Force

	Yes	No	Remarks
155. Is there a security or guard force?			
156. Is it adequate for the security and protection needed?			
157. Is the force reviewed periodically to ascertain its effectiveness?			
158. Can the guards use the communications equipment properly?			
159. Do the guards meet minimum qualification standards?			

Part XVII: Guard Force (continued)

	Yes	No	Remarks
160. Are the guards on duty armed? Describe their weapons.			
161. Are the weapons inspected periodically?			
162. Are guards required to complete basic courses in the use of firearms?			
163. Is there in-service training on security and firearms?			
164. Does each guard carry a flashlight?			
165. Do the activities of the guards follow established policy?			
166. Does each guard write a daily report?			
Comments:			

Part XVIII: Product Controls (Shipping and Receiving)

	Yes	No	Remarks
167. Are all thefts, shortages, and other possible problems reported immediately?			
168. Are truck drivers allowed to wander about the area?			
169. Are shipping and receiving doors used by employees to enter or leave the facility?			
170. Is protection provided for loaded trucks awaiting shipment?			
171. Are trailers secured by seals?			
172. Are seal numbers checked for correctness against shipping papers?			
173. Is a separate storage location utilized for overages, shortages, and damaged goods?			
174. Is parking prohibited from areas adjacent to loading docks or emergency exit doors?			

Part XVIII: Product Controls (Shipping and Receiving) (continued)

	Yes	No	Remarks
175. Is any material stored in the exterior of the building? If so, how is it protected?			
176. Are trailers or shipments received after closing hours? If so, how are they protected?			
177. Are all loaded trucks or trailers parked within a fenced area?			
Comments:			

Part XIX: Personnel Identification and Control

	Yes	No	Remarks
178. Are background investigations conducted on any employees?			
179. If so, who conducts the background investigations?			
180. Are new employees given any security or other type of orientation?			
181. Do newly hired employees execute a corporate briefing form for inclusion in their personnel file?			
182. Are exit interviews conducted with terminating employees?			
183. Is an identification card or badge used?			
184. Is a picture of the employee on the badge?			
185. Is the picture updated?			
186. Is there a standard operating procedure for the identification system?			
187. Are personnel knowledgeable about the system?			
188. Is special identification required for high-security areas?			
189. Are visitors issued a visitor's pass or badge?			

Part XIX: Personnel Identification and Control (continued)

	Yes	No	Remarks
190. Can this badge be used only in a designated area?			
191. Is everyone required to wear an identification badge at all times in the facility?			
192. Do guards at entrances and exits compare the badge photo to the bearer?			
193. Are badges recorded and controlled by an accountability procedure?			
194. Are replacement badges identifiable as such?			
195. Are temporary badges used?			
196. Are rosters of lost badges posted at guard control points?			
197. Are badges distinct in appearance for different areas?			
198. Do procedures ensure the return of identification badges upon termination of employment or transfer?			
199. Is the identification system under the supervision and control of security officers?			
200. Is there a visit escort policy?			
201. Are visitor arrivals recorded?			
202. Must a visitor's identification badge be displayed at all times?			
203. Are visitors allowed to move about the facility unattended?			
204. Must visitors turn in identification passes when leaving the facility?			
205. Is visitor departure time recorded?			
206. What is the procedure if a visitor fails to turn in an identification pass?			
207. Are permanent records of visitors maintained?			

Part XIX: Personnel Identification and Control (continued)

208. Are restriction notices displayed prominently at appropriate entrances?			
209. Is there inspection of all packages and materials carried into and out of the facility?			
Comments:			

Part XX: Sensors and Switches

	Yes	No	Remarks
210. Are there sensors and switch devices?			
211. Where are they located?			
212. Are the security devices adequate for the degree of security required?			
213. Is there an operation of a photographic or closed-circuit television identification camera in security-sensitive areas?			
214. Where is the monitor located?			
215. Who monitors the screens?			
216. What is the working condition of the system?			
217. Is it a manual or timed sequence system?			
218. Are security devices adequately protected against attacks?			
219. Are these security devices inspected regularly to ensure that they are working properly?			
220. Are the security devices connected to a silent alarm?			
221. Are local alarms loud enough to alert a civic-minded person in the area?			
222. Would a police force nearby respond to a sounding alarm?			
223. Who is responsible for the security devices at the facility?			

Part XX: Sensors and Switches (continued)

224. Is there an auxiliary power source for the alarm system?			
225. Are all wires for the alarm system underground so they are tamper resistant?			
226. Are the alarm systems designed, and are locations recorded, so repairs can be made rapidly in an emergency?			
227. Is there someone available at all times to make repairs to the alarm system?			
228. Is there someone available at all times to make repairs to the communications system?			
229. Note other deficiencies or irregularities.			
230. Note security measures implemented but not listed above.			
231. Recommendations:			
Comments:			

Source: Data from R. Atlas, Site Security Planning and Design Criteria (Paper presented at the American Society for Industrial Security International Meetings, Las Vegas, NV, September 1999); R. Borum et al., "Threat Assessment: Defining an Approach for Evaluating Risk of Targeted Violence," *Behavioral Sciences and the law 17,* no. 3 (1999): 323–337; J. F. Broder, *Risk Analysis and the Security Survey* (Woburn, MA: Butterworth-Heinemann, 1984), W. C. Church, Writing Dynamic Security Management Plans (Paper presented at the American Society for Industrial Security International Meetings, Las Vegas, NV, September 1999); R. A. Fein et al., *Threat Assessment: An Approach to Prevent Targeted Violence,* National Institute of Justice Research in Action (Washington, DC: U.S. Department of Justice, Office of Justice Programs, July 1995), NCJ 155000; J. Granger, Physical Security: Threats-Vulnerability Assessment and Survey (Paper presented at the American Society for Industrial Security International meetings, Las Vegas, NV, September 1999); T. W. Leo, "Site Security Evaluation," *Security Concepts,* September 1994, 11, 23, 30, T. A. Ricks et al., *Principles of Security* (Cincinnati, OH: Anderson Publishing Company, 1994), esp. pp. 436–456; C.A. Roper, *Physical Security and the Inspection Process* (Boston, MA:

Part XXI: Procedures for Major Systems Failures for the Following:

	Yes	No	Remarks
Telephone			
Computer			
Water supply			
Electric supply			
Gas supply			
Food supplies			
Medical supplies			
Generator fuel supplies			
Support services (ambulances, etc.)			

Butterworth-Heinemann, 1997), esp. pp. 217–239, 241–279; C. A. Sennewald, *Effective Security Management* (Los Angeles: Security World Publishing, 1978); Threat Analysis Group, Apartment Security Survey; D. B. Tweedy, *Security Self-Assessment: Security Program Design and Management: A Guide for Security-Conscious Managers.* (Westport, CT: Quorum Books, 1989), pp. 255–279.

Part XXI: Procedures for Major Systems Failures (continued)

Road closures			
Civil disturbances			
Comments:			

Company X Request for Proposal:
Contract Security Service Specifications

Company X, hereinafter called "the Company," desires to engage a Contract Security Officer provider, hereinafter called "the Contractor," to perform security services for those certain spaces, offices, service centers, and other activities located in the buildings situated at the below given addresses:

I. THE DESIRED COVERAGE

The coverage described herein shall be performed by the Contractor's personnel in accordance with a schedule and in the manner specified in a Post Orders Manual. Said Post Orders Manual will be produced as a joint effort between the Contractor and the Company.

A. *Coverage by Type:* Coverage will be provided for the above described facilities, as outlined below, 24 hours per day, seven (7) days per week, and the above-described facilities will share Management, Supervisory, and Patrol services, which will be located at Corporate Headquarters, 9595 Pine Tree Blvd., Hobart, ME 04000.

1. The Company will require six full-time Security Officers per day at the corporate office building, two officers from 0700 to 1500, two officers from 1500 to 2300, two officers from 2300 to 0700, a total of 48 hours of coverage per day, 7 days per week for a total 336 hours per week.

2. In addition, the Company will require two full-time Security Officers to fill two shifts each day at other facilities from 0700 to 1500, a total of 16 hours of coverage per day, 7 days per week, for a total of 112 hours per week.

3. The Company will also require two part-time Security Officers to fill two shifts per day, from 1500 to 1900, a total of 8 hours of coverage per day, 7 days per week for a total of 56 hours per week.

4. The Company will also require two external full-time Patrol Officers to patrol all of the above-described facilities Monday through Friday, a total of 16 hours of coverage per day, from 0700 to 1500 and from 1500 to 2300, 5 days per week for a total of 80 hours per week. The Company will also require 1 additional part-time, 9-hour external patrol person on each Saturday and Sunday for a total of 18 hours of coverage. Total weekly hours for Patrol Officers will be 98 hours.

5. The Company will also require one Account Manager to oversee operations at all the facilities, Monday through Friday, for a total of 8 hours of coverage each day, 5 days per week for a total of 40 hours per week.

6. The Company will require one full-time Lead Officer Monday through Friday for 8 hours per day, five days per week for a total of 40 hours per week.

B. *Total Coverage Per Week*

1. Security Officers—8 full-time, 2-part-time, for a total of 448 hours per week.
2. Patrol Officers—2 full-time, 1 part-time, for 98 hours per week.
3. Lead Officer—1 full-time supervisor, 40 Hours per week.
4. Account Manager—1 full-time manager, 40 hours per week.

II. STAFFING RESPONSIBILITIES

The following is a brief outline of the expected duties of the Account Manager, Lead Security Officer, Patrol Officers, and Security Officers. The detailed job descriptions for each of these positions will appear in the Post Orders Manual.

A. *Account Manager*   Basically works the day shift Monday through Friday, 7:00 A.M. to 4:00 P.M. and will be a salaried employee of the Contract Company. This employee will be on a cell phone and expected to provide immediate response to his or her subordinates 24 hours per day, 7 days per week.

B. *Lead Security Officers*   Must work the evening shift, Monday through Friday, from 2:00 P.M. to 10:00 P.M. with no specified lunch period or break period, and all lunches and breaks are to be working lunches and breaks. This employee is never off-duty during their work shift and may be interrupted during any lunch period or break for emergency response or any request for assistance. This officer is expected to work overtime when necessary and to leave the facility only when the evening shifts have been filled.

C. *Patrol Officers*   Will work from 7:00 A.M. to 3:00 P.M. and from 3:00 P.M. to 11:00 P.M. Monday through Friday. Patrol Officers will work from 10:00 A.M. to 7:00 P.M. on each Saturday and Sunday. This employee is never off-duty during their work shift and may be interrupted during any lunch or break for emergency response and requests for assistance. This officer is expected to work overtime when necessary. These employees are not allowed to take breaks or lunches off site or to make personal side trips off their patrol routes during their shift.

D. *Security Officers* Will work 8-hour shifts or 4-hour shifts as specified by their work schedule, with no off-duty periods for lunch or breaks. All lunches and breaks will be considered working breaks and may from time to time be interrupted by emergencies or calls for assistance. Officers will respond to emergencies and assistance calls during any break they may be taking.

III. FITNESS FOR DUTY AND LENGTH OF SHIFT

The Company feels that fitness for duty for Security Officers is greatly diminished after 12 hours of continuous duty, on a regular basis. Therefore it is required that no Security Officer shall be regularly scheduled for more than 9 hours per day and unauthorized overtime should not be scheduled except under the most urgent situation. With this provision, it is the desire of the Company to allow an existing Security Officer to stay on duty until a fellow officer replaces the existing officer. However, it is also the desire of the Company that the contractor shall not, on a regular basis, use overtime to fill any shift at the Company. It is the expectation of the Company that any officer on overtime will be relieved before the end of the 16-hour maximum time limit imposed herein.

A. In the event of an emergency, a Security Officer scheduled for 8 hours may work unauthorized overtime hours, up to but not to exceed a total of 16 hours in any one 24 hour period. (*Note:* All unauthorized overtime is to be paid by the Contractor and the Company shall be held harmless for payment of same).

B. No security personnel shall work a shift that is more than sixteen 16 hours in length, and no Security Officer shall work more than 56 hours in a 6 day period. No full-time Security Officer shall work more than 6 consecutive days without a 24-hour period off duty before the start of another regular 5-day schedule.

C. All security personnel will have at least eight 8 hours off between shifts. No Security Officer shall work at this Company with less than 8 hours off work immediately following working any hours at this Company or any other Company. If the Contractor "flex force" personnel are used to fill shifts at this Company, the "flex force" officer used for that purpose must have had at least 8 hours off from working any hours at any Company before working at this Company.

D. This rule on maximum hours of work only applies to the full-time security personnel. The 4-hour part-time security personnel may be used to fill in for the full-time security personnel.

IV. OUTSIDE ASSIGNMENTS

Full-time security personnel will not be provided permanent assignments to work at other Contractor client sites without the approval of the Company representative. The Contractor will be responsible for the discipline of full-time security personnel who are found to be working other security positions, proprietary or contract.

A. The Contractor shall supply the specified number of people who have been trained according to State of Maine applicable Laws and Rules. The Contractor shall assure that all security personnel are competent to perform the services required hereunder and assure that each employee is free of a criminal background according to the State of Maine applicable laws on background checks. All persons providing contract security services are, and shall be deemed employees of the Contractor, and not the Company. Such employees shall at all times be under the Contractor's direction and control.

B. The Contractor assumes all responsibility for timely compliance with all relevant local, state, and federal laws, including, but not limited to, Fair Labor Standards Acts, Occupational Safety and Health Acts, the Americans With Disabilities Act, Federal and State withholding tax laws, Workers' Compensation insurance, FICA and Federal and State unemployment insurance laws, the EEOC and AA regulations. If any violations of such laws occur, the cost, fines, and penalties resulting if any shall be paid by the Contractor without reimbursement by the Company and the Contractor shall hold harmless the Company for any such violations of laws in the performance on this contract.

V. ADDITIONAL SECURITY COVERAGE

The Contractor will provide additional security personnel from time to time as is needed for special events. The Contractor must receive prior verbal or written authorization from the Company representative or his designee for any additional coverage.

VI. STAFF DUTIES

The following duties are general duties and more specific sob descriptions will be formed and published in the "Post Orders Manual."

A. *Account Manager:* The Account Manager will oversee the day-to-day operations of the security department and security operations at the facilities identified by address in this specification. The Account Manager will act as liaison between the Company and Contractor. The Account Manager may be responsible for the operations of certain specialized equipment, the preliminary investigation of criminal incidents and accidents, and provide general response to day-to-day security care needs of each Company facility. The Account Manager shall be responsible for the supervision of his or her subordinates including but not limited to training, supplying, supervising, scheduling, and supporting the subordinates in ways that will assure successful operations.

B. *Lead Security Officer:* The Lead Security Officer shall oversee the operation of the shift and assure compliance with the Post Orders. The Lead Security Officer directs activities of the Security Officers on the shift in all facilities identified by address in this specification. The Lead Security Officer shall report directly to the Account Manager and follow the direction of the Account Manager. The Lead Security Officer will assist the Account Manager with the supervision of Security Oficers, including, but not limited to, training, supplying, scheduling, and supporting the subordinates in ways that will assure successful operations.

C. *Patrol Officer:* The Patrol Officer shall patrol the parking lots and provide security outside of each facility. The Patrol Officers shall issue parking tickets and place parking warning stickers on vehicles of parking rules violators. They will have illegally parked cars towed from time to time. The Patrol Officer will provide escort service for escorting employees to their vehicles when requested to do so. The Patrol Officer will provide interfacility courier service from time to time when urgency requires same. The Patrol Officers shall report to and follow the directions of the Account Manager. They will assist the lead officers with tasks if that assistance does not interfere with their primary external security duties.

D. *Security Officer:* The Security Officers will follow the direction of the Lead Security Officer. The Security Officers will perform access control and CCTV and alarm monitoring as well as periodic interior building patrol. They will assist with emergency response and will respond to reasonable requests for assistance from Company personnel.

E. *Post Orders:* A draft of a Post Orders Manual for each facility will be produced by the Contractor within thirty (30) days of the contract start date and must be agreed to by the Company. These Post Orders Manuals will contain all services that will be provided by the Contractor as well as all security related policies and procedures authorized by the Company.

VII.   SUPPLIES AND EQUIPMENT

The contractor shall furnish any and all supplies, equipment, uniforms, and/or materials whatsoever which may be necessary for the performance of these specifications. All such materials and supplies shall be of first quality only. No lethal or less-than-lethal weapons shall be issued to any of the Contractor's employees or brought to the premises other than locked in the trunk of a Contractor vehicle before entering upon the Company property. No armed personnel shall enter any Company building for any purpose at any time during the period of the contract without the express permission of the Company representative.

A. The following security equipment is proprietary to the Company and will not be of any cost to the Contractor:
    1. All Card Access Equipment
    2. All CCTV Equipment
    3. All Alarm Systems
    4. All Locking Equipment and Key Control Equipment
    5. All Security Lighting
B. Contractor shall be responsible for the use of all Company equipment in their possession. All repairs or replacement due to neglect, abuse, vandalism, theft, or misplacement of said equipment by a Contractor employee shall be replaced or repaired by the Contractor at the Contractor's expense. Unless otherwise specified, the Company, at no cost to the Contractor, shall provide the regular maintenance of all such equipment. All such equipment furnished by the Company shall not leave the Company property without written authorization from a representative of the Company.
C. Contractor employees shall not use any offensive or defensive weapons of any kind, and the Contractor or the Company will provide none. The Contractor will be responsible for the discipline of security personnel to be found in possession of any such weapon. Weapons mentioned above include, but are not limited to, the following: firearms of all kinds, batons, handcuffs, chemical incapacitation sprays, electronic incapacitation devices, or other lethal or less-than-lethal weapons.
D. The Contractor will provide a patrol vehicle for external patrol of the facilities described in this specification, and its costs will be billed to the Company as described below.
E. The Contractor will provide two hand-held portable two-way radios and one two way radio base station for the dispatch office. These radios will be set to the Contractor's FCC Licensed Frequency. This equipment cost will be billed to the Company as specified below.
F. The Contractor will provide one cell phone for the Patrol Officer and one cell phone for the Account Manager and the costs therefore will be billed to the Company as specified below.

VIII. UNION STATUS

A. Contractor must provide the Company with notice of any union affiliation within the bid.
B. Contractor, if affiliated with a union, must also list any and all possible union conflicts with these specifications within the bid.

IX. UNIFORMS

All uniforms will be designed and provided by the Contractor, in keeping with current state laws regarding same. Contractor will provide the Company with a selection of types of uniforms to pick from.

X. AGREEMENT TO INDEMNIFY, INSURANCE

A. The Contractor shall indemnify and save the Company and hold the Company harmless from and against any and all liabilities, obligations, damages, fines, penalties, claims, demands, cost, charges, judgments, and expenses, including, but not limited to, attorneys' fees, which may be imposed upon or incurred or paid by or asserted against the Company or any interest therein by reason of or in connection with, directly or indirectly, the performance of the services provided, and/or any acts or omissions of the Contractor, its employees, and agents, whether or not acting within the scope of their employment or agency.
B. The contractor agrees to provide and maintain at all times during the term of any Agreement the following insurance:
   1. Worker's Compensation as required by law and Employer's Liability for a minimum limit of $100,000.00 per occurrence.
   2. Automobile Liability for owned, nonowned, and hired vehicles for a minimum limit of $1,000,000.00 combined single limit per occurrence.
   3. Comprehensive General Liability for premises/operations, broad form property damage, blanket contractual liability, and independent Contractors for a minimum $2,000,000 combined single limit per occurrence for consequential damagers.
C. At least fifteen (15) days prior to the commencement of the services and until the expiration of any such policy of insurance, Contractor shall provide to the Company a certificate of insurance evidencing and requiring thirty (30) days prior written notice of cancellation, material change, or nonrenewal. Such insurance shall not derogate from Contractor's indemnification obligation to the Company set forth above.

XI. ENGAGEMENT TERMS

A. Subject to and on the terms and conditions of this specification, the Company will engage the Contractor as an independent Contractor. The Contractor will accept such engagement, to perform and provide the services, as defined in these specifications, in respect to the properties for a period commencing in late summer or early fall 2000 and for a period of one (1) year.

B. The company may terminate any Agreement at any time upon thirty (30) days prior written notice thereof to the Contractor without cost and without cause. Contractor may terminate any Agreement at any time by giving written notice thereof to the Company stating the date on which such termination shall be effective, which date shall be the last day of any month and at least sixty (60) days after the date such notice is given. The fees payable shall be prorated as of any such termination.

C. In consideration of the full and timely performance by Contractor of the Services, Company shall pay Contractor in accordance with the provision of said contract, with the exception of overtime created by the Contractor unless requested or approved by the Company representative. A charge back of $10.00 per hour will be billed to the Contractor for every hour worked by security personnel in excess of sixteen (16) hours.

D. Invoices for said $10.00 back charges shall be submitted by the Contractor every two weeks at the end of each payroll period for the Company to cover work performed during said month, and shall be payable within thirty (30) days.

XII. CONTRACTOR RECORDS

The Contractor must submit a sufficient amount of documented information so the Company can evaluate the Contractor. The Contractor shall submit the following:

A. State of Maine Protective Agents License

B. Proof of Contractor's Financial Stability

C. Contractor's history

D. List of the names of each certified trainer

E. Copy of the certified preassignment training curriculum

F. Copy of the letter from the Private Detective and Protective Agents Board indicating that the preassignment training curriculum has been certified

G. References from past and present clients where similar services are provided

H. The Contractor shall provide the Company with a brief biographical sketch of all operational management personnel. This information regarding each member of Contractor's management staff must be submitted with the bid to include length of tenure within your Company and within the management position assigned.

I. The Company will also reserve the right to visit, announced and unannounced, the Contractor's offices to meet management personnel and see Contractor's operation first hand.

J. An organizational chart of the Contractor's local and corporate management group must also be included with the proposal, including the names, titles, and telephone numbers of each officer of the Contractor's Company listed in the organizational chart.

XIII. OFF-SITE SUPERVISION

A. The Contractor must be able to provide adequate "off-site" supervision to insure the Contractor's span of control over the "on-site" security personnel. Contractor will provide the Company with an outline of how "off-site" supervision is maintained and provided by the Contractor.

B. The security Contractor must be able to provide 24 hours communication for employees and clients.

C. The Contractor must provide for monthly communication, training, and supervision meetings with all security personnel and the Company representative.

D. The Company reserves the right to personally supervise, motivate, and make "on-the-spot" corrections and discipline of the Contractor's performance.

XIV. EMPLOYEE SELECTION

Contractor's employee selection process must be submitted with the proposal. This process must meet with Maine State laws regarding the hiring of security personnel. Each law must be mentioned by reference, including the individual provisions which affect the hiring of security personnel and how the Contractor intends to meet the expectations of each of those pertinent provisions.

XV. TRAINING

A. Contractor must provide 12 hours Security Officer Preassignment Classroom Training prior to "on-site" training. This training will consist of no less than the following topics or equivalent topics:
    1. Introduction to Security
    2. The Role and Importance of the Security Officer

    3. Legal Issues Affecting Security Officers

    4. Security Officers and Human and Public Relations

    5. Communications Skills

    6. Patrolling Techniques

    7. General Security Officer Duties

    8. Report Writing

    9. Fire Prevention and Control

   10. Emergency Situations and Procedures

   11. Safety Issues: How to Recognize Hazards for the Client

   12. State Laws Pertaining to Private Security

B. "On-site" training will be conducted by a registered certified trainer and will be no less than twenty-four (24) hours in length at the Contractor's expense and will consist of no less than the following:

    1. Facility Orientation

    2. Specific Shift Duties

    3. Life Safety Procedures

    4. Fire Emergencies

    5. Medical Emergencies

    6. Police Calls for Assistance

    7. Severe Weather Emergencies

    8. Reading and Sign Off on Post Orders Manual

    9. Successful Completion of a Post Orders Exam

XVI. ON-SITE TRAINING MANUAL

A "training manual" will be produced by the Contractor and will outline all items and procedures that will be taught during the "on-site" training. All training will be documented and copies provided to the Company representative. All "on-site" training will be conducted by a State Certified Trainer.

XVII. SECURITY PERSONNEL CONDITIONAL PLACEMENT

All Security Officer placements at this Company will be conditioned upon each Security Officer meeting the following conditions:

A. A biographical sketch of all new Security Officers must be presented to the Company representative prior to "on-site" training.

B. The Company reserves the right to request removal of any security personnel without cause and replacement must be made within 3 days under normal conditions and immediately for violation of "zero tolerance" policies. The Company representative reserves the right for determination of immediate removal of any security personnel with cause and replacement must be made immediately.

C. The Contractor must provide for a reserve of personnel "flex-force," at the Contractor's expense, who are fully trained and competent to fill in as security personnel in the event temporary replacement of existing trained personnel is required.

XVIII. SECURITY PERSONNEL WAGE INCREASES

Wage increases must be earned by security personnel and not just given due to time in service at the properties. The Account Manager must conduct a performance review before a wage increase is requested. A request with documentation must be given to the Company representative for final approval.

XIX. INCENTIVE PROGRAM

Security contractor must produce or provide an incentive program to reward exceptional performance of security personnel. This incentive program will also include career advancement opportunities and training provided for security personnel beyond the training mentioned previously.

A. Benefits
   1. Vacations: One (1) week after one (1) year of service, two (2) weeks after (2) years of service. The Account Manager will receive 2 weeks vacation after one year.
   2. Holidays: The Company recognizes six major holidays for contractors and employees: New Years Day, Memorial Day, Independence Day, Labor Day, Thanksgiving Day, and Christmas Day. Time and one-half will be paid to security personnel working those holidays chargeable to the Company.
   3. Health Insurance: A medical insurance program for the security personnel must be submitted with the proposal.
   4. Uniforms: Uniforms must be provided by Contractor but not be at the expense of the security personnel. A uniform deposit does not constitute an expense to security personnel.
   5. Miscellaneous: A savings plan, such as 401K automatic savings deduction, must be provided for security personnel.

XX. RATES:

A. All rates should be indicated on a per hour basis. Separate rates for holidays must also be shown. Contractor will show separate rates to include raises for each of the following categories of employee:
   1. Account Manager
   2. Lead Officers
   3. Patrol Officers
   4. Security Officer
B. Each rate should be broken down according to the attached forms.
C. Rates for additional equipment should be shown separately and at a per invoice rate.

XXI. AUDIT AND REVIEW

The company reserves the right to interview Contractor's security personnel and to review all Contractor's records as they pertain to wages, benefits, personnel selection process, and training of security personnel.

XXII. COMPLIANCE WITH LAWS AND REGULATIONS

A. The Contractor agrees to comply with all federal, state, and local laws, ordinances, and/or rules and regulations, including, without limitation, obtaining all licenses and permits, in connection with the performance of the services. Contractor represents and warrants to the Company that it holds all licenses and permits necessary to perform the above services.
B. The Contractor further agrees to comply with any and all Company internal rules and regulations, which may be existing or issued or promulgated by Company from time to time.

XXIII. ASSIGNMENT

The Contractor may not, voluntarily, by operation of any law or otherwise, assign, subcontract, or otherwise transfer in whole or in part any Agreement or any of its rights or obligations hereunder. Subject to the foregoing, any Agreement shall be binding on and insure to the benefit of the parties hereto at their option.

XXIV. NOTICES

A. ALL notices under this specification shall be deemed to have been fully given made or sent when deposited in the United States Mail, certified or registered, and prepaid and addressed as follows:

> Director, Corporate Security
> Corporate Headquarters
> 9595 Pine Tree Blvd.
> Hobart, ME 04000

B. The address to which any such notice may be given, made, or sent to either party may be changed by written notice given by such party as above provided.

XXV. GOVERNING LAW

The laws of the jurisdiction in which the Building is located herein shall govern any agreement.

XXVI. CONTRACT AFFIXATION PROHIBITED

Security Service will not be associated with or affixed to the contract for Building Maintenance.

XXVII. ITEMS TO INCLUDE WITH PROPOSAL

A. Union affiliation (if any)
B. Union conflicts with specifications (if any)
C. One (1) copy of Contractor's license
D. Proof of Contractor's Financial Stability
E. Three (3) present client references
F. Two (2) past client references
G. Biographical sketches on all personnel hired to work at this Company
H. "Off-site" supervision program
I. Employee selection procedure
J. Security Officer preassignment training curriculum
K. List of Certified Security Trainers
L. Letter from the State Board of Protective Agents regarding training certification
M. Security personnel incentive program outline
N. Major Medical insurance program

O. Organizational chart of local management
P. Biographical sketches on all local office personnel
Q. Billing rates/Appendix A, B, and C plus equipment charges

Contract Security Service Specifications

SECURITY OFFICER	START	6 MO	12 MO	18 MO	24 MO
Rate of pay	$	$	$	$	$
Overtime pay					
Total pay					
Other					
Other					
Holiday pay					
Vacation pay					
Sick pay					
Funeral pay					
Gross pay					
Other					
Other					
FICA tax					
State/fed. unemployment tax					
General liability insurance					
Workmen's' Comp. Insurance					
Total payroll cost					
Other					
Other					
Health and welfare					
Uniform replacement					
Uniform maintenance					
Supervisory wages & P/R taxes					
Other expense					
Administrative expenses					
Total cost					
Profit at M%					
Customer rate					
Other					
Other					

Contract Security Service Specifications

PATROL OFFICER	START	6 MO	12 MO	18 MO	24 MO
Rate of pay	$	$	$	$	$
Overtime pay					
Total pay					
Other					
Other					
Holiday pay					
Vacation pay					
Sick pay					
Funeral pay					
Gross pay					
Other					
Other					
FICA tax					
State/fed. unemployment tax					
General liability insurance					
Workmen's' Comp. Insurance					
Total payroll cost					
Other					
Other					
Health and welfare					
Uniform replacement					
Uniform maintenance					
Supervisory wages & P/R taxes					
Other expense					
Administrative expenses					
Total cost					
Profit at M%					
Customer rate					
Other					
Other					

Contract Security Service Specifications

LEAD OFFICER	START	6 MO	12 MO	18 MO	24 MO
Rate of pay	$	$	$	$	$
Overtime pay					
Total pay					
Other					
Other					
Holiday pay					
Vacation pay					
Sick pay					
Funeral pay					
Gross pay					
Other					
Other					
FICA tax					
State/fed. unemployment tax					
General liability insurance					
Workmen's' Comp. Insurance					
Total payroll cost					
Other					
Other					
Health and welfare					
Uniform replacement					
Uniform maintenance					
Supervisory wages & P/R taxes					
Other expense					
Administrative expenses					
Total cost					
Profit at M%					
Customer rate					
Other					
Other					

Contract Security Service Specifications

ACCOUNT MANAGER	START	6 MO	12 MO	18 MO	24 MO
Rate of pay	$	$	$	$	$
Overtime pay					
Total pay					
Other					
Other					
Holiday pay					
Vacation pay					
Sick pay					
Funeral pay					
Gross pay					
Other					
Other					
FICA tax					
State/fed. unemployment tax					
General liability insurance					
Workmen's' Comp. Insurance					
Total payroll cost					
Other					
Other					
Health and welfare					
Uniform replacement					
Uniform maintenance					
Supervisory wages & P/R taxes					
Other expense					
Administrative expenses					
Total cost					
Profit at M%					
Customer rate					
Other					
Other					

APPENDIX

Protection Officer Code of Ethics

The Protection Officer Shall

Respond to employer's professional needs
Exhibit exemplary conduct
Protect confidential information
Maintain a safe & secure workplace
Dress to create professionalism
Enforce all lawful rules & regulations
Encourage liaison with public officers
Develop good rapport within the profession
Strive to attain professional competence
Encourage high standards of officer ethics

PROTECTION OFFICER CODE OF ETHICS

Today business and the public expect a great deal from the uniformed security officer. In the past there has been far too little attention paid to the ethical aspects of the profession. There has to be solid guide lines that each officer knows and understands. More importantly, it is essential that each manager and supervisor perform his or her duties in a manner that will reflect honesty, integrity and professionalism.

Every training program should address the need for professional conduct on and off duty. Line officers must exhibit a willingness to gain professional competency and adhere to a strict code of ethics that must include:

LOYALTY

To the employer, the client and the public. The Officer must have a complete and thorough understanding of all of the regulations and procedures that are necessary to protect people and assets on or in relation to the facility assigned to protect.

EXEMPLARY CONDUCT

The officer is under constant scrutiny by everyone in work and public places. Hence it is essential that he/she exhibit exemplary conduct at all times. Maturity and professionalism are the key words to guide all officers.

CONFIDENTIALITY

Each officer is charged with the responsibility of working in the interests of his/her employer. Providing protection means that the officer will encounter confidential information which must be carefully guarded and never compromised.

SAFETY & SECURITY

The foremost responsibility of all officers is to ensure that the facility that must be protected is safe and secure for all persons with lawful access. The officer must fully understand all necessary procedures to eliminate or control security and safety risks.

DEPORTMENT

Each officer must dress in an immaculate manner. Crisp, sharp, clean and polished are the indicators that point to a professional officer that will execute his/her protection obligations in a proficient manner and will be a credit to the profession.

LAW ENFORCEMENT LIAISON

It is the responsibility of each officer to make every effort to encourage and enhance positive relations with members of public law enforcement. Seek assistance when a genuine need exists and offer assistance whenever possible.

STRIVE TO LEARN

To become professionally competent, each officer must constantly strive to be knowledgeable about all his/her chosen career. How to protect people, assets and information must always be a learning priority for every officer.

DEVELOP RAPPORT

It is necessary to be constantly aware of the image that our profession projects. All officers can enhance the image of the industry, their employer and themselves. Recognize and respect peers and security leaders throughout the industry.

HONESTY

By virtue of the duties and responsibilities of all officers, honest behavior is absolutely essential at all times. Each officer occupies a position of trust that must not be violated. Dishonesty can never be tolerated by the security profession.

PREJUDICE

The job of protecting means that the officer must impose restrictions upon people that frequent the security workplace. All human beings must be treated equally: with dignity and respect, regardless of color, race, religion or political beliefs.

SELF DISCIPLINE

With the position of trust comes the responsibility to diligently protect life and property. These duties can only be discharged effectively when the officer understands the gravity of his/her position. Self discipline means trying harder and caring more.

CONCLUSION

The job of protecting life and property focuses much attention on the individual Security Officer. Hence, it is essential to be aware of the need for professional conduct at all times. By strictly adhering to each section in this code of ethics, it may be expected that we as individuals and the industry as a whole will enjoy a good reputation and gain even more acceptance from the public as well as private and government corporations. You as the individual officer must be a principle in this process.

ASIS CODE OF ETHICS

PREAMBLE

Aware that the quality of professional security activity ultimately depends upon the willingness of practitioners to observe special standards of conduct and to manifest good faith in professional relationships, the American Society for Industrial Security adopts the following Code of Ethics and mandates its conscientious observance as a binding condition of membership in or affiliation with the Society:

Source: IFPO, *Protection Officer Training Manual*, 6th ed. (Butterworth-Heinemann, Boston), pp. 12–13.

CODE OF ETHICS

1. A member shall perform professional duties in accordance with the law and the highest moral principles.
2. A member shall observe the precepts of truthfulness, honesty, and integrity.
3. A member shall be faithful and diligent in discharging professional responsibilities.
4. A member shall be competent in discharging professional responsibilities.
5. A member shall safeguard confidential information and exercise due care to prevent its improper disclosure.
6. A member shall not maliciously injure the professional reputation or practice of colleagues, clients, or employers.

ARTICLE I

A member shall perform professional duties in accordance with the law and the highest moral principles.

Ethical Considerations

I-1   A member shall abide by the law of the land in which the services are rendered and perform all duties in an honorable manner.

I-2   A member shall not knowingly become associated in responsibility for work with colleagues who do not conform to the law and these ethical standards.

I-3   A member shall be just and respect the rights of others in performing professional responsibilities.

ARTICLE II

A member shall observe the precepts of truthfulness, honesty, and integrity.

ETHICAL CONSIDERATIONS

II-1   A member shall disclose all relevant information to those having the right to know.

II-2   A right to know is a legally enforceable claim or demand by a person for disclosure of information by a member. Such a right does not depend upon prior knowledge by the person of the existence of the information to be disclosed.

II-3   A member shall not knowingly release misleading information nor encourage or otherwise participate in the release of such information.

ARTICLE III

A member shall be faithful and diligent in discharging professional responsibilities.

Ethical Considerations

III-1   A member is faithful when fair and steadfast in adherence to promises and commitments.
III-2   A member is diligent when employing best efforts in an assignment.
III-3   A member shall not act in matters involving conflicts of interest without appropriate disclosure and approval.
III-4   A member shall represent services or products fairly and truthfully.

ARTICLE IV

A member shall be competent in discharging professional responsibilities.

Ethical Considerations

IV-1   A member is competent who possesses and applies the skills and knowledge required for the task.
IV-2   A member shall not accept a task beyond the member's competence nor shall competence be claimed when not possessed.

ARTICLE V

A member shall safeguard confidential information and exercise due care to prevent its improper disclosure.

Ethical Considerations

V-1   Confidential information is nonpublic information, the disclosure of which is restricted.
V-2   Due care requires that the professional must not knowingly reveal confidential information or use a confidence to the disad-

vantage of the principal or to the advantage of the member or a third person, unless the principal consents after full disclosure of all the facts. This confidentiality continues after the business relationship between the member and his principal has terminated.

V-3   A member who receives information and has not agreed to be bound by confidentiality is not bound from disclosing it. A member is not bound by confidential disclosures made of acts or omissions which constitute a violation of the law.

V-4   Confidential disclosures made by a principal to a member are not recognized by law as privileged in a legal proceeding. The member may be required to testify in a legal proceeding to the information received in confidence from his principal over the objection of his principal's counsel.

V-5   A member shall not disclose confidential information for personal gain without appropriate authorization.

ARTICLE VI

A member shall not maliciously injure the professional reputation or practice of colleagues, clients, or employers.

Ethical Considerations

VI-1   A member shall not comment falsely and with malice concerning a colleague's competence, performance, or professional capabilities.

VI-2   A member who knows, or has reasonable grounds to believe, that another member has failed to conform to the Society's Code of Ethics shall present such information to the Ethical Standards Committee in accordance with Article VIII of the Society's bylaws.

Source: ASIS, *ASIS Dynamics*, May/June 2000, News for and about members of ASIS, p. 34.

Security Time Line

ANCIENT CIVILIZATIONS

1860 BC Sumerian Codes

1750 BC Code of Hammurabi (Babylon)

            Code of Justinian (Rome)

            Code of Draco (Greece)

EUROPEAN HISTORY AS RELATED TO THE UNITED STATES

1066	Normandy (France) shires—areas are divided into districts for protection.
1100	Gunpowder is developed in China.
1150	Iceland issues first fire and plague insurance.
1167	First classes take place at Oxford University.
1215	Magna Carta is completed.
1250	"Premium"-based insurance is first offered.
1260	Guns and cannons come into use.
1285	Statute of Westminster is completed.
1348	Bubonic Plague (Black Death) devastates Europe.
1455	Johann Gutenburg publishes the Gutenburg Bible. It is one of the first examples of printing from movable type in Europe.
1492	Christopher Columbus sails to the New World (now known as America).
1500s	Organization of life insurance begins.
1580	First noted life-insurance policy is sold in England.
1640	Nitric acid, essential to explosives, is invented by Johann Glauber.
1664	Isaac Newton discovers and defines gravity.
1680	Fire insurance is introduced in London, England, after the Great Fire of 1666. It is offered by The Fire Office insurance company.
1682	Bank checks are first used in London, England.
1748	Henry Fielding (Bow Street Runners) is appointed magistrate at Bow Street in London.

1765	First savings bank opens in Brunswick, Germany.
1769	James Watt patents the steam engine.
1800	Italian physicist invents the electric battery.
1803	First steam locomotive is built in England.
1829	Sir Robert Peel ("Bobbies") establishes a police organization that is used as a model by the United States.
1830	First all-steam railroad is operational in England.
1896	Radioactivity is discovered.
1901	Guglielmo Marconi's electromagnetic wave gives rise to wireless communication.
1922	British Broadcasting Corporation is founded.
1939	Igor Sikorsky builds and flies the first helicopter designed for mass production.
1949	Soviets test their first atomic bomb.
1952	First British atomic bomb is made.
1956	The first nuclear power plant (Calder Hall) opens in England.
1957	Soviets launch first earth satellite (184-pound *Sputnik*).
1957	First Soviet intercontinental ballistic missile is made.
1959	Soviet Union reaches moon with the first unmanned rocket.
1961	Berlin Wall goes up.
1967	First cash dispenser issuing paper vouchers is installed at Barclays Bank in the United Kingdom.
1971	First space station (USSR Salyut1) is completed.
1972	First cash dispenser to use magnetic strip cards (developed by IBM) is installed at Lloyds Bank in the United Kingdom.
1986	Chernobly nuclear accident (Ukraine, USSR) takes place.
1989	Berlin Wall falls.
1997	First successful clone of adult mammal (sheep) occurs.
1998	India, Pakistan test nuclear weapons.
2000	Air France Flight 4590 crashes in Paris after catching fire shortly after takeoff. This is the first crash of a Concorde aircraft. All 109 onboard are killed.

UNITED STATES

1692	Salem witch trials are held in Massachusetts colony. Twenty people believed to be witches are put to death.
1732	The Friendly Society, the first U.S. insurance company, is formed in Charles Town (now Charleston), South Carolina. It insures houses and tenements.
1733	First circulating library is founded in North America by Benjamin Franklin.

1739	Benjamin Franklin creates the first municipal police force in Philadelphia.
1751	Benjamin Franklin discovers electricity while flying a kite in a thunderstorm.
1770	Boston Massacre occurs over a disturbance between American colonists and British troops.
1775	American War of Independence begins.
1776	Declaration of Independence is signed in Philadelphia.
1781	American Revolution comes to an end when General Cornwallis surrenders.
1785	The dollar is declared the official currency of the United States by Congress.
1787	The Constitution arises from the Philadelphia Convention.
1791	The First Bank of the U.S. is formed and modeled after the Bank of England.
1800s	Several U.S. cities organize local police agencies.
1802	U.S. Military Academy is established at West Point to train officer corps in the case of invasion.
1812	War of 1812 between the U.S. and Britain begins.
1816	The Second Bank of the U.S. is formed.
1821	First tuition-free public high school in the United States opens in Boston.
1837	Michigan Act allows for a banking system free of government control.
1838	Samuel Morse perfects an electrical telegraph system.
1850	Pinkerton opens a detective agency in Chicago.
1852	Wells, Fargo and Company is established.
1858	Edwin Holmes invents the first electronic security alarm.
1859	W.P. Brinks security company is established.
1863– 1864	National Banking Acts attempt to assert some degree of federal control over the banking system.
1864	U.S. Treasury establishes an investigative unit.
1865	President Lincoln is assassinated by John Wilkes Booth at Ford's Theater.
1869	Inauguration of the Trancontinental Railroad.
1876	Alexander Graham Bell sends a speech through wires with the telephone.
1879	Thomas Edison invents the incandescent lamp.
1881	President Garfield is assassinated by Charles J. Guiteau.
1885	Rock Spring massacre of Chinese miners in Wyoming takes place.
1901	President McKinley is assassinated by Leon Czolgosz.

1903	Wright brothers' first flight takes place in Kitty Hawk, North Carolina.
1909	William J. Burns Detective agency is established.
1912	*Titanic* ocean liner sinks, killing over 1500.
1913	Federal Reserve Act sets up regional reserve banks.
1914	World War I begins: Total wartime losses include 8 million military and 6 million civilian. About 21 million are wounded.
1915	First transatlantic phone call (Virginia to Paris, made by Bell Telephone is placed.
1917	First armored car is used.
1917	United States declares war on Germany and becomes involved in World War I.
1918	World War I ends.
1919	Prohibition (18th Amendment) is ratified by states.
1926	Physicist Robert Goddard launches the first liquid-fueled rocket (to a height of 200 feet).
1927	Charles Lindbergh flies solo across the Atlantic (New York to Paris).
1928	First working color television is used.
1929	Stock market crashes October 24, precipitating the Great Depression.
1930	Frank Whittle patents first turboject engine.
1932	The baby of Charles A. Lindbergh is kidnapped from the family home. The child is found months later dead in the woods near the home.
1933	Dust bowel begins in Texas, Oklahoma, and Kansas (continued through 1939).
1933	Prohibition ends with 21st Amendment.
1934	Joseph Stalin begins the "Great Purge" (1934–1939); millions are killed.
1939	World War II begins: Germany invades Poland, and Japan conquers coastal China.
1940	United States begins work on atomic bomb.
1941	United States becomes involved in World War II after Japan bombs Pearl Harbor.
1942	President Franklin D. Roosevelt approves the Manhattan Project; atomic bomb builing begins.
1942	President Franklin D. Roosevelt orders the internment of 110,000 Japanese Americans
1943	The first fully electronic computer (*"Colossus"*) is built.
1943	Payroll deductions begin for U.S. income tax.
1943	Allied forces in World War II break German war code.

1944	D-Day—invasion takes place in Normandy.
1945	United Nations is founded.
1945	NBC creates first television network; it links New York, Philadelphia, and Schenectady.
1945	World War II ends. Germany surrenders (May 8); United States atomic bomb destroys Hiroshima (August 6) and Nagasaki (August 9); Japan surrenders (August 15).
1946	The first programmable electronic digital computer is completed (ENIAC—Electronic Numerical Integrator and Comparator).
1949	North Atlantic Treaty Organization (NATO) is founded.
1950	Korean War begins; it lasts until 1953.
1951	The first credit card is introduced by Franklin National Bank in New York.
1951	The first commercial computer is introduced.
1952	First Hydrogen bomb is completed.
1952	Department of Defense strengthens security requirements for defense industries.
1954	U.S. Supreme Court outlaws segregation (*Brown* v. *Board of Education*).
1955	Disnetland opens.
1956	Rosa Parks helps ignite U.S. civil rights movement by refusing to take a back seat on a Montgomery, Alabama bus.
1958	First U.S. satellite (*Explorer I*) is created.
1960	First laser is built at the Hughes Aircraft Company by Theodore Maiman.
1960	American U-2 spy plane is shot down over Russia.
1961	First people go into space (USSR—Yuri Gargarin orbited Earth [April 12]; U.S.—Alan Shepard [May 5]).
1962	Cuban Missile Crisis (October 22–December 2). Soviets place nuclear missiles in Cuba, and the United States blockades Cuba; war is narrowly averted.
1962	First U.S. citizen (John Glenn) orbits earth.
1962	Semiconductor lasers are invented at GE, IBM, and The Massachusetts Institute of Technology.
1963	President John F. Kennedy is assassinated by Lee Harvey Oswald in his presidential motorcade through Dallas, Texas.
1965	U.S. involvement in Vietnam War officially begins.
1967	First Superbowl is played.
1968	Martin Luther King, Jr. is assassinated.
1968	Robert Kennedy is assassinated.
1969	Neil Armstrong and Edwin Aldrin are first people to walk on the moon.

1969   Precursor to the Internet is created.

1969   First cash dispenser is installed in the United States.

1970   U.S. Environmental Protection Agency is founded.

1970   Ohio National Guard kills four antiwar protesters at Kent State University.

1970   First microchip (Intel) is completed.

1972   Watergate break-in at Democratic National Headquarters.

1972   DDT banned in the United States.

1973   Six month (Arab) oil embargo cripples world economy.

1973   U.S. Supreme court legalizes abortion in *Roe* v. *Wade*.

1974   Nixon resigns as president.

1975   First personal computer is created.

1975   First home VCR is created.

1975   First ATMs in United States to offer more than just cash dispensing are installed.

1976   Smallpox is eradicated worldwide.

1977   Aids epidemic begins.

1977   Microsoft is founded.

1979   Partial meltdown at Three Mile Island (Pennsylvania) nuclear plant.

1980   Mount St. Helens volcano erupts in Washington State.

1981   President Reagan is shot and seriously wounded.

1981   IBM launches the personal computer.

1984   DNA fingerprinting discovered.

1985   President Reagan and Gorbachev take steps to end the Cold War.

1986   U.S. space shuttle *Challenger* explodes—seven astronauts are killed.

1987   Black Monday (October 19): Dow Jones industrials drop record 22.6 percent.

1989   Exxon *Valdez* oil tanker spill occurs in Alaska—the worst oil spill in U.S. history.

1989   World Wide Web is launched.

1990   Hubble Space Telescope is launched.

1992   Hurricane Andrew devastates Homestead, Florida area.

1993   World Trade Center building in New York City is damaged by a bomb planted by terroists. Six people die, while more than 1000 are injured.

1993   Eighty-six die in federal police raid on Branch Davidian Complex in Waco, Texas.

1993   The Global Positioning System is completed.

1995   Bombing of federal building in Oklahoma City kills 168 and damaged 220 buildings in the area.

1996   TWA flight 800 explodes off Long Island shortly after takeoff, killing 230.

1996   New series of currency that is more difficult to counterfeit is introduced.

1997   At Health High School in West Paducah, Kentucky, three students are killed and five wounded when someone opens fire on their prayer circle in the hallway.

1998   Five people are killed and 10 injured during a false fire alarm when two students open fire from the woods near the school in Jonesboro, Arkansas.

1998   Swissair Flight 111 crashes into North Atlantic Ocean. All 229 on board die.

1999   Columbine High School shooting in Littleton, Colorado. Fifteen people are killed.

2000   Alaska Airlines Flight 261 plunges vertically (nose first) into the Pacific Ocean, 20 nautical miles of Los Angeles. All 88 passengers are killed.

Source: Data from C. Allbritton, "Virus Threat Ebbs Slightly: Melissa Clones Not Quite as Insidious," *http://abcnews.go.com/sections/tech/DailyNews/virus990331.html* (March 26, 1999), accessed September 28, 2000; J. Borland and G. Sandoval, February 8, 2000, "Attack Knocks Out Buy.com" *http://www.canada.cnet.com/news*, accessed September 28, 2000; R. Fischer and G. Green, *Introduction to Security,* 6th ed. (Boston: Butterworth-Heinemann, 1998; M. Geller, "1000 2000: A Thousand Years," *Christian Science Monitor,* October 28, 1999, 12–15; History channel, "Insurance," *http://historychannel.com/index/html,* accessed February 10, 2000; J. Hu, "Outrage a Deliberate Attack, Yahoo Says," *http://www.canada.cnet.com/news* (February 7, 2000), accessed September 28, 2000; Kathy Bayes Insurance Agency, "History of Insurance in America" *http://www.insurance4texus.com/history.htm* (November 2, 1999), accessed February 10, 2000; Mastercard, "About Our Company Corporate Overview," *http://www.mastercard.com/about/corp,* accessed February 10, 2000; P. Purpura, *Security and Loss Prevention: An Introduction* (Woburn, MA Butterworth-Heinemann, 1998); G. Sandoval, T. Wolverton, "Leading Web Sites Under Attack," *http://www.canada.cnet.com/news* (February 9, 2000), accessed September 28, 2000; C. E. Simonsen, *Private Security in America: An Introduction* (Upper Saddle River, NJ: Prentice Hall, 1998); Union Pacific Railroad, "Facts, Figures and History: Chronological History," *http://www.uprr.com/uprrfjh/history/uprr-chr.shtml,* accessed February 17, 2000; G. Welling, "A Hypertext on American History," *http://odur.let.rug.nl/~usa* accessed February 10, 2000.

Index